Digital Projects for Musicians

Twenty exciting, useful, and educational projects for studio or stage.

by Craig Anderton, Bob Moses, and Greg Bartlett
Foreword by Herbie Hancock

Amsco Publications
New York • London • Sydney

Parts Kit Information

PAVO offers the following MIDItools Computer hardware support:

- MIDItools computer kits with all components, circuit boards, and one EPROM of your choice (box enclosure sold separately).

- Hand Box and Rack Box enclosures. Custom metal boxes and labels for the MIDItools Computer.

- Etched and drilled printed circuit boards.

- Programmed EPROMs. Each EPROM transforms the MIDItools Computer into a new kind of MIDI tool. As of this writing, there are 20 different EPROMs available for the MIDItools Computer.

- Expansion board kits. These are needed for the Custom Instrument, Relay Driver, and MIDI Patch Bay.

- MIDItools newsletter. A forum for technical support, user feedback, applications notes, upgrade information, etc.

- Data books and other related publications for those who want to get further into programming.

- MIDItools Computer Kit to design and program custom MIDItools devices.

- Custom MIDItools designs.

To request a price list, place an order, or obtain more information, contact PAVO via:

Telephone: 1-800-546-5461 (toll-free, USA and Canada only).

Mail: PAVO, P.O. Box 47, Buchanan, MI 49107-0047.
(Please write to this address if you want to contact any of the authors.)

Electronic Mail: America Online: MIDItools
CompuServe: 73074,2526
Internet: MIDItools@aol.com

(MIDItools, PAVO, and the PAVO logo are registered to Lighthouse Music Group, Inc.)

Please note: to obtain an index of this book, send a self-addressed, stamped envelope with postage for two ounces to PAVO at the address above.

Cover photograph by Comstock Inc.
Cover design and illustration by Dan Earley
Interior design and layout by Don Giller

Order No. AM 91244
US International Standard Book Number: 0.8256.1384.1
UK International Standard Book Number: 0.7119.3487.8

Exclusive Distributors:
Music Sales Corporation
257 Park Avenue South, New York, NY 10010 USA
Music Sales Limited
8/9 Frith Street, London W1V 5TZ England
Music Sales Pty. Limited
120 Rothschild Street, Rosebery, Sydney, NSW 2018, Australia

Printed in the United States of America by
Vicks Lithograph and Printing Corporation

Contents

Foreword

Digital Projects for Musicians is the perfect book for someone like me, who is very interested in technology, but who has never had the time to really get into it deeply. The book covers basic digital electronics theory and then brings it back to musicians—why do we care about this and what does it mean to us? What I really like about the book is that it's very descriptive about the components in electronic gear, what they look like, how they work, and how to actually use them. The book also describes the MIDI protocol and many different kinds of MIDI set-ups in more detail than I've seen anywhere else, and in a very user-friendly way.

Digital Projects for Musicians demystifies all the little boxes that we use when we make music with electronics. It tells you what a microprocessor is and does, and what all of the different kinds of electronic components inside an electronic box are (and how they work): resistors, capacitors, diodes, optoisolators, LEDs, and so on. It explains the difference between RAM, ROM, EPROMs, and EEPROMs, with instructions on how to buy these parts. It then describes binary math and programming languages, teaching you how to draw flow charts, and how to write a special type of program called a state machine. I've had questions for years about what these things are.

One of the things I really like is that the book discusses basic hardware tools such as drills and drill bits, reamers, hole punchers, saws, pliers, wrenches, screwdrivers, vices, and soldering. You learn the best way to apply these tools with all kinds of tips and hints on their use. For example, I've run across other books that tell you how to solder. They'll say: "Don't use too much solder," but they never have any pictures showing you what a proper solder joint is supposed to look like. This book does.

When you understand what's happening inside your gear, you feel a lot more confident using it. You're not left completely in the dark if something doesn't function properly in your MIDI setup, and you'll probably have an idea of what the causes might be. I have a studio technician named Will Alexander who helps me maintain my gear. But everybody doesn't have an opportunity to hire for themselves the talent and knowledge that Will possesses. This book helps you learn how to troubleshoot and fix your MIDI setup yourself.

I'm one of those guys who, when I get a new instrument, I'll fool around with it and I'll ask, "Oh, does it do such-and-such?" and then they'll say, "Well no, it doesn't do that." And then I'll say, "Wow, it'd be great if it would do that." Digital Projects for Musicians explains how to build your own MIDI box, called the MIDItools Computer. The architecture of this box allows you to create your own MIDI events, and frees you to do whatever your creativity directs. The book has projects that explain how to build this computer for 20 different applications. They even have kits available so you can buy all the parts from one source. With the MIDItools Computer you might be able to come a little closer to actualizing some of those dreams that you have. And one of the most important things is that you can do it inexpensively. Let's not forget that. This is not an expensive affair that we're talking about; this is affordable by anyone, from the ground up, because you build it yourself.

From what I've seen, *Digital Projects for Musicians* is the first of its kind. Take it from me, it's very hot. Everything's in here. Everybody should have this on their shelves, whether they read it from cover to cover or keep it only as a reference for when they have questions. This is a perfect reference book for any beginner or intermediate student. Even the seasoned pro might want to check it out and say, "These things I've been using all this time—so this is how they work!" I've never found anything else like it. This is the most complete electronics course that I've seen, and yet it's geared toward musicians. It makes everything so simple.

—Herbie Hancock
Los Angeles, CA

Editor's Preface

It's interesting how books get started. Bob Moses, a well-respected digital engineer at the Rane Corporation, came up with a few clever, simple MIDI projects in the process of researching more complex MIDI applications for Rane. Bob showed his projects to his friend Greg Bartlett, an electrical engineer who had just left his engineering job to pursue his dreams as an electronic musician and studio owner.

Greg thought Bob's little MIDI gadgets were pretty cool, so he designed a bunch of his own. Steve Macatee, one of Rane's top CAD designers, joined the project and got to work laying out circuit boards and building prototypes. Before long, these three guys had created the general-purpose MIDItools Computer, and the twenty projects described in this book.

Since these weren't really Rane-type products, Bob asked what I thought he should do. I suggested he write a book of MIDI projects, much as I had done years ago for analog projects in *Electronic Projects for Musicians*. I became involved when Bob and Greg decided they needed the equivalent of a "producer," and after I added a bunch of material to what they had written, we had a book.

Interesting side note: Bob and Greg got started in audio electronics by reading my projects book, and now they've taught me about digital electronics with *their* projects book. (Life can be so circular sometimes!) In any event, we appreciate your interest in *Digital Projects for Musicians*, and hope that what we've done helps further your musical dreams in some small way.

—Craig Anderton

A Special Credit

There's one more person (not listed as an author of this book) who is a full member of the *Digital Projects for Musicians* team. His name is Steve Macatee. You won't see his name on the cover of this book, because Steve didn't actually write any of the text. But, while Bob, Greg, and Craig were writing, Steve was hard at work building prototypes of the MIDItools Computer and making them work. We want to acknowledge our debt to Steve, and thank him for all the long hours he spent drawing diagrams, etching circuit boards, sawing, drilling, soldering, searching for parts, and troubleshooting. The MIDItools Computer, and therefore this book, would not exist without Steve's help.

Acknowledgments

Any book is a product of more than just the people credited as authors. We'd like to thank the following people for making this book possible (or at least better than it would have been if we'd been left to our own devices):

Dave Hyder at Motorola for generously lending us equipment and a lot of parts.

Dennis Bohn, Steve Brakken, and the rest of the staff at Rane for letting several Ranesters get away with abusing some of their privileges at work (like, for example, taking home all the Rane R&D lab equipment weekend after weekend).

Mark Lacas, Ray Miller, Steve Turnidge, and Dave Warman for bouncing ideas around, commenting on early manuscripts, and keeping us honest.

Herbie Hancock for taking time out from his rigorous recording schedule to spend time with us and write the foreword to this book.

Caitlin Cotter for typing, typing, typing, typing, and more typing.

Craig Rosenberg and Philip "Random" Reay for their cover ideas.

Einar Ask of "The Same" for being the first MIDItools guinea pig, and reminding us why we started this whole project in the first place. (Good luck with the custom percussion controller, Einar.)

Vesta Copestakes for doing the original drawings and photographs of parts and tools for *Electronic Projects for Musicians,* some of which were recycled for this book.

Music Sales for not giving up all hope that this book would ever be finished.

Anne Cotter, who patiently waited three years for her long-lost husband (Bob) to finish this project. (Well, actually, Anne got tired of waiting, went back to school, and got a Master's degree, but that's another story.)

Jill Macatee for not feeding Steve's cold dinner to the cat while waiting for him to come home, late as usual, over the duration of this project.

Pro-Tech Respirators for lending lab facilities.

Tony Walbert for burning lots of EPROMS.

Chris Bartlett for reviewing early MIDItools designs.

Cary Moon for reviewing the ergonomics of the front panel layouts.

Torrefazione Italia for pouring the world's best coffee (and providing a great place to sit and dream up MIDItool devices).

And everyone else who provided encouragement and help in creating this book.

About the Authors

Bob Moses is Rane Corporation's Senior Digital Audio Engineer, where he designs MIDI and digital audio products. Bob has been very active in the MIDI Manufacturers Association (MMA) and the Audio Engineering Society (AES) for more years than he cares to admit, and is currently serving as Chairman of an international standards committee (known as "AESSC SC-10-3" for you bureaucrats out there) which is creating local area network standards for audio systems.

Bob got his start in electronics when his Dad helped him build a Heathkit radio at the age of six, and he's been building audio gadgets ever since (including just about everything ever designed by Craig Anderton). Bob obtained his electrical engineering degree from McGill University in Montreal, specializing in digital audio and music. Bob got involved in early Compact Disc technology at McGill, and designed one of the world's first outboard oversampling digital-to-analog processors. He wrote a paper summarizing his digital audio research which won a slew of engineering awards and landed him a job at Rane. Bob's passions today are skydiving, electronic music, interactive kinetic sculpture, and building custom MIDI tools for his friends. He lives in Seattle with his wife Anne.

Greg Bartlett is Chief Engineer of Pavo, where he designs microprocessor-based utility devices and interfaces for various industries.

Greg began his electronics career building Craig Anderton's mixer (from the book *Home Recording for Musicians)* for his high school band. He received a BSEE and MSEE at M.I.T., where he developed one of the first MIDI sequencers (BART) using a bootlegged Yamaha DX7 and a VAX minicomputer. In 1989, Greg founded Lighthouse Music Group in Seattle and poured his energy into producing demos and teaching classes in MIDI and home recording. He has recently returned to engineering with Pavo. Greg, an independent liquorist, also enjoys Mexican cuisine, travel, writing fiction, and criticizing personal computer designers. He is currently between cities.

Craig Anderton received a guitar from his parents on his tenth birthday, along with a transistor radio kit from his grandmother, and since then has split his life between the technical and artistic. He recorded three albums with the 60s group Mandrake, produced three albums by classical guitarist Linda Cohen, did session work in New York, played on and mixed recordings by new age artists David Arkenstone and Spencer Brewer, and released a solo instrumental album *(Forward Motion,* distributed by MCA) in 1989.

A prolific author who is seldom seen without a notebook computer, Craig has authored articles for magazines such as *Rolling Stone, Byte, Guitar Player, Keyboard,* and *EQ.* He coined the term "electronic musician" and edited the magazine bearing that name for the first five years of its existence. He has also written eleven books, mostly on musical electronics.

Lately Craig is much in demand as a lecturer—work that has taken him to over twenty-two states and six countries. He also consults to manufacturers in the music business and is responsible for some of the sounds you hear coming out of various instruments, as well as some of their design features.

Chapter 1

Introduction

MIDI (the Musical Instrument Digital Interface) has opened up a whole new musical world. Although MIDI's original premise was to translate performance gestures—playing keyboard keys, moving controls, pressing sustain pedals, turning a pitch bend knob—into computer-compatible digital data, MIDI has evolved into much more. It can provide synchronization between rhythmic devices, control theater lighting, automate a recording studio, and even store "snapshots" of an instrument's knob and switch settings in a computer for later recall (or editing). Chapter 3 on MIDI Basics will fill you in on the details of what this powerful protocol can do.

Although many musicians think of MIDI devices as mysterious black boxes, it doesn't have to be that way. With a little bit of knowledge, you can understand not only how this gear works, but even build your own MIDI devices and customize them for particular applications. You'll have fun, you'll save money, but most importantly, you'll take control of the technology—and take pride in your work.

There's more, though. MIDI devices are based on microprocessors, digital electronics, and software—the engines that power today's computers and consumer electronics. So while you're learning how to build nifty musical devices, you're also getting a painless course on what computers are all about. That way, even if your record doesn't go platinum, you'll pick up skills that will serve you well in all kinds of endeavors, and may even open up a lucrative and satisfying career opportunity.

If you're intimidated by the thought of learning digital electronics, don't be. We've made every attempt to make this material accessible to *anyone* who's willing to do a little studying and spend a little time. If you can play a musical instrument, you definitely have the brain power to get into electronics. Although these boxes may seem magic to you, remember that engineers feel the same way about music.

To make life easier, all twenty software projects in this book are based on a single piece of hardware: a general purpose MIDI computer which is surprisingly simple and inexpensive to build. By simply plugging in a chip with different software, this computer can perform a variety of useful functions. As a bonus, it's not difficult to modify these projects if you want to advance even further.

Whether you're an electronics buff with a musical slant who wants to learn how microprocessors work, a "starving musician" who needs to save money by avoiding store-bought boxes, or a pro who wants to create devices that have no commercial equivalents, this is the book for you. Welcome aboard!

How to Read This Book

This book is designed for three types of readers:

• Musicians who simply want to build and use the MIDItools Computer projects and have no interest in learning about computers.

• Those who see the MIDItools Computer as an introduction to understanding the wide world of computers.

• Engineers who already know about computers, but want to get into the musical end of things. For them, the MIDItools Computer is an easy-to-understand hardware platform for writing their own software.

As a result, it's not really necessary to read all the chapters to get what you want from the book. If you only want to build and use the computer, then you can ignore just about everything after Chapter 7, and even some of the introductory material. However, we recommend that you take the time at some point to read the rest of the book. Some of this is a lot easier to understand than it appears at first.

Overview

Part 1, the Basics, covers basic electronics, basic MIDI applications, the tools needed to build the MIDItools Computer, and construction techniques like soldering, fabricating enclosures, and labeling. Putting together electronic devices isn't that much harder than building a model airplane—follow instructions, put parts together in the right order, and you're set. Of course, the main difference is that if you get sloppy with a plane kit, it just looks ugly; getting sloppy with electronics means that the thing might not work. It pays to be careful.

To simplify matters, parts kits, circuit boards, and enclosures are available from PAVO (see Appendix). However, most components are readily available from electronics supply houses (as found in major metropolitan areas) and mail-order suppliers.

Part 2 on The MIDItools Computer gets more specific. Chapter 6 describes MIDItools Computer basics; although this isn't essential reading if all you want to do is build the computer and use the projects, it's worth a look to become familiar with common microcomputer terms.

Chapter 7 presents the twenty software projects that make up the core of this book. For those who already have some familiarity with MIDI, here's a quick preview of what to expect.

Project 1: Universal Transmitter. You can program and send any one-, two-, or three-byte message. It's suitable for an "All Notes Off" panic button, controller reset button, song select button, master controller or sequencer add-on (to transmit any message not supported by a master controller or sequencer), sys ex byte sender, or troubleshooting device.

Project 2: Channel Message Transmitter. This transmits a variety of MIDI voice messages; you select the type of message, then use a slider to select the message values and send them. This project makes a good single-track volume fader or panpot, breath controller substitute, or real-time effects programming device.

Project 3: Programmable Controllers. The data slider can transmit data for up to three continuous controller commands on any MIDI channel. This project is useful for moving on-screen sequencer faders, doing real-time sound editing on synths or special effects boxes, MIDI lighting control, replacing footpedals with hand controls, etc.

Project 4: Custom Instrument. Create a 64-note, velocity-scalable MIDI controller using any type of switches (keyboard, mercury switches, push buttons, etc.). Hook it up to a standard keyboard for a MIDI keyboard controller, or do something more exotic—like mount the switches in a guitar neck, or fashion a percussion controller.

Project 5: Tap Tempo Transmitter. Control sequence tempo by tapping on a switch, which not only gives a more "humanized" feel, but also lets you synchronize playback of your sequence to a live drummer or vocalist. If you speed up or slow down, so does the sequencer; you can also smooth out the tempo if your timing is a little jittery.

Project 6: Sequencer Remote Control. Lets you operate a sequencer remotely, with stop, start, continue, fast forward, rewind, looping, and one autolocation point. One application: put it near your drummer, who can handle the song starts.

Project 7: Data Monitor. This troubleshooting tool for MIDI systems monitors the MIDI data stream and displays all types of MIDI messages (channel, program change, system exclusive, pressure, clock, etc.). Use this inline monitor to know what channels are being used, if a timing clock is present, if active sensing is clogging the MIDI data stream, and so on.

Project 8: Relay Driver. Triggers four relays from MIDI commands. These could drive lights, substitute for footswitches, or the paranoid could create a MIDI-controlled home security system.

Project 9: Control Thinner. This thins the amount of continuous controller data by a variable amount, to prevent overloading synthesizers with too much data, or to economize on sequencer memory.

Project 10: Channel Filter. Lets you pass or reject MIDI messages on different channels. Use this to solo an instrument, do remote muting, monitor MIDI channel messages, etc.

Project 11: Data Filter. Analyzes the MIDI data stream and passes or rejects specific MIDI messages (note, program change, system exclusive, system common, system realtime, poly pressure, mono pressure, pitch bend, modulation wheel, controllers).

Project 12: Channel Mapper. Lets you map incoming messages on one MIDI channel to a different channel. Use this project to enhance inexpensive synthesizers and drum machines that restrict you to using certain channel numbers.

Project 13: Controller Mapper. Filters out particular controller messages from the data stream, and re-inserts them with a different controller number. For example, if you want your mod wheel (controller 1) to control master volume (controller 7) of another device, this project is the answer. This is a great way to generate any continuous controller number from an inexpensive or old keyboard with limited controller options.

Project 14: Keyboard Mapper. Note messages can be mapped to one, two, or three channels, according to velocity or note number. This lets you split any MIDI keyboard into three splits, as well as trigger different modules on different channels according to velocity. One option would be to have a hard-hit snare on one channel and a softer-hit snare on another. (*Voilà!* A velocity-switched drum sample!)

Project 15: Translating Randomizer. Alters MIDI note numbers, velocity, and/or program changes. It can also translate certain controller messages into other messages. This can change music into interesting new permutations, some parts of which might even be pretty catchy.

Project 16: Multi-Effector. This multieffects unit for MIDI data includes compression, limiting, gating, and delay. The effects are similar to analog devices, but work on the MIDI data itself. Use this project to eliminate bad notes in real time, compress tracks with "booming" notes, and the like.

Project 17: Sequencer Helper. Tack this on your sequencer's output, and you can transpose all notes (except for drums) to match a vocalist's range, reset all controllers, do smooth master volume fades (in or out), or even use it as a "panic button" to unstick stuck notes.

Project 18: Chord Player. Play a single note, and this box will generate chords in accompaniment. What's more, these can be "strummed" to give guitar effects, arpeggiated, or played all at once.

Project 19: System Exclusive Folder. You can save sys ex to a non-volatile folder, then transmit the sys ex later at the touch of a button.

Project 20: MIDI Patch Bay. Patch each of four MIDI outputs to any one of four MIDI inputs—your basic system connection router.

Finally, for particularly brave (or insatiable) readers, Part 3 goes over number theory, computer hardware and software, MIDI details, the basis of the MIDItools software, how to speak the microprocessor's language, and where to learn more. But don't worry about that for now—let's just jump right in and get started.

Chapter 2
Basic Electronics

A Little Theory

You don't need to understand internal combustion engines to drive a car, and you don't need to know lots of electronics theory to assemble the MIDItools Computer. Besides, there's no point in getting *too* thorough here, since there are already plenty of books on electronics theory in libraries and electronics stores.

However, knowing a little theory makes it easier to understanding proper construction techniques, and is invaluable when troubleshooting. We'll look at four important concepts:

- Voltage

- Current

- Resistance

- Capacitance

It's not necessary to understand all this completely; just get a feel for the language. Many of the concepts will fall into place later as you apply what you're learning.

After explaining the basic concepts, we'll look at electronic components in more detail, and then learn how to read schematic diagrams.

Basic Electrical Concepts

Simply stated, electricity is what happens when electrons start moving around. Electrons are all around us as component parts of atoms, but when they're located inside the atoms of certain materials known as *conductors* (such as wire, or other metals), you can make those electrons do useful work on your behalf.

Electrons moving in a conductor resemble traffic flow down a freeway. Wire is a "freeway" for electrons; electrons are like little cars. If a bunch of cars are in the middle of a highway but out of gas, not much will happen. But give them a little energy, direct them (*i.e.,* stay to the right, pass on the left, stop at red lights), and you have a working freeway. Same with electrons: give them some energy, tell them what to do, and you have a working conductor, which is the first step toward creating a circuit.

The opposite of a conductor is an *insulator*. Rather than encourage the flow of electrons, it inhibits the flow—much as removing a section of highway prevents cars from traveling over that particular section.

Current is analogous to the number of cars going down the road. Bumper-to-bumper cars means heavy traffic; bumper-to-bumper electron flow is heavy current. The measurement unit for current is the *ampère* (amp or A for short), named after the French scientist André Marie Ampère.

Voltage is a more elusive phenomenon to explain; it relates to the intensity of electron flow, rather than just the number of electrons going down a conductor. With our automobile analogy, voltage is like the car's horsepower.

The place(s) in a circuit where no voltage is present is referred to as *ground,* or minimum possible intensity (zero volts—the volt, abbreviated V, measures voltage). There are still just as many electrons, but they have no intensity, and don't do anything. A more intense level of activity translates into higher voltage.

What provides this intensity? Well, electrical circuits require an area that lacks electrons and wants to acquire some, and an area that has a surplus of electrons. (The best example of this is a battery: one terminal is loaded with electrons just waiting to get out, whereas the other terminal is begging to have electrons come in.) As the electrons move through the wire to their destination, they create a flow of current. The intensity with which the electrons want to get from one end to the other is the voltage. The medium through which the electrons make their journey from one area to another is the *conductor.*

Another way to look at voltage is to think of water flowing into the ocean. The ocean, which is at sea level, represents "ground" potential. If the stream is at sea level, then there isn't any appreciable current flow. But if the stream flows down from a mountain, current will flow to the ocean. The altitude is analogous to the amount of voltage. The higher the altitude for a given distance to the ocean, the more intense the flow.

However, the stream might encounter dams, lakes, and other obstacles along the way that slow the flow, just as traffic can run into road repairs. These concepts segue neatly into *resistance.*

When the electrons try to get from one area to the other through the conductor, they are always trying to move as quickly as they can, so you have to control them in some way. One way to do this is with *resistors,* small electrical parts that when inserted into a circuit, inhibit the flow of current. This is the electrical equivalent of putting a 40-mph zone in the middle of a highway. We'll have more on this shortly.

Resistance is measured in *ohms* (named after Georg Simon Ohm, a German physicist of the 1800s), abbreviated by the Greek letter omega (Ω), and can cover a wide range. Ten million ohms will turn an electrical stream into a trickle, whereas 4Ω won't slow things down much at all.

Capacitance is the last term we need to investigate for now. Capacitors store energy—sort of like miniature, very low power batteries. They consist of two metal plates, separated by a thin insulator; connecting a voltage source to these plates creates an electric field between them. Storing energy in this field is called *charging* a capacitor, whereas drawing the energy out (say, through a conductor or resistor) is called *discharging.*

This charge-discharge action allows a current to flow, even though the plates are insulated. Because a capacitor can react to alternating (charging and discharging) current, capacitors often serve to block direct current (DC, the kind that stays steady, like from a battery) but let alternating current, audio-type signals through. More capacitance indicates more energy storage capability.

Resistors

The most common resistors are carbon-composition and metal film types. Metal film resistors are quieter and more stable in the face of temperature fluctuations than carbon-comp types, which makes them ideal for audio applications. For the hobbyist market, the price difference between the two types is negligible.

Resistors all look pretty similar (Fig. 2-1): they're small, brown or tan cylinders with colored bands going around them (metal film resistors aren't exactly cylindrical, but are shaped more like a leg bone—the ends are more bulbous).

The first three colored bands, reading from the resistor's outside to the inside, form a code that indicates the resistor's approximate value in ohms. Precise resistance values are generally not that critical in electronic circuits; using the speed zone analogy given earlier, you don't see 33.7-mph speed limits since 35 mph is close enough.

The fourth band will be gold or silver, and indicates the resistor's *tolerance (i.e.,* how much it can vary from its stated value). A silver band indicates 10% accuracy; a gold band, 5%. If there is no fourth band, the resistor has 20% tolerance.

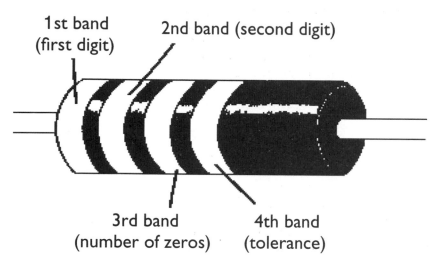

1st band (first digit) | 2nd band (second digit) | 3rd band (number of zeros) | 4th band (tolerance)

Fig. 2-1

Each number from zero to nine has an associated color:

0 = black
1 = brown
2 = red
3 = orange
4 = yellow
5 = green
6 = blue
7 = violet
8 = gray
9 = white

The first band is the first digit of the resistor value, the second band is the second digit, and the third band is the *number of zeros* that follow the first two digits. What if the resistor value is less than three digits (*e.g.,* 6.8Ω)? If the third band is gold, multiply the value of the first two bands by 0.1. If the third band is silver, multiply the value of the first two bands by 0.01.

For example, if the bands read "blue-gray-red-gold," the first digit is blue (6); the second digit is gray (8); and the red band means that two zeros follow the first two digits. Putting it all together, you get 6-8-00, or 6800Ω. The gold band indicates that the real-world value is within 5% of 6800Ω.

You may sometimes see what appears to be a resistor, but with a single black band. This is a 0Ω resistor that provides a jumper wire to "jump over" the traces on a circuit board. The reason why it's shaped like a resistor is so that it can be inserted by automated insertion tools. Electrically speaking, a piece of bare wire does the same job.

To simplify matters, there are certain standard resistor values. The first two digits of any 10% tolerance resistor will be one of the following: 10, 12, 15, 18, 22, 27, 33, 39, 47, 56 68, 82. For example, you won't run across a 19,000Ω, 10% resistor because the first two digits are not standard 10% values.

So that electronics aficionados don't spend a large portion of their time drawing zeros in resistor values, there are two commonly used abbreviations: k (short for kilohm) and M (short for megohm). M stands for a million, and k for a thousand. For instance, the following values are the same:

22,000Ω = 22k

or

1,800,000Ω = 1.8M

Note that computers sometimes express memory in kilobytes, using a capital K. This is because a kilobyte is actually 1,024 bytes, due to the nature of the binary numbering system (as explained in Chapter 8). So usually, k means 1,000 and K means 1,024, but not everyone observes this protocol.

International Resistor Nomenclature

Schematics from Europe and most other parts of the world abbreviate resistor values a little differently from American schematics. When a resistor value includes a decimal point (*i.e.,* 2.7k, 1.2M), the k or M in the international standard inserts where the decimal point would normally appear in the American. Here are some examples of American nomenclature and the international equivalents:

American	International
2.7k	2k7
4.7k	4k7
2.2M	2M2
5.6M	5M6

If there is no decimal point in the resistor value, then the metric and American designations are the same.

Resistor Wattage (Power) Ratings

In addition to a resistance rating, resistors have a power rating (expressed in watts) to indicate how much energy they can handle. Slowing down electron flow dissipates energy, which has to go somewhere—usually into heat. For example, a 2 watt resistor can handle more power than a 1W type. However, the projects in this book don't use heavy currents, so we'll mostly use 1/4W resistors.

Resistors rated for more wattage are okay providing there's enough room for them on the circuit board, but don't use resistors rated at a lesser wattage. An underrated resistor can overheat, thus changing its value and possibly damaging the circuit to which it connects.

Fig. 2-2 shows two other types of resistors: power resistors (not just 1W—sometimes 10W or 20W in hefty power supplies), and precision resistors (where 5% tolerance isn't good enough).

1/4W resistor

1/2W resistor

1W resistor

metal film, precision resistor

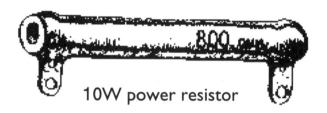

10W power resistor

Fig. 2-2: Different types of resistors.

Potentiometers

Potentiometers (or *pots,* as they're commonly called) are members of the resistor family, except that they are variable resistors. Referring to Fig. 2-3, a potentiometer is a circular resistance element with a sliding conductor called a *wiper* going across it. A pot serves the same function in electrical circuits that a faucet does in plumbing, namely, to regulate current flow. Potentiometers that use a straight resistance element are usually called slide pots (or *faders* in audio applications).

There are actually two variable resistors in a pot. As the resistance between terminals 1 and 2 decreases due to moving the sliding conductor toward terminal 1, the resistance between terminals 2 and 3 increases. Moving the wiper in the opposite direction produces opposite results.

You usually need to use both resistance elements, but sometimes you'll only use one. If you connect up terminals 2 and 3 or 1 and 2 only, you have a two-terminal variable resistor. However, to simplify matters we'll refer to anything that's a variable resistance control as a pot.

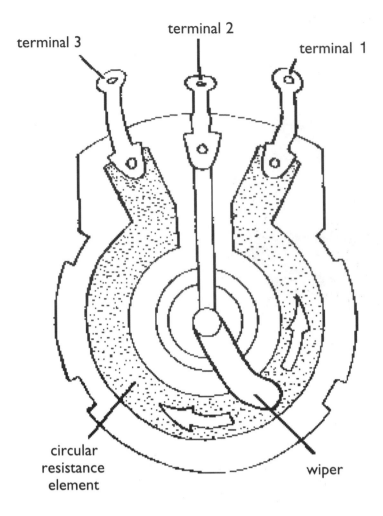

terminal 3   terminal 2   terminal 1

circular
resistance
element   wiper

Fig. 2-3

Potentiometer Taper

One other characteristic of pots, *taper,* can be a source of confusion. This describes the rate at which the resistance element changes. A *linear* taper yields a linear change in resistance when you move the pot—turning it halfway gives half the resistance, a quarter of the way gives a quarter of the resistance, and so on.

However, a *log* taper pot (also known as an audio taper pot) changes resistance logarithmically from one end to the other. Turning the pot up halfway covers only about 10% of the pot's total resistance, and turning the pot up two-thirds of the way covers about 40% of the total resistance. As it gets past this point, each degree of control rotation continues to cover a progressively greater amount of resistance. This taper is necessary because with the human ear, for a sound to appear to steadily increase in volume, you have to actually increase the sound in progressively larger amounts—or logarithmically, in mathematical terms (Fig. 2-4).

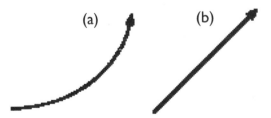

(a)   (b)

Fig. 2-4: A volume change like (a) sounds like (b) to your ear.

In computer-based gear, linear pots are common because the software itself can change the taper by assigning different values to different points in the pot's rotation, including tapers that go beyond simply log or linear changes. The MIDItools Computer uses linear pots.

Different Potentiometer Types

There are many different types of pots (Fig. 2-5); sometimes one or more potentiometer elements are combined, producing a two-section (or greater) ganged pot. Pots occasionally have an on/off switch mounted on the back.

Trimpots are miniature pots for set-and-forget-type applications. These are electrically equivalent to regular pots, but are physically tiny and not designed for continuous handling. They usually mount with other components on a printed circuit board.

Fig. 2-5: Clockwise from upper-left hand corner: a dual-section ganged pot, a single-section rotary pot, a rotary pot with an on/off switch mounted on the back, a miniature trimpot, and a linear slide pot.

Good pots are relatively expensive, but they will give longer service and perform reliably. Some pots are sealed from the outside air to prevent dust and pollution from coating the resistance elements and interrupting the resistance change (this produces a "scratchy" sound with audio circuitry). Most common pots, however, are not hermetically sealed and are more easily subject to deterioration. Fortunately, chemical sprays (such as DeoxIT from Caig Laboratories) can clean and renew the resistance surface of old pots to a remarkable degree.

Capacitors

The three most important capacitor characteristics are:

- Value (amount of capacitance)

- Working voltage (how much voltage the capacitor can withstand)

- Size and type (capacitors vary widely in size)

A capacitor's value is expressed in *farads,* with one complication. A farad is a whole lot of capacitance, therefore, capacitors are usually rated in microfarads (abbreviated μF), which equals one-millionth of a farad (0.000001 farad). There are even some very low capacitance capacitors with values in picofarads or pF (a millionth of a millionth of a farad—pretty tiny!).

International Capacitor Nomenclature

As with resistors, schematics in most other parts of the world designate capacitor values differently from American schematics. First of all, in addition to the μF and pF, these schematics frequently use the term nanofarad (abbreviated nF), which equals 0.000000001 farad. Here are some common capacitor values, expressed in μF, pF, and nF:

0.001μF = 1,000pF = 1nF
0.01μF = 10,000pF = 10nF
0.1μF = 100,000pF = 100nF

When a capacitor value includes a decimal point (*i.e.,* 1.2 µF, 4.7 pF, 2.2 nF), the µ, p, or n goes where the decimal point would normally appear. Here are some examples of American nomenclature and the international equivalents:

American	International
1500pF	1n5
4.7µF	4µ7
0.22µF	220nF
6.8pF	6p8

While the international nomenclature may appear more complex, it is actually a more efficient and less ambiguous way to designate resistor and capacitor values. It's almost impossible to put a decimal point in the wrong place accidentally, as the international nomenclature avoids using decimal points; and you don't end up with big numbers—an otherwise clumsy 3900pF becomes 3n9 in metric.

Working Voltage

Working voltage simply means the voltage up to which a capacitor will work reliably. If a 10V capacitor gets hit consistently with 15V, you will end up with a warm or nonfunctioning capacitor. You can use a capacitor with a working voltage higher than the one specified. In most any circuit, as long as the capacitors have a higher working voltage than the voltage of the power supply feeding the circuit, you're covered.

Different Capacitor Sizes and Types

Capacitor size (as a rough rule of thumb) increases with either higher capacitance or working voltage. Because of the importance of small components in today's miniaturized gear, electronic parts catalogs frequently specify capacitor dimensions along with working voltage and capacitance.

There are two basic types of capacitors (caps): *discs* and *electrolytics* (Fig. 2-6). Disc capacitors all look pretty much the same—a round, fairly flat ceramic blob of variable size with two wires coming out of it. They generally have relatively high working voltages (ratings of 500V are common), but their capacitance seldom exceeds 0.2µF. Disc capacitors can even provide very small values like 5 or 10pF.

Electrolytic capacitors are tubular, and have either *axial* or *radial* mounting (Fig. 2-6 shows both). With radial mounting both wires come out of the same end of the capacitor. Axial mount caps lie flat against circuit boards, while radial ones mount "standing."

Electrolytic caps are also *polarized*, meaning that they have a positive (+) and negative (-) end, just like a battery—and like a battery, if you hook up the positive and negative backwards, the part won't work right. On most capacitors, only one lead is marked for polarity.

A lot of capacitance can be squeezed into an electrolytic— 40,000µF or more. Unfortunately electrolytics age, because of internal chemicals that eventually dry up, over anywhere from several years to many decades.

Although resistors and disc capacitors aren't polarized, many other electronic parts are, and it's important to hook the ends up correctly. One of the more common errors encountered in building electronic gear is to miss the polarity of an electrolytic capacitor, a transistor, or what have you; so be careful.

Other types of capacitors include *mylar* types, which are similar to discs but less susceptible to temperature changes and other variables. *Polystyrene* types are generally small and provide stable capacitance values in the pF range; they're often tubular, plastic, and silvery.

The premium capacitors for large capacitance values are *tantalum* types, which can be quite expensive unless purchased surplus. Like electrolytics, they are polarized; unlike electrolytics, they don't dry out over time, and generally are able to pack a larger amount of capacitance in a smaller physical space. Tantalum capacitors are reliable, and perform well in critical circuits.

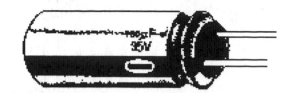

radial mounting electrolytic capacitor
(negative or minus lead marked)

mylar capacitor

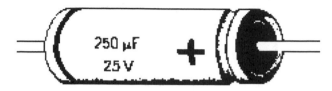

axial mounting electrolytic capacitor
(positive or plus lead marked)

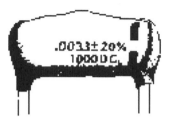

dipped mylar capacitor

tantalum capacitor

polystyrene capacitor

tantalum capacitor

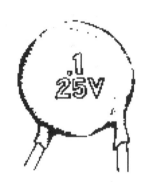

ceramic disc capacitor

Fig. 2-6

Basic Semiconductors

In addition to conductors and insulators, there is a third class of material that exhibits properties of both. Under some conditions, it acts as an insulator, and under other conditions it's a conductor. This phenomenon is called *semiconducting*—hence the name *semiconductor*—and allows a variable control over electron flow, forming the cornerstone of modern electronics. Semiconducting devices can provide switching, making them ideal for the on/off nature of digital electronics. Transistors, light-emitting diodes (LEDs), integrated circuits, and many more parts are based on semiconducting materials.

Semiconductors are called *active* components. Unlike resistors, capacitors, and other *passive* components, active components can (under the right conditions) put out more signal than is put in. This is called *gain,* which means semiconductors can amplify as well as switch.

Three important precautions apply to all semiconductor devices:

* Solder with care, as excess heat damages semiconductors. Most semiconductors can be inserted in matching sockets to eliminate the need for soldering; the socket gets soldered to the board, and the leads plug into the socket without any soldering.

- Be careful not to apply either excess voltage or voltage of the wrong polarity to a semiconductor.

- Avoid handling a semiconductor's terminals. The human body can accumulate enough static electricity to "zap" the part, which is why many semiconductors are packaged in conductive foam. (Chapter 4 on Tools mentions how a ground strap can help prevent zapping a chip while handling it.)

Diodes

The *diode* (Fig. 2-7) is the simplest kind of semiconductor we'll use. It acts as an electronic switch.

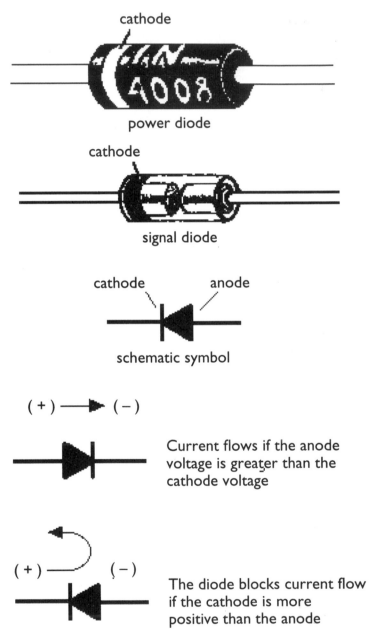

Fig. 2-7

Diodes come in two basic types: *signal* diodes and *power* diodes. Signal diodes are usually small cylinders, a bit smaller than the average resistor, but made out of glass and sporting only one band. This band is the *cathode* and indicates diode polarity the way a (+) and (-) identify battery polarity. The other lead is called the *anode*.

If the anode is more positive than the cathode (or depending on your viewpoint, if the cathode is more negative than the anode), current will flow through the diode. For example, if a diode's cathode connects to ground and the anode connects to a battery's (+) terminal (Fig. 2-8A), current will flow from the battery, through the diode, and to ground.

However, if you reverse the diode, no current will flow because the cathode is more positive than the anode (Fig. 2-8B). If the voltage on the anode or cathode is AC (voltages in both positive and negative quadrants), one half of the AC will be lopped off (in Fig. 2-8C, voltages in the positive quadrant make it through the diode).

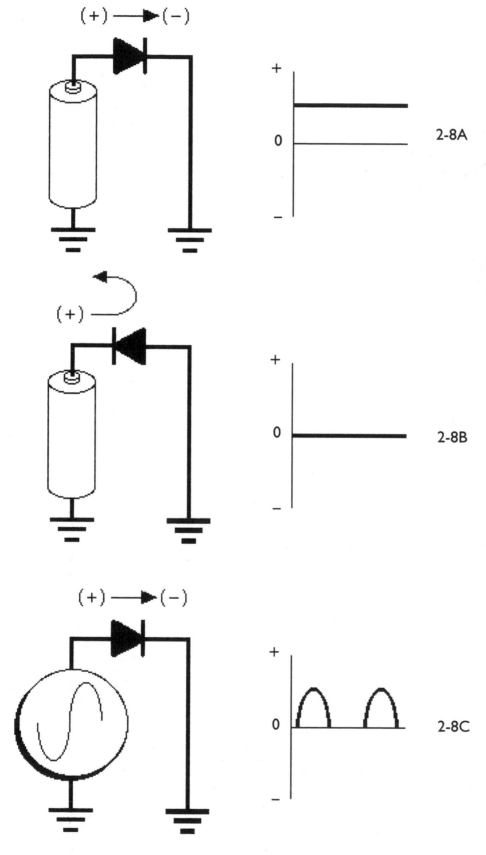

Fig. 2-8

Power diodes are somewhat larger than signal diodes, although those with 1 Amp to 4 Amp ratings are fairly small. They will also substitute for signal diodes, but can be more expensive.

Diodes are rated according to voltage-handling and current-handling ability. It's common practice to use a diode that's considerably over-rated, because the cost difference isn't significant, and the reliability can be higher.

Light-Emitting Diodes

Fig. 2-9 shows several *light-emitting diodes (LED),* which emit light when you feed them some current. Available colors are red, green, yellow, orange, blue (very expensive and current-hungry), and bicolor red/green types. The latter fall into two types: in one, the cathodes are common and the anodes are brought out separately. In the other, the two LEDs are connected "back-to-back." This type is sometimes considered a "tricolor" LED because passing AC through it lights up both the red and green elements, which combine to form an orange/yellow color.

LEDs don't burn out under normal use. Additionally, because LEDs don't have a skinny little filament like a regular light bulb, they're virtually immune to vibrations and shock. However, they can be destroyed if too much current goes through them. Also, because they are polarized (like any diode), if hooked up backwards they won't light.

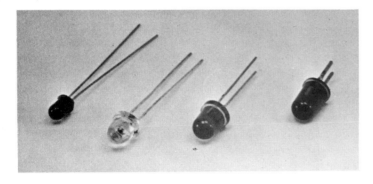

Fig. 2-9: LEDs in several different case styles.

LEDs generally have a flat spot on the case or dot of paint to indicate the cathode. If the manufacturer doesn't follow this convention, the packaging will usually indicate which lead is the cathode.

Liquid Crystal Display (LCD)

Like LEDs, this type of display is also based on semiconducting material although the principle of operation is completely different. LCDs are made from a "nematic liquid crystal" which is a fluid of little crystal rods. Normally these rods are aligned in a certain orientation (on the molecular level) such that light reflects off of them and gives that characteristic gray look.

Subjecting the fluid to an electric field rotates the crystals so the light does not reflect back, darkening the LCD. By applying the electric field selectively to the fluid, we can create black and gray areas that resemble letters, numbers, pictures, etc. This is admittedly an oversimplification, but it is a basically accurate description.

The MIDItools LCD (Fig. 2-10) can display up to 16 characters on 2 lines. Each character is derived from an 8 X 5 matrix of dots (pixels); turning on certain pixels forms a particular character, as shown in the inset.

An oscillator drives the LCD to put the pixels into a "standby" mode, and several pins carry the logic signals required to form the characters. The MIDItools Computer uses 16 LEDs and a single LCD to indicate the unit's status.

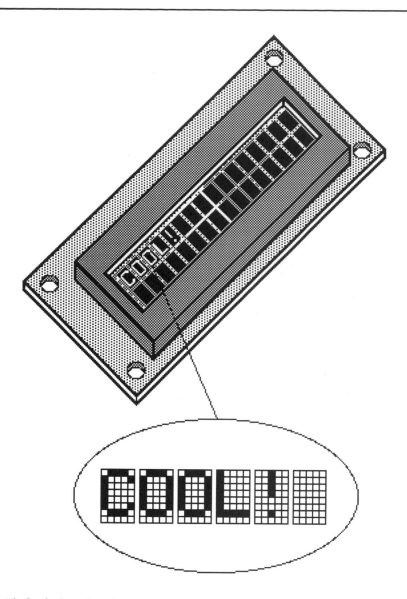

Fig. 2-10: *The first five letters have the correct pixels turned on to spell the word "Cool!" An alphanumeric (letters and numbers) LCD arranges the pixels in 8X5 grids, separated into individual letters. Larger LCDs often consist of a huge matrix of dots and can therefore represent graphics.*

Transistors

A standard *bipolar transistor* has three terminals: the *collector, base,* and *emitter.* One terminal emits electrons, another terminal collects them, and a third terminal acts as a control element. Transistors come in a variety of case types, from small, epoxy-plastic types (see Fig. 2-11) to large, metal models (power transistors).

Fig. 2-11: *The transistor on the left is in a metal case; the one on the right is in an epoxy-plastic case.*

Transistors make good drivers, switchers, and current boosters, but we don't use very many transistors in the MIDItools Computer system. The real work in the computer world is done by integrated circuits, described later.

Incidentally, there are many other types of transistors (unijunction transistor, phototransistor, etc.). One of the most common variations is the field-effect transistor (FET), which also has three terminals (drain, source, and gate) and performs functions similar to bipolar transistors. Each transistor family has particular characteristics that make it better-suited to some applications than others.

Optoisolators

An optoisolator combines a photo-sensitive transistor and LED in a small, light-tight package (usually shaped like a six- or eight-pin integrated circuit, as described in the next section). The most interesting aspect of the optoisolator is that it can transfer current from one place to another without any direct electrical connection—it's all done with light. Typically, a "transmitter" stage drives the LED, while the phototransistor connects to the "receiver" stage. As the LED shines brighter, it causes the photo-sensitive transistor to conduct more current.

Why bother with isolation? MIDI uses optoisolators to prevent the possibility of ground loops, a condition where noise gets into the ground line and therefore into your mixer (and eventually, your master tape—oops!). Because no ground connection is required with an optoisolator, you can't get a ground loop. A thorough discussion of ground loops is beyond the scope of this book, but suffice it to say that optoisolators are an essential part of the MIDI interface. For more information about ground loops, write the Rane Corporation (10802 47th Ave. West, Mukilteo, WA 98275) and ask for Rane Note 110.

Integrated Circuits

An integrated circuit (IC) performs a complete function, such as to amplify or to perform logical operations. It is like any other circuit, except for an incredible parts density—it packs the equivalent of tens of thousands, or even millions, of transistors in a piece of silicon smaller than your littlest fingernail. It does this by depositing a bunch of transistors, diodes, and other materials that mimic the functions of resistors, capacitors, and switches on a single crystalline base called a *substrate*.

You can find almost any electronic function in an IC, from computer memory cells to low-noise audio preamplifiers to complete computers-on-a-chip. Many chips include several independent circuit building blocks, whose only common connections are to the pin's power connections. More than anything else, the IC has contributed to the low cost and small size of today's electronic gear.

There are two major families of ICs, *linear* and *digital*. Digital ICs are used in computers, calculators, digital clocks, and other decision-making or number-counting circuits—such as the MIDItools Computer. Typical digital ICs are memory chips, microprocessors (computer-on-a-chip), and chips that provide simple logic functions.

Linear ICs amplify, oscillate, filter, and do other interesting things. All audio equipment is based on linear circuitry, although sometimes linear circuitry is under digital control.

Some people wonder why other parts are necessary in addition to ICs. The answer is twofold: certain parts are difficult to fabricate on an IC, and ICs are usually set up as general-purpose devices. Other parts define particular characteristics such as the amount of gain, current drain, and frequency response.

IC Packaging

ICs are commonly packaged in a dual in-line package (DIP), a rectangular, thin block with rows of pins on either side of the package (Fig. 2-12). The number of pins can vary widely, but the widths (while they vary) fit standardized dimensions. The MIDItools Computer uses ICs with as few as eight pins and as many as forty.

Fig. 2-12: The IC at left is packaged in an 8-pin minidip, the IC at center in a TO-5 round package (seldom used), and the IC at right is in a 14-pin DIP.

IC Pin Numbering

Each IC terminal is assigned a number for identification purposes. The numbers are assigned as follows: looking at the IC from the top (i.e., with the pins pointing away from you), you will see some kind of notch, dot, or other identifying mark at one end of the IC. With this notch pointing up, as in Fig. 2-13, the pin in the extreme upper left corner is pin 1. The pin below it is pin 2; continue counting down until you reach the end of the row. At this point, jump over to the bottom of the next row and continue counting, but this time count up. The highest number pin is therefore in the upper right corner.

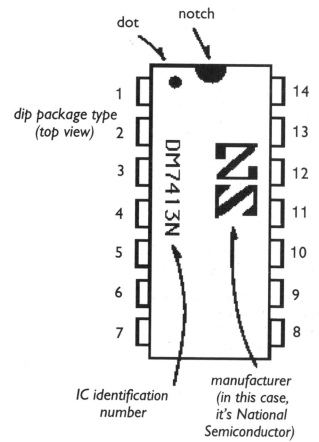

Fig. 2-13: Identifying IC pins. Note how the lowest-numbered pin is in the upper left, and the highest-numbered pin in the upper right.

IC Nomenclature

IC nomenclature varies from manufacturer to manufacturer. A part's basic name will be consistent, but different manufacturers add different prefixes to parts—for example, if an IC part number starts with MC, it was originally made by Motorola; LM indicates National Semiconductor. Some manufacturers use different prefixes for different parts types, and often append suffixes that indicate variations on a standard IC design such as the type of packaging, whether a part is designed for military or consumer use, and other characteristics.

Sometimes letters are also inserted in the middle of an IC to give further information about the IC. For example, a 7404 chip may also show up as a 74LS04, which is a low power version.

Crystals

No, we're not getting New Age on you here. Crystals are based on piezoelectric materials, and provide a highly accurate frequency reference (Fig. 2-14). Connecting a crystal to a microprocessor provides a "clock" to which the microprocessor operations synchronize. The concept of the clock will be covered in more detail—a mind-boggling amount of detail, in fact—in Chapter 13 on the MC68HC705C8 microprocessor.

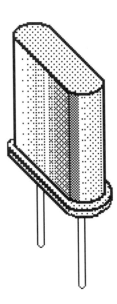

Fig. 2-14

Wire

The simplest kind of wire (Fig. 2-15 shows different types of wire) is bare wire—a solid, fairly thick piece of copper alloy which lets electrons migrate from one place to another. This kind of wire is popularly called *bus wire*.

The next step up in complexity is *insulated* wire—wire covered with a plastic sleeve or insulator that keeps it from shorting out to any other wires. One handy feature is that the insulation comes in different colors for color-coding.

Stranded wire consists of many thin bare wires covered with a plastic sleeve that insulates the entire bunch of wires and holds them together. Stranded wire has the advantage of being sturdier if the wire gets pushed around a lot; if you bend solid wire too much or too often, it can break.

Gauge is the proper term for wire diameter. The best range for wire in these circuits is from #22 (largest practical) to #28 (smallest practical). The higher the gauge number, the thinner the wire.

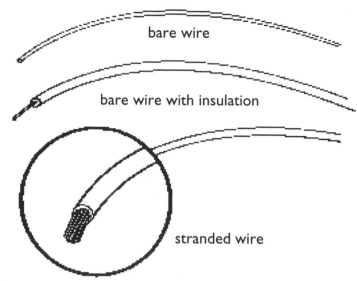

Fig. 2-15: Different wire types.

Ribbon Cable

The three types of wire mentioned above are used for most point-to-point wiring, but to simplify life, the MIDItools Computer makes extensive use of ribbon cable that groups bunches of wires together and attaches the end to DIP plugs. These then plug into sockets (Fig. 2-16). We'll loosely define cable as more than one insulated wire inside a plastic sheath (or which are otherwise connected into a single entity).

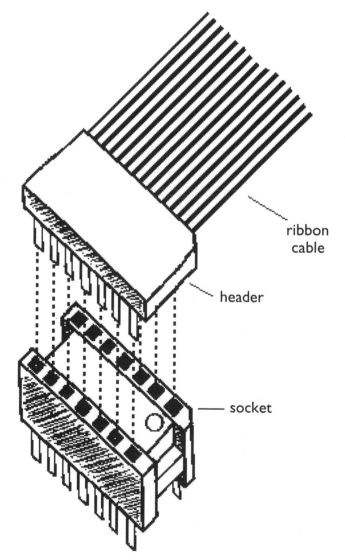

Fig. 2-16: Multiconductor ribbon cable attaches to a DIP "header" (plug) that plugs into a standard IC socket.

For example, suppose you need to connect 16 wires between two different circuit boards. You could either laboriously solder 16 wires (32 connections) between the two boards, then bundle the wires together so they don't look too much like a rat's nest. Or, you could bring the points that need to connect together on each board to a 16-pin socket, and run a commercially-available 16-conductor ribbon cable from one socket to the other by simply plugging each end of the cable into the appropriate socket. The latter approach will save you time (and possibly gray hairs).

Shielded Cable

Most musicians are familiar with *shielded cable,* as used in guitar cords. Shielded cable has one (and sometimes more) insulated conductor(s), wrapped or covered by some form of conductive shield. This shield is usually made of conductive foil or a crisscrossing pattern of very fine protective wires (Fig. 2-17). By connecting the shield to a ground point, the wires it encloses are less susceptible to stray hum or radio signals. The wire inside the shield is referred to as *hot* compared to the shield, which is grounded (no volts—remember?). Sometimes shielding is not required, in which case the cable is simply referred to as *multiple-conductor* cable.

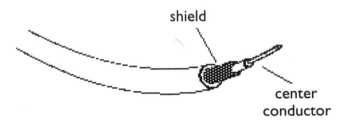

Fig. 2-17: With shielded cable, the center conductor is covered by a shield of fine wires or foil.

Twisted Pair Cable

Twisted pair is similar to shielded cable; by using a pair of wires, twisting them, and connecting one to ground, the other one is somewhat shielded.

Though not as effective as the wrapped type, twisted pair cable is still useful for many applications. Computer cables that use two conductors surrounded by a shield, such as MIDI cables, often wrap the shield around a twisted pair. This not only provides shielding, but the twisting of the cables lessens interference between the two hot lines.

Zip Cord

Zip cord is the wire (usually brown) found on toasters, lamps, radios, and other appliances that plug into the wall (Fig. 2-18); the two heavily insulated conductors can carry a reasonable amount of current. It's useful for both speaker wires and power supply wires. One fact many people don't know: the two different conductors of zip cord are coded. Usually, one side of the conductor's insulation is ridged, while the insulation on the other side is smooth.

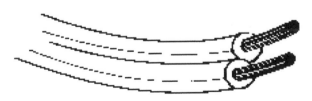

Fig. 2-18: Zip cord has two conductors and is used primarily for AC and speaker wiring.

Mechanical Parts

DIN Plugs and Jacks

DIN plugs are named after Deutsch Industry Norm, a European standards committee that created the specification for DIN connectors. DIN connectors are relatively low-cost, multipin connectors designed for consumer electronics equipment.

MIDI uses 5-pin, 180 degree DIN plugs (Fig. 2-19). Notice that there are also 270 degree types, with the pins arranged in an arc of 270 degrees instead of 180 degrees. These are not compatible with MIDI gear, so make sure you get the right kind of connector.

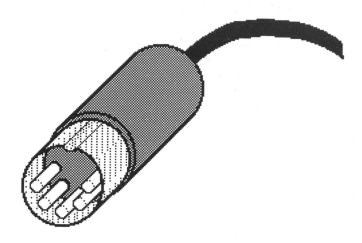

Fig. 2-19: 5-pin DIN plug as used for MIDI and other applications.

DIN jacks are the companion pieces to DIN plugs. There are three main styles: in-line (where the jack connects directly to the end of a cable), chassis mount, and PC mount (Fig. 2-20).

Fig. 2-20: 5-pin MIDI jack. This particular type is designed to solder directly to a printed circuit board.

The MIDItools Computer circuit boards are designed to accept MIDI jacks with PC (printed circuit board) mounting connectors; their terminals solder directly to the circuit board. This is much easier than running wires from the board to the connectors, but requires that the board be mounted so that the connectors are flush against the enclosure to allow for unobstructed plugging and unplugging of cables.

DC Power (Coaxial) Plugs and Jacks

These are two-conductor connectors designed for consumer gear. Most "wall wart" wall transformers terminate in a DC power plug. This has a metal tube surrounded by an insulator, which is in turn surrounded by a metal sleeve (Fig. 2-21).

The matching jack has a pin that goes into the tube, and a metal flange that presses against the plug's metal sleeve. DC power plug connectors come in several different sizes, so it's important to get matched plugs and jacks. Some non-matching plugs and jacks will fit together, but the connection may be loose and cause intermittent operation.

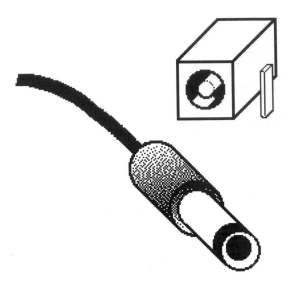

Fig. 2-21: A DC power plug (left) and jack (right).

Transformers

Fig. 2-22 shows a typical "wall wart" power transformer. Since 115V will often fry semiconductors, the transformer converts the AC coming out of your wall to a lower AC or DC voltage (6, 12, 15, or some other low voltage). With DC output wall warts, the plug is polarized. However, DC power jacks are not standardized; some expect a positive voltage on the tip (inner conductor), while others expect a negative voltage. (Hopefully, the device you're plugging into will have some kind of indication which type it is; usually there's a graphic to indicate the polarity, as shown in Fig. 2-22.) The MIDItools Computer will accept AC or DC inputs (of any polarity) between the range of 9V to 15V.

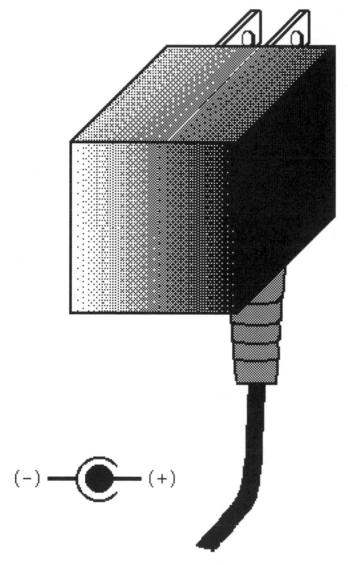

$(-)$ ————◐———— $(+)$

Fig. 2-22: A "wall wart" transformer. Some of these output DC, and some AC. With DC-powered gear, there will usually be a graphic similar to the one in the figure that shows whether the tip has a positive or negative polarity.

Wall warts with AC outputs simply consist of a transformer. Those with DC outputs include internal diodes to perform the AC-to-DC conversion.

Programming Pins

These have a number of tall, fairly strong pins arranged in a row or block (Fig. 2-23) that solder to the circuit board. Several points in the circuit connect to these pins, and a companion "programming jumper" fits over two or more pins. Jumpering between different pins sets up different default conditions.

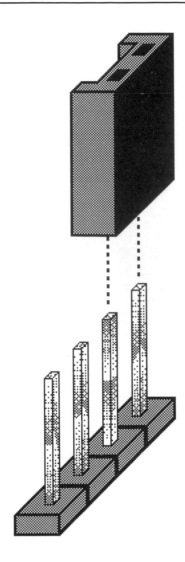

Fig. 2-23: The jumper is about to be placed over two of the programming pins, thus shorting them together and programming a particular condition.

Toggle Switches

Switches generally complete or interrupt a circuit. Fig. 2-24 shows a simple *toggle* switch schematic. With the switch open, A and B are insulated from each other; close the switch, and a conductor connects wires A and B.

open SPST switch

closed SPST switch

Fig. 2-24: SPST switch.

Most on/off switches are of this type. They are called single-pole, single-throw switches (or SPST) because one wire (the pole) can switch to one other wire (the throw). A single-pole, double-throw type (SPDT) can switch a wire to two other wires (Fig. 2-25).

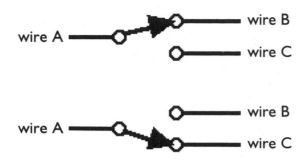

Fig. 2-25: *The two possible SPDT switch positions: wire A can connect either to wire B or wire C.*

A double-pole, double-throw (DPDT) switch (Fig. 2-26), can switch each of two wires to two other wires. A toggle switch has each of the poles and throws brought out to individual solder terminals, usually in a logical way, and comes in regular or miniature sizes.

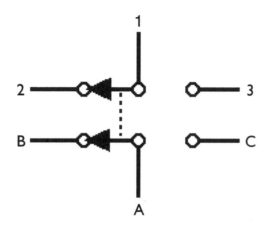

Fig. 2-26: *DPDT switch: as 1 connects to 2, A connects to B; when 1 connects to 3, A connects to C.*

Fig. 2-27 shows which terminals connect together when you push the switch toggle in different directions for a miniature toggle switch. Note that pushing the toggle *down* connects the middle and upper terminals together, while pushing the toggle *up* connects the middle and lower terminals together. Also, note that any DPDT switch can be used as an SPDT, DPST, or SPST switch by simply not using all the available terminals.

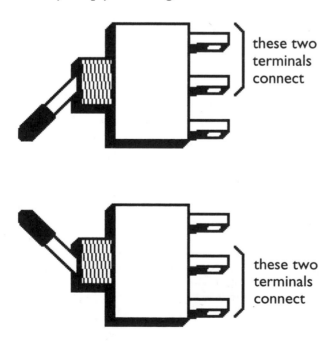

Fig. 2-27: *The terminals that connect together for the two toggle positions of a typical miniature SPDT switch.*

Fig. 2-28 shows a number of switches. The slide switch is less expensive (but also somewhat flimsier) than toggle types. They can be hard to mount, and their non-airtight construction tends to pick up dust and dirt.

Fig. 2-28: Six different switch types. The switch at center is a DPDT miniature toggle switch; clockwise from the left side, there's a DPDT footswitch as used in "stomp boxes," regular-size slide switch, heavy-duty toggle switch, rotary switch, and 7-position DIP switch.

Pushbutton Switches

Pushbutton switches perform a switching function when you push down on a button. Usually the pushbutton switch circuit is open, and pushing on the button closes the circuit. However, sometimes the circuit is normally closed and pushing on the button opens the circuit. A computer, of course, can change the response in software—in other words, it can "act" as if the switch is open when it's closed, or vice-versa.

Pushbuttons are used for the MIDItools keypad and for the on/off switch, but the two types are subtly different. The keypad switches are momentary—the circuit is closed only as long as the button is pressed. The on/off switch has a *latching* action; push once to close the circuit, push again to open it.

Rotary Switches

More complicated switching requires a *rotary* switch. We don't use any in the MIDItools Computer, but it's worth talking about these types of switches because you'll run into them often; besides, you may get an idea for a MIDItools modification that would require the use of a rotary switch.

A rotary switch has phenolic or ceramic wafers with terminals brought out for the poles and throws. Usually the mechanism works similarly to the one detailed in Fig. 2-29, with a detent mechanism hooked up so that the rotary switch clicks as you turn it around and the various conductors line up. Single-pole, 6-throw (SP6T), double-pole, 12- throw (2P12T), and other exotic switching combinations are possible.

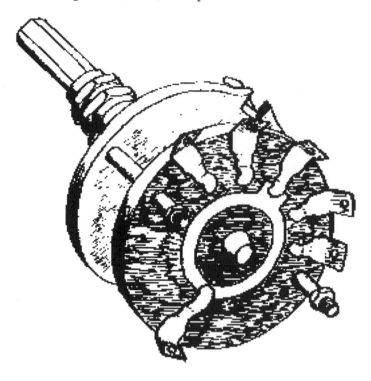

Fig. 2-29: *With a rotary switch, rotating the wiper connects pole connection with any one of several throws. This switch is a 1 pole, 5 throw type.*

With rotary switches and some other switch types, which terminals connect together in various switch positions may not be entirely obvious. To find out, use a continuity tester or ohmmeter to check for continuity (a completed circuit, in other words) between the various switch terminals; make a note of which terminals connect together in various switch positions.

DIP Switches

Our final switch type is the *DIP switch*. The one in Fig. 2-28 contains seven miniature on/off switches in a case not much bigger than a conventional 14-pin IC.

In fact, DIP switches are size-compatible with standard IC sockets. DIP switches are not really intended as front panel switches; they have the same relationship to regular switches as trimpots have to regular potentiometers.

Switch Ratings

It's sometimes important to know the current rating of the switch, as well as the switching configuration. Most toggle switches can safely handle 2 or 3 Amps of current at 125V, which means that they can control a fair amount of juice (about 250W). Any switch can handle the voltages we'll be dealing with here; however, DIP switches are *never* suitable for switching 115V AC.

Switch Screw Terminals

On some switches and other parts, you'll see screw terminals. Wrapping a wire around the screw and tightening it down is just not as reliable as soldering, so either avoid these, or remove the screws and solder anyway.

Sockets

Sockets are "go-betweens" between an IC and circuit board (Fig. 2-30). In other words, you could plug an IC directly into a circuit board and solder it in place, but this can lead to three problems:

- Heat can damage semiconductors

- Replacing a defective IC is very time-consuming

- Upgrading or changing a part can also be a pain

Instead, you solder the socket to the board (which is relatively impervious to heat), and plug the IC or other compatible component (DIP switch, ribbon cable, etc.) into the socket. Replacing the IC simply involves removing it from the socket and plugging in the new chip.

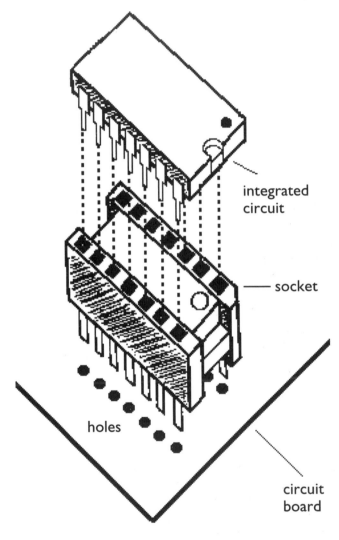

integrated circuit

socket

holes

circuit board

Fig. 2-30: The circuit board has holes drilled to accommodate the socket pins. The IC is plugged into the socket once the socket has been soldered to the circuit board.

Sockets are nice, but not perfect. Sometimes the connection between the IC and socket will oxidize, giving an intermittent contact. Simply pulling out the IC part way then reinserting it will usually solve this problem; stubborn cases may require contact cleaner. Also, sometimes ICs can come loose from their sockets if shaken or vibrated to excess. Pushing down on the IC so that it seats firmly in the socket usually solves this.

When you need to change a chip often (for example when prototyping, or changing memory chips in the MIDItools Computer), consider using a zero insertion force (ZIF) socket. Unlike regular sockets, these have an "arm" that, when switched in one direction, opens up the contacts that grab the IC pins. When open, you can insert a chip without any force because you're not working against the mechanical resistance of the contacts. Pushing the arm in the other direction closes the contacts and pushes them against the IC pins to provide good contact.

Heat Sinks

Semiconductors that need to handle a lot of power often generate significant amounts of heat. Since excessive heat can shorten a component's life, a *heat sink* draws the heat away and dissipates it into the air. The MIDItools Computer requires a heat sink on the voltage regulator IC, as this is the component that converts the wall wart voltage to the 5V DC that powers all the internal circuitry.

The typical heat sink clamps over an IC, or screws onto the case (Fig. 2-31). The better the thermal connection between the IC and heat sink, the better the heat dissipation. Smearing a thin layer of silicone grease between the heat sink and IC improves the heat transfer.

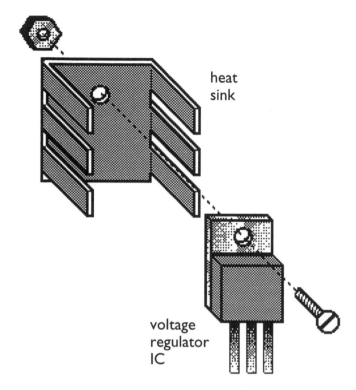

heat sink

voltage regulator IC

Fig. 2-31: A nut and bolt attach the heat sink to the voltage regulator IC.

Knobs

Everybody knows what a knob is, but you may not know that there are different methods to hold knobs onto pot and switch shafts. Cheap knobs simply put grooves on the inside plastic wall that mate with matching grooves on the pot shaft. Types with a setscrew in the back are somewhat better, but the best are the kind with two setscrews, placed ninety degrees apart. This dual retaining action holds the knob tightly and securely on its shaft. Sometimes the setscrews use standard screwdriver slots, and sometimes hex nuts. To take off a knob with hex nuts requires a tool called an Allen wrench. Chances are, though, that you won't run into these too often, as hex nuts generally are indicative of a high-priced knob.

Grommets

Grommets (Fig. 2-32) are little rubber or plastic doughnuts. They are installed in pass-through holes for wires in metal panels, principally to keep the wire's insulation from scraping against the sharp metal that often surrounds a drilled hole. You'll see that most AC line cords pass through grommets on their way to the electronic innards of whatever they're powering.

Fig. 2-32

Nuts and Bolts

The most popular sizes for electronic work are 4-40 and 6-32. It's a good idea to buy nuts and bolts in assorted sizes, so that you always have hardware around. Common screw lengths for electronic construction are 9.3 mm (3/8"), 6.2 mm (1/4"), and 21.8 mm (7/8"). The 6-32 types are a little heavier duty, and good for mounting parts like transformers and panels. The 4-40 size is good for attaching solder lugs and mounting circuit boards.

Lockwashers

Lockwashers go between a nut and the surface being screwed through (see Fig. 2-33). Lockwashers hold the screw tightly and keep it from becoming undone by vibration or other sinister forces.

Solder Lugs

Solder lugs (Fig. 2-34) mount to a metal chassis with a screw through one end; the other hole is for attaching wires and making solder connections. Actually, you can call anything that is metal and designed to have wires soldered to it a solder lug. For example, a potentiometer has three terminals which can be thought of as solder lugs. The terminals coming out of switches are also solder lugs.

Cases

Most cases (or chassis) are made of metal for two reasons: one, metal is a conductor, so the case may be treated as a big ground area; two, metal is far stronger than plastic or phenolic, the other popular choices for cases. Your best bet is to stick to the aluminum type. Steel eats through drill bits like crazy and requires more effort to drill.

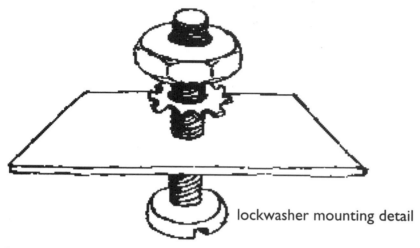

lockwasher mounting detail

Fig. 2-33: Three different types of lockwashers, and how a lockwasher mounts between the nut and chassis.

Fig. 2-34

Reading Schematic Diagrams

Now you know what kinds of parts we'll be working with, what they look like, and what their important characteristics are. Before we finish, we should talk about relating these parts to *schematic* diagrams.

Schematics are simply shorthand wiring diagrams. Instead of drawing a wire, you draw a line. When connections go to ground, rather than drawing a line connecting all the ground points together, you just hang a ground symbol on whatever needs to be grounded.

Each part is identified by its own symbol, except for integrated circuits. Fig. 2-35 shows the schematic equivalents for the main parts we've talked about.

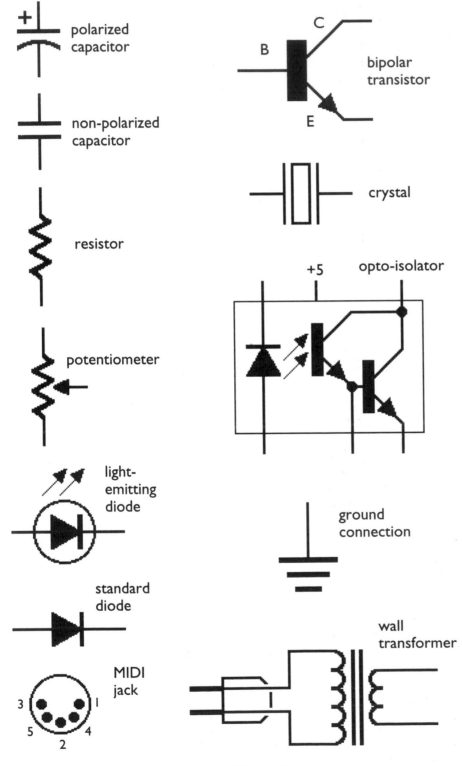

Fig. 2-35: Schematic symbols for the main parts used in the MIDItools Computer.

Integrated circuits have nearly as many schematic representations as there are ICs, but we'll use the two most popular approaches.

One way is to simply draw a box with pin numbers. This is common for complex parts such as microprocessors. Sometimes the part will be drawn realistically, whereas in other instances the box will be more symbolic (Fig. 2-36). The latter approach doesn't constrain you to having the pins in a particular physical place, so you can group together pins with related functions.

MC68HC705C8

30	TD0		$\overline{IRQ}$	2
29	RD1			
			$\overline{SS}$	34
			SCK	33
			MOSI	32
			MISO	31
1	$\overline{RESET}$		PA0	11
			PA1	10
			PA2	9
			PA3	8
			PA4	7
39	OSC1		PA5	6
38	OSC2		PA6	5
			PA7	4
			PB0	12
			PB1	13
			PB2	14
			PB3	15
			PB4	16
3	V_{PP}		PB5	17
40	V_{CC}		PB6	18
			PB7	19
20	V_{SS}		PC0	28
			PC1	27
			PC2	26
			PC3	25
			PC4	24
			PC5	23
37	TCAP		PC6	22
35	TCMP		PC7	21

Fig. 2-36: This schematic diagram of the MC68HC705 doesn't look much like the chip itself, but allows for grouping related pins together (e.g., the PB, PA, and PC lines) for easier understanding, even if the pins are not located near each other physically.

For simpler ICs, such as logic functions, each part of the IC may be shown as a separate symbol with associated pin numbers. For example, the 7404 IC contains six subcircuits in a single, 14-pin package. In this case, we can still draw a skeleton outline (Fig. 2-37, left) that shows each subsection of the IC, but it's frequently less cumbersome to show the individual subcircuits and their associated pin numbers (Fig. 2-37, right).

You'll notice that the power leads, pins 7 and 14, come out of the top and bottom of one of the subcircuits. The power supply connection lines could come out of any of the subcircuits; the reason it doesn't matter is that the power lines are generally common to all subcircuits within an IC.

Frequently it is not necessary to show all the IC pins, since some pins are not of interest in many applications, and some aren't even connected to

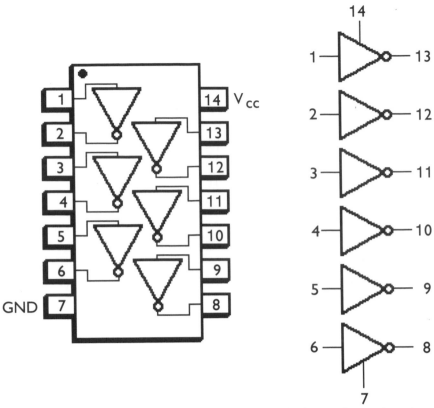

Fig. 2-37: The representation on the left is typically used in data books to make the part's function clearer, but most schematics use the approach shown on the right.

anything inside the IC. In fact, if you see some schematics and notice unconnected IC pins, don't worry; to save space, sometimes the drawing shows only the pins you need.

However, proper engineering practice is to show *all* unused pins and label them as NC (no connection). Also, if an IC has several subcircuits, it's a good idea to show all the subcircuits, even if they're not all used. (Incidentally, the inputs to the unused subcircuits are usually tied to either ground or the supply voltage so that they are electrically disabled and don't affect the other subcircuits.)

Wiring Diagrams vs. Schematics

For small circuits, in some ways it's easier to build a circuit from a wiring diagram; however, schematics give a clearer understanding of what the circuit does. For the MIDItools Computer, you don't really need a wiring diagram since the parts can be mounted on a circuit board, reducing the required wiring to a bare minimum. Therefore, we'll show schematic representations exclusively.

Chapter 3
MIDI Basics

Since we're going to build a MIDI computer, we need to understand what MIDI can do. Even if you're a MIDI veteran, it's still a good idea to skim this section since it also covers some MIDItools Computer applications. You'll get your reward later in Chapter 11, which covers the MIDI spec from a more technical standpoint.

Virtually all electronic instruments built since the early 80s—synthesizers, drum machines, sequencers, and so on—have some type of small computer inside. Although it may seem unusual to mix high-tech number-crunching with art, remember that music is a close relative of mathematics. This concept goes back at least as far as Pythagoras (the Greek philosopher and mathematician), who became fascinated with the mathematical properties of different scales and tunings.

Orchestras tune up to A 440, where the 440 stands for a specific number of sound waves per second. Tempos are given in a certain number of beats per minute, and notes are expressed as fractions—quarter notes, eighth notes, sixteenth notes, and so on. Songs last for a certain number of measures, and particular sections of a song will often repeat a certain number of times within the song. Even the rate of vibrato, the frequency response of an instrument, and the harmonic structure of a vibrating string can all be expressed as numbers. Computers are right at home with music thanks to their common mathematical heritage.

In the early '80s, far-sighted engineers in the music industry started a cooperative effort to better tap the potential of the computers inside these new musical instruments, as well as insure compatibility among gear produced by different manufacturers. The result of their work was introduced in 1983 as MIDI (Musical Instrument Digital Interface), an internationally-recognized specification that expresses musical events (notes played, vibrato, dynamics, tempo, etc.) as a common "language" consisting of standardized *digital data*. This data can be understood by MIDI-compatible computers and computer-based musical instruments. You can think of MIDI as a communications system (see sidebar).

Conceptually, MIDI is like "sheet music for computers." Before the electronic age, communicating musical ideas required translating musical parameters into special symbols (music notation) to indicate a note's pitch, rhythmic value (duration), dynamics (with crescendo/decrescendo marks), and the like. With MIDI, a computer translates musical parameters into digital data that can convey the type of information shown on sheet music, and much more.

Just one example of a MIDI message that has no equivalent in sheet music is the *program change* command. This message selects different sounds in a synth, presets in a signal processor, "scenes" in a MIDI lighting controller, etc.

Meet the MIDItools Computer

The MIDItools Computer is a single-board computer (*i.e.,* all the main computer elements fit on a single circuit board) designed specifically to generate, receive, and process MIDI data. It is relatively easy to build and use; you don't have to be a computer scientist to make it work. The twenty projects in this book provide a variety of useful MIDI functions that can be helpful in any MIDI system, whether it consists of a single MIDI keyboard or a roomful of state-of-the-art gear.

Furthermore, you can change the MIDItools Computer's function simply by replacing one IC with another, and in some cases, adding expansion boards. If you want a more generic computer, you can populate it with *all* the optional components and just change EPROMS.

One more item: for those who want to learn more about MIDI, computers, and software, the MIDItools Computer is an ideal training tool since it lends itself to software and hardware modifications.

MIDI Connections

Virtually every MIDI-equipped device has a *MIDI In* and *MIDI Out* jack. It may also have a *MIDI Thru* jack, which provides a duplicate of the signal at the MIDI In jack. Thru jacks are not required by the MIDI specification, and will be discussed later; the MIDItools Computer includes all three MIDI connections.

MIDI data is different from normal audio signals in that MIDI data doesn't make sounds, but rather, consists of digital control signals that represent *what you play* (Fig. 3-1). "Play" can be taken pretty loosely—we don't just mean notes. You can also "play" a tune's mix using MIDI-compatible volume faders, or "play" timbral changes in a signal processor with a footpedal.

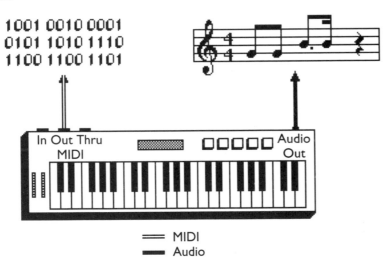

Fig. 3-1: The Audio Out produces musical sounds that feed an amplifier, and which the listener eventually hears. The MIDI Out produces digital data representing your performance (notes played, modulation, pitch-bending, etc.). The MIDItools Computer, MIDI-compatible PCs, and other MIDI devices can receive and understand this data.

The MIDI Out jack transmits MIDI control signals to another MIDI device. Example: Suppose you're playing a keyboard with a MIDI Out jack. Data that corresponds to your playing flows out that jack at an extremely rapid rate. Press down a D♯, and a piece of data that stands for "D♯ has been pressed" exits via the MIDI Out. If the keyboard responds to dynamics, the message will include dynamics information as well.

Release the note, and another piece of data goes out that says "D♯ has been released." If you add pitch bend, vibrato, or other changes, the MIDI Out jack transmits corresponding pieces of data for these too.

As expected, when the MIDItools Computer is generating data, it sends this data via the MIDI Out jack. Example: If you set up MIDItools to transmit a test signal to a piece of MIDI gear, the MIDI test message will appear at the MIDI Out.

The MIDI In jack receives MIDI data from another device. This data might tell a synthesizer which notes to play, but MIDI data can also include timing messages to which rhythmically-oriented units (such as drum machines and sequencers) can synchronize.

The MIDI Thru jack transmits a copy of the MIDI messages received at the MIDI In. We'll discuss the thru function in detail later in this chapter. Fig. 3-2 summarizes what these three jacks do.

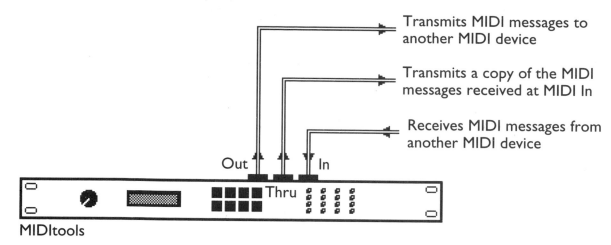

Fig. 3-2: Functions of the three different MIDI connectors.

MIDI jacks are different from audio jacks not only in the information they carry but also in appearance. MIDI jacks use 5-pin DIN connectors, which are different from regular audio jacks to avoid confusion.

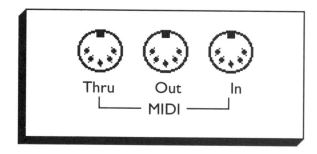

Fig. 3-3: Typical MIDI connection panel on a synthesizer or other MIDI device.

MIDI Applications

So what is all this good for? Following are just some of MIDI's many applications on stage and in the studio. The MIDItools Computer can be a useful addition to all of these applications.

Keyboard Doubling

Suppose you want to create a "bigger" sound by having two keyboard synthesizers play together (e.g., combine a string sound from one synthesizer with a choir sound from another). You could play one keyboard with one hand and the other keyboard with the other hand, but that's somewhat limiting.

MIDI lets a single keyboard play *both* synthesizers. The *master* keyboard's MIDI Out connects to the *slave* keyboard's MIDI In (Fig. 3-4). Since the master keyboard sends out data that corresponds to your playing, and the slave responds to that data, the slave will follow along and double whatever you play on the master. (Remember, the slave keyboard receiving the MIDI In data responds just as if you, not the MIDI data, were playing the synthesizer.)

In addition to providing richer, fatter sounds, this layering technique allows for some unusual effects—for example, combining sampled and synthesized timbres.

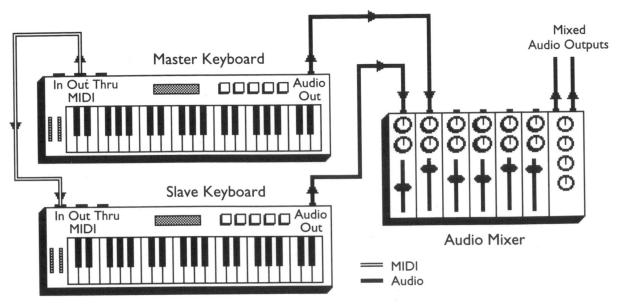

Fig. 3-4: *Layering two keyboards together. A mixer combines the two keyboard audio outputs into stereo (or mono, if desired) audio outputs suitable for feeding an amplifier.*

Inserting the MIDItools Computer between the master MIDI Out and slave MIDI In lets you process the notes going to the slave. For example, Project 13 remaps (transforms) controllers to different controller numbers, Project 14 remaps the note messages coming from the keyboard to different channels, Project 16 provides a variety of special effects (compression, limiting, delay, etc.), and Project 18 generates chords in response to playing a single note. Projects 15 (Randomizer), 9 (Control Thinner), and 11 (Data Filter) are also useful for processing keyboard messages.

Compact Live Performance Setups

In Fig. 3-4, note that the slave unit's keyboard is redundant since all the playing occurs from the master keyboard. To complement MIDI setups, several manufacturers make keyboardless *expander modules* (also called *sound modules* or *tone modules*) that contain only a synthesizer's sound-generating circuitry. It's assumed that expander modules will be triggered by signals appearing at the MIDI In connector. This approach reduces size, weight, and cost compared to using multiple keyboards.

Before MIDI, musicians who wanted to obtain many sound colors when playing live had to use a "stack" of expensive, heavy keyboards. You can now do the same thing with one master keyboard and several compact sound modules (Fig. 3-5).

Alternate Controllers

You don't have to be a keyboard player to use MIDI. Several MIDI-compatible guitars convert what you play to MIDI data, which then typically feeds an expander module of some kind. Drum controllers are also commonly available, as are violin-to-MIDI, bass-to-MIDI, voice-to-MIDI, wind-to-MIDI, fader-to-MIDI (for doing automated mixdowns), and a variety of other MIDI-compatible controllers. Project 4, the Custom Instrument, provides a good foundation for creating your own alternate controllers.

One problem with many alternate controllers is that they produce a lot more controller data than regular keyboards. MIDItools Project 9 can reduce the amount of controller data without adversely affecting the sound quality.

Incidentally, the word "controller" has a couple of different meanings, which we should clear up now to avoid confusion. Controller can mean either a physical device that generates MIDI data (keyboard, MIDI guitar, modulation wheel, footpedal, etc.) or a particular type of MIDI message. Fortunately, the context usually makes it obvious which meaning is intended.

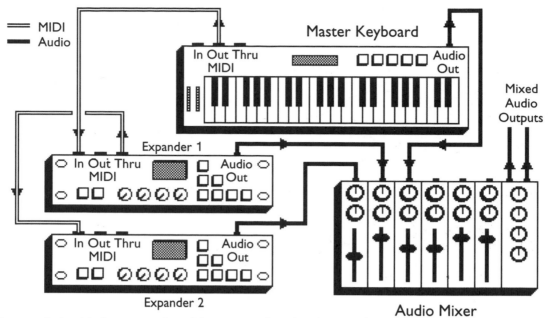

Fig. 3-5: One master keyboard feeding two expander modules. A mixer combines the audio outputs from the master keyboard and the two expander modules.

Signal Processor Control

Many signal processors and multieffects devices respond to MIDI messages. You can therefore control processors via remote footswitches, hand controls, or even computer-automated setups. One typical application is for a guitarist's footswitch to transmit MIDI program change commands that call up different preset effects, or for sound engineers to "tweak" MIDI equipment used on stage. The MIDItools Computer can generate a variety of MIDI messages with Projects 1 and 2, so it works well as an inexpensive "universal MIDI remote."

Sequencing

Sequencing, the computer equivalent of tape recording, is another common MIDI-based application. Here's how it works.

As mentioned before, when you play a MIDI keyboard, digital computer data representing your performance appears at the MIDI Out jack. Suppose we can route that data into a computer, and load the computer with a program that instructs the computer to *remember the order in which this data appeared at the MIDI In jack.* The computer then acts like a recorder, since it stores numbers that represent the notes you played, and the exact order in which you played those notes.

What happens if you play a chord? Each note in the chord gets its own piece of data, and these are sent one right after the other. In fact, all MIDI data (notes, pitch bend, vibrato, etc.) is transmitted *serially*—one piece of data after another. However, this happens so fast that these numbers appear (for all practical purposes) to occur at the same time as your playing.

To play back the recorded data, we patch the computer's MIDI Out jack to the instrument's MIDI In, and data flows from the computer back into the instrument. This is analogous to a player piano, but instead of punching holes in paper, we've "punched" data into the computer. The computer remembers the order in which we played a series of notes, and then plays back the notes (numbers) from memory. Like a player piano, the keyboard plays the sounds triggered by those numbers—except, of course, the keys don't need to move up and down.

Possibly the best aspect of computer-based sequencing is *editing.* For example, we might tell the computer to add 1 to every number's pitch value, thereby transposing the performance up a semitone. If we tell the computer to add 12 instead, the part will shift up one octave (12 semitones). If we subtract 12 (or add -12) to every number, the part will shift down one octave.

Transposition is only one example of editing. Note duration, loudness, and many other parameters can all be edited easily as MIDI data. This is why having a standardized specification is so important—since all manufacturers agree to the exact meaning of different pieces of data, the information coming out of one manufacturer's MIDI Out will make perfect sense when it hits the MIDI In of a different manufacturer's gear.

The MIDItools Computer can help out sequencing in several ways. Project 5 (Tap Tempo Transmitter) lets you control the sequence tempo by finger tapping, Project 6 (Sequencer Remote Control) can operate a sequencer remotely, Project 15 (Translating Randomizer) alters MIDI note numbers, velocity, and/or program changes, and Project 17 (Sequencer Helper) performs a variety of functions (transposition, reset all controllers, do fadeouts and fadeins, and send an "all notes off" message to turn off "stuck" notes).

How the MIDItools Computer Uses MIDI Connections

The MIDItools Computer can use one, two, or all of the MIDI connections. Here are some examples:

- MIDItools MIDI message generation. This is a very simple application: the MIDItools MIDI Out goes to the MIDI In of the device that's intended to receive the message. Fig. 3-6 shows the MIDItools Computer sending program changes to a signal processing unit to call up different sounds.

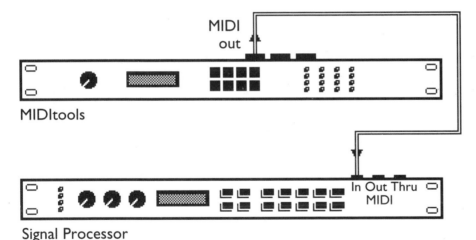

Fig. 3-6: Using the MIDItools Computer as a signal generator.

- When using the MIDItools Computer as a MIDI data monitor to see what type of data a device generates, the MIDItools MIDI input receives data from the output of the MIDI device being tested (e.g., a master keyboard). Suppose you also want to send the master keyboard's MIDI data to a sound module. In this case, you would hook up the MIDItools Computer's MIDI Thru to the sound module's MIDI In (Fig. 3-7).

- The MIDItools Computer can also be an *in-line* device; in other words, it inserts in a MIDI line to process the data going through it (for example, to create harmonies from notes played on a MIDI keyboard). In this case, the MIDI In receives the data to be processed, the MIDItools Computer adds the harmonies, then sends the processed data to the MIDI Out as shown in Fig. 3-8. (Additionally, the MIDI Thru could send the unprocessed signal elsewhere, if desired.)

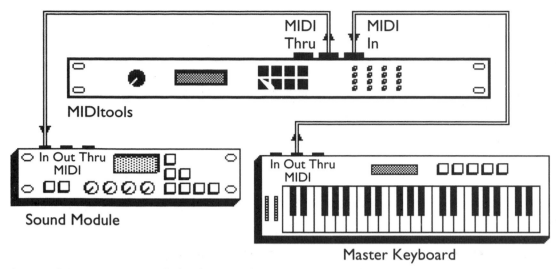

Fig. 3-7: Using the MIDItools Computer to monitor a keyboard's MIDI signal on its way to a sound module.

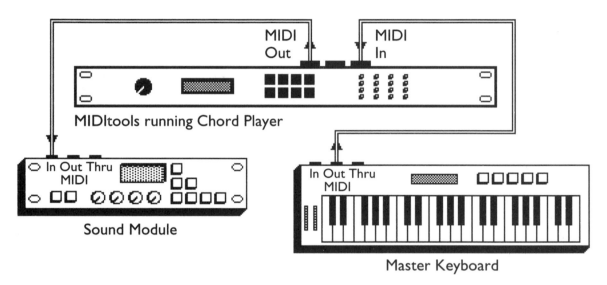

Fig. 3-8: The MIDItools Computer processes the keyboard output, then transmits the processed signal via the MIDI Out.

- The MIDItools Computer can also *merge* the signal appearing at the MIDI In with data generated by the computer itself. The merged combination of signals then appears at the MIDI Out.

"Daisy-Chaining" MIDI Thru Connections

Since the MIDI Thru connector carries the same signal as the one present at the MIDI In, you can "daisy-chain" multiple devices together (Fig. 3-9) if you want one master device to control several other devices simultaneously.

In this example, the MIDItools Computer is sending program changes to three different signal processors: distortion, delay, and reverb. When the distortion unit changes to a particular sound, the delay and reverb change to complementary sounds. Each signal processor receives the same data from the MIDItools Computer, since this data has been passed from one MIDI Thru to the next.

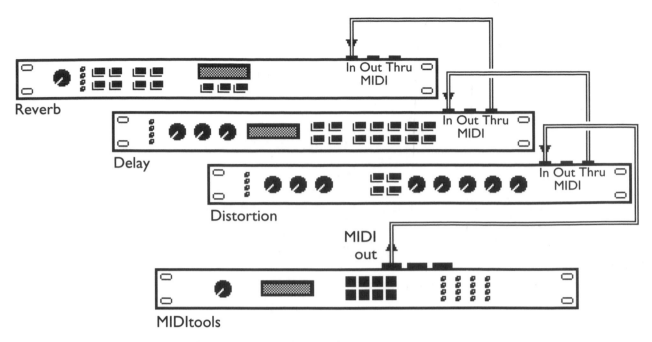

Fig. 3-9: Using MIDI Thru connections to drive multiple signal processors from a single MIDI Output.

Daisy Chain Limitations

To insure accurate data transfer, no more than four or five MIDI devices should be daisy-chained together. Each time the MIDI signal passes from the MIDI In to the MIDI Thru jack, a slight amount of distortion occurs due to physical limitations of the components used in the MIDI interface. The more times a signal goes through this circuitry, the greater the amount of distortion. If the distortion is severe enough, data can be lost or altered.

Note that the problem of data distortion is sometimes erroneously referred to as "MIDI delay." Actually, the delay caused by going from MIDI In to MIDI Thru is only a few microseconds (millionths of a second). This amount of delay is not audible, even when daisy-chaining many MIDI devices.

The alternative to excessive daisy-chaining is the MIDI Thru Box, which splits a single MIDI In into several (not just one) MIDI Thru connections (Fig. 3-10). A MIDI Thru box eliminates the need to use multiple Thru jacks on multiple pieces of MIDI gear, thus minimizing MIDI distortion problems. *MIDI Projects for Musicians*, a companion volume to this book, includes plans for building two different types of MIDI thru box.

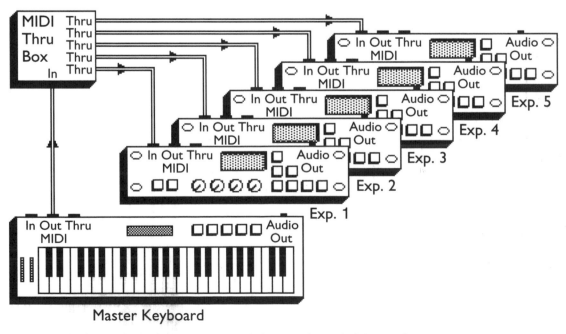

Fig. 3-10: Using a MIDI Thru box to split a single MIDI Output into multiple outputs that can feed, for example, expander module inputs.

MIDI Language Basics

Since its inception, the computer "language" called MIDI has often been treated as some sort of complicated black magic that mysteriously makes synthesizers and other MIDI devices "talk to each other." In reality, the data that makes up MIDI is neither complicated nor mysterious, and is actually quite simple if broken down to its most basic elements. These basic elements are *Channels, Messages,* and *Modes.* Let's look at each element individually.

MIDI Channels

MIDI includes 16 channels; each channel can carry its own unique set of MIDI data. You can think of these channels as similar to a television. When you watch TV, you tune in the channel that you want to see, even though there may be signals from dozens of channels being picked up by the TV's antenna (Fig. 3-11). With MIDI, you "tune in" the channel from which the synthesizer should receive data. Like a TV, when you tune in a channel that isn't transmitting, nothing interesting happens.

Channel 7
("I Love Lucy" reruns)

Channel 3
(Talk Show: "How to Apply Eye Makeup")

Channel 4
(Movie: "Star Wars")

Channel 13
(Network News)

Fig. 3-11: TVs tune in one channel out of many; MIDI channel selection works similarly.

Although you might think that MIDI would need sixteen cables to carry data for sixteen channels, only one cable is required to carry a system's MIDI data. This is because the channel identification is part of the data generated by a MIDI device. Examples: If you program a keyboard to transmit over channel 7, all its data will be "stamped" with an ID of channel 7. If you program a keyboard to transmit over channel 5, all data will be "stamped" with an ID of channel 5.

Channel identification makes multitrack sequencing possible. A bass part could be recorded in channel 1, a string part in channel 2, and a lead part in channel 3. On playback, the bass synthesizer would be set to channel 1 and play back only the data associated with channel 1; the string synthesizer would be set to channel 2 and play back only the channel 2 data, and the lead synthesizer would be set to channel 3 and play back only the channel 3 data. All this data appears serially, over one cable.

MIDI is different from your typical television in that most MIDI units can transmit MIDI data on the MIDI channel as well as receive data (another difference is that MIDI data will not bombard you with commercials).

MIDI gear varies considerably as to channel assignment flexibility. Some units can receive many channels at the same time, but transmit only over one fixed channel. Some units send and receive on any of the 16 channels, while still others can send on one channel while receiving on another. (This is explained further in the section on "MIDI Mode Messages.") Project 12, the Channel Mapper, can help overcome these types of limitations by taking incoming MIDI messages on one channel and transforming them to another channel. Project 14 (Keyboard Mapper) allows any MIDI keyboard to transmit on as many as three channels at once.

The currently selected channel is called the *basic channel*. Usually, when an instrument is first "powered-up," the basic channel is 1.

The Different Types of MIDI Messages

There are two main types of MIDI messages: *Channel* messages and *System* messages. Channel messages are channel-specific and consist of *Voice* and *Mode* messages. System messages, which are not encoded with channel numbers and are therefore received by all units in a system, consist of *Common, Real Time,* and *Exclusive* messages.

Voice Messages

The sound-generating elements in synthesizers are called *voices*. Each voice consists of some kind of tone generator, as well as various modules that can alter the tone generator's timbre and dynamics (*e.g.,* make the sound decay rapidly like a struck drum, attack slowly like a wind instrument, etc.).

Generally each voice can play one note at a time. Example: A six-voice synthesizer lets you play up to six keys (notes) simultaneously. If you press more than six keys, the instrument won't have any voices left to play those notes. Likewise, an eight-voice synth can play up to eight notes simultaneously, and a 16-voice synth can play up to 16 notes at the same time. If you play more than the available number of notes, older notes are "stolen" (which cuts off their sound, even if they're still sustaining) in order to free up voices that can be assigned to the new notes.

MIDI Voice messages describe what notes are being played, their dynamics, and durations. But they can also communicate what sound has been selected, whether any pitch-bending has been added, and whether controllers such as *aftertouch (i.e.,* pressure applied to a keyboard after the key is down) or *modulation* (usually, but by no means always, vibrato) are being used. A MIDI voice message is stamped with a MIDI channel number, so each channel can carry independent voice messages. Voice messages include:

Note On—Occurs when a note is played by hitting a keyboard's key, striking a MIDI drum pad, etc. The allowable range of note numbers extends from 000 (lowest note) to 127 (highest note). Middle C is 60.

Note Off—Occurs when a note is released. The allowable range is from 000 (lowest note) to 127 (highest note).

Velocity—Corresponds to the dynamics of your playing; playing softly gives less velocity, and playing hard gives more velocity. A MIDI keyboard usually derives this value by measuring the time it takes for a key to go from the full up to full down position. It assumes that faster times mean you're hitting the keys harder. Velocity usually affects the level of the note being played and possibly other parameters too. Velocity values range from 001 (minimum velocity) to 127 (maximum velocity). A velocity value of 000 is equivalent to a Note Off.

Some keyboards offer Release Velocity, which measures the time it takes for a key to go from the full down to full up position. Values range from 000 (minimum release velocity) to 127 (maximum release velocity). However, this feature is rarely implemented, either in keyboards or sound generators.

Pressure (also called Aftertouch)—Indicates how much pressure is being applied to a keyboard after a key is down. Example: On a guitar patch, aftertouch can let you bend pitch when you press down on a key. This gives a more physical, guitar-type feel. (Project 15, the Translating Randomizer, can add aftertouch-to-bend translation to any MIDI controller.)

There are two kinds of aftertouch: *Mono* (also called *Channel)* aftertouch, where the aftertouch data represents an average of all keys being pressed down, and *Polyphonic* or *Key* aftertouch, which sends out individual aftertouch data for each key being pressed down. Aftertouch values range from 000 to 127.

Program Change—Remember when we mentioned controlling multiple slave devices from a single master keyboard? If you change sounds on the master, you'll probably want the slaves to change sounds too. Example: Suppose your master is set to play program 1 (a violin sound), and the slave's program 1 produces a cello sound. Let's assume that when you switch the master over to program 2 (choir), you want the slave to play a brass sound.

Simply store a brass program in the slave's program 2 memory slot. When you call up program 2 on the master, a Program Change command will tell the slave to go to program 2, and you'll hear the desired combination of choir and brass. MIDI allows for 128 Program Change command numbers.

Incidentally, you'll often hear the term *patch* as well as program. This is a holdover from the early days of synthesis, when you had to physically route patch cords between different connections to create new sounds. Although creating sounds on synths these days is more like programming a computer—hence the term *program*—you'll see both terms used in the real world, as well as in this book.

Note that while Program Change messages are standardized, the way different synthesizer manufacturers number their programs is not. One synthesizer might number 100 programs as 00-99, and another as 001-100. Some synths number their programs in banks of eight (1-1 for the first patch, 1-2 for the second, and so on until you hit 1-8 for the eighth program. The ninth program would be 2-1, which stands for Bank 2, 1st patch).

Confused? That's okay, it *is* confusing. Fortunately, whatever program gets called up on a slave synth will at least be consistent. Some musicians make up a reference chart to show what programs are selected on a slave when you call up particular programs on the master.

Many synthesizers also let you *remap* program changes. This means that selecting program 1 on your master controller doesn't have to call up program 1 on a slave sound generator; the message could be remapped at the slave to call up any program number—2, 56, 127, 362, etc.

This is particularly helpful because the original MIDI spec allowed for only 128 different program changes, but modern synthesizers often provide memory for more than 128 programs (synths with 300, 400, or even 500 programs are becoming more common). So, you can set up a map where the 128 program changes generated by a master controller can choose any 128 programs from an available palette of hundreds of programs.

Bank Select—This represents another way to get around MIDI's 128 program change limit. MIDI Bank Select messages, a relatively recent addition to the MIDI spec, select up to 128 individual banks. These can contain up to 128 programs each, thus letting you select up to 16,384 programs.

Pitch Bend—A synthesizer's pitch bend wheel (or lever, joystick, footpedal, etc.) changes the pitch much like the way a guitarist "bends" a string or whammy bar to change pitch. In addition to being used for bent string effects, slight pitch-bending is a characteristic of wind instruments.

Bending pitch on a master will also cause a suitably-equipped slave to bend, but note that both synths should be set to the same pitch bend range for best results. In other words, you don't want a pitch bend of four semitones on the master to create a pitch bend of three semitones on the slave (well, sometimes you do—but that's another story!). Most synthesizers have a pitch bend range adjustment to allow for this.

Control Change—Pitch bend is not the only control signal generated by MIDI instruments. Footpedal, modulation wheel, and breath controller (where blowing into a device gets converted to MIDI messages—it's great for simulating brass sounds) are just some of the ways to add more expressiveness to your playing. Typically, turning up the modulation wheel will inject vibrato into a signal but it might also change level, open a filter, affect some other part of the sound, or control multiple aspects of the sound simultaneously.

MIDI allows for 64 continuous controllers (these act like potentiometers in that you can choose from many different values) and 58 continuous/switch controllers (these can act like continuous controllers but some are assumed to choose between two possible states, such as on/off). The remaining six controller numbers are dedicated to Mode messages (see next section). Some controllers are standardized; for example, modulation wheel is controller 01, and master volume is 07.

Do not confuse controller numbers with channel numbers; each channel can carry its own set of controllers. Example: Channel 1 could be carrying volume (controller 07) messages, while Channel 2 carries its own volume messages as well as modulation (controller 01) and footpedal (controller 04) messages.

Each type of controller is stamped in software with its own controller identification number. Not all controller numbers have been standardized for specific functions, but some have been. Chapter 11 has a complete listing of controller assignments, but these are the most common.

1	Modulation Wheel
2	Breath Controller
4	Foot Controller
5	Portamento Time
6	Data Slider
7	Main Volume
8	Balance
10	Pan
11	Expression
64	Sustain Pedal
65	Portamento On/Off
96	Data Increment
97	Data Decrement

Controllers tend to generate a lot of data, since doing something like sweeping a pitch bend wheel can send out dozens or even hundreds of pitch bend messages. Several MIDItools projects relate to controllers: Project 9 thins the amount of controller data in the MIDI data stream by discarding data according to various options, Project 11 lets you filter out different types of controllers from the MIDI data stream, and Project 13 can transform controller messages from one controller number to another, in real time. For example, if you wanted your mod wheel (controller 1) to control master volume (controller 7) of another device, this project could do it.

Mode Messages

There are two voice messages that choose the MIDI mode *(i.e.,* how the MIDI device will receive MIDI data). The *Omni* message determines how many channels will be recognized. Omni on means that data from all channels will be received. Omni off limits the number of channels, usually to one.

The *Mono/Poly* message deals with voice assignment within the synthesizer. In Mono mode, only one note at a time plays in response to voice messages, regardless of how many message are received. In Poly mode, as many voices as are available can play notes.

Combining these two messages in various ways produces the four main operating modes for MIDI equipment (however, most devices do not support all modes). The modes are selected either from the front panel, and/or with MIDI commands.

Transmitters and receivers operate differently under the different modes, as explained next.

Omni On/Poly (Mode 1)—The *receiver* responds to voice messages from *all* channels. These are assigned to the synthesizer's voices, and are played polyphonically up to the device's internal voice limit (naturally, the synthesizer cannot play more notes than it has voices).

The *transmitter* sends MIDI channel voice messages on its Basic channel (generally set by a front panel operation). It can send multiple notes at the same time (polyphonic, or poly, transmission), up to the internal limits of the device.

Omni On/Poly Mode is usually a synthesizer's default after power-up, and is most frequently used when layering several synths together (Fig. 3-12) from a master keyboard. Since all slaves receive their MIDI messages from only one source, setting them to Omni On/Poly mode eliminates the need to set particular channel assignments.

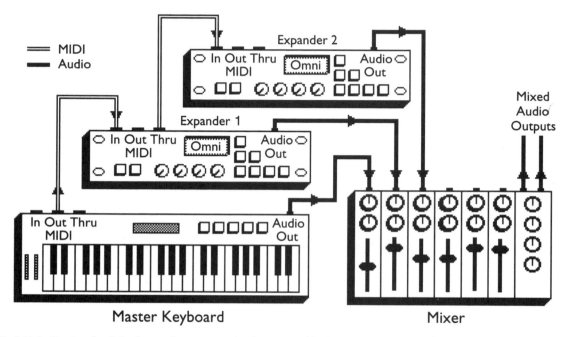

Fig. 3-12: *In Omni mode, all the slave synthesizers respond to data generated by the master keyboard.*

Omni On/Mono (Mode 2)—The *receiver* responds to voice messages on all channels, but plays only one note in response (no, this is not particularly useful, and that's why this mode is almost never implemented). The *transmitter* sends MIDI channel voice messages on its Basic channel and transmits only one note at a time.

Omni Off/Poly (Mode 3)—The *receiver* responds to voice messages occurring over a single assigned channel, and assigns these polyphonically to the synthesizer's voices. In other words, several notes at once can play on one MIDI channel. Messages usually will be transmitted on the same channel over which messages are being received, but this is not always the case—some devices can receive and transmit over different channels. The *transmitter* works the same as in Mode 1.

Omni Off/Poly is by far the most commonly-used mode with sequencers, since all synthesizers connected together in the system receive on only one channel at a time so as not to receive parts played on other channels.

This mode is also useful live when you want to drive different sounds from different ranges of the keyboard. Project 14 (Keyboard Mapper) can assign different note ranges to different channels, which are then picked up by different synthesizers. Fig. 3-13 shows how the MIDItools Computer "picks off" different note ranges and routes them to the various keyboards.

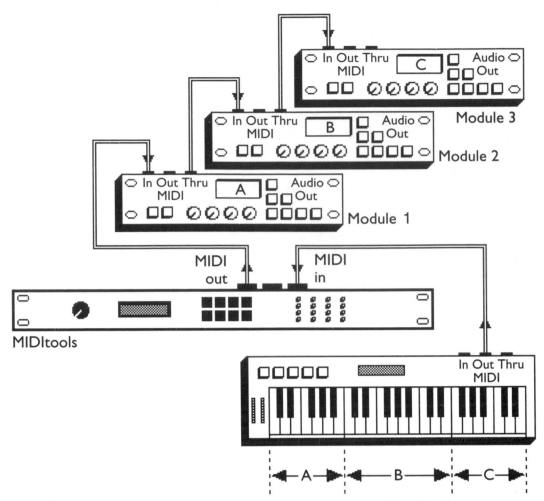

Fig. 3-13: In this example, the MIDItools Computer splits the master keyboard into zones A, B, and C, which we'll assume transmit on MIDI channels 1, 2, and 3 respectively. Notes falling within a particular range are sent on the range's MIDI channel. Set sound module 1 to receive on channel 1 and it will play back notes within range A; similarly, sound module 2 plays back notes within range B, and sound module 3 plays back notes within range C.

Omni Off/Mono (Mode 4)—The *receiver* responds to voice messages received over a specified range of channels. It supports monophonic playback of only one note at a time (mono), per channel, up to the synthesizer's voice limits. The *transmitter* sends MIDI channel voice messages on a specified range of channels. It transmits only one note at a time (mono), per channel.

An example should help make Mode 4 a little clearer: Let's assume a MIDI guitar controller assigns each string to its own MIDI channel—for example, channel 1 for the first string, channel 2 for the second string, and so on up to channel 6 for the sixth string. Furthermore, remember that you can play only one note at a time on a guitar string (monophonic response).

A synthesizer set to receive in mono mode will assign the data coming in over each of the six channels to one voice in the synthesizer. So, one voice will play the monophonic data coming in on channel 1, another voice will play the monophonic data coming in on channel 2, and so on up to channel 6. (With a guitar synthesizer set to transmit in Mode 4, the synthesizer receiving the guitar data will never need more than six voices.)

Omni Off/Mono is used occasionally with *multi-timbral* synthesizers (one capable of assigning a different patch or program to each voice) in an effort to save voices. For example, a bass line, single note lead, and percussion part will usually require only one note each at a time. Suppose the bass line is programmed on channel 1, the single note lead on channel 2, the percussion part on channel 3, and a polyphonic piano part on channel 4. With an eight-voice multi-timbral synthesizer, one voice could be set to a bass sound and assigned to channel 1, another voice to a lead sound and assigned to channel 2, and a third voice set to a percussion sound and assigned to channel 3. Note that we still have five voices available; these could be all be assigned to channel 4 so that the piano part could play up to five notes at a time.

However, applying a technique called *dynamic allocation* greatly increases mono mode's usefulness. Some synthesizers will respond to several different channels, but can receive *polyphonic* data over each channel as needed. In other words, a channel will "grab" as many voices as it needs to play a part. This is very useful for sequencer work, where one instrument can play back polyphonic parts appearing over several different channels. With synthesizers boasting an ever-increasing number of voices and more efficient dynamic allocation schemes, note-stealing problems are becoming less and less of an issue.

Local Control On/Off—This message is designed for synthesizers that include both a keyboard and internal sound generators. Referring to Fig. 3-14, with Local Control On any controller data goes to the internal sound generators *and* to the MIDI Out jack. With Local Control Off, the controller data appears solely at the MIDI Out and does not drive the internal sound generators. This has several uses; one of the most important lets you play a keyboard with Local Control Off in order to trigger an expander module without triggering the keyboard's internal sound generators.

Another application is that you can turn off Local Control and route the keyboard's MIDI Out through a MIDI data processor, then feed this processed data back into the synth through the MIDI In. (This is conceptually like the "effects loops" found in guitar amps.) For example, Project 16 (Multi-Effector) can compress, limit, gate, and delay keyboard data—just like standard analog audio processors—on its way to the internal sound generators. Project 18, the Chord Player, generates chords in response to a single note inputs.

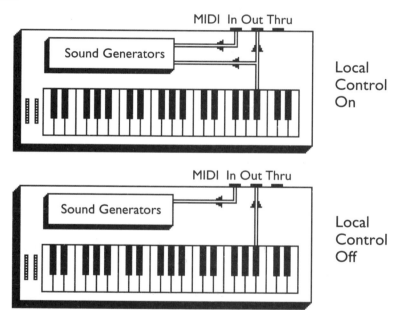

Fig. 3-14: How local control affects a synthesizer's internal sound generators.

All Notes Off—This is the "shut up" command and turns off all notes currently on. You can program this message into Project 1, the Universal Transmitter, and send an All Notes Off command to a MIDI system in case any notes get "stuck" on (this can happen if MIDI information is going into a synthesizer faster than the synth can handle it, thereby causing the synth to miss a Note Off message). Other projects also incorporate an All Notes Off option.

System-Wide Messages

System Common messages are not encoded with channel numbers, and are intended for all units in a system. System Real Time messages are also intended for all units in a system, but since they control timing and synchronization, may be sent at any time—even sandwiched in the middle of other data. System Exclusive messages start with a manufacturer's ID code and are intended only for equipment made by a specific manufacturer. This allows MIDI to translate non-universal data, such as a particular manufacturer's way of encoding patch information, into something that can be sent down a MIDI cable and into a computer.

System Common Messages

System Common messages include:

Song Position Pointer (SPP)—This message keeps track of how many "MIDI beats" (sixteenth notes) have elapsed since the beginning of a piece, up to 16,384 total. Thus, if a sequencer can send Song Position messages and a drum machine can receive them, you could start the sequencer at any point in a song. Before actually starting to play, it would first send out a Song Position Pointer message, which the drum machine would use to autolocate itself to the same point in the song. After sending out the Song Position, the sequencer would then go into play mode and the drum machine would follow along.

Song Select—This message tells devices such as sequencers and drum machines which song to play.

Tune Request—This asks all synthesizers in the system to tune themselves. It doesn't tune them to a standard; rather, the synthesizers just act as if you had pressed their front panel "tune" buttons. This message is a holdover from the earlier days of synthesis; modern digital synthesizers do not go out of tune and do not respond to Tune Request.

MTC 1/4 Frame Message—This provides MIDI systems with timing messages based on SMPTE Time Code. For more information, see the section on basic synchronization.

EOX—This is used as a "flag" to indicate the end of a System Exclusive transmission (defined later in this chapter).

System Real Time Messages

These System messages contain rhythmically-related timing information that synchronizes the units in a MIDI system, along with some other "utility" messages such as System Reset and Active Sensing.

The MIDI specification includes extensive synchronization capabilities; synchronization occurs through digital timing messages that are exchanged between pieces of equipment via MIDI. There's more information on synchronization toward the end of this chapter; following are the basic messages.

Timing Clock—MIDI sends out 24 timing messages per quarter note to which all devices synchronize. Thus, if the master sends out a timing clock, all other units advance by 1/24th of a quarter note. Clock messages have priority over all other messages to insure accurate timekeeping. (Project 5, the Tap Tempo Transmitter, lets you control the timing clock by tapping on a switch to give a more "humanized" feel; the tempo can also be smoothed if your timing isn't perfect.)

Start—This tells sequencers, drum machines, and such when to start playing since you want all these units to start playing at the same time.

Stop—This is the opposite of Start, and tells each system element when to stop playing.

Continue—After a Stop command has been issued, sending a Continue message re-starts the units from where they were stopped. This is different from a Start command, which always re-starts a drum machine or sequencer from the beginning of a song. (After two units autolocate to each other via Song Position Pointer messages, the master usually sends a Continue message to the slave to start them both from that common point.)

Project 6, the Sequencer Remote Control, generates Start, Stop, Continue, Rewind, Fast Forward, Loop Play, and Jump commands for controlling sequencers and drum machines from a simple, hand-held remote.

System Reset—Initiating this from a master source causes all devices in a MIDI system that respond to this command to return to their initialized (default) state.

Active Sensing—This optional message sends a "dummy" message approximately every third of a second whenever there is no other MIDI activity. These messages let any device that receives Active Sensing know that the MIDI lines of communication are available, even if there is currently no MIDI activity.

This message is left over from the early days of MIDI to cover those situations when someone would disconnect a MIDI cable while a synthesizer's notes were still sounding. With the cable disconnected, the synthesizer could not receive any Note Off messages, and the synth would drone on until someone re-connected the cable or muted the voices.

Active sensing was designed to solve that by having a synth turn off all its notes if it didn't receive Active Sensing messages, under the assumption that the reason it didn't receive Active Sensing messages was because the MIDI cable was pulled out or otherwise interrupted.

Active Sensing is not used much any more, and synthesizers that do include this feature usually let you disable it. This is a plus, because if active sensing is enabled, its constant background "babble" gets in the way of the various MIDI conversations and can confuse things. The MIDI Data Monitor (Project 7) shows whether or not a device sends active sensing.

System Exclusive Messages

These messages usually contain information that is not universal, but applicable only to a certain piece of gear. This type of data is called "exclusive" because each instrument has its own unique format for receiving system exclusive data (sys ex for short). Example: a sys ex message that sets the delay time for a MIDI-controlled signal processor probably won't make any sense to an analog synthesizer.

System exclusive information often encodes a synthesizer's parameter settings. In other words, it takes a "snapshot" of all of the synthesizer's parameter values. This data is compatible with *librarian* software programs that run on a personal computer and can store (on commonly available and inexpensive floppy disks) all of a synthesizer's parameters for later recall. This is useful if you fill up a synth's memory banks; you can save the contents with the librarian program, clear the memory, and create a whole new bank of sounds. Project 19, the System Exclusive Folder, can store sys ex messages and play them back later.

System Exclusive messages are also used with computer-based *editing* programs, which display all of a synthesizer's patch parameters on a computer screen for easy editing. Since each synthesizer has different parameters, there is no standardized way to include this information in the main MIDI specification. System Exclusive provides a way to communicate this data over MIDI.

MIDI Extensions

The MIDI Specification is a living document that changes when technology changes, yet doesn't render obsolete previously-made MIDI gear. One of the reasons MIDI has been so successful is because any proposed changes must undergo extensive discussions by the members of the two organizations charged with maintaining the MIDI spec, the MIDI Manufacturer's Association (MMA) and the Japan MIDI Standards Committee (JMSC). All Manufacturer ID Numbers are assigned by these groups.

System Exclusive messages have been particularly useful in expanding the MIDI spec. When an ID Number is assigned, the System Exclusive codes used by the manufacturer must be implemented and published within one year. This satisfies one of the fundamental MIDI precepts: that publishing equipment information leads to greater compatibility.

Any MIDI equipment manufacturer may use the System Exclusive codes of any existing product without permission. For example, if a company makes a software-based editor for the Rane MAP 33 MIDI-controlled acoustic preamp, that editor can use the MAP 33 sys ex codes to store presets, edit parameters, etc.

When MIDI was first introduced, one of its stated goals was to be open-ended enough to allow for future growth. This goal has been realized, and over the years there have been several additions to the MIDI spec. Some of the most significant are:

- Standard MIDI Files. A Standard MIDI File follows a particular sequence file format that virtually all computer-based sequencers can generate and read. In other words, we can use Sequencer "A" to create a sequence, save it as a Standard MIDI File, then import this file into Sequencer "B." Standard MIDI Files have been a boon for those who work with different sequencers on different computer platforms (or who collaborate with people who use different programs), as well as for those who telecommunicate musical files.

- Sample Dump Standard. This allows digital audio signals to be sent over MIDI (albeit very slowly), and is mostly used with samplers. For example, suppose samplers "Y" and "Z" support the Sample Dump Standard. If you have a superb guitar sample that you sampled on "Y," you can transfer it to sampler "Z" over MIDI. Note that only the audio itself and loop points are sent—no filter, envelope, or other "front panel" settings.

- SCSI Musical Data Interchange. This addresses the slow transfer time of standard sample dumps by sending sample data over SCSI (Small Computer System Interface), speeding up transfers between computer and sampler by a factor of 50.

- MIDI Time Code. Intended primarily for audio-for-video applications, MIDI Time Code bridges the gap between MIDI and SMPTE (Society of Motion Picture and Television Engineers), the timing specification used in film and video. We don't need to go over this right now, but it is an important topic if you get into post-production. MIDI Time Code is also used extensively for synching sequence playback to analog and digital audio tape.

- MIDI Show Control. Now you can control theatrics—fireworks, lighting, hydraulics, scene changes, and much more—from MIDI (and who among us hasn't wanted to jump on a footswitch and unleash a pyrotechnics display?).

- MIDI Machine Control. MMC allows MIDI to control studio devices such as audio/video tape recorders and hard disk recorders. Applications: Use a sequencer to control punch in and out, do "intelligent" tape motion (e.g., rewind at the end of the second chorus and start playing from the first verse), and/or autolocate to specific points in a song.

- General MIDI. Although MIDI always seemed like a good way to distribute music by releasing diskettes with MIDI data, in practice this has been problematic because there was no standardization among program changes. For example, program 11 might call up a trumpet on one synthesizer and a harpsichord on another. So, manufacturers decided on a "General MIDI" set of program numbers and drum sound note assignments to insure that a sequence played back through any General MIDI-compatible machine will sound more or less the same. General MIDI is entirely optional; some synthesizers can be made into "General MIDI" devices simply by loading patches and drum sounds that follow the General MIDI specification.

- Tuning. The subject of alternate tunings is extremely intriguing, and modern computer technology is making it easier to revive this lost art. The MIDI specification now accommodates a standardized way to create alternate pitch tables for MIDI instruments.

Basic Synchronization

Suppose you have two rhythmically-oriented devices, such as a sequencer and drum machine, and want to make sure that they play together (*i.e.,* when the sequencer starts playing, the drum machine starts at the exact same time); and if the sequencer plays through a certain number of measures, the drum machine will have played through exactly the same number of measures.

You might try to simply set both units to the same tempo, and press their Play buttons at the same time. However, this won't work very well, for two reasons.

- It is unlikely that you will be able to push both Play buttons at precisely the same time, so one unit will probably start a bit late compared to the other.

- If the tempo of one of the units drifts by even a tiny amount (which is not just possible, but probable), by the end of a tune the two units will no longer be playing together. The answer to both these problems is *synchronization.*

Synchronization is often considered difficult to understand, but actually, synchronization is something that all musicians already use. When you play to a metronome, or with a drummer, the metronome or drummer serves as a master tempo "clock," and you try to synchronize your rhythm to that of this master clock. Electronic synchronization works similarly: you appoint one device as a master timekeeper ("tempo clock" or just "clock" for short), and have all other devices (the "slaves") respond to the tempo data generated by the master rather than following their own internal clock. This insures one master tempo which all devices follow.

MIDI Sync

The MIDI specification includes extensive synchronization capabilities. MIDI synchronization occurs through digital timing messages, as described previously, that are exchanged between pieces of equipment over the MIDI line.

SMPTE-to-MIDI Conversion

SMPTE stands for Society of Motion Picture and Television Engineers, the group that devised a time code system (based on a protocol developed by NASA for logging data from space probes) for synchronizing audio to film and video. A *SMPTE Time Code generator* generates "timing markers" that are recorded on tape (or some other recording medium) at regular intervals. Each marker describes the running time in hours, minutes, seconds, and *frames.*

A frame's duration varies for different applications. For film work, there are 24 frames per second (*i.e.,* each frame equals 1/24th of a second). For black and white video, the rate is 30 frames per second in the USA and 25 frames per second in Europe. For NTSC color "drop frame," the rate is 29.97 frames per second (for reasons far too complicated to go into here). Most of the time, if you live in the USA you will find yourself working with 30 or 24 frames per second; in Europe, 25 or 24 frames per second.

SMPTE Time Code is based on *absolute* time in hours, minutes, second, and frames. Musical rhythm, on the other hand, is based on measures and beats, which is a *relative* time system. For example, with 4/4 music at 40 beats per minute, each measure lasts six seconds; with 4/4 music at 120 beats per minute, each measure lasts two seconds. Therefore, we need a way to convert absolute time (as represented by SMPTE) into "musical time," which brings us to SMPTE-to-MIDI conversion. Sometimes dedicated boxes provide this function; sometimes conversion is built into MIDI interfaces used with sequencers, and some instruments perform the conversion internally.

SMPTE-to-MIDI converters can read SMPTE code from tape and convert this data into MIDI Time Code, Song Position Pointer messages, or both (virtually all MIDI sequencers can sync to one or the other). When working at a 30 frames per second rate, the SMPTE timing data is updated every 1/30th of a second.

Wherever you start a piece of tape, the SMPTE reader can tell you (or a piece of equipment) the precise tape location within 1/30th of a second. The SMPTE-to-MIDI converter will read the SMPTE time, translate it to MIDI Time Code or Song Position messages, send a Continue command after figuring it out, and *voilà*—your MIDI gear is synchronized to tape. What's more, should the tape become slightly damaged in one or two places so that SMPTE data is lost, most SMPTE boxes will "guess" where the markers would have been until the real markers appear again.

SMPTE is the synchronization system of choice in the film and video industries. As a result, SMPTE sync is commonplace in major studios.

MIDI Time Code (MTC)

This extension to the original MIDI specification can communicate SMPTE times directly over MIDI, thus allowing MIDI devices to respond to absolute times (hours, minutes, seconds, etc.) as well as musical times (bars, beats, etc.). An example will help get the point across.

Suppose you're scoring a commercial, and also providing some sampled sound effects to be played back from a sampler. You sync your sequencer to the video, and start creating the sound track. Then as you see where specific effects are to take place—a door slam, car crash, crowd applause, etc.—you play the corresponding keys on the sampler that trigger those sounds, and record those keypresses into the sequencer. Perfect—on playback, the tune is in sync with the video, and all the effects are triggered in just the right places.

Then the producer comes in next day, and thinks you've done a great job—but wants the tempo sped up by 5%. So you speed up the sequence tempo, but now the rate at which the sound effects occur speeds up too, to the point where they no longer match the film. The problem is simple: the sound effects relate to absolute time—in other words, the door should slam at perhaps 12 seconds and 11 frames into the film, regardless of what the music is doing. The music runs on relative time.

With a MIDI Time Code-equipped sampler, you could trigger the samples via MIDI Time Code at specific times, and drive the sequencer from a SMPTE-to-MIDI converter. Problem solved; if you need to change the sequence you simply edit it, yet the MIDI Time Code values remain constant, since they relate directly back to SMPTE. Therefore, the samples will be triggered at the specified times regardless of what happens with the sequencer.

MIDI Implementation Charts

The manufacturer is responsible for informing users of a piece of gear's MIDI implementation *(i.e.,* which MIDI messages trigger which actions). This is important because not all gear implements all aspects of the MIDI spec; for example, some keyboards provide channel pressure, some key pressure, and some don't generate pressure messages at all.

MIDI Implementation Charts were developed to provide a standard format for reporting a piece of equipment's MIDI capabilities. These charts are extremely useful when comparing various MIDI receivers and transmitters.

A chart must be included in a MIDI device's documentation; it's usually toward the back of the operating manual. It will look something like the example chart in Fig. 3-15.

```
UNIVERSAL TRANSMITTER                        Date: 9-30-92
MIDItool 1        MIDI Implementation Chart  Version: 1.0
```

Function		Transmitted	Recognized	Remarks
Basic	Default	***	***	note 1
Channel	Channel	1-16	***	note 2
	Default	***	***	
Mode	Messages	O	X	
	Altered	***	***	
Note		O	X	
Number	True Voice	***	***	
Velocity	Note ON	O	X	note 3
	Note OFF	O	X	note 4
Aftertouch	Key	O	X	
	Channel	O	X	
Pitch Bend		O	X	
Controllers		O	X	
Program		O	X	
Change	True #	***	***	
System Exclusive		O	X	
System	SPP	O	X	
Common	Song Select	O	X	
	Tune Request	O	X	
System	Clock	O	X	
Realtime	Commands	O	X	
Aux	Local ON/OFF	O	X	
	All Notes Off	O	X	
	Active Sensing	O	X	
	Reset	O	X	

```
Notes:
1: There is no default transmit channel setting
2: Transmit channel is programmable and optional
3: Note On velocity is programmable (0-127)
4: Note Off velocity is programmable (0-127)


Mode 1: Omni On, Poly     Mode 2: Omni On, Mono      O:Yes
Mode 3: Omni Off, Poly    Mode 4: Omni Off, Mono     X:No
```

Fig 3-15: Typical MIDI implementation chart (in this case, for MIDItools Project 1). At a glance, it's obvious from this chart that the device can transmit, but not receive, MIDI messages.

Following are explanations of the MIDI implementation chart's various sections:

Header—The chart header shows the device name, model number, date, and version.

Symbols—The standard chart symbols are:

O means Yes, a message is implemented
X means No, a message is not implemented
***, N/A, or a blank indicates that the function is not applicable

The bottom of the chart should have a key to these symbols as well as MIDI mode numbers.

Transmitted/Recognized Column—These columns give the appropriate Yes/No symbol or description, and describe the MIDI messages that the device can receive and transmit.

Remarks Column—This column provides further explanations for a given row.

Notes—These are explained in the notes section at the bottom of the chart.

Function Column—This column lists each MIDI message type along with certain useful subheadings.

Basic Channel—The Default subheading specifies the transmit and receive channels the device assumes on power-up. Often, it will memorize the current channel settings when power is turned off.
The Channel subheading indicates which channels can be set manually by the user.

Mode—The Default subheading specifies the MIDI operating mode the device assumes on power-up. The default mode is often user-assignable.
The Messages subheading indicates which MIDI Channel Mode messages the device understands. Some equipment, although allowing modes to be set manually, will not recognize the corresponding MIDI messages.
The Altered subheading indicates which mode is selected when the device receives a MIDI Channel Mode message for a mode that is not supported.

Note Number—The appropriate column shows the range of note numbers transmitted and/or recognized by the device.
The True Voice (sometimes called Sound Range) subheading gives the range of notes available when Middle C is set to note number 60.

Velocity—The Note On and Note Off subheadings indicate which velocity values can be transmitted and/or recognized. The range of acceptable values may be included.

Aftertouch—The Key (or Key's) and Channel (or Ch's) subheadings show which of the two types of aftertouch is implemented.

Pitch Bend—This section indicates whether or not Pitch Bend messages are transmitted and/or recognized.

Control Change—This section shows whether or not Control Change messages are transmitted and/or recognized. Subheadings may be given for individual controller numbers. Typically, a range of numbers is provided with a note or remark dictating which controllers can be assigned or disabled. Controller functions may also be named or described.

Program Change—This section defines whether or not Program Change messages are transmitted and/or recognized.
The True # subheading specifies the range of device presets selected by each program change number.

System Exclusive—This indicates whether or not System Exclusive messages are transmitted and/or recognized.

System Common—The Song Position Pointer (SPP), Song Select, and Tune Request subheadings indicate which of these messages are implemented. The Remarks column should note any Data byte value restrictions.

System Realtime—The Clock subheading indicates whether or not MIDI Timing Clock messages are transmitted and/or recognized.
The Commands subheading indicates whether or not MIDI Start, Stop, and Continue messages are transmitted and/or received.

Auxiliary Messages—The Local On/Off, All Notes Off, Active Sensing, and Reset subheadings indicate which messages are implemented.

The Power of Imagination

Remember, MIDI messages are only numbers: manufacturers can process MIDI messages any way they see fit. A Note On message might inspire Device A to make a sound while Device B energizes a floodlight and Device C unmutes a mixer channel.

Since it is impossible to assign a finite number of message types to every possible musical and non-musical event, the specification only considers common musical applications. For manufacturers of non-musical equipment, message types can be assigned to other functions (as long as they don't violate the specification). For example, one of the authors of this book designed a device for monitoring firefighters' respirators using the MIDItools Computer.

One thing's for certain: MIDI will continue to evolve, and has yet to reach its peak despite being introduced to the public way back in 1983. When you think about how few other technical marvels from 1983 are still with us, MIDI's contribution becomes that much more obvious. The music industry can be proud of itself for creating and maintaining a workable, useful standard with a minimum of politics and a maximum of compliance.

Communication Systems

MIDI is a communications system, so let's consider these types of systems in general. Every communication system consists of four basic components:

- The Transmitter(s) generates, then sends, the information to be exchanged. Communication systems can have several transmitters.

- The Receiver(s) receives information from a Transmitter and decides what to do with the data (process it, ignore it, store it, translate it, etc.). Communication systems can have multiple receivers.

- The Communication Medium provides a defined path along which information travels from the transmitter(s) to the receiver(s).

- The Protocol defines a set of rules that control the exchange of messages. The entire system must abide by these rules to ensure the intelligibility of the received information. This Protocol might specify the relationships among Transmitters and Receivers, the direction and rate of transmissions, what action should take place if an error occurs, how to address multiple receivers, and similar communications-oriented issues.

In addition to these basic elements, there must also be a common language so that there is no ambiguity between transmitter and receiver. Any attempted interchange of information (*i.e.*, communication) will succeed when the transmitter and receiver both understand the structure (grammar) and data (vocabulary) of the language. Languages can consist of words, sounds, symbols, quantities, numbers, smells, etc.

A Quick Comparison of Communication Systems

To help illustrate the components of communication, let's summarize three typical systems.

Component	Human Speech System	Television System	MIDI System
Transmitter	Mouth	TV Tower	Keyboard
Receiver	Ear	TV Set	Sound Module
Medium	Air	Air	MIDI Cable
Protocol	serial 5 words/sec bidirectional	parallel 30 frames/sec unidirectional	serial 31,250 bytes/sec bidirectional
Typical message	"Let's go to the movies!"	"Make this pixel red!"	"Play note #100!"
Language reference	Dictionary	NTSC Standard	MIDI Specification

The spoken word is not a very efficient communications medium; it takes a long time to transfer information at a rate of 5 words per second, and people are often careless about using language.

Television can send 30 frames (distinct images) in one second, which, given the power of images, conveys a fair amount of information.

MIDI transmits significant quantities of data, especially considering its low cost and simple technology. It is possible to send over 1,000 notes in one second, or a lesser number of notes combined with other messages (*e.g.*, 500 notes and 500 pitch bend messages).

Chapter 4
Using Tools

Before you start building, you need good tools and the know-how to care for them. This chapter covers drills, hole punchers, nibblers, hacksaws, files, pliers, cutters, strippers, screwdrivers, soldering equipment, IC insertion/extraction tools, care of tools, and safety tips.

The parts cost of electronic projects isn't too high, but you will need to spend some money on tools. This initial investment will pay for itself if you plan to get into music and electronics (and you might have some of the required tools already). Luckily, no really expensive or hard-to-find tools are necessary to build the MIDItools Computer; and if you buy the parts kit, all you really need is a needlenose pliers, set of screwdrivers, wire cutter, and soldering iron.

Drilling Equipment

Your biggest expense will probably be a good drill (Fig. 4-1). Choose one that can take a 3/8" bit. Though slightly more expensive than the 1/4" variety, a 3/8" drill usually implies a heavy duty machine. Variable speed is also helpful (if it has a smooth action from minimum to maximum speed); some variable speed drills can even reverse the drill bit rotation at the flick of a switch.

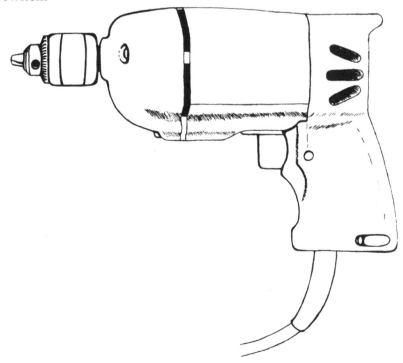

Fig. 4-1: Typical electric, hand-held drill.

You'll also need a set of bits (Fig. 4-2) to go along with your drill. These are often available inexpensively in sets, with typical drill bit diameters ranging from 1/16″ to 1/4″. They won't last forever, but if you're only drilling aluminum and plastic they'll drill a lot of holes before they dull out. If you don't want a full set, you can pretty much get by with three bits: 1/16″ (for drilling pilot holes); 1/8″; and 9/64″ or 5/32″.

Fig. 4-2: Drill bit.

If you're drilling holes for potentiometer or rotary switch shafts, you'll also need a 3/8″ bit. For DIN connectors, a 5/8″ bit does the job (a 9/16″ or 1/2″ bit should also work, but you may need to enlarge the hole with a file or tapered reamer, depending on the DIN connector). Tapered reamers (Fig. 4-3) aren't too expensive and are useful for deburring or enlarging previously drilled holes.

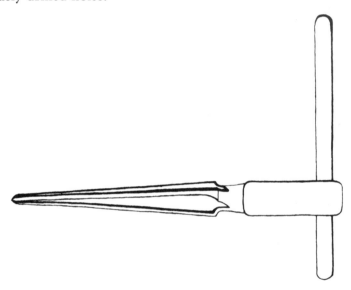

Fig. 4-3: Turning the reamer while pushing forces the reamer further into the hole, thus enlarging the hole's diameter.

Tapered drill bits are available that let you drill virtually any size hole—just push the drill bit in further to enlarge the hole. However, knowing when to stop can be difficult, and tapered bits can be harder to use properly than standard bits.

Your final piece of drilling equipment is a center punch (Fig. 4-4). This lets you punch a small dimple (indentation) in metal or plastic by tapping it with a hammer on the non-pointed side. This dimple keeps the drill bit centered during its first few revolutions. You can get by with a nail in an emergency, but a real center punch is far more accurate.

Fig. 4-4: Center punch.

Hole Punches

Drilling small diameter holes is usually simple, but what about square or rectangular holes, or holes with really large diameters? Although you can use a file to turn a round hole into a square one, it takes a lot of work and usually yields a less-than-professional look. Pros use chassis punches, which work along the principle shown in Fig. 4-5.

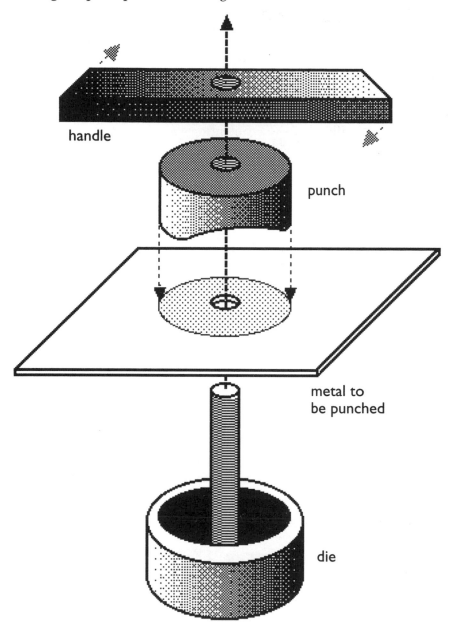

Fig. 4-5: The die's shaft inserts through a small hole in the metal to be punched. The punch, which has sharp edges, goes over the threaded screw; screwing the handle onto the shaft and rotating the handle forces the punch down through the metal. The area to be cut is shown in light gray.

The device consists of two parts, the punch and the die. You drill a hole through the panel to be punched, sandwich the panel between the punch and die, and insert a threaded screw through the punch, panel, and die. Tightening the handle or nut on the end of the screw with a wrench draws the punch closer to the die, causing the punch to pierce the panel cleanly and without burrs. (Rectangular punches may have multiple screws, which have to be tightened down in order.)

This is a very basic type of punch. There are also hand punches whose two handles, when squeezed together, punch through a panel (for smaller holes—up to about 1/4″ or so), as well as industrial-strength punching machines.

Punches can be circular, square, or even cut out in the shape of a multipin, computer-style connector. Generally, the more unusual the shape or the larger the size, the more expensive the punch. Be forewarned: the fancy punches get very pricey—but if you have to make a lot of holes for MIDI connectors and the like, a punch can save much time and effort.

Nibblers

For those on a tight budget, a nibbling tool makes it easy to cut square and rectangular holes (as long as they aren't too small). A nibbler is hand operated; you first drill a hole to make room for the nibbler shaft, then use what looks like a miniature guillotine to take pieces out of the metal. It's much slower than using a punch, but is easier (and can make straighter lines) than using a file to enlarge holes.

Sawing and Filing

You'll also need a hacksaw (Fig. 4-6), principally for cutting potentiometer shafts to length. Almost any kind will do, but use a blade with fairly fine cutting teeth. While you're at it, get a spare blade—you'll need it at some unexpected later moment.

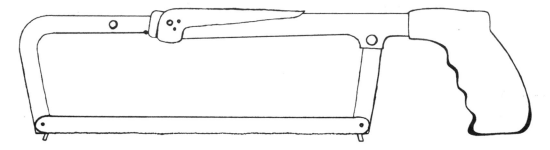

Fig. 4-6: Hacksaw with blade

Files can not only enlarge holes as mentioned previously; you can use a file to get rid of the little burrs that are left around the perimeter of a newly-drilled hole or cut. You only really need two files: a rat's tail file, and a half-round type (Fig. 4-7). Don't get big files, since electronics work involves tight spaces most of the time.

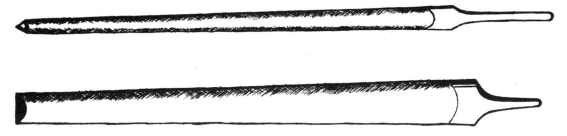

Fig. 4-7: The rat's tail file (above) is good for deburring. The half-round file (below) is so called because one side is flat, and the other side is semi-circular.

Pliers, Wire Cutters, Screwdrivers, Wrenches

For dealing with wire, bending components, and other light assembly work, you'll need needlenose pliers (Fig. 4-8), diagonal cutters (Fig. 4-9), and a wire-stripping tool for removing insulation (Fig. 4-10).

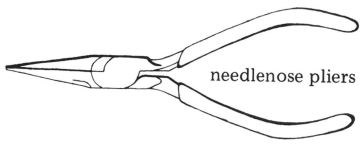

Fig. 4-8: Needlenose pliers.

Check the pliers jaws for accurate alignment and smooth action before buying anything, no matter how little or how much the item may cost. Remember you'll be working with tiny parts, so get small pliers and cutters.

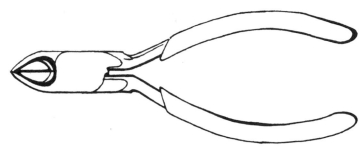

Fig. 4-9: Diagonal cutters for cutting hookup wire.

Fancy semi-automatic wire strippers are available, but unless you're doing small-scale production you may find they're not worth the extra expense compared to simpler models.

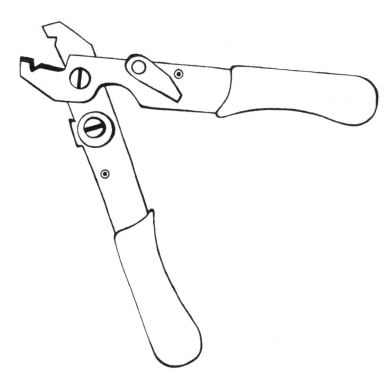

Fig. 4-10: Simple wire stripper. With this type, there's a small cam underneath a setscrew. You can loosen the setscrew and adjust the cam so that the wire strippers cannot close more than a certain amount, thus allowing you to strip the insulation without nicking the wire.

Next, your tool kit should include a medium-size straight screwdriver and a Phillips-head screwdriver, as well as a set of small jewelers' screwdrivers (Fig. 4-11). These are handy for the setscrews in knobs, but have many other uses like poking, prying, and scraping.

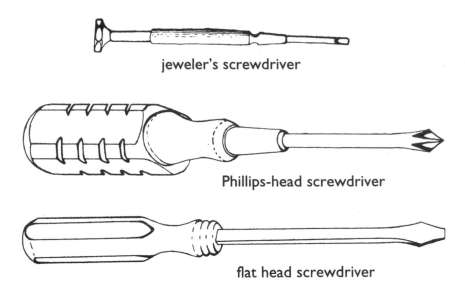

jeweler's screwdriver

Phillips-head screwdriver

flat head screwdriver

Fig. 4-11: *Several types of common screwdrivers.*

You'll also want a small crescent wrench (Fig. 4-12) for tightening nuts on pots and screws and, although it isn't really necessary, a pair of vise grips (Fig. 4-13), which is a wonderful tool to have (especially if your kitchen plumbing goes bonkers one Sunday morning and there are no plumbers around—this is something we know from experience).

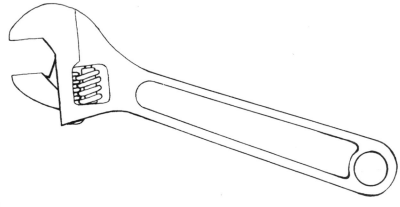

Fig. 4-12

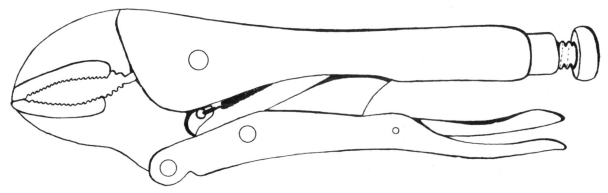

Fig. 4-13

To round out your selection of mechanical tools, get a small vise to hold parts for soldering, sawing, or filing (Fig. 4-14).

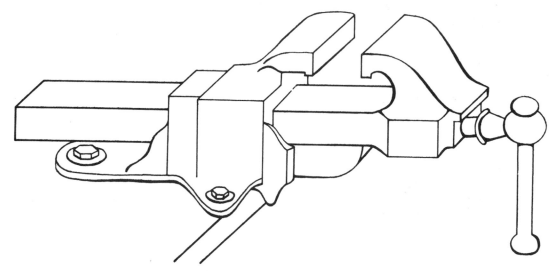

Fig. 4-14

Soldering

Now to soldering equipment. You'll need a 40 watt to 60 watt soldering pencil (Fig. 4-15; soldering "iron" may imply a big beastie that will probably burn out heat-sensitive parts) and some spare tips. Look around for something with a fairly small tip, that way you'll save yourself a lot of aggravation in tight places

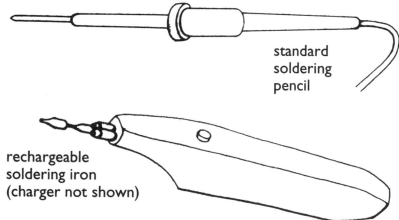

standard soldering pencil

rechargeable soldering iron (charger not shown)

Fig. 4-15: Two types of soldering pencils.

If you have the bucks, a temperature-controlled soldering station is the deluxe way to go (Fig. 4-16). The most sophisticated versions of this type of soldering device apply as much heat as is necessary to properly solder a connection; for example, they will pump out lots of heat if you're soldering a jack, and much less if you're soldering the pins on an IC socket. Tips are available in different temperature ratings as well (700 degrees works well for most electronic work).

The type of solder you buy can make or break a unit's operation—and we mean "break" literally! Do not under any circumstances purchase acid-core solder, since it's designed for plumbing applications, not electronics, and can damage electronic circuits. The kind you want is 60/40 rosin-core solder (preferably the "multi-core" type). The "60/40" refers to the mixture of metals in the solder. Thinner solder is easiest to use, and a much better choice than thicker solder.

If the rosin core flux is "activated" or "water-soluble" (cleanup using water), be certain that the flux is completely cleaned off the board after soldering. These fluxes are highly corrosive in the presence of humidity; the corrosion will someday short traces together and ruin your board.

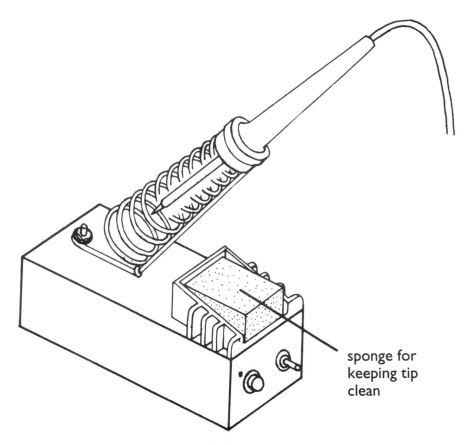

Fig. 4-16: Soldering station with temperature-controlled tip.

sponge for
keeping tip
clean

In addition to soldering, you might also want a desoldering tool. They come in all shapes, complexities, sizes, and costs, but the simplest kind is a squeeze bulb with a Teflon tip (Fig. 4-17). Chapter 5 contains much more information about soldering and desoldering techniques.

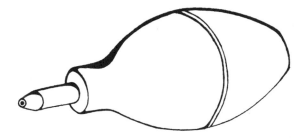

Fig. 4-17: One of the simplest desoldering tools. Squeeze the bulb while the tip is against a molten solder connection then release the bulb; the suction draws the liquid solder into the bulb. The bulb tip, which is usually made of Teflon so that the solder doesn't stick, should be cleaned periodically with a thin, solid wire to prevent clogging.

IC Insertion/Extraction Tools

You need to insert ICs during the course of building a project, and remove them should they need replacement. Using sockets makes this easier, but you do need to be careful; IC pins are fragile, and if while inserting the chip they get bent under the IC, they could break when you try to unbend them.

To avoid this problem, an IC insertion tool straightens the pins and makes it easy to push the IC into the socket (make sure the insertion tool is made of antistatic material).

The simplest extractor tool is simply a spring "tweezers" whose ends hook underneath the IC and pull it up (Fig. 4-18). These work just fine, but if you want to go more upscale, for ICs up to 16 pins you can get extractors that clip under *all* the pins and make it very easy to pull out chips.

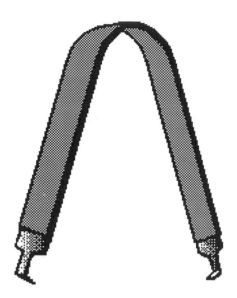

Fig. 4-18: Inexpensive IC extractor. Squeezing on the spring forces the clips together, which are inserted between the chip and socket. Rocking and pulling gently upward pulls the IC out of its socket.

Some companies offer combination inserter/extractor tools, and separate IC pin straighteners. Just about all these devices do the job.

Incidentally, if you don't have an extractor you might be tempted to poke a screwdriver between an IC and socket, and use the blade as a lever to remove the IC. Don't! Sometimes there will be circuit board traces on the top of the circuit board, underneath the chip. It's too easy to scratch them or even break the trace or socket, so . . . spend the $3 it costs for a simple IC extractor.

Preventing IC Static Blowout

Since we're talking about inserting ICs, remember that all semiconductor devices are sensitive to static electricity, and that during a dry day it's easy to accumulate enough static charge to fry a chip if you handle it incorrectly.

The best preventive maintenance is to wear a conductive *ground strap*. One end goes around your wrist, and the other end clips to the device's chassis ground through a resistor. If you don't use a ground strap, at least touch a metal ground to discharge any static electricity from yourself before handling any chips, and don't do anything that could accumulate a charge while you're inserting, removing, or storing the chip. Combs, rugs, and snack-food wrappers are especially vicious enemies.

Testing, Testing

Believe it or not, there is a chance that what you build won't work the first time you turn it on. In that case, you'll want something that can test the wiring, make sure the power supply is producing sufficient voltage, etc. The tool of choice is a hand-held Digital Multimeter (DMM), which can show resistance, voltage, and current on a digital readout (typically 3-1/2 digits, meaning three regular digits and a most significant digit that can read either 0 or 1). The price ranges from dozens to hundreds of dollars, but even the inexpensive models will suffice to do basic MIDItools tests. DMMs are available at any electronics store.

Analog multimeters, which feature large analog meters (you know, the kind with pointers, like old VU meters) are also available. However, these aren't really cost-effective compared to the average digital multimeter.

The Care and Feeding of Tools

There are a few general rules for taking care of tools:

- If any of them come with instructions, *read them*. Your drill will come with instructions about lubrication, proper handling, and so on. These instructions should be followed, as should any directions that come with your soldering iron or DMM.

- Never use a tool for a purpose other than the one for which it was intended. For example, screwdrivers make lousy chisels, and soldering irons are not available to little brothers or sisters for wood burning.

- Drill bits respond well to sharpening at regular intervals, and you may want to pick up an oilstone to keep them happy.

- Make sure that your screwdriver fits tightly into the screw slot. Using too small a screwdriver will tear up the screw, and may lead to premature death of the screwdriver itself.

- Needlenose pliers are for fine work and wire bending. Don't use them on big clunky jobs where you should be using vise grips or the like, or you'll knock the jaws out of alignment and have to get a new set of pliers. The same goes for diagonal cutters; they're for cutting fine to medium gauge wire. If somebody asks you to cut a piece of copper tubing with your cutters, politely decline and hacksaw through it instead.

- Incidentally, a Swiss Army knife can be an excellent investment. You can't take your tool kit everywhere you go, but you can do quite a few field repairs with the various knives, screwdrivers, pliers, and files available in the more complete knives.

Safety First

Before moving on, let's talk safety. Tools that are designed to slice through metal can slice through human flesh even easier, and flying bits of metal or plastic can lodge in your eyes, lungs, or possibly even unmentionable parts of your body. The point is this: *tools are dangerous*. Treat them with respect, and remember that one wrong move could cause an accident with the potential to haunt you for the rest of your life.

Arguably, the most dangerous tool you'll be using is the drill. Here are some rules to follow:

- Keep your hair out of the way! Tie it back or whatever, but be careful. Some people have gotten into real trouble by not remembering this rule.

- Remove any jewelry—rings, bracelets, watches, etc.—when drilling.

- When you drill, don't hold the object you're drilling with your hands! Hold it with a vise, or vise grips, or anything suitable—should the drill bit slip or skid, you want it attacking the vise and not your hand.

- Make sure the drill bit is always perpendicular to whatever it is you're drilling. You can apply a light amount of downward pressure on the drill bit to speed up the drilling process a little bit, but you have to be very careful—a broken drill bit is not only annoying, but dangerous.

Here are some other tips:

- Always use all three conductors of anything requiring a three-wire cord. The one on the bottom is ground, and three-wire AC stuff is far safer than sticking on a three-to-two adapter and plugging that into your wall. If you don't have a three-wire outlet, use an adapter but take the wire coming out of the adapter and connect it to the screwplate on your AC outlet (Fig. 4-19). The screw should go to ground and effectively does the same thing as the ground wire of a three-wire outlet—assuming that the plate was properly grounded when it was wired. If you absolutely must use a two-wire setup, even though you shouldn't, don't stand on wet concrete barefoot, okay? You'll zap yourself unless the tool is properly insulated.

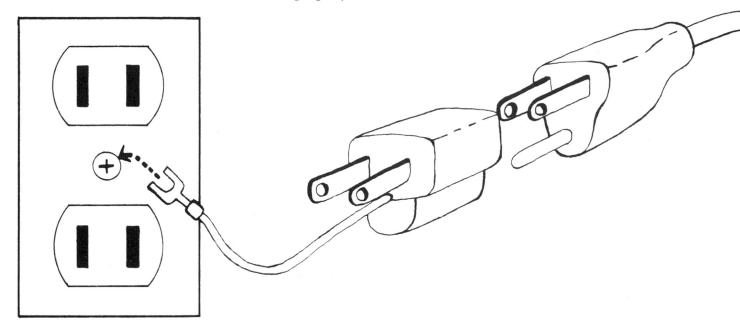

Fig. 4-19: Adapting a two-wire outlet to a three-conductor cable.

- Don't solder with shorts on. Sometimes the rosin spits out and hits you on the leg; not horrifyingly bad, but not fun either.

- For similar reasons, wear eye protection when soldering. Glasses with plastic lenses give a certain degree of protection, but clear plastic goggles are cheap insurance for your eyesight.

- Be careful where you lay down your soldering iron—don't put it where it can burn through its AC cord (this happens; don't laugh!).

- Make sure you always know where the tip of your iron is. These babies are hot.

- Sometimes it's a good idea to wear sturdy gloves when using screwdrivers or pliers. This protects your skin from rubbing against the tool.

After this scary talk, it's probably worth mentioning that most electronics hobbyists don't do any damage to themselves; be careful and use some common sense, and you probably won't have any trouble either. Hands are precious to the musician, and proper care will keep them unscarred and unscathed.

Chapter 5

Building the MIDItools Computer

This chapter tells how to turn a pile of parts into an attractive, reliable, smoothly functioning unit. Don't be intimidated if you've never built anything electronic before—it's really not that difficult if you just follow the steps and *be patient*.

Introduction

The process of building any electronic device can be broken down into several logical steps. Performing these steps in order saves time and promotes better results; one step of planning can indeed save two in execution. Here are the steps for building the MIDItools Computer:

Step 1: Gather together the required parts, hardware, and tools.

Step 2: Fabricate or purchase a circuit board for mounting the electronic components.

Step 3: Mount the various components on the circuit board then solder them in place.

Step 4: Select an enclosure big enough to hold the circuit board, pot, connectors, switches, expansion boards, etc. It's better to have too large an enclosure than too small an enclosure, as working in a cramped space can be frustrating. (The PAVO prototype rack enclosure is one rack space high and 8.25″ deep.)

Step 5: Drill and/or punch holes in the enclosure for the various panel components (connectors, LEDs, pushbuttons, LCD, pot, etc.) as well as for small screws that hold the boards in place.

Step 6: Add any wires or ribbon connectors to boards that will be difficult to connect to once they are mounted in place.

Step 7: Mount the circuit board(s) in the chassis, and complete any interboard connections by plugging in the appropriate ribbon cable ends.

Step 8: Add knobs, and label the various panel components.

Step 9: Test for proper operation. (Lack of smoke is always a good sign.)

We'll go through these steps one at a time. But first, let's look at how to solder, since this is such an important part of electronic construction.

The Art of Soldering

Proper soldering is paramount. Perhaps the majority of problems with projects are due to poor soldering. Here are four important points to consider:

- Select the right tools. Don't use irons under 30 or over 60 watts, and don't use acid-core solder under any circumstances. The only acceptable solder is *rosin core solder* that's expressly designed for electronic work. See Chapter 4 for additional information on choosing a soldering iron and solder.

- Keep your soldering iron tip in good condition. The main rule of tip care is *not* to let your iron sit in a warmed-up condition without having a thin layer of solder on the tip; otherwise, the tip will oxidize and work less efficiently. Here's how to get your iron ready for soldering:

  (1) Wrap a turn of solder around the tip of your iron before plugging it in or turning it on. Then when the tip comes up to temperature, it will melt the solder and form the protective layer of solder we just mentioned.

  (2) Have a slightly wet sponge sitting next to your iron (in a coffee can lid, ash tray, or the like). Just before soldering, wipe the tip across the sponge to remove any excess solder from the tip. This produces a clean tip, permitting better heat transfer for faster, more efficient soldering. When you're about to put the iron aside after soldering some connections, do *not* clean off the tip first; only clean the tip just before soldering a connection.

- Make sure the surfaces you'll be soldering together are clean. For example, if you make your own circuit boards, you'll find that copper forms a layer of oxidation when exposed to the air and this layer resists solder. The remedy is to rub the board lightly with fine steel wool. Component leads can also become dirty or oxidized; use a rubber eraser, light sandpaper, or steel wool to clean off the scum.

- Heat up the area to be soldered before feeding in the solder. Don't just use the point of the iron's tip to solder; use the whole tip to heat the surfaces to be joined (Fig. 5-1). After heating up the joint for a couple of seconds, feed in some solder and keep the iron in position until the solder flows freely over the connection. The key: both surfaces to be soldered (component lead and circuit board pad) must be at a temperature above the solder's melting point or your joint will be weak.

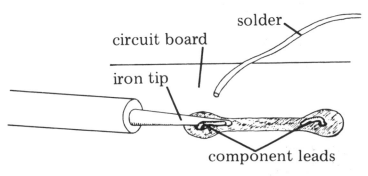

Fig. 5-1: The soldering iron's tip heats the component lead, the circuit board trace, and the solder.

The time required for the joint to heat up depends on the type of connection. Circuit board connections require little heat since it's necessary to heat up only a thin strip of copper and a component lead. Ground lugs, on the other hand, usually require a fair amount of heat since the chassis tends to draw heat away from the lug.

When soldering diodes, transistors, and other heat sensitive parts, try clipping an alligator clip on the lead being soldered, as close to the body of the part as possible (Fig. 5-2). This will draw away heat from the part, and often is enough to prevent heat damage.

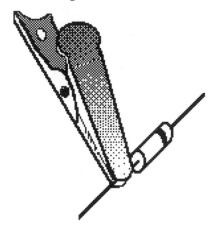

Fig. 5-2: An Alligator cliposaurus attacking a baby diode. No, that's not really it. The alligator clip draws heat away from the diode during soldering.

- Leave the iron on for an additional second or so after the solder flows freely, then remove the iron from the connection. *Do not disturb the connection in the process, or this will weaken the joint.* Should this happen, wait about 15 seconds, then reheat the connection while feeding in a tiny bit more solder.

One of the most common solder joint problems is a *cold joint,* where not enough heat was applied to make the solder flow smoothly. Also, the rosin inside the solder (which smells a little like musk incense) cleans dirt and grease from the connections. If it isn't brought up to temperature, then the connection isn't going to get properly cleaned, which can also give a bad joint. If the proper temperature is achieved, the rosin core flux will do its cleaning job, and then politely evaporate.

Important: Flux vapor is mildly toxic, as are lead particles (found in the solder) that float in the air and remain on your fingertips. Always have good ventilation when you are soldering. Also, wash your hands after soldering.

Good solder connection

...solder flows smoothly over the area being soldered, and the component lead outline is clearly visible.

not enough heat, or dirty component lead

too little solder

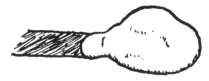

too much solder (component lead outline is not visible)

Fig. 5-3: Different types of solder connections.

Fig. 5-3 shows a variety of solder connections—what to strive for and what to avoid. A good connection looks smooth, round, and shiny. Poor solder connections look dull, tend to ball up, and are often grainy in appearance. One thing's for sure: If you can pull the lead out of its solder connection, the connection is no good. A good mechanical connection helps create a better electrical connection.

Now that you understand soldering basics, here's a simple project to extend the life of your iron's tip (and save electricity): a "standby" switch so that your iron doesn't stay at maximum juice while unused. It works on the same principle as light dimmer switches that give a bright and low position, but please note that this device is *not* for soldering irons that use a transformer or electronic controlling circuitry, and can damage them.

Fig. 5-4 shows the schematic for the heat control, which consists of a diode (a 1N4003 or any heavier-duty diode will work just fine, and in this application the polarity doesn't matter) and an SPST switch rated at a minimum 115V, 1A. Closing the switch applies full power to the iron; opening the switch diverts power through the diode, which cuts down the energy going to the iron and thus reduces the heat.

When hooking up the 3-wire AC cord the ground lead goes to the AC socket ground, one AC cord hot lead goes to S1, and the other hot lead to one of the AC socket's *non-grounded* terminals.

You'll find when experimenting that there are lots of times when you'll solder for several minutes straight, then quit for 10 to 15 minutes. That's when to use the reduced power. After you flick the switch to max, it takes only a few seconds for the iron to reach maximum heat again.

If you build one of these, be *extremely* careful because *standard house current is potentially lethal.* Make sure all connections are well-insulated, double-check your wiring before plugging it in, and plug into a fused outlet (just in case!). If you have any doubts about your ability to successfully complete this project, don't build it.

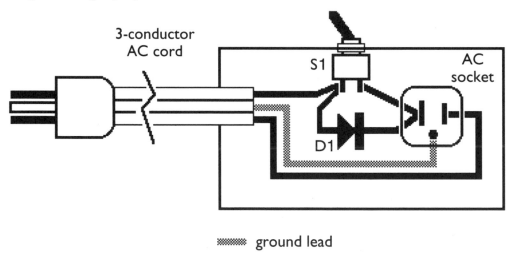

Fig. 5-4: Soldering iron heat control, which saves energy and wear and tear on the iron. Open the switch to run the iron at reduced power.

Desoldering

From time to time you'll need to unsolder a component from the board. This can happen if, for example, you need to replace a defective (or incorrectly installed) part.

Begin by removing as much solder as possible from the connection using one of the methods described next. Then, remove the part by gently pulling on its leads with a pair of needlenose pliers. If the part still won't come out, try to get rid of some more solder. In extreme cases, pull out the part while applying heat to the connection to liquify the solder.

To prevent damage to a part or circuit board, use the minimum amount of heat necessary and remember that desoldering takes more care than soldering: *be patient.* It's crucial not to overheat the circuit board; copper pads can delaminate (peel up off the board), leaving no place to which you can re-solder. Here are three popular ways to remove unwanted solder.

- Desoldering squeeze bulb with Teflon tip (see Fig. 4-17 in Chapter 4). While heating up the solder that needs to be removed, you squeeze the air out of the bulb. Then hold the Teflon tip up against the solder blob, and let the air back in the bulb, pulling the molten solder with it. These are inexpensive and easy to use, but one drawback is that you must periodically clean out the tip.

- "Solder sucker." This works on the same principle as the squeeze bulb, but semi-automates the process. You push down on a spring-loaded cylinder, hold the Teflon tip up to the heated solder connection, then press a release button or lever. The retreating cylinder creates a vacuum and sucks up the solder.

- Solder wicks. These are pieces of braided wire that are especially designed to suck up solder. To use a solder wick, you heat the solder connection while holding the wick up against that connection; the wick removes virtually all of the solder by capillary action. You then cut off this section of the braid after the solder has cooled, thereby exposing more of the wick for desoldering your next connection. This generally does the best job.

Step 1: Gathering Parts

One of the biggest stumbling blocks for electronic hobbyists is finding the parts necessary to build a project. However, this need not be difficult; in fact, all the parts for the MIDItools Computer are available from a number of sources. You can obtain parts by mail, from retail electronics dealers, or a mix of the two.

The Authorized MIDItools Computer Parts Kit

For those who don't want to take the time to chase down parts or fabricate boards and enclosures, PAVO is endorsed by the authors as the official MIDItools support source. The company offers complete kits as well as selected individual parts (EEPROMs for different projects, circuit boards, enclosures, pre-programmed 6805 microcontrollers, LCDs, etc.). A repair service is also available should problems crop up. PAVO also serves as a "clearinghouse" for those who come up with new applications for the MIDItools Computer.

Buying Parts by Mail Order

Few towns have enough electronics experimenters to support a large electronics retail store; you'll tend to find these only in larger metropolitan areas, and even then they may not offer a wide selection of parts. As a result, many hobbyists rely on mail-order shopping as an alternative to buying through retail outlets—particularly for locating ICs, which can be extremely difficult to find locally.

The best way to locate mail-order outlets is to visit your local library or newsstand and check out some of the magazines published expressly for electronics hobbyists *(Popular Electronics, Electronics Now, 73*, etc.). Look in the back pages of these magazines, and you'll see numerous ads for mail-order hobbyist supply houses. These ads generally include a partial listing of parts and prices, as well as instructions on how to obtain a catalog. Many times this just involves circling a number on a reader service card bound into the magazine; a few weeks later, the catalog will arrive at your door. Mail-order companies often have lower prices and a wider selection of parts than local stores.

People generally have two main reservations about mail-order houses:

- You have to wait for the order to be processed and sent back to you, which can try your patience when you're hot to get started on a project.

- There have been cases of mail-order fraud (few involving electronics suppliers, however), and people are suspicious about sending off large amounts of money to some post office box halfway across the country.

Fortunately, these reservations are not really justified. Many suppliers turn orders around in 24 hours, and offer accelerated delivery (via Federal Express, UPS, etc.) for an additional fee. Companies often have toll-free or 24-hour answering services to take credit card or COD orders, and this can also speed up the turnaround time. Sometimes parts are back ordered, but that can also happen when dealing with a retail store if it doesn't have what you want in stock.

Concerning fraud, companies do mess up an order from time to time, but this is usually due to human error rather than malevolence—a polite letter or phone call generally straightens out any difficulties. Paying with a credit card can also help prevent problems, and stringent mail-order laws have helped weed out some of the more marginal companies anyway.

Here are a few tips for getting the best results from mail-order companies.

- Put your name and address on the order itself—simply including it on the envelope return address isn't good enough. Companies get really frustrated when they have a check, a list of parts, and no address.

- Keep any correspondence separate from orders if you want your order processed as quickly as possible.

- Although COD eliminates some element of risk, it costs more money and will also delay your order.

- If you have trouble with a company, write them. Even the best mail-order houses cannot avoid an occasional goof; they have no way of knowing there's a problem unless you tell them.

- If you're asking for advice, technical help, or something beyond a simple request for price lists or catalogues, include a self-addressed stamped envelope. This encourages a prompt (and often friendlier) response.

Finding Local Parts Sources

Check the phone directory's Yellow Pages under "Electronic Equipment and Supplies—Dealers" and "Electronic Equipment and Supplies—Wholesale."

Dealers are retail stores who want your business, whether large or small. The prices are generally close to list prices because they do small volume compared to wholesale firms. Frequently they sell consumer equipment, such as stereos, calculators, and burglar alarms, as well as parts.

A variation on the independent local retailer is the chain store. For example, Radio Shack carries a line of parts, but you can also find chains that are more regionally oriented.

At retail stores, you can usually ask questions about parts and electronics without getting funny looks. Frequently the person on the other side of the counter, and sometimes even the manager, will know less about electronics than you will after you've read this book, but they may be able to introduce you to either somebody in the store who knows the subject, or to a regular customer who's into electronics.

Wholesale stores serve the industrial and/or repair market, and cater to professionals. They don't want to bother with somebody who walks in and just wants one IC (although there are exceptions). If you can go into a wholesale place and specify exactly what you want and act like you know what you're doing, they'll be more inclined to deal with you.

Remember, though, that these stores are set up for the professional and that the employees have neither time nor the inclination to do any thinking for you. If you're lucky, there will be a wholesale outlet in your community that also has an over-the-counter section for nonindustrial users. Here, the counter people are more likely to know about electronics, and if you are polite and look green enough, nine times out of ten they'll try to help you with any questions.

One way to be welcomed at wholesale stores is to obtain a resale number. Wholesalers interpret resale numbers as an indication of a sincere and professional interest in electronics, and some wholesale outlets won't even let you through the door unless you have one. The state you live in issues resale numbers, which allow the professional manufacturer or distributor to avoid paying sales tax on parts, since the parts will be resold as part of a finished product and sales tax will be collected on that. If you intend to make anything for sale, a resale number is a valid permit to obtain. However, certain legal obligations must be complied with.

- Some states will require a deposit; for small businesses, though, this deposit is nominal.

- If you sell something to somebody you must collect the prevailing sales tax, and send it to your state tax board on a regular basis.

- If you buy parts for your own use and not for resale, you must declare them as taxable and pay the sales tax.

The above does not substitute for legal advice, but represents general guidelines. Check your county government (see the phone book under "Government Offices—Sales Tax") for more information.

Another branch of the wholesale tree is the electronics distributor. These exist mostly to serve the industrial market; they expect orders that require hundreds or even thousands of parts, and carry products from specific companies. If you're extremely lucky, there may be one in your area that offers over-the-counter sales.

Surplus electronics stores also deserve a look. Some sell a wide selection of really high-quality parts at extremely good prices; others sell trash and rejects without giving you any real cash advantage. Remember that the reason why something is in a surplus store in the first place is because the original buyer didn't want it, due to any number of reasons (change in styling, defects, business failure, and so on). So, there is a definite "let the buyer beware" implied in dealing with surplus stores. This is not necessarily because of any dishonesty; rather, these stores don't have time to go through all their parts, which leaves it up to the customer to determine whether or not a part is suited for the intended application. Most of the time, surplus stores will cheerfully take back any defective components, but others don't, and you can't really blame them. People frequently will get an exotic part, blow it up through lack of knowledge, then blame the store.

Now that all these warnings are out of the way, let's examine the benefits of surplus outlets.

- The price is right.

- The parts are frequently difficult to obtain elsewhere and are of good quality. A part that may be obsolete for the space program may be perfect for the experimenter, and the savings are substantial.

- Companies will sometimes go out of business and sell their inventory for peanuts to surplus dealers to minimize their losses. This saving gets passed on to you.

- The employees at surplus stores are far more likely to know about electronics than the people at retail stores, since their very livelihood depends on being able to examine a batch of parts and determine whether it's something on which people would want to spend money.

An emergency parts source, although limited in scope, is your local electronics/TV repair shop (again, the Yellow Pages are a great help).

Because they are not in business to sell parts they don't have many on hand for experimenters, and if you do request something it will sell for list price. This is only fair, because they have to make a living somehow and can't afford to deplete their parts stock unless they make something from it. So, although it's a last resort, it's still worth checking out, and you might meet some interesting and knowledgeable people that way (you may also meet a grouch or two).

Getting the Best Prices

One of the best ways to keep parts costs down is through quantity buying. If you can locate fellow enthusiasts in your area and pool orders, you can save a lot—a jack that costs $1 in single quantities may cost 80¢ if you buy 10, and 60¢ if you buy 100. This is also why commercial parts kits can sometimes cost less than buying the parts yourself, since companies have more purchasing clout than individuals.

Another way to stock your lab is to scrutinize the ads in the back of electronics magazines. One company might make a great buy on capacitors, and offer them at a lower price than the competition for a period of a few months. Another company might have low prices on resistors, while another specializes in ICs.

There is one caveat, though. Some companies offer "untested" semiconductors that are sold at rock-bottom prices because most of the time they work marginally, if at all. Although experimenters can have fun with untested parts, it's best you steer clear of anything marked "untested" unless you know how to test for functionality.

Step 2: Printed Circuit Boards

Although printed circuit boards speed up assembly time, they require a time-consuming production process. For this reason, many giant electronic manufacturers have their circuit boards made by firms that specialize in PC board manufacture rather than deal with the problem themselves. With the MIDItools Computer, a commercially-available circuit board is available for those who want to get going with minimal time and effort. However, learning to make your own circuit boards can be a worthwhile skill if you decide to get further into electronics, so let's see what's involved.

Basic Principles

You start out with a piece of insulator that's flat, about 1.6 mm (1/16") thick, and has copper (a conductor) bonded to one side (sometimes both sides, but we don't need to know about that for this book). Fig. 5-5 shows a blank circuit board.

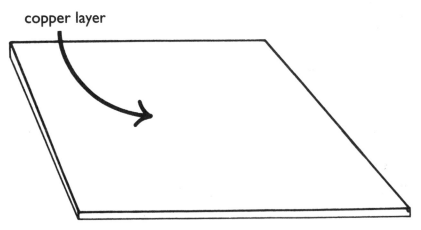

copper layer

Fig. 5-5: Blank circuit board, copper clad on one side.

Next, copper can be etched away and dissolved by a not-too-dangerous chemical called ferric chloride, which we'll call ferric for short. If you take a blank circuit board and throw it into a tank of ferric, within about 45 minutes there won't be any copper left. By covering the copper with something that defeats the etching action (*e.g.*, tape or paint; see Fig. 5-6), you can etch away selectively at the blank board. This creates areas of insulators (etched areas) and conductors (unetched areas). These conductors are called *traces,* and take the place of wires in a circuit.

Although ferric is the "old standby" for etching, a newer option, ammonium persulfate, is less messy, and unlike ferric, remains relatively clear during the etching process so that you can see how the board is doing. Most electronic suppliers offer both; you're probably best off with the ammonium persulfate.

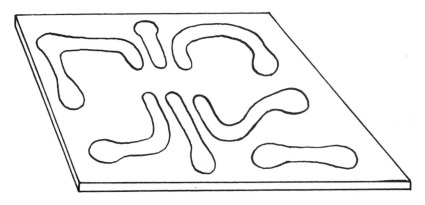

Fig. 5-6: Lay down etch resist (tape, enamel paint, photoresist, etc.).

After etching the unwanted copper, you then strip off the resist and drill holes in the finished board (Fig. 5-7).

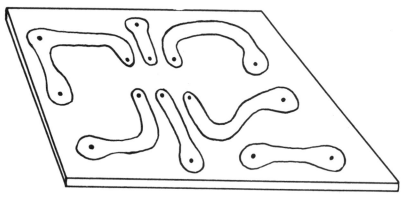

Fig. 5-7: Etch away unwanted copper, remove any resist, then drill holes.

Next, insert component leads through the board (the leads come out on the *copper* side of the board; see Fig. 5-8).

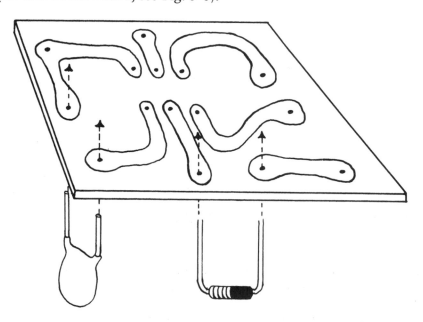

Fig. 5-8: Insert parts through the board as indicated on a parts layout diagram.

Now bend the wires over to hold the part in place, and cut off any excess lead length. Be careful not to scrape the trace with the wire cutter tip.

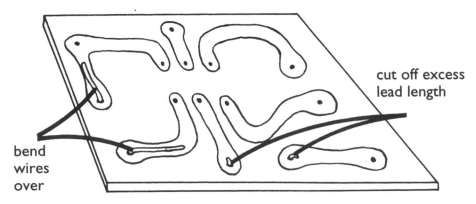

Fig. 5-9: When cutting off excess length, leave enough to make good contact with the circuit board, but not so much that it shorts out against an adjoining trace.

By soldering these leads to the traces, you now have a completed circuit (Fig. 5-10). Incidentally, many experimenters prefer to insert the part, bend the leads over, solder, and then cut. The advantage of this approach is that the part will tend to stay more solidly in place as you solder; the disadvantage is that it's easier for solder to stray along the lead, and possibly create a solder bridge.

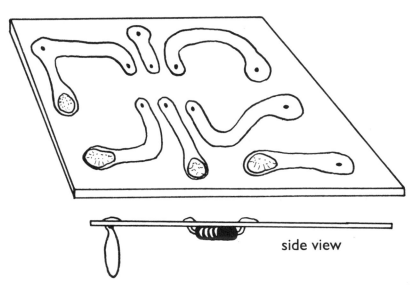

Fig. 5-10: Solder lead to the circuit board pads. Note the side view, which shows how components are snug against the board.

The catch to the whole process is how to avoid etching away the parts of the copper you want to keep, so let's delve into that subject next.

Resisting the Etchant

The least sophisticated way to resist etchant is to just put little pieces of tape down directly on the copper, then dunk the board into an etching bath. The tape prevents any solution from getting to the copper. The drawback here is the inability to do fine work, which ICs require.

An easier way is to use a resist pen, although this still isn't precise enough for working with ICs. Resist pens are like felt-tip markers; in fact, you can even use some stock felt-tip pens as resist pens. With this method, you lay ink down on the copper, let it dry, then toss the board in an etching bath. The dried ink keeps the etchant from the copper in those places where appropriate. But there's a problem here too, since the ink has to be on really thick to withstand sitting in the bath for twenty to thirty minutes; some of it can wear away and expose the copper underneath, which naturally starts to etch.

So, you switch to thicker ink in this case—enamel paint seems to work well (you know, the kind for model airplanes that comes in little glass bottles). Get yourself a really fine brush, and paint on where you want the conductors to be. The enamel is very effective against etchant when you throw the board into the etch bath, although now you have the problem of getting the enamel paint off before you can solder to the copper. A variety of noxious and harmful chemicals do the job really fast, like ethyl acetate or toluene. You can also use paint thinner; saturate a little steel wool with a chemical of your choice and strip off the paint. However, these are environmentally nasty chemicals that also generate extremely toxic vapors. It's worth taking the extra minute or so to sand off the enamel gently instead of using chemicals.

If you insist on using toxic chemicals, wear rubber gloves during the whole process to prevent absorption through the skin. However, whatever strips off enamel paint also seems to have it in for rubber gloves, so move fast. Make sure you work in a room with plenty of ventilation, and of course, dispose of any chemicals properly, in accordance with local environmental guidelines.

After giving the board a rinse and letting it dry, give a *light* final polish (you don't want to take off too much copper) with some clean steel wool and you're ready to go.

Note that you need to keep the copper clean as you prepare for etching—sometimes a fingerprint will resist the ferric chloride and give uneven results. Similarly, keep dust and sticky surfaces away from the printed circuit board.

Pro-Level Circuit Boards

The previous methods have major drawbacks, so professional circuit board manufacturers use photographic techniques. Here are the basic steps:

(1) Make a photographic negative of the circuit board pattern on transparent, thin plastic.

(2) Place the negative over a piece of copperclad board that has previously been sprayed with *photoresist*. Applying photoresist is almost like spraying a piece of photographic film on the circuit board. That way, when you place the negative over the board and expose it to light, an impression of the negative pattern forms in the layer of photoresist.

(3) After exposing, immediately throw the board into a developing bath, where a developer chemical combines with the photoresist to form a protective coating, thus protecting the copper traces.

(4) As in the previous methods, wash the board in etchant, watch the copper etch away, strip the photoresist that's left on the circuit board by using a stripping solution, and lightly scour with steel wool to keep the copper clean and free of grease for soldering.

Incidentally, before mounting and soldering parts it's generally a good idea to lightly steel wool any printed circuit board that has exposed copper. However, if the traces are silvery (as most commercially-manufactured boards are), then they've already been "tinned" and are ready to be soldered to. They should *not* be scrubbed with steel wool.

To make boards using photographic techniques, you first need a negative. Photocopy shops, blueprint stores, and other photography-oriented vendors (time for another Yellow Pages plug, and no, we don't get a kickback) can produce a negative for you if you take them the MIDItools printed circuit pattern. The price is usually not too steep, but chances are a friend with a darkroom can do a satisfactory job for much less.

The Etching Process

No matter which method you choose to make PC boards, the etching process remains pretty much the same. Use plastic, rubber, or glass trays (dishwashing trays do just fine, as do small plastic garbage cans), since the ferric will eat away at metal.

Ferric works best at higher temperatures, but don't heat it or you'll get some nasty fumes. It's best to etch outside, because of the ventilation and the warming action of the sun.

While etching, it's a good idea to agitate the etch solution as much as possible. The idea is to put in just enough ferric to keep the board covered, then jostling the plastic tray (or what-have-you) so that fresh ferric continually washes over the copper. This hastens the etching process, and the board tends to etch more evenly.

Although ferric won't burn your skin if you come into contact with it, you will acquire a brown stain that's hard to get rid of. Ferric can also permanently stain clothes, as well as modify the color of small furry animals. Wear rubber gloves and an apron, and etch somewhere away from any activity.

After the etching process is all over and there's no more unwanted copper on the board, it's a good idea to put the board in a plastic bucket of cold water for at least a minute. This washes off any excess ferric, while the cold stops the etching action totally. After removing the board from the cold water, dry it off and check for any flaws or unetched areas before stripping the resist.

In some cases the etchant may etch away a piece of the trace. Should this happen, you can solder a small wire bridge to reconnect the trace (Fig. 5-11).

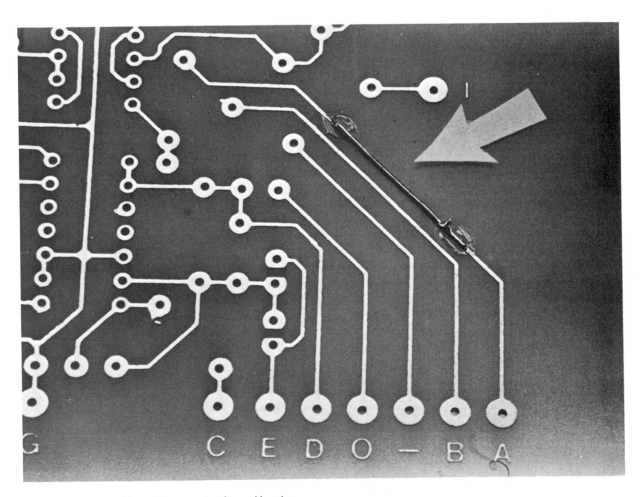

Fig. 5-11: Use a piece of bare wiring to repair a damaged board trace.

Many electronic stores carry kits with detailed instructions for making PC boards. If you want to get into making circuit boards, this is probably the best introduction. Just remember to take your time, follow the directions, and resign yourself to the almost certain knowledge that your very first board will be a total disaster. Your third, however, will probably be quite good—no missing resist, no incomplete etching, sharp edges on the traces, and all the other qualities that make a trouble-free and good-looking circuit board.

Step 3: Loading the Circuit Board

Now it's time to do some actual construction. Referring to the CPU board parts layout (Fig. 5-12, next page), mount the various parts in the following order (other boards are assembled similarly).

Begin by mounting the resistors, jumper wires (or "0W resistors"), and diodes. Bend the leads at right angles to make insertion into the holes of the PC board a little easier, and insert *all* components from the noncopper-clad (or nonfoil) side of the board. These parts should hug the board as closely as possible; for example, resistors should mount flush against the board as shown in the upper drawing of Fig. 5-13, and not "float" as shown in the lower drawing. The one exception is components that generate significant heat, as floating somewhat over the circuit board gives improved ventilation.

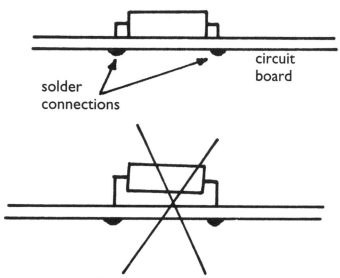

Fig. 5-13: Resistors and other parts should not "float" above the board unless they generate heat.

Now bend the leads down against the copper side and solder the lead to the pad. Cut off any excess lead length (don't scrape the traces) so that it doesn't short against the other copper traces and pads. Also, make sure your solder blob hasn't bridged across to any other traces. This is called a *solder bridge* and is a member of the short-circuit family—avoid solder bridges if you want your project to work.

Next, install any IC sockets. Note that the socket will have an indentation or mark to indicate the pin 1 corner of the socket. Don't try to save a few pennies by soldering ICs to the board without a socket; not only do sockets make repairs and upgrading easier, but one of the prime causes of IC failure is excessive soldering heat, and a socket eliminates this possibility.

Mount the capacitors next after the resistors, jumpers, diodes, and sockets are on the board. Capacitors are not overly sensitive to heat, but solder them fairly rapidly, consistent with a good solder joint. Then mount and solder the remaining parts—crystal, MIDI jacks, trimpot, on-off switch, DC power jack, programming pins, etc.

Now that the components are mounted and soldered in place, check that all polarities are correct, that the solder joints are good, and that there aren't any solder bridges or board defects. If everything checks out, you're ready for the next step. By the way, don't plug any ICs in their sockets just yet; wait until all the outboard wiring is completed.

Set your board(s) aside for now.

Step 4: Selecting an Enclosure

There are several ways to package your equipment so that it looks good and works well. Choose a method that gives you adequate work room, yet isn't overly large. It's important to gather together all your parts before choosing a chassis—with the items in front of you, it's easier to estimate what size you'll need to contain the parts comfortably.

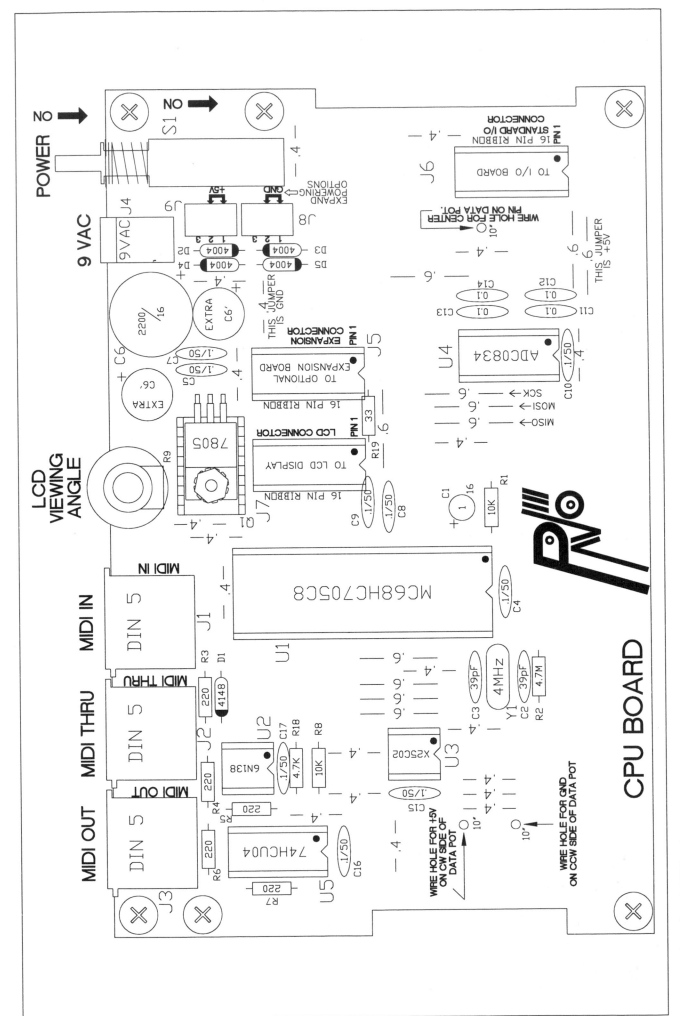

Fig. 5-12: Parts layout for main CPU board.

There are two suggested enclosure styles for the MIDItools Computer:

- Single rack space box (Fig. 5-14A). This is a standard 1U, rack mountable box that holds the CPU board (it's located toward the rear panel), the rack version of the Human Interface board (mounted flush against the front panel), and one optional expansion board (the cutout in the rear panel accommodates expansion board connectors and I/O).

- The Hand Held box (Fig 5-14B). This is a small box, designed for sitting on the top of consoles, racks, etc. It holds the CPU board and the hand-held version of the Human Interface board (there's a different version of this board for each of the two enclosures). As you can see from Fig. 5-14C, an interior view, there is no room for expansion boards in the hand held box.

Many electronic outlets sell commercial boxes, finished and painted in different colors. These enclosures are easy to find and use, although they also tend to be expensive (especially for large enclosures). Enclosures are available from PAVO.

Rack mountable enclosures have a standard width of 48.75 cm (19.5"), but the height can vary from 4.4 cm (1.75") and up. Screw holes are spaced at standardized intervals.

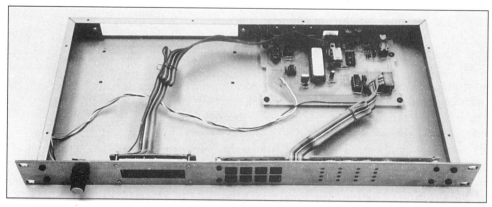

Fig. 5-14A: Single rack space box.

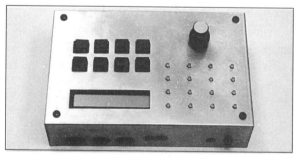

Fig. 5-14B: Hand Held box.

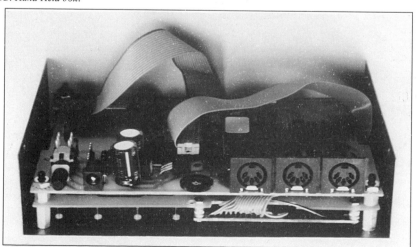

Fig. 5-14C: Interior view of Hand Held box.

This approach allows for *modularity;* for example, you can build the MIDItools Computer on one panel, a MIDI thru box on another panel, and a MIDI patch bay on yet a third panel, then mount them all in a rack mount frame. If you want to replace your patch bay later on with a model that has more inputs and outputs, no sweat— just pop out the old patch bay, build the new patch bay, and put it in where the old one used to be (leaving the other panels as they were).

Rack panels, incidentally, are available in a wide variety of colors, and a choice of either steel or aluminum. *Stick with aluminum!* Steel is really a hassle to work on.

Step 5: Drilling and Punching

The drilling process requires a template to indicate where the holes are to be drilled, and a center punch to make a small indentation the drill bit can follow.

The easiest way to get everything lined up correctly is to draw the template on graph paper. After you've made the template, tape it to the chassis (use masking tape to avoid leaving a residue and/or pulling off the finish), support the back of the panel with a piece of wood, and use the center punch on each of the hole guides. When using the center punch on plastic, don't hit too hard or the plastic may crack. On metal, you can tap a little harder, but don't do it hard enough to deform the metal around it. All you want is a neat little space to center the drill bit during the first few turns of the drill.

You now have the center holes punched. Take off the template, and drill your holes. If you're drilling a hole larger than 6.2 mm (1/4"), it pays to drill a 1.6 mm (1/16") pilot hole first, then use the big bit. Otherwise, the bit may "walk," even with the center-punched guide.

Keeping the drill as vertical as possible, start it up at a fairly low speed (you decided on a variable speed drill, right?) to make sure it's centered in the pilot hole. When the drill starts to penetrate into the metal, speed up, but back off when you feel you're reaching the end. Oftentimes, the bit will start to grab when you reach the end. Keep on drilling, but remember *NEVER hold the object being drilled with your hand!* It's hard to explain exactly why on paper, but if you ever end up with the drill grabbing onto a chassis and twirling it round and round at 2500 RPM, you'll see the logic of the statement. After you've drilled all your holes, use a file to clean off any burrs.

If you're using a chassis puncher, the procedure is to drill the hole(s) required by the puncher, then punch the hole. (See Fig. 4-5 in Chapter 4 and its accompanying text.)

While you're in a metal-working frame of mind, cut any pot shafts to length. Hold the shaft in a vise (Fig. 5-15) and cut with a hacksaw. Never hold the body of the pot/switch! Be careful, also, to leave enough shaft length to fit comfortably into whatever knobs you've chosen.

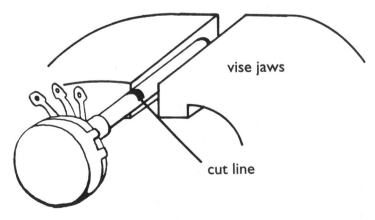

Fig. 5-15: Proper technique for cutting a potentiometer shaft.

Step 6: Wiring

The MIDItools Computer requires very little point-to-point wiring. Most "wiring" between components is handled by the circuit board traces and jumpers, and ribbon cables take care of the inter-board wiring. However, you will need three wires to go to the pot, as well as to any optional faders or other outboard parts you use. Solder these wires to the board *before* it's mounted in the enclosure; make sure the wires are longer than needed, as you can always cut them to length later (save the trimmings—you never know when you'll need a short piece of hookup wire).

You will also need to connect a ribbon cable to the LCD board. There's not enough room on the LCD board for a socket, so one end of a ribbon cable terminates in a 16-pin DIP plug that connects to the main MIDItools board. The leads from the cable's other end solder directly to the LCD board (Fig. 5-16).

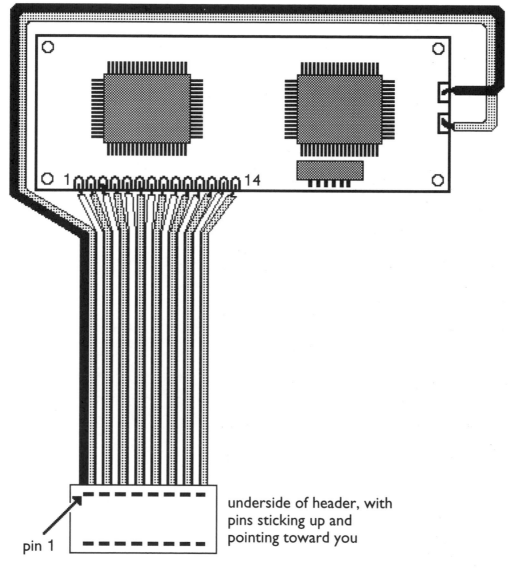

underside of header, with pins sticking up and pointing toward you

pin 1

Fig. 5-16: Soldering the ribbon cable to the LCD board.

For point-to-point wiring, use stranded—not solid—wire, because it's more flexible. The thickness of the wire is assigned a number, called the *gauge*. For general electronics construction, #24 to #26 gauge is about optimum.

The first consideration when wiring with insulated wire is removing the insulation. Use a wire-stripping tool to remove about 6 mm (1/4") of insulation. Removing too much can lead to accidental shorts; removing too little can make for a poor connection, as excess insulation melts into the solder. When using wire strippers, be careful not to cut or nick the wire itself, or you'll end up with a weakened connection.

Note that mounting the Human Interface board against the front panel makes it impossible to use a ribbon cable socket on the H/I board. The ribbon cable connector must be soldered directly to the H/I board.

Step 7: Mounting the Circuit Board in the Enclosure

PC boards mount to enclosures and panels with long screws, spacers, lockwashers, and nuts (Fig. 5-17). Method 1 uses L-brackets to mount a small board vertically; method 2 uses long screws and spacers to mount a board horizontally.

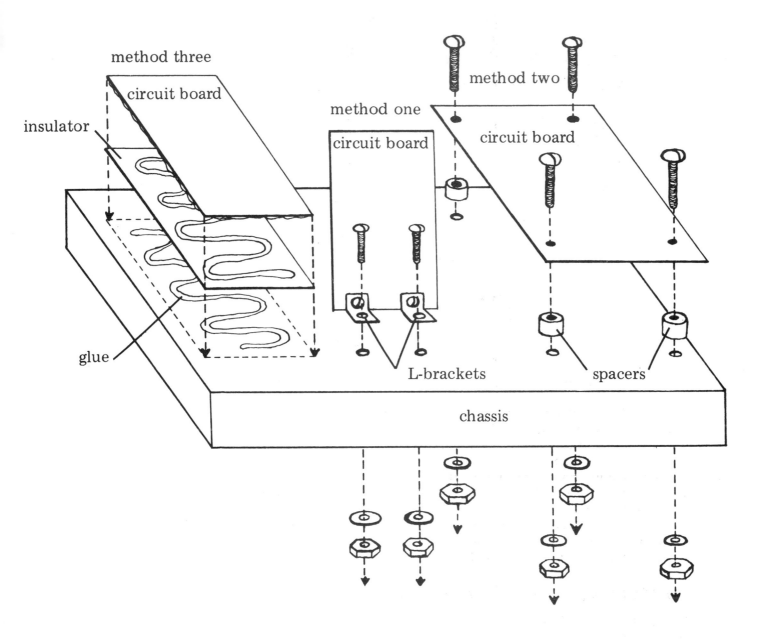

Fig. 5-17: Two ways to mount circuit board. Method 2 is much more common.

Boards can "stack" together by using an extra spacer to isolate the two stacked boards (Fig. 5-18). The amount of spacing depends on whether components on the lower board generate heat; more space gives more ventilation.

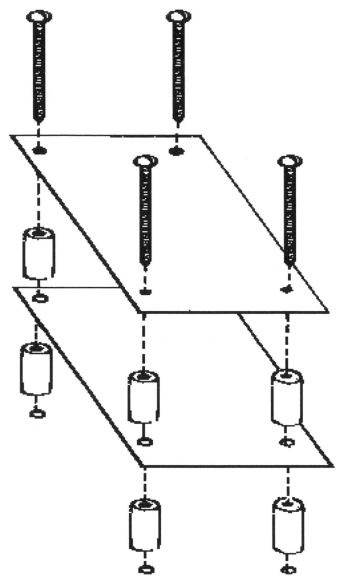

Fig. 5-18: Stacking two boards. Note the need for long screws.

For best results, install all mounting screws, then the spacers, then slip the board over the screws, then add lockwashers and nuts. Tighten them "finger-tight" at first, make sure the board is sitting properly on the mounting screws *(e.g.,* it's not flexed or obstructed by other parts), then tighten the nuts down. Do not tighten one nut all the way before moving on to the next one; give one nut a couple turns, then the next, then the next, and so on until all the nuts are tight.

Incidentally, in a pinch empty Bic pens are a good source for spacers. Remove the point along with its ink reservoir, then use a fine-toothed hacksaw to cut the pen into spacer-sized cylinders.

Step 8: Add the Knobs and Label the Functions

Putting on a knob shouldn't require an explanation. One note of caution, though—use the correct-size screwdriver on setscrews *(i.e.,* the biggest jeweler's screwdriver that fits). If the screwdriver is too small, there will be a tendency to bite and deform the screw, which nine times out of ten will not be made of the strongest metal in the world.

Concerning labeling, each project shows a recommended front panel layout template. If you're not too concerned with looks, you can photocopy the template, and tape it on the front panel. Using instant lettering on a clear plastic overlay looks classier, but requires significantly more work. Either of these approaches works well if you plan to switch EPROMs frequently and try out different projects.

If you're going to dedicate the MIDItools Computer to one particular function, consider making some permanent labels. The fastest and cheapest way to label is with a commercial label making device (check your local office supply store). However, it doesn't look as good as some other options.

A popular approach is to use dry transfer lettering and apply it directly on the chassis (however, you should do this *before* mounting any parts in the enclosure). Transfer lettering sheets are available at art supply stores; ask to see a dry transfer lettering catalog. The catalog will also explain how to put the stuff on in greater detail than is worth going into here. After transferring the letters onto the chassis, spray a coat of clear acrylic over them for protection.

Although this is a popular way to letter, there are some problems. Instant lettering doesn't adhere to metal well; it's designed to go on paper, or other slightly textured surfaces (a painted enclosure is much easier to label than an unfinished one). Also, the acrylic spray doesn't protect very well against deep scratches.

To get around these problems, here's a somewhat different labeling process. Fig. 5-19 graphically shows the various steps.

(1) Choose an appropriate color of adhesive-backed contact paper, and transfer your letters to it.

(2) Get a piece of clear adhesive contact paper and cover over the letters you've just transferred. This gives excellent protection for the letters, and adds a subtle kind of matte finish.

(3) Cut out the contact paper sandwich you've just created.

(4) Peel the backing off the sheet of contact paper on which you did the original lettering, and press the whole sandwich on your panel. If you don't get it centered quite right the first time, *carefully* peel if off and reposition. You can't do this too many times, though, as the adhesive will lose its sticking power.

And now, a few words about the importance of æsthetics. Some electronic experimenters just throw together a bunch of parts in a chassis, label it with a commercial labelmaker, and forget about it. Many times the device will work just as well as if it were carefully done, but the extra time spent on beautiful packaging is well worth it. Music, after all, is all about creativity and beauty—carry that into your electronics, too.

Aside from the inspirational value of playing with a beautiful piece of equipment, it's also worth more. Often the difference between a superior guitar and an ordinary model is workmanship, plated hardware, delicate inlays, and choice woods. Naturally, you'll play just as well on an axe that doesn't have beautiful inlays, but there is a great deal of satisfaction to be derived from playing a beautiful instrument, and even more satisfaction and confidence if you can point to it and say, "I made that."

Step 9: Testing 1-2-3

Yes, the Big Moment has arrived. Check your work over one last time, plug the ICs into their sockets (remember the cautions about static electricity and IC pin orientation), plug the wall wart plug into the power jack, and turn the on/off switch to on.

If there's nothing on the display, first trying rotating the LCD contrast control—if it's set incorrectly, you may not see anything on the display. However, if at any point you see smoke, hear sputtering noises, smell something heating up, or notice the transformer humming loudly, *shut down power immediately.*

Ideally, you should be rewarded with a greeting on the display, followed by the messages mentioned for the individual projects (described in Chapter 7). You're ready to go! Start learning what the thing can do, and have a good time.

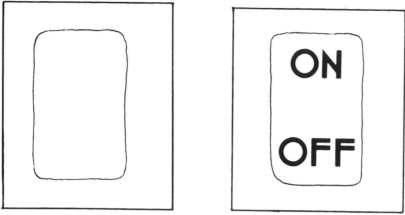

draw the label outline on a piece of backing contact paper,
then transfer the lettering

cover with clear contact paper

cut out the label, take off the
adhesive backing, and affix
to the equipment

Fig. 5-19: Creating easy, good-looking custom labels

If a project doesn't work at first, don't get discouraged. A digital electronic circuit is like a combination lock where every number has to be correct before it will work. It's easy to miss a solder connection, or a jumper wire, or hook up a wire to the wrong place. Begin checking things over from square one, and you'll probably find a solution.

Most problems with electronic gear trace back to human error, but sometimes components will be bad. The most common mistakes (in no particular order) are:

- ICs inserted backwards

- Polarized components not properly polarized

- Missing jumper wire

- Red is mistaken for orange (or vice-versa) with resistor color codes

- Cold solder joint

- Solder bridge (connects two traces accidentally)

- Ribbon cable plugged in backwards

- Programming pins set incorrectly

- No power at AC outlet (don't laugh, this happens!)

- Incorrectly set LCD contrast control

- Chip pins folded under or sticking out of socket

Remember that it takes time to understand how to use any electronic device effectively. As a result, you shouldn't expect to obtain the best results immediately as soon as you plug in and turn on power. For example, it's not just enough to have the Universal Transmitter work; you also have to know how to program it with a byte to make it do something useful.

Always allow yourself a period of time to become familiar with the various options to learn exactly what they can, and cannot, do. This shouldn't be too surprising a concept—every musician knows that you have to practice an instrument to get good at playing it.

Chapter 6
Understanding the MIDItools Computer

Before we build the MIDItools Computer, let's get to know a little bit about how it works. You don't have to understand this chapter to build and use the MIDItools Computer, but it's useful background and helps de-mystify the project a bit. Take in as much as you can; what you don't "get" at first will make sense eventually.

Design Rules

All the MIDItools are based on a generic *embedded* computer, which is built into a device and provides the intelligence necessary to perform that device's functions. In the case of MIDI devices, an embedded computer processes the MIDI data, and interfaces with the human operator (that's you).

The MIDItools Computer follows some basic design rules:

- Generic operation. Since this one computer provides many different MIDItools, it must be flexible enough to accommodate them all.

- Modularity. The computer is built around a number of modular circuit boards. These provide a "building block" approach so that the individual pieces can be built, tested, and changed independently; also, resources which are not required for a particular application can be left out of the computer, thus saving money and effort.

- Simplicity. There's no point in building a cool MIDI computer if it's frustrating to build, use, or modify. Besides, there are plenty of expensive computers with correspondingly expensive MIDI software. The object here is not to provide the Sequencer of the Gods, but rather a set of useful, simple, and desirable tools.

- Inexpensive and easy-to-find parts. The parts required to build the MIDItools Computer are commonly available through electronics distributors and many mail-order catalogs. Parts kits with all components needed to build the projects, as well as professionally machined and punched enclosures, are also available from PAVO (see Appendix).

About the MIDItools Computer

The three MIDItools Computer modules (circuit boards) are:

- CPU board

- Human Interface board (H/I board)

- Optional Expansion board

They interconnect with standard 16-wire ribbon cables, which eliminates messy point-to-point wiring. Fig. 6-1 shows the MIDItools Computer's overall block diagram.

Let's get the big picture for each board. We won't get too detailed since this info isn't absolutely necessary to make the MIDItools Computer work; for more information, check out the books mentioned in Chapter 14, as well as the Appendix.

The CPU Board

The CPU board (Fig. 6-2) contains the guts of the MIDItools Computer.

MC68HC705C8 ("6805C8") Microcontroller

The MC68HC705C8 is a particular version of a family of microprocessors called the "6805." MC68HC705C8 is a long name, so we'll simply call it the "6805C8" instead. (The suffix "C8" describes which peripherals are added to the generic MC68HC705 processor.)

The 6805C8 contains most of the resources needed by the MIDItools (it requires only a few external components for operation), including:

- Plenty of RAM and ROM

- Lots of I/O ports

- A Serial Communications Interface (UART)

- Gobs of CPU power for implementing sophisticated MIDI processing functions

- Oscillator

However, the 6805C8 doesn't contain everything we need—and we wouldn't want it to, since implementing some of the resources outside the microcontroller allows for greater flexibility. For example, referring to the block diagram in Fig. 6-1, the components most likely to change (switches, LEDs, LCD, and ADC) are external to the 6805C8.

Buses

Peripheral devices connect to the 6805C8 via four buses, as follows:

- Serial Peripheral Interface (SPI) bus

- Parallel Data bus

- Switch bus

- Control bus

SPI Bus

The SPI bus connects the 6805C8 to devices with serial data interfaces. (Note for tech types: the MC68HC705C8 uses three SPI signals, MOSI, MISO, and SCK.) The SPI bus is especially useful for interfacing between PC boards since it requires only three wires for two-way data communication. The downside is that each bit is sent serially, so data transfer is considerably slower than the Parallel Data bus, which transfers groups of bits simultaneously.

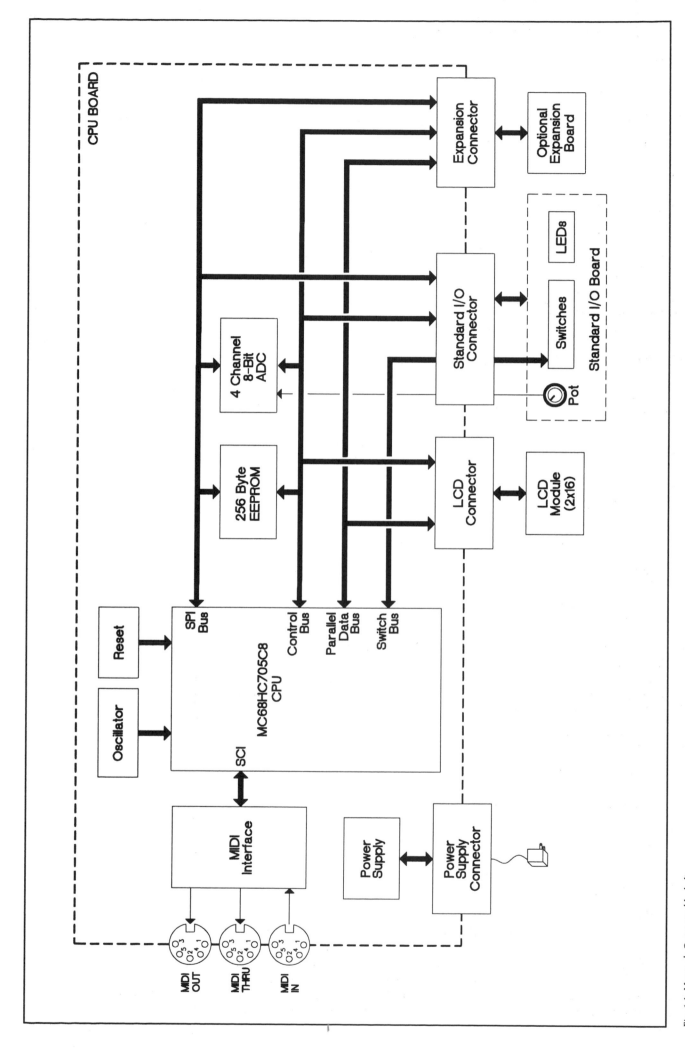

Fig. 6-1: MIDItools Computer block diagram.

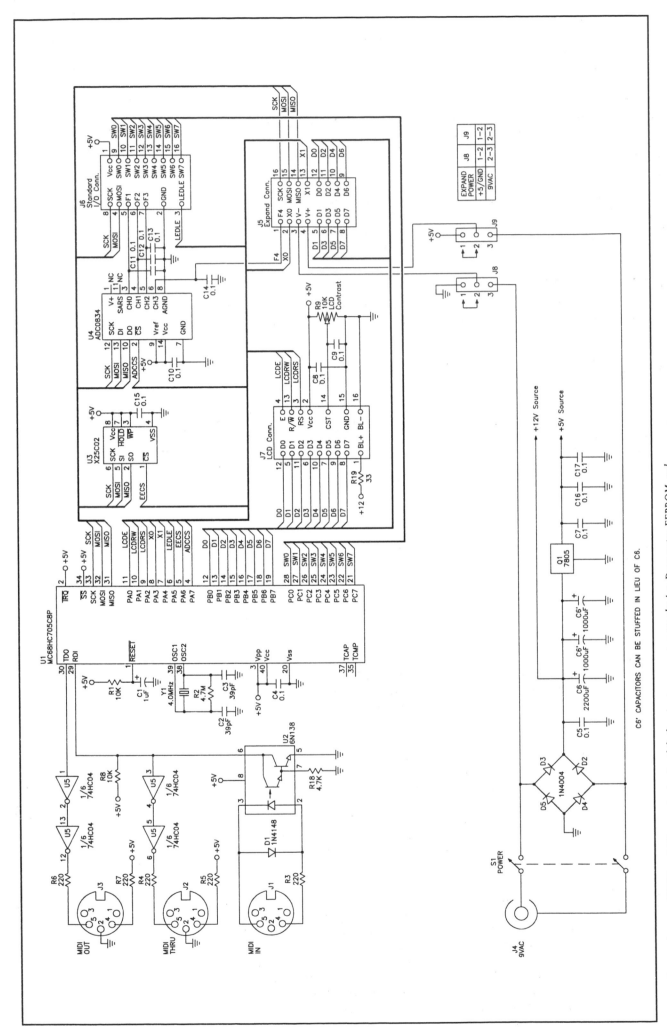

Fig. 6-2: Schematic diagram of CPU board. The MIDI circuitry is at left, the microprocessor at center, the A to D converter, EEPROM, and connectors at right, and the power supply (based around the 7805 voltage regulator) lines the bottom.

Parallel Data Bus

The Parallel Data bus is a general purpose bi-directional *(i.e.,* it can transmit and receive) parallel bus that connects the 6805C8 to devices with parallel data interfaces. It contains 8 lines (D0-D7).

Switch Bus

The Switch Bus connects switches to the 6805C8. One switch connects to each of the 8 lines of the Switch bus (SW0-SW7).

Control Bus

The Control Bus could be considered the "miscellaneous" bus; it contains the various control signals required by the computer's assortment of peripheral devices. For example, all devices on the SPI and Data buses require a unique control signal to tell them when the data on the buses is intended for them, and the control bus takes care of it.

Peripherals

As we've already mentioned, the 6805C8 is cool, but it can't do everything. Here are some of the peripherals on the main CPU board that help it do more.

MIDI Interface

The MIDI interface conforms to the MIDI specification, and provides MIDI In, Out, and Thru ports via 5-pin female DIN connectors. The MIDI In signal passes through optoisolator U2, which translates the current flowing through the MIDI line into a voltage compatible with the 6805C8's Serial Communications Interface (SCI). The MIDI Out and Thru connections are "buffered" from the outside world by U5 (a 74HC04 IC) so that if there's any gross abuse to the system (like someone plugging the MIDI Out into the AC line), the buffer chips get fried instead of the 6805C8.

Electrically Erasable PROM (EEPROM)

Turning off power to the 6805C8 causes any data in RAM to disappear. EEPROM peripheral U3, a XICOR X25C02, stores up to 256 bytes of data external to the 6805C8 and is non-volatile *(i.e.,* it never loses data, even when power is turned off). The EEPROM connects to the 6805C8 via the SPI and Control buses.

Analog to Digital Converter (ADC)

Potentiometers (and many other control sources) are inherently analog devices, so the pot's position needs to be converted into digital information before the computer can understand it. This is the job of the ADC0834 Analog to Digital Converter (ADC), a four channel, 8-bit converter from National Semiconductor.

The ADC converts analog signals ranging from 0 to +5 volts DC at each of its four analog inputs to an 8-bit number, and connects to the 6805C8 via the SPI and Control buses. Each change of 19.5 mV (5 volts DC divided by 256) on an analog input corresponds to a change of "1" in the digitized measurement.

In the MIDItools Computer, the ADC converts three analog inputs coming from the Human Interface board (one for the potentiometer, and two for future expansion) and a fourth input from the optional expansion board.

Liquid Crystal Display (LCD)

The LCD gives you a "window" into the computer's brain so you can communicate with it. The MIDItools Computer uses a 2 row by 16 character LCD for the Human Interface, and connects to the 6805C8 via the Parallel Data and Control buses. Fortunately, most LCD manufacturers have standardized on one LCD control interface that accommodates all different sizes, from 1 row by 8 character, up to the big 4 row by 80 character types. You can easily upgrade to one of these alternative sizes.

To provide maximum flexibility the LCD doesn't mount directly to the CPU board, but off-board where most appropriate. Normally, it attaches to the enclosure's front panel, but you can mount it anywhere you want—just run a 16-wire ribbon cable to connect the LCD to the CPU board's LCD connector.

To set the LCD contrast (also called "viewing angle"), rotate the potentiometer mounted on the rear of the CPU board. This pot sticks out the back of the two standard MIDItools enclosures (rack and hand box) so you can adjust it without taking the box apart.

Light Emitting Diodes (LEDs)

The MIDItools Computer controls up to 16 LEDs, which connect to a latch that the 6805C8 controls via the SPI and Control buses.

Switches

The MIDItools Computer reads up to eight switches, which connect to the 6805C8 via the Switch bus.

Expansion Port

The Expansion Port interfaces the CPU board with an optional Expansion board via a 16-wire ribbon cable. The interface carries the important signals in the computer: the SPI bus, the Parallel Data bus, one input to the ADC, two general purpose control signals (X0, X1), and power. These are enough signals to allow for all kinds of expansion.

Oscillator

The oscillator provides the computer's basic heartbeat and determines its timing. Just as an engine's pistons force wheels to spin, the oscillator forces the 6805C8 to perform fetch/execute cycles. Although much of the oscillator is built within the 6805C8, it does require an external crystal for operation.

Human Interface Connector

The Human Interface connector connects the Human Interface board to the CPU board via a 16-wire ribbon cable. This cable carries all the signals required by the Human Interface board: the SPI bus, Switch Bus, multiple control lines, and power.

Power Supply

The power supply consists of two parts: the external line transformer ("wall wart"), and the internal rectifier/regulator circuit.

To provide maximum flexibility, the power supply can come from any AC step-down transformer whose output voltage ranges from 7 to 18 volts. More is not better—it's good to stay as close to 7 volts as possible, since the extra voltage at the input is essentially "thrown away" as heat. We recommend transformers or AC adapters that put out 7-12 volts AC.

You can also feed the MIDItools Computer from a 7 to 18 volt DC source, such as a battery eliminator or AC adapter. It should be able to deliver at least 1 Amp of current.

After entering the CPU board, the voltage from the external transformer goes to the bridge rectifier. This part serves two purposes: if the wall wart outputs AC, the rectifier turns it into DC. If the wall wart outputs DC the rectifier polarizes the positive and negative leads so that the MIDItools cannot be subjected to a reverse power supply voltage, which can be lethal to many parts.

The 7805 +5 volt regulator takes the rectified input voltage and turns it into a constant +5 volts DC, which fuels the MIDItools Computer.

The Human Interface Board

The Human Interface board (Fig. 6-3, following pages) is your "control panel" for the MIDItools Computer. It provides up to:

- 8 push button switches

- 16 LEDs

- 3 potentiometers

Switches

The switches connect to the 6805C8 via the Switch bus. The standard switch is a "normally open" pushbutton switch. Other types of switches can be used, but pay attention to the voltages feeding the 6805C8. The 6805C8 considers a logical 1 (+5 volts DC) on a Switch bus line to represent the switch in its "on" position; logical 0 (0 VDC) represents an "off."

LEDs

The 16 LEDs are powered from two 74HC595 *serial to parallel shift register* chips. These accept a serial input from the SPI bus, and convert the data to 8 parallel outputs. The LEDs connected to the outputs turn on or off as each bit is set to logical 1 or 0 respectively. One 74HC595 only has 8 outputs, and the Human Interface has 16 LEDs, so it takes two of the chips to handle the full 16 bits of LED data.

Potentiometer

The Human Interface board's potentiometer feeds one ADC input. Rotating the pot from one extreme to the other changes the voltage going to the ADC from 0 to 5 volts DC. The ADC digitizes this voltage, and therefore takes a relative reading of the pot's position. The pot normally controls parameters in the MIDItools Computer.

Three of the four ADC inputs connect to the Human Interface board, and two are currently unused. The experimentally-minded among you can connect these two inputs to analog voltages that vary from 0 to 5VDC, and program the computer to read them.

Expansion Boards

The remaining PC boards are optional expansion boards that contain the unique circuitry required by a particular tool. There are currently three expansion boards:

- MIDI Patch Bay board (provides connections for instruments connected to the patch bay)

- Relay board (contains relays that are triggered by MIDI data)

- Custom instrument board (your own real-world-to-MIDI-converter!)

We'll go into more detail on each of these when we discuss the specific tools that use them.

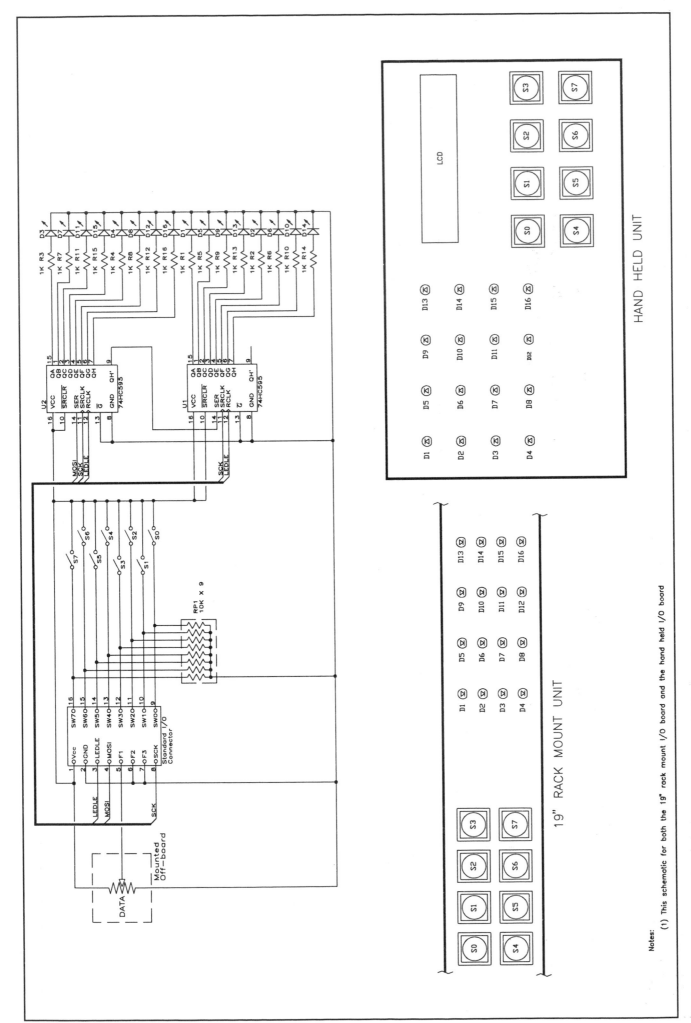

Fig. 6-3: Schematic Diagram and component layout (rack mount and hand-held versions) for the Human Interface board

Notes:

(1) This schematic for both the 19" rack mount I/O board and the hand held I/O board

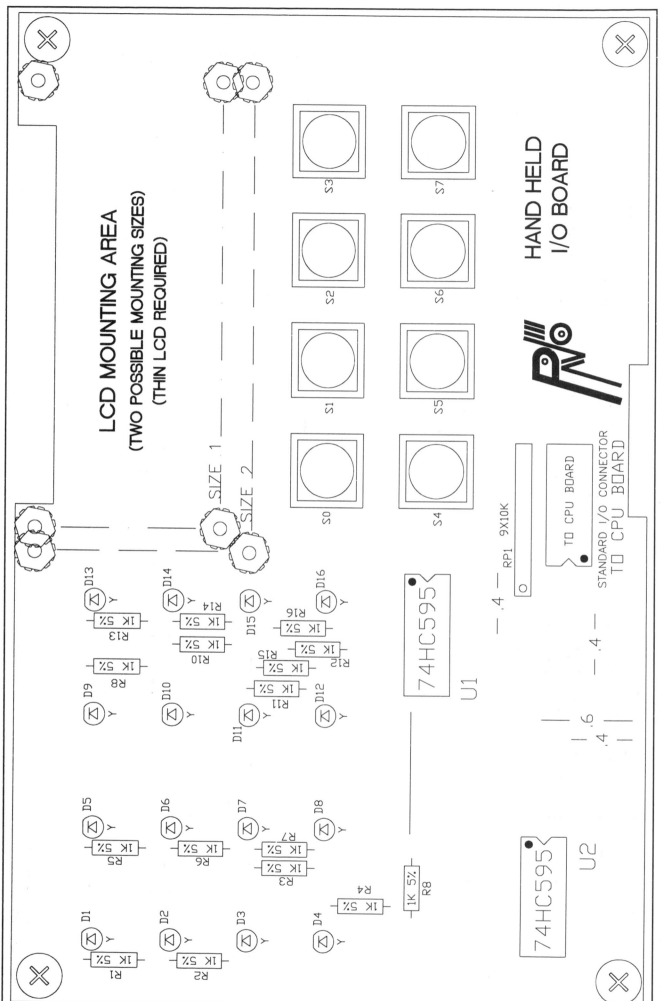

Fig. 6-3, continued.

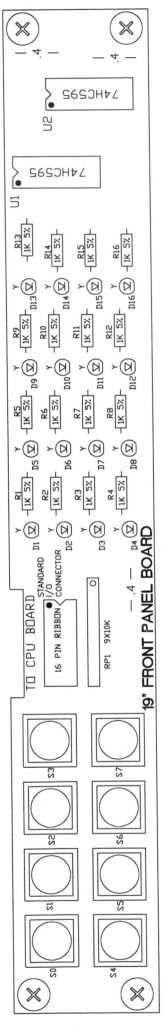

Fig. 6-3, continued.

Chapter 7

The Twenty MIDItools Software Projects

We've finally arrived at our main destination—the twenty MIDItools projects. Each one is presented as a "mini-manual" with several different sections.

As usual, software is an ongoing endeavor. The projects in this book have all been tested and used, but it seems we can never leave well enough alone, so every now and then a new feature or two might get added; and new projects are being designed around the MIDItools computer as more people get their hands on the hardware. Contact PAVO (see Appendix) for an up-to-the-minute listing of available projects. Also, if you come up with any design ideas or software, contact PAVO for details regarding how to share your design with other MIDItools enthusiasts.

Here's a preview of the information included with each project description.

Introduction

This gives some background about the project's intended function, as well as several representative applications.

Specs

This summarizes the MIDItool's main talents and requirements. Following are descriptions of the various categories.

Function

A brief description of what the tool does. Each MIDItool fits in one of the following functional categories:

- *Monitor* MIDItools receive MIDI messages and display them without doing any alterations. Monitors are "inline" devices: all received messages are retransmitted without delay or modification. (There's more on inline devices shortly.)

- *Storage* MIDItools place received MIDI messages in non-volatile memory for reviewing and later retransmission. Received messages are not altered.

- *Filter* MIDItools discard received MIDI messages of the type specified by the filter name. Messages of all other types are retransmitted without delay or modification. Filters are inline devices.

- *Modifier* MIDItools receive MIDI messages, alter their status and/or data bytes, and retransmit the new message without delay. Modifiers are inline devices.

- *Generator* MIDItools create and transmit MIDI messages. They may or may not operate as inline devices. Some generators have internal merging capabilities so that generated messages are properly merged with incoming messages. This eliminates the need for a separate merge box.

- *Translator* MIDItools receive MIDI messages and use them to control non-MIDI devices *(e.g.,* control signal buses, relays). Since they interface with other hardware, they are not operated as inline devices.

Transmit/Receive/Both

Each MIDItool can transmit MIDI messages from its MIDI Out port, receive MIDI messages at its MIDI In port, or do both. This line indicates whether the MIDItool is a MIDI Transmitter (Tx), MIDI Receiver (Rx), or MIDI Transceiver (Both).

Note: any device that receives MIDI at the MIDI In port will retransmit the received messages out the MIDI Thru port without delay or modification. Even though these messages are "transmitted" from the MIDI Thru port, we will consider MIDItools to be MIDI Transmitters only if MIDI messages are generated or modified internally and then transmitted from the MIDI Out port.

Inline Device

If yes, the MIDItools computer inserts between a master device's MIDI out and a slave unit's MIDI in. If no, the MIDItools computer is either the source of MIDI data, or the end recipient.

Internal Merging

For Generator inline devices with internal merging, messages are received at the MIDI In port, merged with generated messages, and retransmitted in realtime from the MIDI Out port. The external running status from the master device is preserved.

If there is no internal merging, data appearing at the MIDI In is not merged with the MIDItools-generated data.

PC Boards Required

There are six printed circuit boards available in the MIDItools "toolbox." Each MIDItool uses one CPU board and one Human Interface board. In addition, some MIDItools use an expansion board. Expansion boards are mentioned if needed, and described in a sidebar included elsewhere in the project text.

Here's a brief description of the available boards:

- CPU Board. This is the heart of the MIDItool. It contains a microprocessor, an EEPROM, an analog-to-digital converter, an optoisolator, MIDI ports, power supply regulation and control, and associated circuitry.

- Human Interface (H/I) Boards. Choose either the Hand or Rack H/I board based on which enclosure you're going to use. Both boards accommodate eight momentary pushbutton switches, sixteen LEDs, a potentiometer (the Value fader), and LED driver circuitry.

- Relay Driver Expansion Board. This board (used in MIDItool 8, the Relay Driver) contains four relays, control circuitry for turning them on and off, and four 1/4" stereo jacks.

- External Keys Expansion Board. This board (used in Miditool 4, the Custom Instrument) contains circuitry for communicating between an external keyboard and the CPU board. The external keyboard can support up to 64 momentary pushbutton switches.

- Patch Bay Expansion Board. This board (used in Miditool 20, Midi Patch Bay) contains logic and control circuitry, four Midi In jacks, and four Midi Out jacks.

Inputs

This lists the various ways that signals and commands get into the Miditools computer from the outside world. Each tool has a power supply input (see Chapter 6), On/Off switch for applying and removing power, and an LCD Contrast control to adjust for the most readable display at different viewing angles. The functions of all other inputs, as described below, are project-specific.

- Midi In. These are used by Midi Receivers, Transceivers, and inline tools to receive Midi messages.

- Panel Switches. Enter commands into the Miditools computer with the various switch functions. Up to eight are available for use.

- Value Fader. This provides a fast means of data entry. An 8-bit analog-to-digital converter encodes the variable voltage present at the potentiometer's wiper to one of 256 numeric values.

- External Keys. You can connect up to 64 external momentary switches (keys) to the Miditools computer (Project 4 uses this feature as the basis of a custom keyboard instrument).

Outputs

Miditools presents information to the outside world via various outputs. Each project uses an LCD to convey status and operational information; the functions of all other outputs are project-specific.

- LEDs. Up to sixteen (16) LEDs are available as indicators.

- Midi Out. This 5-pin DIN output transmits Midi messages.

- Midi Thru. Echoes each Midi message received at the Midi In port without delay or modification.

- Relay. Four 1/4″ stereo jacks are available for use as relay outputs. The three jack terminals correspond to the relay's single pole, double-throw switch connections.

Enclosure

The Hand Box (approximately 4″W x 6″L x 1″H) accommodates all Miditools except three; the Rack Box accommodates all Miditools. This enclosure is a standard single rack space enclosure with a minimum depth of approximately 4″.

Complexity

Due to the modular nature of the system (i.e., you build the Miditools computer and then select your desired "program"), the hardware complexity varies little from one Miditool to the next. Any Miditool with an additional expansion board is therefore considered more complex than those without.

Complexity falls into one of three categories: Low (simple), Medium, or High (complicated). The easiest Miditool programs to modify are those with Low complexity.

Panel Layouts

These layouts show the switch and LED labels for the rack box and (if applicable) hand box. An up arrow indicates the + key, and a down arrow the - key. Unused buttons are shown in white.

Setup

This describes what you need to do to get the MIDItool ready to do useful work, such as patching into ancillary gear, or plugging in expansion boards.

Operations

How to make the MIDItool do wondrous things. Several typical LCD screens help illustrate the described procedures.

Default Settings

What the MIDItool does when you first power it up. If the MIDItool remembers its status when last powered-up, the default setting may vary somewhat from the diagram.

Advanced Applications

If you're interested in hacking the code and adding your own improvements, here are suggestions on some of the more "doable" possibilities.

Software Summary

This section gives a brief summary of the software used in the MIDItool, and describes the following elements:

- States. These are the possible "modes" the MIDItool can be in. A state defines what the MIDItool is *doing right now*.

- Actions. These define the various tasks the MIDItool performs. Many actions update the values of variables in the device, others write text to the LCD display, or send MIDI messages.

- Events. These define input to the MIDItool, such as button pushes, knob turns, and MIDI reception.

- State Matrix. The State Matrix organizes States, Actions, and Events into a table describing which action is performed in response to each possible event during each state. The columns of the state matrix represent each state, while the rows represent each event. At the intersection of a column and row is the next state the device will enter when that event occurs during that state, and which action is performed.

If you want to change a MIDItool's functionality, you will generally add (or subtract) states, actions, and/or events from the state matrix for that tool. If you add an action, you'll have to write the small subroutine that performs it. See Chapter 12 (MIDItools Software) for more details.

MIDI Implementation Chart

This summarizes what elements of the MIDI spec are implemented in each MIDItool.

Now let's look at the projects.

Project 1: Universal Transmitter

Use this tool to program and transmit any one, two, or three-byte message to your MIDI system. You first select the bytes to be programmed, then use either the +/− keys or Value fader to choose the byte values (or use the Null key to inactivate a byte, if needed). You can then send or clear the message. Typical uses include:

- "All Notes Off" panic button. This MIDI command instructs synthesizers to turn off all notes, which is an excellent way to "unstick" stuck notes. (Stuck notes occur if a device receives a note-on command but does not receive a note-off command. This can happen if the instrument receives too many notes at one time and loses its mind, or if the MIDI In cable is disconnected before the note-off occurs.)

- Controller reset button. Another MIDI command can reset all controllers to their nominal value—pitch bend to center, and all controllers to 0. This is particularly handy when you stop a sequence in the middle of a controller or pitch bend change, since otherwise the MIDI device will retain the value(s) at the time the sequence was stopped. In the case of pitch bend, this could cause an instrument to sound out of tune.

- Song select button. Many sequencers and drum machines respond to the song select message, which can call up any of 128 songs. Use the Universal Transmitter as a remote control to select a song.

- Master controller or sequencer add-on to transmit messages not supported by the controller or sequencer. Example: your sequencer may not send MIDI mode messages (omni, poly, mono) to configure a keyboard controller. Patch the sequencer output into the Universal Transmitter input to merge it with the transmitter output, and you'll be able to send mode messages along with the sequencer output.

- Sys ex byte sender. You can even program and transmit system exclusive data.

- Troubleshooting device. The Universal Transmitter can provide MIDI messages, allowing you to determine if a device responds to particular messages. Example: Does a rack mount device respond to polyphonic pressure? Send some polyphonic pressure messages and find out.

Universal Transmitter Specs

Function: Generate MIDI messages
Transmit/Receive/Both: Transmit
Inline Device: Yes
Internal Merging: Yes
PC Boards required: CPU, Hand H/I or Rack H/I
Inputs: MIDI In, Panel Keys (8), Fader, DC Power, On/Off Switch, LCD Contrast
Outputs: LCD, LED(1), MIDI Out, MIDI thru
Enclosure: Hand Box or Rack Box
Complexity: Low

Panel Layouts

rack mount front panel

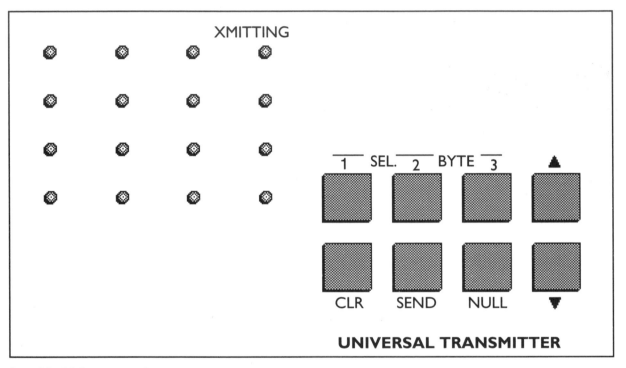

hand held front panel

Setup

1. Connect a suitable power supply (see Chapter 6) to the MIDItool power supply input.

2. Patch the MIDItool MIDI Out to the MIDI In of a slave device or thru box.

3. To merge a MIDI signal with the Universal Transmitter output, patch the MIDI Out providing the signal to be merged into the MIDItool MIDI In.

4. Turn on the power switch.

5. Adjust the LCD Contrast control for the best contrast.

Universal Transmitter Operations

Default Settings

When power is first applied, the screen shows:

The default settings are:

- All Bytes are inactive—the Universal Transmitter won't send anything, even if you ask it to.

- The device is ready for you to program the first byte.

Create a Message

The LCD's upper line shows the byte values in hex; the lower line shows the byte being programmed.

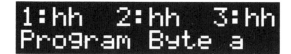

The possible variable values are:

hh = Byte value in hex, from $00–$FF (Dashes = inactive byte)
a = Byte number (1, 2 or 3)

1. Select the byte number to be programmed with the Select Byte keys (1, 2, or 3).

2. Program the hex value of the selected byte with the +/– keys and/or the Value fader.

Inactivate Byte

1. Select the byte number to be deactivated with the Select Byte keys (1, 2, or 3).

2. Press the Null key. The byte display should show — to indicate that the byte is inactive and will not be transmitted.

3. Press the +/– keys or move the Value fader to reactivate the byte.

Send the Message

1. Press the Message Send key to transmit active bytes. If MIDI messages are present at the Universal Transmitter's MIDI In, they will be merged with the Universal Transmitter output.

2. The Transmitting LED will flash.

Clear the Message

1. Press the Message Clear (Clr) key. The LCD briefly flashes "Message Reset":

2. All three bytes are reset to their inactive state and the screen shows:

Byte Information

Here are the bytes you need to program to perform specific functions. "n" stands for the channel number, and ranges from $0–$F.

All Notes Off: $Bn 7B 00

Reset All Controllers: $Bn 79 00

Program Change: $Cn hh (hh= $00–$7F, or 0–127)

Local Control Off: $Bn 7A 00

For example, programming the bytes to show:

and pressing the "send" button sends program change 14 (0E) on channel 2.

Advanced Applications

Here are some suggestions for modifications of the Universal Transmitter:

- Display the valid status byte name.

- Allow multiple messages to be programmed, stored, and recalled.

- Triggering from an external event (MIDI, handclap, footswitch, etc.).

- Allow messages to be transmitted automatically at periodic intervals (timing clock, active sense, etc.).

- Allow messages with more than three bytes (for system exclusive messages, etc.).

- Disallow undefined status bytes so that you can't enter bytes that MIDI devices don't recognize.

Software Summary

States

Name	Objective
StB1	Configure Byte 1
StB2	Configure Byte 2
StB3	Configure Byte 3

Actions

Name	Activity
IDLE	No Action
B1INC	Increment Byte 1 value
B1DEC	Decrement Byte 1 value
B1FDR	Set Byte 1 value with fader
B2INC	Increment Byte 2 value
B2DEC	Decrement Byte 2 value
B2FDR	Set Byte 2 value with fader
B3INC	Increment Byte 3 value
B3DEC	Decrement Byte 3 value
B3FDR	Set Byte 3 value with fader
B1OFF	Inactivate Byte 1
B2OFF	Inactivate Byte 2
B3OFF	Inactivate Byte 3
MSGCLR	Inactivate all bytes and reset display
MSGSND	Transmit message
B1DISP	Update display for programming Byte 1
B2DISP	Update display for programming Byte 2
B3DISP	Update display for programming Byte 3

Events

Name	Interface
EvIdle	Idle
EvByte1	SELECT BYTE 1 key
EvByte2	SELECT BYTE 2 key
EvByte3	SELECT BYTE 3 key
EvPlus	+ key
EvClear	MESSAGE CLEAR key
EvSend	MESSAGE SEND key
EvNull	NULL key
EvMinus	- key
EvValue	VALUE fader

State Matrix

Event	State 0:StB1 NextSt,Act	State 1:StB2 NextSt,Act	State 2:StB3 NextSt,Act
EvIdle,	StB1,IDLE,	StB2,IDLE,	StB3,IDLE
EvPlus,	StB1,B1INC,	StB2,B2INC,	StB3,B3INC
EvMinus,	StB1,B1DEC,	StB2,B2DEC,	StB3,B3DEC
EvValue,	StB1,B1FDR,	StB2,B2FDR,	StB3,B3FDR
EvNull,	StB1,B1OFF,	StB2,B2OFF,	StB3,B3OFF
EvClear,	StB1,MSGCLR,	StB1,MSGCLR,	StB1,MSGCLR
EvSend,	StB1,MSGSND,	StB2,MSGSND,	StB3,MSGSND
EvByte1,	StB1,IDLE,	StB1,B1DISP,	StB1,B1DISP
EvByte2,	StB2,B2DISP,	StB2,IDLE,	StB2,B2DISP
EvByte3,	StB3,B3DISP,	StB3,B3DISP,	StB3,IDLE

MIDI Implementation Chart

UNIVERSAL TRANSMITTER   Date: 9-30-93
MIDItool 1   MIDI Implementation Chart   Version: 1.0

Function		Transmitted	Recognized	Remarks
Basic	Default	***	***	note 1
Channel	Channel	1-16	***	note 2
Mode	Default	***	***	
	Messages	O	X	
	Altered	***	***	
Note		O	X	
Number	True Voice	***	***	
Velocity	Note ON	O	X	note 3
	Note OFF	O	X	note 4
Aftertouch	Key	O	X	
	Channel	O	X	
Pitch Bend		O	X	
Controllers		O	X	
Program		O	X	
Change	True #	***	***	
System Exclusive		O	X	
System	SPP	O	X	
Common	Song Select	O	X	
	Tune Request	O	X	
System	Clock	O	X	
Realtime	Commands	O	X	
Aux	Local ON/OFF	O	X	
	All Notes Off	O	X	
	Active Sensing	O	X	
	Reset	O	X	

Notes:
1: There is no default transmit channel setting
2: Transmit channel is programmable and optional
3: Note On velocity is programmable (0-127)
4: Note Off velocity is programmable (0-127)

Mode 1: Omni On, Poly   Mode 2: Omni On, Mono   O:Yes
Mode 3: Omni Off, Poly   Mode 4: Omni Off, Mono   X:No

Project 2: Channel Message Transmitter

This transmits a variety of MIDI voice messages (program change, pitch bend, channel aftertouch, mod wheel, breath controller, footpedal, portamento time, data entry, main volume, balance, pan, and expression) over the channel of your choice.

After selecting the channel and message type, you then select the value with the fader or +/− keys. Updating the value sends a message for each updated value, so the fader can provide real-time control over whichever MIDI parameter you selected.

Typical Channel Message Transmitter uses include:

- MIDI master controller add-on. Transmit any message type not supported by your master controller.

- Single-track volume fader. Select master volume (controller 7), and program fades, mutes, and other level changes into a sequencer by recording the MIDItool fader moves.

- Single-track panpot. Select pan (controller 10), and pan a single sequencer track or instrument in real time for mixing or live performance.

- Breath controller substitute. Some sound modules have programs that require a breath controller to control certain parameters. If you don't have a breath controller, this project can send out messages that "look" like breath controller data.

- MIDI wa-wa substitute. Some signal processors have "wa-wa" presets whose filter frequency is controlled by a MIDI foot pedal. This project can produce suitable messages and allow for hand control.

- Remote control. Program sound modules remotely using program change messages and data entry messages.

- MIDI effects processor programmer. Modern signal processors allow for controlling several parameters of your choice with MIDI controllers. Set your 10 favorite parameters to be controlled by the controller types generated by this project (don't use program change or main volume, however, as these are generally dedicated to other uses). You can now program the most important signal processor parameters directly from the Channel Message Transmitter's fader. Note, however, that many signal processors do not respond to pitch bend.

- Gonzo "wave sequencing." Since the value transmitted by this project gets updated every time the value changes, you can generate a bunch of program changes very rapidly by moving the fader. This can create some truly bizarre effects when playing synthesizer, and has the bonus side effect of frightening away small animals.

Channel Message Transmitter Specs

Function: Generate 12 different types of channel messages
Transmit/Receive/Both: Transmit
Inline Device: Yes
Internal Merging: Yes
PC Boards required: CPU, Hand H/I or Rack H/I
Inputs: MIDI In, Panel Keys (5), Fader, DC Power, On/Off Switch, LCD Contrast
Outputs: LCD, MIDI Out, MIDI Thru
Enclosure: Hand Box or Rack Box
Complexity: Low

Panel Layouts

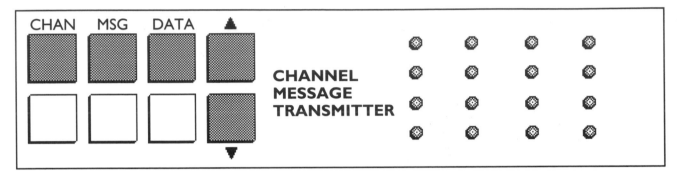

rack mount front panel

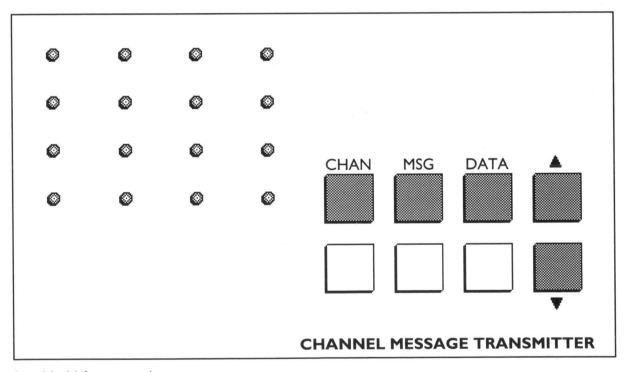

hand held front panel

Setup

1. Connect a suitable power supply (see Chapter 6) to the MIDItool power supply input.

2. Connect a MIDI cable from the MIDItool MIDI Out to the target device's MIDI In or a MIDI Thru box.

3. Since this project allows for merging, you can optionally patch a master device's MIDI Out to the MIDItool's MIDI In. For example, this is useful if you want to use the Channel Message Transmitter in conjunction with a master keyboard.

4. Turn on the power switch.

5. Adjust LCD Contrast for the best contrast.

Channel Message Transmitter Operations

Default Settings

Turn on the juice, and the screen shows:

The default settings are:

- Transmit Channel—Channel 1.

- Message Type—Program Change

- Data Value—0

- Operational status—Transmit Channel is available for editing.

Set the Transmit Channel

1. Press the Setup Chan key. An arrow points at the channel number to show that it is available for editing.

2. Select the MIDI transmit channel using the +/– keys and/or the Value fader. The LCD always displays the current transmit channel.

Select the Message Type

1. Press the Setup Msg key.

2. Select the message type using the +/– keys (the Value fader is inactive for message type selection). The following message types are available:

Program Change
Pitch Bend
Channel Aftertouch
Modulation Wheel (Controller 1)
Breath Controller (Controller 2)
Foot Controller (Controller 4)
Portamento Time (Controller 5)
Data Entry (Controller 6)
Main Volume (Controller 7)
Balance (Controller 8)
Pan (Controller 10)
Expression (Controller 11)

The following screens show the message types and range of values you can program for each message. Note that pitch bend values are transmitted in 128 discrete steps over the full range of possible values; the LCD shows this range as –64 to +63.

```
CHANNEL          nn      CHANNEL          nn
PROGRAM          bbb     PITCH BEND       PPP

CHANNEL          nn      CHANNEL          nn
CH AFTCH         bbb     MOD WHEEL        bbb

CHANNEL          nn      CHANNEL          nn
BREATH CTL       bbb     FOOT CTL         bbb

CHANNEL          nn      CHANNEL          nn
PORTA TIME       bbb     DATA ENTRY       bbb

CHANNEL          nn      CHANNEL          nn
MAIN VOL         bbb     BALANCE          bbb

CHANNEL          nn      CHANNEL          nn
PAN              bbb     EXPRESSION       bbb
```

The possible variable values are:

nn   = Channel number, 1–16
bbb = Controller value, 0–127
ppp = Pitch bend, –64 to +63

Transmit Data

1. Press the Data key. An arrow points at the message value to show that it is available for editing.

2. MIDI messages (of the selected type) are transmitted each time the data value is modified with the +/– keys and/or the Value fader.

Advanced Applications

Here are some suggestions on modifications for the Channel Message Transmitter:

- Allow simultaneous multi-channel transmission.

- Allow simultaneous multi-message transmission.

- Replace the fader with a foot pedal.

- Replace the fader with a control voltage jack to allow for control-voltage-to-MIDI conversion.

- Allow more control change message types.

- Support internal message thinning.

- Support three additional faders.

- Allow message type selection via MIDI commands.

Software Summary

States

Name	Objective
StCh	Set transmit channel
StMsg	Set message type
StData	Transmit message

Actions

Name	Activity
IDLE	No action
CHINC	Increment channel
CHDEC	Decrement channel
CHFDR	Set channel with fader
MSGINC	Increment message type
MSGDEC	Decrement message type
DATINC	Increment data value and transmit it
DATDEC	Decrement data value and transmit it
DATFDR	Set data value with fader and transmit
CDISP	Update display for changing channel
MDISP	Update display for changing message
DDISP	Update display for setting data value

Events

Name	Interface
EvIdle	Idle
EvChan	SETUP CHAN key
EvMsg	SETUP MSG key
EvData	DATA key
EvPlus	+ key
EvMinus	- key
EvValue	VALUE fader

State Matrix

Event	State 0:StCh NextSt,Act	State 1:StMsg NextSt,Act	State 2:StData NextSt,Act
EvIdle,	StCh,IDLE,	StMsg,IDLE,	StData,IDLE
EvPlus,	StCh,CHINC,	StMsg,MSGINC,	StData,DATINC
EvMinus,	StCh,CHDEC,	StMsg,MSGDEC,	StData,DATDEC
EvValue,	StCh,CHFDR,	StMsg,IDLE,	StData,DATFDR
EvChan,	StCh,IDLE,	StCh,CDISP,	StCh,CDISP
EvMsg,	StMsg,MDISP,	StMsg,IDLE,	StMsg,MDISP
EvData,	StData,DDISP,	StData,DDISP,	StData,IDLE

MIDI Implementation Chart

CHANNEL MESSAGE TRANSMITTER   Date: 9-30-93
MIDItool 2   MIDI Implementation Chart   Version: 1.0

Function		Transmitted	Recognized	Remarks
Basic	Default	1	***	
Channel	Channel	1-16	***	note 1
	Default	Mode 3	***	
Mode	Messages	X	X	
	Altered	***	***	
Note		X	X	
Number	True Voice	***	***	
Velocity	Note ON	X	X	
	Note OFF	X	X	
Aftertouch	Key	X	X	
	Channel	O	X	
Pitch Bend		O	X	
Controllers	1	O	X	mod wheel
	2	O	X	breath cont
	4	O	X	foot cont
	5	O	X	portamento
	6	O	X	data entry
	7	O	X	main volume
	8	O	X	balance
	10	O	X	pan
	11	O	X	expression
Program		O	X	
Change	True #	***	***	
System Exclusive		X	X	
System	SPP	X	X	
Common	Song Select	X	X	
	Tune Request	X	X	
System	Clock	X	X	
Realtime	Commands	X	X	
Aux	Local ON/OFF	X	X	
	All Notes Off	X	X	
	Active Sensing	X	X	
	Reset	X	X	

Notes:
1: Transmit channel is programmable

Mode 1: Omni On, Poly   Mode 2: Omni On, Mono   O:Yes
Mode 3: Omni Off, Poly   Mode 4: Omni Off, Mono   X:No

Project 3: Programmable Controllers

This project transmits up to three different MIDI continuous controller commands on up to three MIDI channels. You can also transmit three different controller types on one channel, or two different controllers on one channel and another controller on a second channel.

After selecting the channel and controller number, the +/− keys or Value fader change the controller value.

Being able to transmit a variety of MIDI controllers is useful for electronically varying parameters normally controlled by faders on sequencers, synths, lighting controllers and special effects boxes, or replacing footpedal control with hand control. Typical applications include:

- MIDI master controller add-on. Transmit any controller messages not supported by your master controller.

- MIDI lighting controller programmer. Manipulate stage lighting in real time with the Value fader.

- MIDI effects processor programmer. Since newer signal processors usually allow for controlling various parameters with MIDI controllers, you can use the Programmable Controllers MIDItool to program effects remotely. For example, if you're working with an echo patch, you could assign delay time, delay feedback, and delay mix to three separate controllers. To program the delay time, select the associated controller on the Programmable Controllers box and vary the fader to dial in the desired amount of delay time. Follow the same procedure for the other parameters, then save the program at the effects unit to make these changes permanent.

- MIDI equalizer programmer. Some graphic equalizers can assign each band to its own MIDI controller. Adjusting these is usually a hassle using the effect's standard interface, where you often have to hit +/− keys repeatedly to select the band to be edited, and then again to change the value. It's a lot easier to adjust the equalizer bands with a fader; follow the same basic procedure as outlined in the previous paragraph on programming effects.

- Multitrack panpot. Control placement in the stereo field of up to three sequenced tracks (one in real time).

- Multitrack volume fader. Control volume levels (mutes, fades, etc.) of up to three sequenced tracks (one in real time).

Programmable Controllers Specs

Function: Generates up to three continuous controllers on up to three channels
Transmit/Receive/Both: Transmit
Inline Device: Yes
Internal Merging: Yes
PC Boards required: CPU, Hand H/I or Rack H/I
Inputs: MIDI In, Panel Keys (8), Fader, DC Power, On/Off Switch, LCD Contrast
Outputs: LCD, MIDI Out, MIDI Thru
Enclosure: Hand Box or Rack Box
Complexity: Low

Panel Layouts

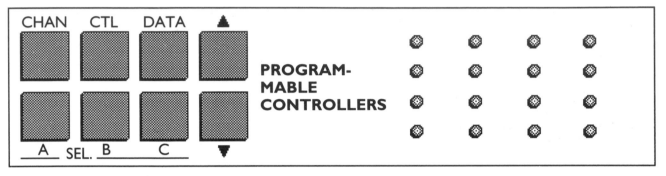

rack mount front panel

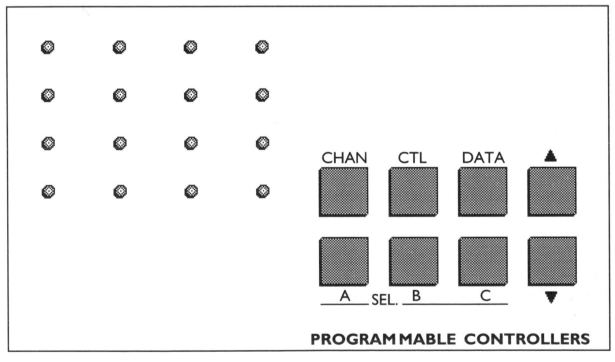

hand held front panel

Setup

1. Connect a suitable power supply (see Chapter 6) to the MIDItool power supply input.

2. Connect a MIDI cable from the MIDItool MIDI Out to the target device's MIDI In or a MIDI Thru box.

3. Since this project allows for merging, you can optionally patch a master device's MIDI Out to the MIDItool's MIDI In. This is useful if you want to use the Programmable Controllers transmitter in conjunction with a master keyboard or drum machine.

4. Turn on the power switch.

5. Adjust LCD Contrast for the best contrast.

Programmable Controllers Operations

Default Settings

Turn on power, and the screen initially shows:

The default settings for all controllers are:

- Transmit Channel—1

- Controller Number—0

- Data Value—0

- The display shows Controller A's parameters.

- Operational status—Controller A's Transmit Channel is available for editing, as indicated by the arrow pointing at the Channel parameter.

Select A Controller

Press the desired Controller Select key (A, B or C) to choose one of three independent controllers for programming and/or use. As soon as you select one of the three controller options, an arrow points to the Data parameter to show it's ready to transmit controller data in real time.

The LCD's upper line shows the parameters for one of three controllers (channel number, controller number, and controller value data). The lower line displays each parameter's value.

The possible variable values are:

x   = One of the three controllers (A, B, or C)
nn   = Channel number, 1–16
bbb   = Controller value and number, 0–127

The arrow always points to the parameter that will be modified by the +/– keys and Value fader.

Set the Selected Controller's Transmit Channel

1. Press the Setup Chan key; an arrow points at the Channel parameter to indicate it is ready for editing.

2. Adjust the MIDI transmit channel using the +/– keys and/or the Value fader.

Set the Selected Controller's Number

1. Press the Setup Ctl key. An arrow points at the Controller Number parameter to indicate it is ready for editing.

2. Assign the controller number using the +/– keys and/or the Value fader.

Transmit Messages Using the Selected Controller

1. Press the Data key. An arrow points at the Data value to show that it is available for editing.

2. Controller messages are transmitted each time the data value is modified with the +/– keys and/or the Value fader. The LCD shows all parameters and transmitted data values for the selected controller.

3. Generated data is merged with any incoming MIDI messages.

Advanced Applications

Here are some suggestions on modifications for the Programmable Controllers:

- Replace the single fader with three faders, one for each controller.

- Replace the fader with a foot pedal.

- Replace the fader with a control voltage jack to allow for control-voltage-to-MIDI conversion.

- Provide two faders for LSB/MSB programming.

- Allow simultaneous transmission (3 at once).

- Display the selected control change name.

- Implement other controllers (pitch bend, etc.).

Software Summary

States

Name	Objective
StCh	Set transmit channel
StCtl	Set controller number
StData	Transmit controller messages

Actions

Name	Activity
IDLE	No Action
CHINC	Increment channel
CHDEC	Decrement channel
CHFDR	Set channel with fader
CTLINC	Increment controller number
CTLDEC	Decrement controller number
CTLFDR	Set controller number with fader
DATINC	Increment data value and transmit msg
DATDEC	Decrement data value and transmit msg
DATFDR	Set value with fader and transmit msg
CHDISP	Update display for changing channel
CTDISP	Update display for changing controller
DTDISP	Update display for setting data value
ADISP	Update display with Controller A data
BDISP	Update display with Controller B data
CDISP	Update display with Controller C data

Events

Name	Interface
EvIdle	Idle
EvChan	SETUP CHAN key
EvCtl	SETUP CTL key
EvData	DATA key
EvPlus	+ key
EvA	CONTROLLER SELECT A key
EvB	CONTROLLER SELECT B key
EvC	CONTROLLER SELECT C key
EvMinus	- key
EvValue	VALUE fader

State Matrix

Event	State 0: StCh NextSt,Act	State 1: StCtl NextSt,Act	State 2: StData NextState,Act
EvIdle,	StCh,IDLE,	StCtl,IDLE,	StData,IDLE
EvPlus,	StCh,CHINC,	StCtl,CTLINC,	StData,DATINC
EvMinus,	StCh,CHDEC,	StCtl,CTLDEC,	StData,DATDEC
EvValue,	StCh,CHFDR,	StCtl,CTLFDR,	StData,DATFDR
EvChan,	StCh,IDLE,	StCh,CHDISP,	StCh,CHDISP
EvCtl,	StCtl,CTDISP,	StCtl,IDLE,	StCtl,CTDISP
EvData,	StData,DTDISP,	StData,DTDISP,	StData,IDLE
EvA,	StData,ADISP,	StData,ADISP,	StData,ADISP
EvB,	StData,BDISP,	StData,BDISP,	StData,BDISP
EvC,	StData,CDISP,	StData,CDISP,	StData,CDISP

MIDI Implementation Chart

PROGRAMMABLE CONTROLLERS   Date: 9-30-93
MIDItool 3   MIDI Implementation Chart   Version: 1.0

Function		Transmitted	Recognized	Remarks
Basic	Default	***	***	note 1
Channel	Channel	1-16	***	note 2
	Default	Mode 3	***	
Mode	Messages	X	X	
	Altered	***	***	
Note		X	X	
Number	True Voice	***	***	
Velocity	Note ON	X	X	
	Note OFF	X	X	
Aftertouch	Key	X	X	
	Channel	X	X	
Pitch Bend		X	X	
Controllers		O	X	note 3
Program		X	X	
Change	True #	***	***	
System Exclusive		X	X	
System	SPP	X	X	
Common	Song Select	X	X	
	Tune Request	X	X	
System	Clock	X	X	
Realtime	Commands	X	X	
Aux	Local ON/OFF	X	X	
	All Notes Off	X	X	
	Active Sensing	X	X	
	Reset	X	X	

Notes:
1: All three controllers default to channel 1
2: Transmit channel is programmable
3: Control number can be assigned to any of three
   programmable controller faders

Mode 1: Omni On, Poly   Mode 2: Omni On, Mono   O:Yes
Mode 3: Omni Off, Poly   Mode 4: Omni Off, Mono   X:No

Project 4: Custom Instrument

This project serves as the basis of a 64-note MIDI master controller using normally open momentary switches. These switches could be arranged in custom keyboard configurations, mounted in a guitar neck, or used for any of the following typical applications:

- Performance artist master controller. Use tape switches on the floor as the external keyboard for controlling sample playback and sound module playback.

- MIDI keyboard controller. Hook this project into a standard keyboard (or even build a strap-on remote keyboard).

- Analog keyboard MIDI retrofit. Use the keys found in any analog keyboard (Fender Rhodes, spinet piano, etc.) to trigger switches that drive a MIDI sound generator.

- Esoteric instrument. Use pressure switches, magnet (reed) switches, photodetectors, infrared detectors, motion detectors, and/or other transducers to create a truly unique musical instrument.

- Lighting controller. Customize your stage lighting setup by making a custom keypad to control each lamp and special effect (fog machine, flashpot, etc.)

- MIDI drum controller. Use it with drum trigger switches to retrofit a drum kit for control of drum samples.

- Educational keyboard. Use it to create a small inexpensive keyboard for sight reading training, piano instruction, or MIDI basics tutoring.

Custom Instrument Specs

Function: Generator
Transmit/Receive/Both: Transmit
Inline Device: No
Internal Merging: No
PC Boards required: CPU, Rack H/I, External Keys
Inputs: Panel Keys (5), Fader, External Keyboard, DC Power, On/Off Switch, LCD Contrast
Outputs: LCD, MIDI Out
Enclosure: Rack Box only
Complexity: High

Panel Layout

rack mount front panel

Setup

1. This tool uses the External Keys expansion PC board (see sidebar) to interface to the external keys. Connect the Expansion Keys board to the CPU board's expansion connector with a ribbon cable.

2. Connect a suitable power supply (see Chapter 6) to the MIDItool power supply input.

3. Connect a MIDI cable from the MIDItool's MIDI Out to a sound module or signal processor's MIDI In.

4. Turn on the power switch.

5. Adjust LCD Contrast for the best display contrast.

Custom Instrument Operations

Default Settings
Turn on the power, and the display shows:

- Transmit Channel—Channel 1

- Note Number Offset—0

- Velocity—64

- Operational status—the Transmit Channel is available for editing.

Changing the Custom Instrument Parameters
The LCD's upper line shows the parameters you can program (MIDI transmit channel, note number offset, and note velocity). The lower line displays each parameter's value.

The possible variable values are:

nn = Channel number (1–16)
ssss = Note number offset (–128 to +127)
bbb = Velocity value (0 to 127)

Set the Transmit Channel

1. Press the Setup Chan key. An arrow points at the channel number to show that is it available for editing.

2. Select the MIDI transmit channel with the +/– keys and/or the Value fader. The LCD always displays the current transmit channel.

Set the Note Number Offset

1. Press the Setup Offset key. This function shifts the base note in semitone increments for easy transposition.

2. Select the desired degree of offset for all note messages with the +/– keys and/or the Value fader.

Set the Velocity for All Notes

1. Press the Setup Vel key. This function sets the velocity value that the custom instrument will transmit.

2. Set the velocity for all Note On messages with the +/– keys and/or the Value fader. Velocity can be adjusted in real time while notes are being played.

Advanced Applications

Here are some ideas for possible Custom Instrument modifications:

- Allow more than 64 keys.

- Support program change message transmission.

- Replace the velocity fader with a foot pedal.

- Include a channel message transmitter.

- Allow the keyboard to be split.

- Provide for simultaneous multi-channel transmission.

- Allow a pressure-indicating input (aftertouch).

Software Summary

States

Name	Objective
StCh	Set transmit channel
StOff	Set offset
StVel	Set velocity

Actions

Name	Activity
IDLE	No action
CHINC	Increment channel
CHDEC	Decrement channel
CHFDR	Set channel with fader
OFFINC	Increment offset
OFFDEC	Decrement offset
OFFFDR	Set offset with fader
VELINC	Increment velocty
VELDEC	Decrement velocity
VELFDR	Set velocity with fader
SCAN	Scan key matrix and transmit notes
CDISP	Update display for changing channel
ODISP	Update display for changing offset
VDISP	Update display for changing velocity

Events

Name	Interface
EvIdle	Idle
EvChan	SETUP CHAN key
EvOff	SETUP OFFSET key
EvVel	SETUP VEL key
EvPlus	+ key
EvMinus	- key
EvValue	VALUE fader

State Matrix

Event	State 0:StCh NextSt,Act	State 1:StOff NextSt,Act	State 2:StVel NextSt,Act
EvIdle,	StCh,SCAN,	StOff,SCAN,	StVel,SCAN
EvPlus,	StCh,CHINC,	StOff,OFFINC,	StVel,VELINC
EvMinus,	StCh,CHDEC,	StOff,OFFDEC,	StVel,VELDEC
EvValue,	StCh,CHFDR,	StOff,OFFFDR,	StVel,VELFDR
EvChan,	StCh,SCAN,	StCh,CDISP,	StCh,CDISP
EvOff,	StOff,ODISP,	StOff,SCAN,	StOff,ODISP
EvVel,	StVel,VDISP,	StVel,VDISP,	StVel,SCAN

MIDI Implementation Chart

CUSTOM INSTRUMENT   Date: 9-30-93
MIDItool 4   MIDI Implementation Chart   Version: 1.0

Function		Transmitted	Recognized	Remarks
Basic	Default	1	***	
Channel	Channel	1-16	***	note 1
	Default	Mode 3	***	
Mode	Messages	X	X	
	Altered	***	***	
Note		O	X	note 2
Number	True Voice	28-91	***	note 3
Velocity	Note ON	1-127	X	note 4
	Note OFF	O	X	
Aftertouch	Key	X	X	
	Channel	X	X	
Pitch Bend		X	X	
Controllers		X	X	
Program		X	X	
Change	True #	***	***	
System Exclusive		X	X	
System	SPP	X	X	
Common	Song Select	X	X	
	Tune Request	X	X	
System	Clock	X	X	
Realtime	Commands	X	X	
Aux	Local ON/OFF	X	X	
	All Notes Off	X	X	
	Active Sensing	X	X	
	Reset	X	X	

Notes:
1: Transmit channel is programmable
2: Root note value is programmable (0-127)
3: Assuming 64 keys (max), this is the range with middle key
   set to middle C (note number 60)
4: Device transmits Note On message with velocity = 0 to
   turn notes off

Mode 1: Omni On, Poly   Mode 2: Omni On, Mono   O:Yes
Mode 3: Omni Off, Poly   Mode 4: Omni Off, Mono   X:No

About the Expansion Keys Board

Referring to the schematic, this expansion board implements an 8 by 8 key matrix, which allows you to interface up to 64 switches. Keys are normally open (in the off state); there is no velocity sensing, although velocity can be adjusted in real time using the fader.

Each column of the key matrix is turned on (logical 0) consecutively, and the state of all rows is read from the Parallel data bus. By individually enabling each column, we can scan each group of eight keys. By continuously scanning columns in this fashion, we can read all 64 keys.

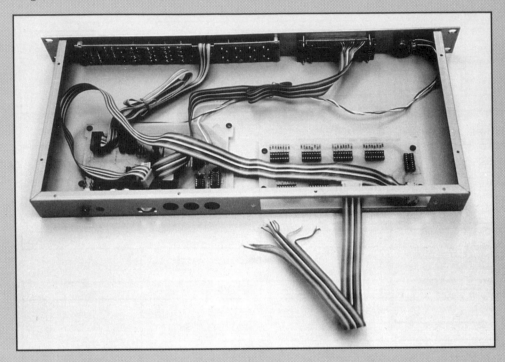

Note the custom instrument expansion board mounted in the lower right corner, with a ribbon cable extending outward. This connects to the custom instrument's switches.

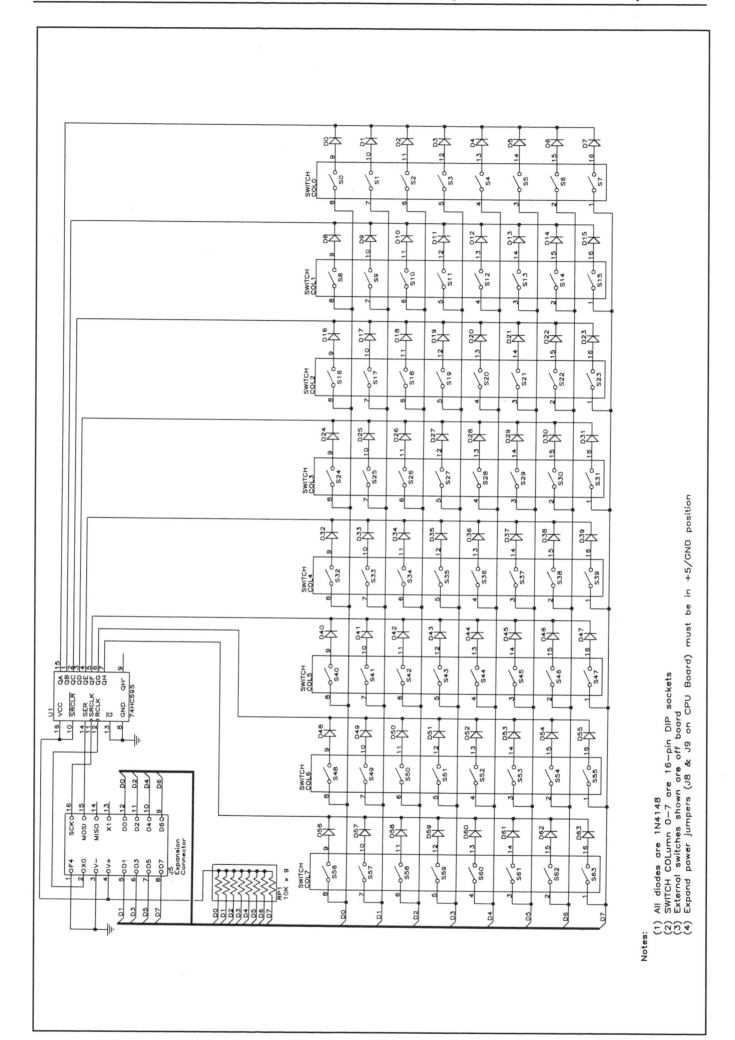

Notes:

(1) All diodes are 1N414B
(2) SWITCH COLumn 0–7 are 16-pin DIP sockets
(3) External switches shown are off board
(4) Expand power jumpers (J8 & J9 on CPU Board) must be in +5/GND position

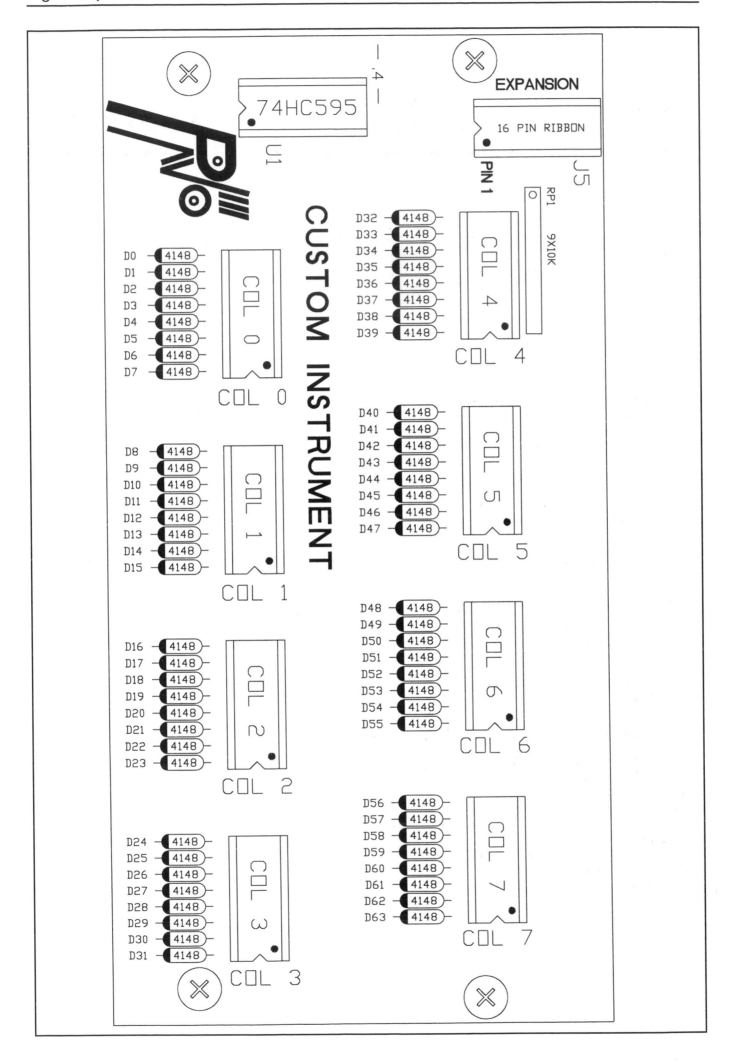

Project 5: Tap Tempo Transmitter

One of the complaints about sequencers and drum machines is that the tempo they produce can be stiff and robotic. Although these devices generally include ways to edit the tempo, this can be a somewhat cumbersome process. Many times, what you really want is the ability to simply tap out the tempo, complete with ritards and accelerandos.

This project lets you do just that. You can "humanize" the sequence's tempo by tapping on a button—if you speed up or slow down, so does the sequencer. It's also possible to smooth out the tempo if your timing is a little jittery.

Typical uses include:

- Human metronome. Control real-time playback of any sequencer, drum machine, or other device that accepts MIDI clocks.

- Human/machine interface. Act as a conductor with the Tap Tempo Transmitter to synchronize sequence playback to live performers (small ensembles, theater orchestras, church groups, etc.)

- Theater music director's helper. Control the synchronization of any sequence to match prescribed movements or actions during a theater performance.

- Sequencer remote control. Initiate sequence playback using the Autoplay mode.

- Live drummer synchronizer. If you've always wanted to synchronize a sequencer to the drummer rather than the other way around, this project does the job.

- Educator's helper. When teaching composition, orchestration, etc., it's often advantageous to control a sequence's playback tempo to allow for easier analysis of particular passages.

Tap Tempo Transmitter Specs

Function: Generates MIDI clock signals
Transmit/Receive/Both: Transmit
Inline Device: No
Internal Merging: No
PC Boards required: CPU, Hand H/I or Rack H/I
Inputs: Panel Keys (8), Fader, DC Power, On/Off Switch, LCD Contrast
Outputs: LCD, LEDs (2), MIDI Out
Enclosure: Hand Box or Rack Box
Complexity: Medium

Panel Layouts

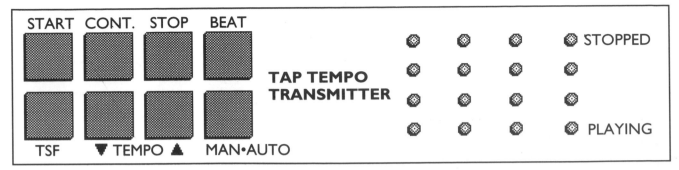

rack mount front panel

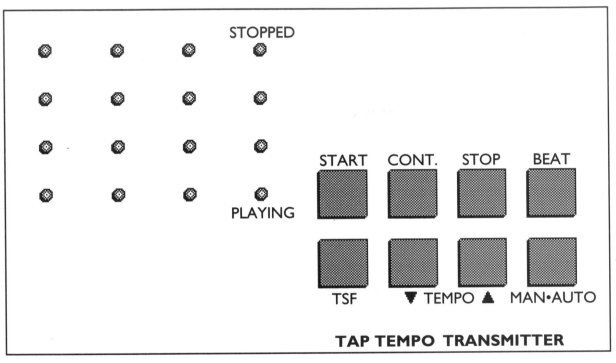

hand held front panel

Setup

1. Connect a suitable power supply (see Chapter 6) to the MIDItool power supply input.

2. Patch the MIDItool's MIDI Out to a drum machine or sequencer's MIDI In.

3. Turn on the power switch.

4. Adjust LCD Contrast for the best contrast.

Tap Tempo Transmitter Operations

Before using the Tap Tempo Transmitter, set your target device (sequencer, drum machine, etc.) to receive external MIDI synchronization. This is generally called External Clock, MIDI Sync, or Chase Lock.

Default Settings

When you first apply power, the LCD shows:

The default settings are:

- Tempo (Quarter Notes Per Minute)—20.

- Playback Mode—Manual.

- Tempo Smoothing Function (TSF)—Off.

- Operational Status—The tempo is available for editing.

Manually Control the Sequence Tempo

The screen's upper line shows the three available parameters, and the lower line, their values.

The possible variable values are:

eee   = Tempo in QPM (20 to 255)
vvv   = Tempo smoothing function (On or Off)
ffffff   = Sequencer playback mode (Manual or Auto)

To tap a song's tempo:

1. Set the Initial (Estimated) Tempo. With the sequencer stopped, enter an estimate of the initial tempo with the Tempo +/– keys and/or the Value fader.

2. Press the Start key. The Tap Tempo Transmitter will issue a start command, and the sequencer will play from the first beat of the first measure.

3. To control the sequence playback speed, press and release the Beat key once for each beat. The LCD shows the approximate tempo in quarter notes per minute (QPM).

Enable Smoothing

You can enable smoothing at any time by pressing the TSF key. The display shows the TSF status.

Freeze and Change Sequence Playback Tempo

1. While the sequencer is playing, press Auto to freeze the current tempo.

2. To change a frozen tempo either use the Tempo +/– keys, or return to manual mode by pressing the Beat key.

Set Constant Tempo (Defeat Manual Function)

1. The Auto key toggles between Manual and Auto modes when the Tap Tempo Transmitter is stopped. Select Auto mode.

2. Use the Tempo +/– buttons or fader to set the tempo.

3. Press Start or Cont to initiate playback at the current tempo.

4. Change the tempo in real time with the +/– buttons or fader.

Stop the Sequencer

Press the Stop key. The sequencer will stop at the end of the current measure. When stopped, you can alter the tempo with the +/– keys and/or Value fader.

Continue Playback from Where It Was Stopped

1. Press the Cont key. The sequencer will start playing from the first beat of the current measure.

2. In manual mode, you can continue playing the sequence with the Beat key. In Auto mode, playback will continue at the current tempo.

Check Playback Status

Two LEDs indicate whether the Tap Tempo Transmitter is Stopped or Playing.

Advanced Applications

Here are some suggested Tap Tempo Transmitter modifications:

- Build a mercury switch in a conductor's wand for the beat key.

- Write more sophisticated tempo algorithms.

- Parallel the beat key with a drum trigger.

- Build an analog circuit that detects a handclap, kick drum, metronome, etc. type of sound and closes an electronic switch paralleled with the beat key.

- Feed an analog drum machine's click tone into the above box so MIDI sequencers can sync with vintage drum machines.

- Allow fractional tempos.

Software Summary

States

Name	Objective
StOp	Sequencer stopped
StPl	Sequencer playing

Actions

Name	Activity
IDLE	No action
START	Send Start message
CONT	Send Continue message
STOP	Send Stop message
TEMINC	Increment tempo
TEMDEC	Decrement tempo
TEMFDR	Set tempo with fader
CLK24	Transmit 24 clocks and calculate QPM
TSFTOG	Toggle Tempo Smoothing Function status
AUTOPL	Set autoplay mode
AUTTOG	Toggle playback mode status
MDISP	Update display with playback mode
TDISP	Update display with tempo value
LEDSTP	Control STOPPED LED
LEDPLY	Control PLAYING LED

Events

Name	Interface
EvIdle	Idle
EvStart	START key
EvCont	CONT key
EvStop	STOP key
EvBeat	BEAT key
EvTSF	TSF key
EvMinus	- key
EvPlus	+ key
EvAuto	AUTO key
EvTempo	TEMPO fader

State Matrix

Event	State 0: StOp NextSt,Act	State 1: StPl NextSt,Act
EvIdle,	StOp,IDLE,	StPl,IDLE
EvStart,	StPl,START,	StPl,IDLE
EvCont,	StPl,CONT,	StPl,IDLE
EvStop,	StOp,IDLE,	StOp,STOP
EvBeat,	StOp,IDLE,	StPl,CLK24
EvTSF,	StOp,TSFTOG,	StPl,TSFTOG
EvMinus,	StOp,TEMDEC,	StPl,TEMDEC
EvPlus,	StOp,TEMINC,	StPl,TEMINC
EvAuto,	StOp,AUTTOG,	StPl,AUTOPL
EvTempo,	StOp,TEMFDR,	StPl,IDLE

MIDI Implementation Chart

TAP TEMPO TRANSMITTER   Date: 9-30-93
MIDItool 5   MIDI Implementation Chart   Version: 1.0

Function		Transmitted	Recognized	Remarks
Basic	Default	***	***	
Channel	Channel	***	***	
	Default	***	***	
Mode	Messages	X	X	
	Altered	***	***	
Note		X	X	
Number	True Voice	***	***	
Velocity	Note ON	X	X	
	Note OFF	X	X	
Aftertouch	Key	X	X	
	Channel	X	X	
Pitch Bend		X	X	
Controllers		X	X	
Program		X	X	
Change	True #	***	***	
System Exclusive		X	X	
System	SPP	X	X	
Common	Song Select	X	X	
	Tune Request	X	X	
System	Clock	O	X	note 1
Realtime	Commands	O	X	note 1
Aux	Local ON/OFF	X	X	
	All Notes Off	X	X	
	Active Sensing	X	X	
	Reset	X	X	

Notes:
1: This device generates System Realtime messages only

Mode 1: Omni On, Poly   Mode 2: Omni On, Mono   O:Yes
Mode 3: Omni Off, Poly   Mode 4: Omni Off, Mono   X:No

Project 6: Sequencer Remote Control

Everyone seems to like remote controls, so this one lets you tell a sequencer to stop, start, continue, fast forward, rewind, go to an autolocation point, or loop. Typical applications include:

- Basic remote control. Control real time playback of any sequence.

- Project studio helper. Control the sequencer when you're laying down guitar tracks, or sitting closer to the keyboards than the sequencer.

- User-friendly sequence player. Loop the sequence when practicing.

- Drummer's song start controller. Drummers can use the remote to start and stop sequences, while another performer or technician loads and monitors the sequence.

- Educator's helper. Control real time playback of any sequence when teaching composition, orchestration, etc.

Sequencer Remote Control Specs

Function: Generator
Transmit/Receive/Both: Transmit
Inline Device: No
Internal Merging: No
PC Boards required: CPU, Hand H/I orRack H/I
Inputs: Panel Keys (8), Fader, DC Power, On/Off Switch, LCD Contrast
Outputs: LCD, LEDs (2), MIDI Out
Enclosure: Hand Box or Rack Box
Complexity: Medium

Panel Layouts

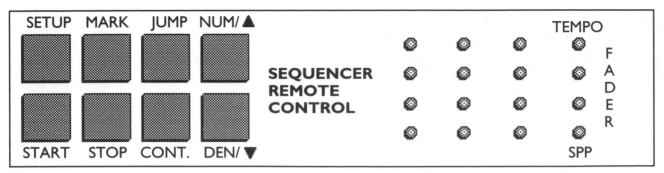

rack mount front panel

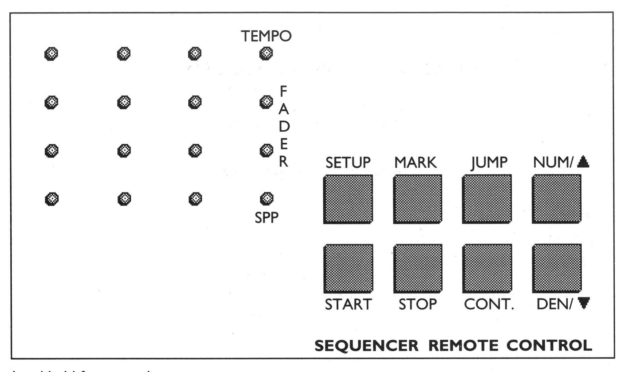

hand held front panel

Setup

1. Connect a suitable power supply (see Chapter 6) to the MIDItool power supply input.

2. Patch the MIDItool's MIDI Out to the sequencer's MIDI In.

3. Turn on the power switch.

4. Adjust LCD Contrast for the most readable display.

Default Settings

On power-up, the display shows:

```
TIME SIG MRK QPM
   4/4        1 100
```

- Time Signature—4/4

- Tempo (Quarter Notes per Minute)—100

- Marked Measure—1

- Measure—1

- Beat—1

- Sequencer Status—stopped

- Operational status—The device is ready to be configured.

Sequencer Remote Control Operations

Before using the remote, your sequencer must respond to external MIDI clock signals (called chase lock mode, external clock, external sync, etc.). Refer to the sequencer's instruction manual for information on how to do this.

Configuring the Remote Control for Your Sequencer

1. Press the Setup key. The display shows:

```
TIME SIG MRK QPM
 nn/dd     eee bbb
```

The LCD's upper line shows the current status (in setup mode, it's Time Signature) followed by the autolocation measure number (marker) and tempo in quarter notes per minute (QPM). The lower line shows the variables; possible values are:

nn = Time signature "numerator" (number of note units per measure; 1–16)
dd = Time signature "denominator" (defines the note unit in relation to the whole note; can be 1, 2, 4, 8, 16)
eee = Marked measure number (1–256; described later)
bbb = Tempo (20–255 quarter notes per minute)

2. Enter the time signature using the Num and Den keys.

3. Set the song tempo with the Value fader. The upper right LED lights when the Value fader controls the tempo.

Play the Sequence from the Beginning

1. Press the Start key (if the status line says "Stopped," press the Start key again). The sequence plays from the first measure and the status line shows "Playing."

```
status    MRK QPM
mmm:cc    eee bbb
```

Possible values are:

status = Playing, Stopped, Looping, or Waiting
mmm = measure number (1–256)
cc = number of beats (1–16)
bbb = tempo (20–255)

2. If desired, adjust the playback tempo with the +/– keys. While playing, the LCD shows the current song measure and beat.

Stop the Sequencer

Press the Stop key. The status says "Stopped." The line below it shows the current song measure and beat. When the sequencer is stopped, this is the last measure and beat that was played.

Go to a Specific Measure

While stopped, use the +/– keys and/or the Value fader to set the Song Position pointer to any measure between 1 and 256, as shown below the status. The lower right LED lights when the Value fader controls the Song Position pointer number.

Continue Playback from the Current Measure

1. Press the Cont key. The sequence will play from the current measure.

2. If desired, adjust the playback tempo with the +/– keys. The LCD shows the current Song Position.

Set the Autolocation Marker

At any time, press the Mark key to save the current song measure number in autolocation memory. The LCD displays the number of the marked measure.

Jump to the Autolocation Point and Continue Playback

While the sequencer is stopped, press the Jump key. The sequencer will jump to the marked measure and resume playback.

Sequence Loop

While the sequence is playing, press the Jump key. The sequence will loop continuously between the autolocation (marked) point and the end of the measure that was playing when you pressed the Jump key. The display shows the loop starting measure (MRK).

Note that if the autolocation point is later than the Jump measure, looping still works but Jump and Mark automatically switch places. The LCD updates accordingly.

Advanced Applications

Here are some ways to enhance the Sequence Remote Control:

*   Replace the sequencer playback controls with footswitches and pedals for hands-free use.

*   Support more sophisticated time signatures.

*   Use a drum trigger for the start key.

*   Allow for an audio or visual tempo indicator.

*   Support tempo mapping.

*   Allow a wider range of tempos as well as fractional tempos.

Software Summary

States

Name	Objective
StSet	Set tempo and time signature
StSht	Shuttle to new location
StPly	Play sequence

Actions

Name	Activity
IDLE	No action (administer loop function)
NUMINC	Increment numerator of time sig
DENINC	Change denominator of time sig
TEMINC	Increment tempo
TEMDEC	Decrement tempo
TEMFDR	Set tempo with fader
MEAINC	Increment song measure
MEADEC	Decrement song measure
MEAFDR	Set song measure with fader
STOP	Stop the sequence
START	Play the sequence from the beginning
CONT	Play sequence from current measure/beat
MARK	Mark the current song measure
JUMP	Jump to the marked measure and play
LOOP	Jump to the marked measure and loop
STDISP	Update display for setup
NMDISP	Display time signature numerator
DNDISP	Display time signature denominator
NRDISP	Update display for normal operation
MSDISP	Display song measure
BTDISP	Display song beat
TMDISP	Display tempo
MKDISP	Display marked measure
MGDISP	Display status message
LEDTEM	Control tempo fader function LED
LEDMEA	Control measure fader function LED

Events

Name	Interface
EvIdle	Idle
EvSetup	SETUP key
EvMark	MARK key
EvJump	JUMP key
EvPlus	+ key
EvStart	START key
EvStop	STOP key
EvCont	CONT key
EvMinus	- key
EvValue	VALUE fader

State Matrix

Event	State 0:StSet NextSt,Act	State 1:StSht NextSt,Act	State 2:StPly NextSt,Act
EvIdle,	StSet,IDLE,	StSht,IDLE,	StPly,IDLE
EvPlus,	StSet,NUMINC,	StSht,MEAINC,	StPly,TEMINC
EvMinus,	StSet,DENINC,	StSht,MEADEC,	StPly,TEMDEC
EvValue,	StSet,TEMFDR,	StSht,MEAFDR,	StPly,IDLE
EvSetup,	StSet,IDLE,	StSet,STDISP,	StSet,STDISP
EvMark,	StSht,NRDISP,	StSht,MARK,	StPly,MARK
EvJump,	StSht,NRDISP,	StPly,JUMP,	StPly,LOOP
EvStart,	StSht,NRDISP,	StPly,START,	StPly,START
EvStop,	StSht,NRDISP,	StSht,IDLE,	StSht,STOP
EvCont,	StSht,NRDISP,	StPly,CONT,	StPly,IDLE

MIDI Implementation Chart

SEQUENCER REMOTE CONTROL   Date: 9-30-93
MIDItool 6   MIDI Implementation Chart   Version: 1.0

Function		Transmitted	Recognized	Remarks
Basic	Default	***	***	
Channel	Channel	***	***	
	Default	***	***	
Mode	Messages	X	X	
	Altered	***	***	
Note		X	X	
Number	True Voice	***	***	
Velocity	Note ON	X	X	
	Note OFF	X	X	
Aftertouch	Key	X	X	
	Channel	X	X	
Pitch Bend		X	X	
Controllers		X	X	
Program		X	X	
Change	True #	***	***	
System Exclusive		X	X	
System	SPP	O	X	note 1
Common	Song Select	X	X	
	Tune Request	X	X	
System	Clock	O	X	note 1
Realtime	Commands	O	X	note 1
Aux	Local ON/OFF	X	X	
	All Notes Off	X	X	
	Active Sensing	X	X	
	Reset	X	X	

Notes:
1: This device transmits System Realtime and Song Position
   Pointer (SPP) messages only

Mode 1: Omni On, Poly   Mode 2: Omni On, Mono   O:Yes
Mode 3: Omni Off, Poly   Mode 4: Omni Off, Mono   X:No

Project 7: Data Monitor

This troubleshooting tool for MIDI systems monitors the MIDI data stream and displays all MIDI messages (channel, program change, system exclusive, pressure, clock, etc.).

There are two modes, Message and Channel. In Message mode, the LCD shows the message type, value, channel, etc. Since this can only show one message at a time, the 16-LED matrix gives an overview of what's being received.

For example, suppose you press a keyboard key, apply pressure, and move the pitch bend wheel while you move a footpedal. The LCD will first show the note-on message, then the aftertouch values, then jump to the pitch bend value when you move the pitch bend wheel and change to the footpedal when you move that (the LCD always gives priority to the newest message). Meanwhile, the note-on LED will flash briefly, then the aftertouch, pitch bend, and controller LEDs will light for as long as you're using those controllers.

Channel mode shows which channels are carrying data on the matrix of 16 LEDs (e.g., if the LEDs for channel 1 and 14 are lit, then data is present on channels 1 and 14). The LCD shows "...monitoring" but is otherwise inactive.

LEDs can be latched if desired. If the LEDs are not latched ("free-running"), then the LEDs will light when messages are present and turn off when there are no messages. If latched, an LED will stay on once it receives a message. As one example of how to use this, suppose you want to see how many sequencer channels are carrying data. You could go into Channel mode, latch the LEDs, run the sequencer, then go do something else while the sequence plays. After the sequence is finished, check which LEDs are lit to see which channels had data.

Other typical MIDI Monitor uses include:

- MIDI Studio Monitor. Leave the monitor on at all times to monitor MIDI messages as they are transmitted.

- System Troubleshooter. Identify MIDI messages to determine whether they contain the desired data.

- SysEx Tool. Verify that System Exclusive messages are being transmitted properly.

- Instrument Verifier. Verify a device's MIDI Implementation Chart.

- Clock/Active Sense Indicator. Check whether MIDI clocks and/or active sense messages are being transmitted.

- MIDI Data Filter Monitor. Verify that data filters are working properly.

- Sequence Monitor. Monitor messages coming out of your sequencer, whether stored in tracks or generated internally (by issuing a Stop command, sending a program change, etc.)

Data Monitor Specs

Function: Monitor the MIDI data stream
Transmit/Receive/Both: Receive data
Inline Device: Yes
Internal Merging: No
PC Boards required: CPU, Hand H/I or Rack H/I
Inputs: MIDI In, Panel Keys (7), Fader, DC Power, On/Off Switch, LCD Contrast
Outputs: LCD, LEDs (16), MIDI Out, MIDI Thru
Enclosure: Hand Box or Rack Box
Complexity: Medium

Panel Layouts

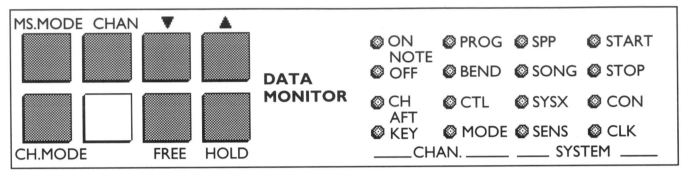

rack mount front panel

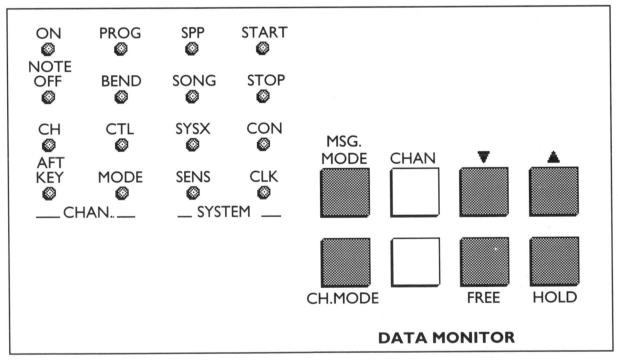

hand held front panel

Setup

1. Connect a suitable power supply (see Chapter 6) to the MIDItool power supply input.

2. Connect a MIDI cable from the MIDI Out of the device being tested to the MIDItool's MIDI In.

3. Connect a MIDI cable from the MIDItool's MIDI Thru to the MIDI In of a slave device or optional thru box.

4. Turn on the power switch.

5. Adjust the LCD contrast control for the most readable display.

Data Monitor Operations

Default Settings

When power is first applied, the screen shows:

The default settings are:

- Monitor Channel—Listens to all MIDI channels.

- Monitor Mode—Message mode.

- LED Mode—Free-running.

- Operational status—The device is waiting for the first message.

If the device under test is emitting MIDI messages, they should show up on the display.

Select the Message Monitor Channel(s)

1. In Message Mode, you can monitor all channels or one particular channel. To adjust this, press the Setup Chan key. The LCD shows:

2. Select the monitor channel using the +/– keys and/or the Value fader. To monitor all channels simultaneously, select 16 and press the + key once, or select 1 and press the – key twice. The LCD will show ALL.

3. To monitor System Messages only, select 16 and press the + key twice, or select 1 and press the – key once. The LCD will show NONE.

Message Mode

Press the Mode Message key. If no MIDI messages are present at the monitor input, the LCD shows:

Message LEDs will light for each occurrence of the associated MIDI message (on the selected message monitor channel[s], if applicable). The matrix of message LEDs indicates the presence of the following messages:

Note On	Prog. Change	Song Pointer	Start
Note Off	Pitch Bend	Song Select	Stop
Mono Pressure	Controller	Sys Ex	Continue
Poly Pressure	Channel Mode	Active Sensing	Clock

LCD Screens

The LCD gives information for the last message received. Timing Clock and Active Sense Messages are not displayed in the LCD.

When messages are received, the LCD shows one of the following screens (abbreviations are explained after the diagrams):

```
TYPE    CH KEY VEL      TYPE    CH KEY VEL
NtOn    nn bbb bbb      NtOff   nn bbb bbb

TYPE    CH KEY VAL      TYPE    CH VAL
KyAft   nn bbb bbb      ChAft   nn bbb

TYPE    CH MSB:LSB      TYPE    CH NUM
PBend   nn bbb:bbb      Prgrm   nn bbb

TYPE    CH NUM VAL      TYPE    CH STATUS
Cntrl   nn ccc bbb      Local   nn yyyyy

TYPE    CH STATUS       TYPE    CH STATUS
OmOff   nn ttttt        OmOn    nn ttttt

TYPE    CH NUM          TYPE    CH STATUS
MonOn   nn    ee        PlyOn   nn ttttt

TYPE    MSB:LSB         TYPE    NUM
SPosP   bbb:bbb         Song    bbb

TYPE                    TYPE
Tune Request           Start

TYPE                    TYPE
Continue               Stop

TYPE                    TYPE
System Exclusive       SysEx EOX

TYPE    CH STATUS       TYPE
AlOff   nn ttttt        System Reset

TYPE    TY VAL          TYPE    CH STATUS
MTC     a  dd           RsCtl   nn ttttt

TYPE          HEX
Undefined     hhh
```

The possible variable values are:

nn	= 1–16
bbb	= 0–127
ccc	= 0–120
hhh	= $00–$FF
yyyyy	= ON, OFF, or undef (undefined)
ttttt	= OK or undef (undefined)
a	= 0–7
dd	= 0–15
ee	= 0–16

The message abbreviations stand for:

NtOn	= Note On
NtOff	= Note Off
KyAft	= Key Aftertouch
ChAft	= Channel Aftertouch
PBend	= Pitch Bend
Prgrm	= Program Change
Cntrl	= Continuous Controller
Local	= Local Control
OmOff	= Omni Mode Off
OmOn	= Omni Mode On
MonOn	= Mono Mode On
PlyOn	= Poly Mode On
SPosP	= Song Position Pointer
Song	= Song Select
AlOff	= All Notes Off
MTC	= MIDI Time Code
RsCtl	= Reset All Controllers

If the MIDI receive buffer fills up, the LCD shows:

```
***WARNING***
Buffer Overflow
```

Channel Mode

Press the Ch Mode key. Channel LEDs will light when messages are received on the associated channel, regardless of which channel has been selected for message monitoring. The LCD shows:

```
CHANNEL MODE
...monitoring
```

Enable LED Hold Display

1. Press the Hold key to enter LED Hold mode. In Hold mode, LEDs will light and stay lit when an associated message is received.

2. Press the key again to clear the LEDs without leaving this mode.

Enable LED Free-Running Display

Press the Free key. After turning off all LEDs, the appropriate LED will blink when a matching message is received.

Advanced Applications

Here are some suggestions on modifications for the Data Monitor:

- Store a certain number of messages for review.

- Support message filtering so that the LCD stays focused on a particular data type.

- Support additional modes (System Common only, All System Messages only, etc.).

- Provide an indication of message timing.

- Provide further Sys Ex data extraction and classification (ID, etc.).

- Provide an indication of MIDI clock integrity.

Software Summary

States

Name	Objective
StMon	Monitor messages and channels
StSet	Set monitor channel for message mode

Actions

Name	Activity
IDLE	No action
CHINC	Increment channel
CHDEC	Decrement channel
CHFDR	Set channel with fader
LHOLD	Clear LEDs and enter LED hold mode
LFREE	Clear LEDs and enter LED free run mode
MSDISP	Parse and display current message
CHDISP	Update display for channel setup
MCDISP	Update display for monitoring channels
MMDISP	Update display for monitoring messages

Events

Name	Interface
EvIdle	Idle
EvMsg	MODE MSG key
EvChan	SETUP CHAN key
EvMinus	- key
EvPlus	+ key
EvCh	MODE CH key
EvFree	LEDs FREE key
EvHold	LEDs HOLD key
EvValue	VALUE fader
EvMsgIn	MIDI message

State Matrix

Event	State 0:StMon NextSt,Act	State 1: StSet NextSt,Act
EvIdle,	StMon,IDLE,	StSet,IDLE
EvPlus,	StMon,IDLE,	StSet,CHINC
EvMinus,	StMon,IDLE,	StSet,CHDEC
EvValue,	StMon,IDLE,	StSet,CHFDR
EvHold,	StMon,LHOLD,	StSet,LHOLD
EvFree,	StMon,LFREE,	StSet,LFREE
EvCh,	StMon,MCDISP,	StMon,MCDISP
EvMsg,	StMon,MMDISP,	StMon,MMDISP
EvChan,	StSet,CHDISP,	StSet,IDLE
EvMsgIn,	StMon,MSDISP,	StSet,IDLE

MIDI Implementation Chart

DATA MONITOR   Date: 9-30-93
MIDItool 7   MIDI Implementation Chart   Version: 1.0

Function		Transmitted	Recognized	Remarks
Basic	Default	***	1-16	note 1
Channel	Channel	***	1-16	note 2
Mode	Default	***	Mode 3	
	Messages	X	O	
	Altered	***	***	
Note		X	O	
Number	True Voice	***	***	
Velocity	Note ON	X	O	
	Note OFF	X	O	
Aftertouch	Key	X	O	
	Channel	X	O	
Pitch Bend		X	O	
Controllers		X	O	
Program		X	O	
Change	True #	***	***	
System Exclusive		X	O	
System	SPP	X	O	
Common	Song Select	X	O	
	Tune Request	X	O	
System	Clock	X	O	
Realtime	Commands	X	O	
Aux	Local ON/OFF	X	O	
	All Notes Off	X	O	
	Active Sensing	X	O	
	Reset	X	O	

Notes:
1: This device receives on ALL channels at once
2: Receive channel is programmable (1-16, ALL or NONE)

Mode 1: Omni On, Poly   Mode 2: Omni On, Mono   O:Yes
Mode 3: Omni Off, Poly   Mode 4: Omni Off, Mono   X:No

Project 8: Relay Driver

Now you can control the world with MIDI by using controller messages to trigger up to four relays. These could drive lights, control a tape recorder's play/stop/fast forward/rewind functions, turn on your MIDI coffee maker, or substitute for footswitches with guitar amps and other non-MIDI devices. (The particularly paranoid could even come up with a MIDI-controlled home security system.) Typical uses include:

- Relay Controller. Control external equipment that allows relay control or switching.

- Tape Deck Synchronizer. Start and stop a tape deck at precise beats in the sequence.

- Lighting Controller. A sequencer can drive relays in time with music (or in time with anything else, for that matter).

- Multi-Media Presentation Coordinator. Use the relays to control slide projectors, laser disc players, or other presentation equipment.

- Footswitch Substitute. Use a relay wherever you want to automate footswitch operation with MIDI commands (this is very useful for triggering guitar preamp or amp channel switching with a MIDI sequencer).

- Computer Interface. Use the relay driver to route and switch phone and data transmission lines.

Caution: The relays used in the MIDItools Relay Expansion Board sold by PAVO are rated for no more than 30 watts (0.3A at 125 VAC). To switch devices that consume more power, use the MIDItools relay to trigger a heavy-duty relay.

Relay Driver Specs

Function: Translator
Transmit/Receive/Both: Receive
Inline Device: No
Internal Merging: No
PC Boards required: CPU, Rack H/I, Relay Driver
Inputs: MIDI In, Panel Keys (8), Fader, DC Power, On/Off Switch, LCD Contrast
Outputs: LCD, LEDs (4), MIDI Thru, Relays(4)
Enclosure: Rack Box only
Complexity: High

Panel Layout

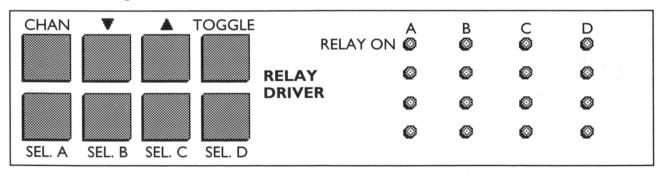

rack mount front panel

Setup

1. This tool uses the Relay Driver Expansion PC board (see sidebar) to provide an interface between the MiDitools computer and the outside world. Connect the Relay Driver Expansion PC board to the CPU board's expansion connector with a ribbon cable.

2. Connect a suitable power supply (see Chapter 6) to the MiDitool power supply input.

3. Patch a MiDi cable from the master device's MiDi Out to the MiDitool's MiDi In.

4. Connect appropriate cables from the MiDitool Relay Outs to relay-controlled hardware.

5. Turn on power.

6. Adjust LCD Contrast for the most readable display.

Relay/Pulse Driver Operations

Default Settings

When you turn on power, the LCD shows:

- Receive Channel—1

- All Relays—Open

- All Controllers—1

- Operational status—The MiDi receive channel is available for editing.

Set the Global MiDi Receive Channel

1. Press the Setup Chan key.

2. Select the global receive channel (1–16) with the Value fader, and/or the +/– keys.

Configure the Relays

1. Press the Select key (A, B, C or D) to select a relay for configuration and/or manual use. (If you are moving to this screen from the MiDi setup channel screen, you may need to press the Select Key twice—once to select the relay configuration screen, and once to select the relay). If A is selected, the display shows:

The arrow points to the currently selected relay. bbb is the currently assigned controller number (0-120).

2. To assign a controller number to a selected relay, use the +/– keys and/or Value fader. For proper operation, each relay should have a unique controller number.

Trigger the Relays

1. To trigger the relays via MIDI, send a controller value of less than 64 to close the relay, and a value of 64 or higher to open the relay. The corresponding Relay On LED lights while the relay is closed.

2. To trigger the relays manually, press the Toggle key. The currently selected relay will change state, as confirmed by the associated Relay On LED.

Advanced Applications

Here are some suggested Relay Driver modifications:

- Allow for higher current loads by driving power transistors and using a separate power supply for the relay coils.

- Replace the keys with footswitches for hands-free control.

- Replace the relays with AC solenoids to drive AC equipment (fans, motors, etc.).

- Allow each relay to operate from its own channel.

- Support other controllers (pitch bend, etc.).

- Build the relay driver board into the equipment being controlled.

Software Summary

States

Name	Objective
StCh	Set receive channel
StRly	Configure relays

Actions

Name	Activity
IDLE	No action
CHINC	Increment channel
CHDEC	Decrement channel
CHFDR	Set channel with fader
ASEL	Select Relay A
BSEL	Select Relay B
CSEL	Select Relay C
DSEL	Select Relay D
CTLINC	Increment Controller of selected relay
CTLDEC	Decrement Controller of selected relay
CTLFDR	Select Controller with fader
TOG	Toggle current relay status
RUPD8	Update relay status
PROC	Process incoming controller messages
CDISP	Update display for changing channel
RDISP	Update display for configuring relays
SDISP	Update relay status display
ARWCLR	Clear LCD cursor arrow

Events

Name	Interface
EvIdle	Idle
EvChan	SETUP CHAN key
EvMinus	SETUP - key
EvPlus	SETUP + key
EvTog	TOG key
EvA	SELECT A key
EvB	SELECT B key
EvC	SELECT C key
EvD	SELECT D key
EvValue	VALUE fader
EvMsgIn	MIDI message

State Matrix

Event	State 0:StCh NextSt,Act	State 1:StRly NextSt,Act
EvIdle,	StCh,IDLE,	StRly,IDLE
EvMinus,	StCh,CHDEC	StRly,CTLDEC
EvPlus,	StCh,CHINC,	StRly,CTLINC
EvValue,	StCh,CHFDR,	StRly,CTLFDR
EvChan,	StCh,IDLE,	StCh,CDISP
EvCtl,	StRly,RDISP,	StRly,IDLE
EvA,	StRly,RDISP,	StRly,ASEL
EvB,	StRly,RDISP,	StRly,BSEL
EvC,	StRly,RDISP,	StRly,CSEL
EvD,	StRly,RDISP,	StRly,DSEL
EvTog,	StCh,TOG,	StRly,TOG
EvMsgIn,	StCh,PROC,	StRly,PROC

Mɪᴅɪ Implementation Chart

RELAY DRIVER   Date: 9-30-93
Mɪᴅɪtool 8   Mɪᴅɪ Implementation Chart   Version: 1.0

Function		Transmitted	Recognized	Remarks
Basic	Default	***	1	
Channel	Channel	***	1-16	note 1
Mode	Default	***	Mode 3	
	Messages	X	X	
	Altered	***	***	
Note		X	X	
Number	True Voice	***	***	
Velocity	Note ON	X	X	
	Note OFF	X	X	
Aftertouch	Key	X	X	
	Channel	X	X	
Pitch Bend		X	X	
Controllers	0-120	X	O	notes 2, 3
Program		X	X	
Change	True #	***	***	
System Exclusive		X	X	
System	SPP	X	X	
Common	Song Select	X	X	
	Tune Request	X	X	
System	Clock	X	X	
Realtime	Commands	X	X	
Aux	Local ON/OFF	X	X	
	All Notes Off	X	X	
	Active Sensing	X	X	
	Reset	X	X	

Notes:
1: Receive channel is programmable
2: Controller numbers are programmable (4 relay triggers)
3: Relays change state using controller values:
   val < 64 closes relay
   val > 63 opens relay

Mode 1: Omni On, Poly   Mode 2: Omni On, Mono   O:Yes
Mode 3: Omni Off, Poly   Mode 4: Omni Off, Mono   X:No

About the Relay Driver Expansion Board

This PC board provides 4 relays, each driven by a transistor connected to an output from a shift register. Relays are turned on and off by shifting data into the shift register, which causes the corresponding outputs to turn on (logical 1) and off (logical 0).

The relays have a single pole, double-throw switching configuration. The stereo jacks are wired so that the ground lead is the pole, the tip the normally open relay connection (*i.e.*, when you apply power to the relay by inputting a controller value <64 this connection closes), and the ring the normally closed relay connection (when you apply power to the relay this connection opens). This will interface with most guitar amp footswitch connections with no modifications, since footswitching jacks generally switch the tip connection to ground. Leave the ring open; it would not be needed for this application.

The relay contacts are rated at 30 watts (1 amp at 30 volts, or 0.3 amps at 125 volts). This is adequate for low-level switching applications such as footswitches, but to control lights and other devices that draw lots of current, it will be necessary to drive these with a heavier-duty relay and use the MIDItool's relays to turn the heavier-duty relay on and off.

You can also use this MIDItool to provide pulsed outputs by wiring the relay to turn on/off the desired voltage.

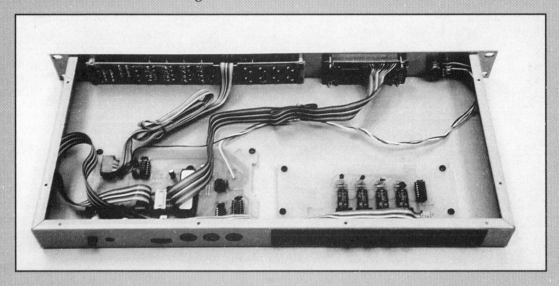

The relay driver expansion board mounts in the lower right corner.

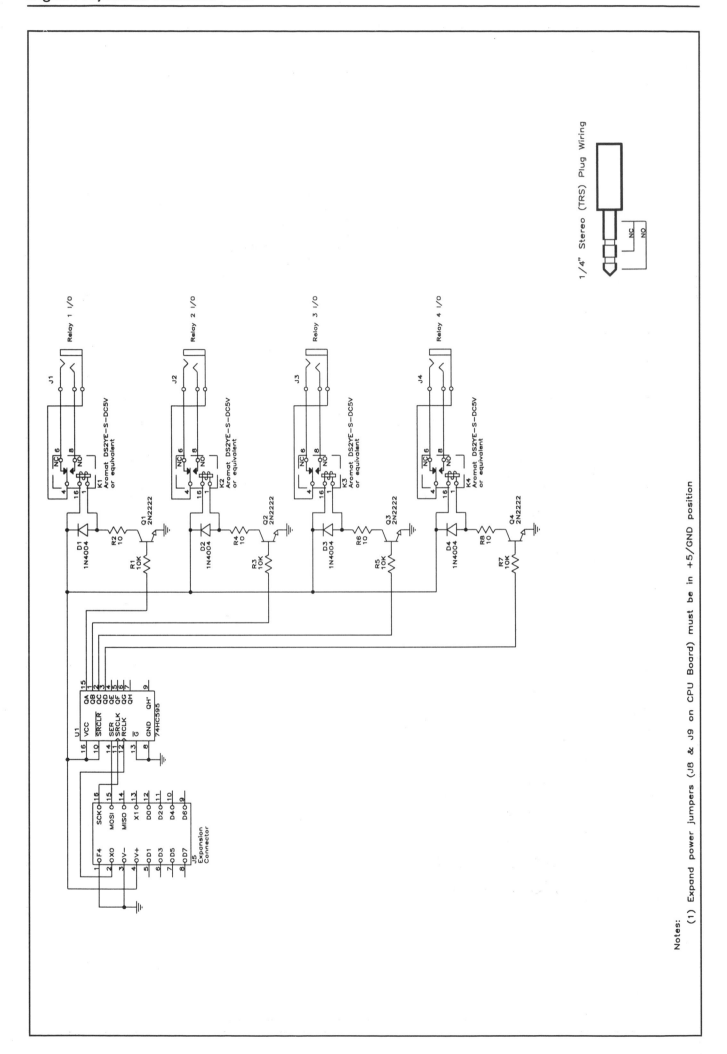

Notes:

(1) Expand power jumpers (J8 & J9 on CPU Board) must be in +5/GND position

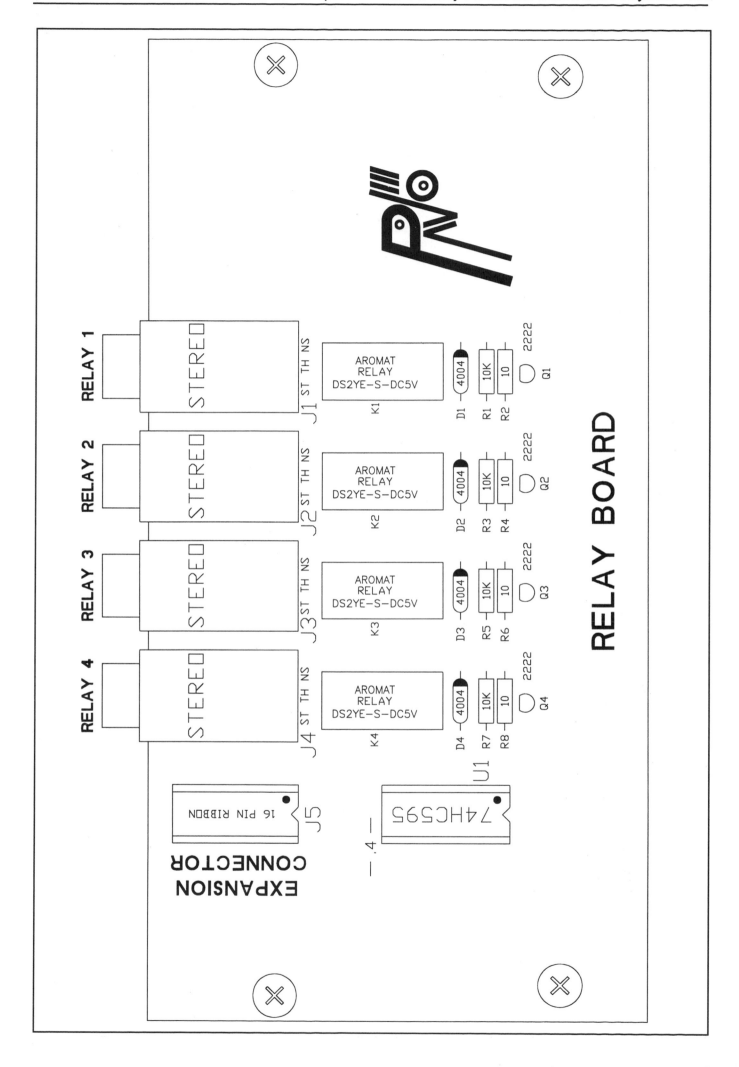

Project 9: Control Thinner

Having too much controller data in the MIDI stream can not only cause jittery timing; it can also overload some synthesizers and use up sequencer memory unnecessarily. Fortunately, much controller data is not really needed, and can be "thinned" without any negative side effects.

This project thins the amount of controller data passing through it, by a variable amount. Typical uses include:

- Sequencer Helper. Patch it after your sequencer's output to thin the number of controller messages emanating from the sequencer.

- MIDI Master Controller Helper. Thin controller data generated by the master controller to minimize the amount of data it takes up in a sequence.

- Data Filter. Filter out control messages by setting the thinning value to 0.

- Troubleshooting Tool. Use the Control Thinner interactively while the sequence is playing to determine if a slave device is being overloaded with MIDI data.

- MIDI Guitar and Wind Controller Tamer. These types of MIDI controllers generate a lot of controller data, which can overload some sequencers and sound modules. Thinning the controller data solves these problems.

- Slave-Specific Thinner. Patch this project at the input of devices that seem most likely to have problems (e.g., multitimbral sound generators and many older pieces of MIDI gear) when presented with too much MIDI data.

- Effects Generator. Apply extensive thinning to create unusual controller responses.

Control Thinner Specs

Function: Filter
Transmit/Receive/Both: Both
Inline Device: Yes
Internal Merging: No
PC Boards required: CPU, Hand H/I or Rack H/I
Inputs: MIDI In, Panel Keys (8), Fader, DC Power, On/Off Switch, LCD Contrast
Outputs: LCD, LEDs (3), MIDI Out, MIDI Thru
Enclosure: Hand Box or Rack Box
Complexity: Low

Panel Layouts

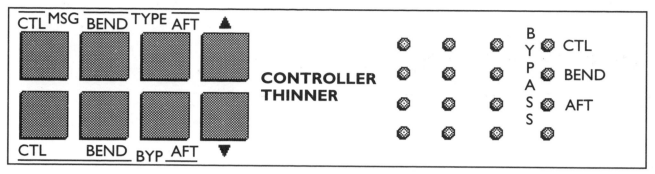

rack mount front panel

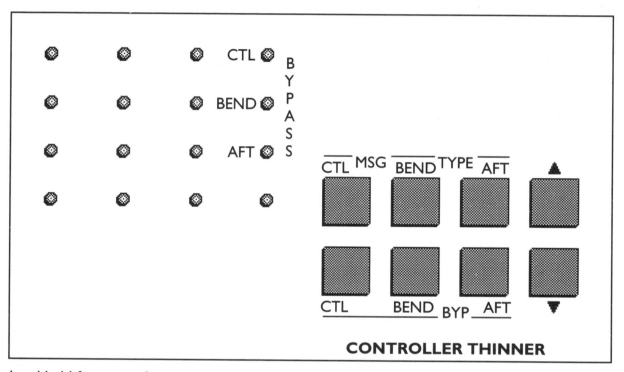

hand held front panel

Setup

1. Connect a suitable power supply (see Chapter 6) to the MIDItool power supply input.

2. Patch the master device's MIDI Out to the MIDItool's MIDI In.

3. Connect a MIDI cable from the MIDItool's MIDI Out to the MIDI In of the slave device or thru box.

4. Turn on the power switch.

5. Adjust LCD contrast control for the most readable display.

Control Thinner Operations

Default Settings
When power is first applied, the screen shows:

- Controller Thin Value—31

- Pitch Bend Thin Value—31

- Aftertouch Thin Value—31

- All Thinners—Active

- Operational status—The controller Thin Value is available for editing.

Select a Message Type and the Amount of Thinning
The LCD's upper line shows the type of data being thinned, and the lower line, the degree of thinning for each data type.

The possible values for nn (thinning amount) range from 0 to 31. Thinning is channel independent; all controller messages are thinned and retransmitted according to the assigned thinning amount.

If nn = 0, every message is thinned (rejected). If nn = 31, every 32nd message of that type is thinned (rejected). In other words, the thinner rejects every nn+1 message; nn also represents the number of messages that will be passed before rejecting the first message.

1. Select a message type with the Message Type keys: Ctl (controllers 0–63), Bend (pitch bend), or Aft (channel and key aftertouch). The arrow points to the parameter being edited.

2. Edit the amount of thinning for the selected message type using the +/– keys and/or Value fader.

Bypass the Thinner
Press the associated Bypass key (Ctl, Bend or Aft) to disable thinning of that message type. The appropriate Bypass LED will light. Pressing the Bypass key again enables thinning and turns off the LED.

Advanced Applications
Here are some ideas on how to modify the Control Thinner:

- Replace the bypass keys with footswitches.

- Allow for the full range of control change numbers.

- Change the thinning algorithm so that messages are retransmitted only if the change is greater than some selected value.

- Allow a greater thinning range.

- Support channel-specific thinning.

- Allow for controller-specific thinning.

- Allow for separate key and channel aftertouch thinning.

Software Summary

States

Name	Objective
StCtl	Select control change thinning
StBnd	Select pitch bend thinning
StAft	Select aftertouch thinning

Actions

Name	Activity
IDLE	No action
CTLINC	Increment control thinning value
CTLDEC	Decrement control thinning value
CTLFDR	Set control thinning value with fader
BNDINC	Increment bend thinning value
BNDDEC	Decrement bend thinning value
BNDFDR	Set bend thinning value with fader
AFTINC	Increment aftertouch thinning value
AFTDEC	Decrement aftertouch thinning value
AFTFDR	Set aftertouch thin value with fader
CTLBY	Toggle control thinning bypass
BNDBY	Toggle bend thinning bypass
AFTBY	Toggle aftertouch thinning bypass
CDISP	Update display for control change
BDISP	Update display for pitch bend
ADISP	Update display for aftertouch

Events

Name	Interface
EvIdle	Idle
EvCtl	MESSAGE TYPE CTL key
EvBnd	MESSAGE TYPE BND key
EvAft	MESSAGE TYPE AFT key
EvPlus	+ key
EvBCtl	BYPASS CTL key
EvBBnd	BYPASS BEND key
EvBAft	BYPASS AFT key
EvMinus	- key
EvValue	VALUE fader

State Matrix

Event	State 0:StCtl NextSt,Act	State 1:StBnd NextSt,Act	State 2: StAft NextSt,Act
EvIdle,	StCtl,IDLE,	StBnd,IDLE,	StAft,IDLE
EvPlus,	StCtl,CTLINC,	StBnd,BNDINC,	StAft,AFTINC
EvMinus,	StCtl,CTLDEC,	StBnd,BNDDEC,	StAft,AFTDEC
EvValue,	StCtl,CTLFDR,	StBnd,BNDFDR,	StAft,AFTFDR
EvCtl,	StCtl,IDLE,	StCtl,CDISP,	StCtl,CDISP
EvBnd,	StBnd,BDISP,	StBnd,IDLE,	StBnd,BDISP
EvAft,	StAft,ADISP,	StAft,ADISP,	StAft,IDLE
EvBCtl,	StCtl,CTLBY,	StBnd,CTLBY,	StAft,CTLBY
EvBBnd,	StCtl,BNDBY,	StBnd,BNDBY,	StAft,BNDBY
EvBAft,	StCtl,AFTBY,	StBnd,AFTBY,	StAft,AFTBY

MIDI Implementation Chart

```
CONTROL THINNER                                    Date: 9-30-93
MIDItool 9              MIDI Implementation Chart   Version: 1.0
```

Function		Transmitted	Recognized	Remarks
Basic	Default	***	1-16	note 1
Channel	Channel	***	***	
	Default	***	Mode 1	
Mode	Messages	X	X	
	Altered	***	***	
Note		X	X	
Number	True Voice	***	***	
Velocity	Note ON	X	X	
	Note OFF	X	X	
Aftertouch	Key	X	O	
	Channel	X	O	
Pitch Bend		X	O	
Controllers	0-63	X	O	
Program		X	X	
Change	True #	***	***	
System Exclusive		X	X	
System	SPP	X	X	
Common	Song Select	X	X	
	Tune Request	X	X	
System	Clock	X	X	
Realtime	Commands	X	X	
Aux	Local ON/OFF	X	X	
	All Notes Off	X	X	
	Active Sensing	X	X	
	Reset	X	X	

```
Notes:
1: Device operates in OMNI mode

Mode 1: Omni On, Poly     Mode 2: Omni On, Mono      O:Yes
Mode 3: Omni Off, Poly    Mode 4: Omni Off, Mono     X:No
```

Project 10: Channel Filter

The Channel Filter sets whether data for each MIDI channel will pass from the Channel Filter MIDI In to the MIDI Out. Each channel can have its own operating status. Typical uses include:

- Sequencer Add-On. Patch the Channel Filter between a sequencer's MIDI Out and the MIDI gear it drives to mute or solo tracks remotely.

- Data Filter. Reduce the amount of data presented to a device's MIDI In by filtering out data on all channels not intended for the device.

- Data Monitor. Use the LEDs to monitor each MIDI channel.

- Global Channel Protector. On devices with a global channel, use the Channel Filter to block data on that channel.

- Channel Message Filter. Filter out all Channel Messages and pass only System Messages.

Channel Filter Specs

Function: Filter
Transmit/Receive/Both: Both
Inline Device: Yes
Internal Merging: No
PC Boards required: CPU, Hand H/I or Rack H/I
Inputs: MIDI In, Panel Keys (6), DC Power, On/Off Switch, LCD Contrast
Outputs: LCD, LEDs (16), MIDI Out, MIDI Thru
Enclosure: Hand Box or Rack Box
Complexity: Medium

Panel Layouts

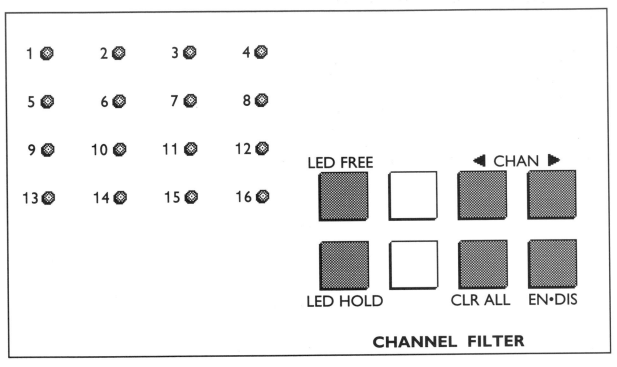

rack mount front panel

hand held front panel

Setup

1. Connect a suitable power supply (see Chapter 6) to the MIDItool power supply input.

2. Patch a MIDI cable from the master device's MIDI Out to the MIDItool's MIDI In.

3. Connect a MIDI cable from the MIDItool's MIDI Out to the MIDI In of the slave device or thru box.

4. Turn on the power.

5. Adjust the LCD Contrast control for the best display contrast.

Channel Filter Operations

Default Settings
On power-up, the LCD shows:

`1234567890123456`

Note that channel 10 is shown by 0, 11 by the rightmost 1, 12 by the rightmost 2, 13 by the rightmost 3, etc. The default settings are:

- All Filters—disabled

- LED Mode—free running

- Operational status—The Channel 1 filter is available for editing (as indicated by the underline)

Select a Channel Filter
Select a filter using the Select < > keys. 16 independent channel filters are available. The cursor underlines the selected filter.

The LEDs monitor the incoming data. If a message is received on a particular channel, the associated LED lights regardless of the filter status.

Enable or Disable the Selected Filter
Press the Enable/Disable key to enable or disable the selected filter. When the filter is enabled (as indicated by an asterisk below the number), all messages received on that channel are rejected (*i.e.,* not transmitted out the MIDI Out port).

Disable All Filters
Press the Clear All key to disable all filters. All asterisks will disappear.

Enable the Data Hold Display
1. Press the LED Hold key. Upon receiving data on a particular channel, the associated LED will light and stay lit.

2. Press this key again to clear the LEDs without leaving the Data Hold mode.

Enable the Free-Running Display
Press the LED Free key. After turning off all LEDs, the appropriate LED will blink when a matching message is received.

Advanced Applications
Here are some ideas for Channel Filter modifications:

- Support a remote data monitor display with larger visual indicators.

- Interchange the LED/LCD displays (Data Monitor/Filter Status).

- Replace the En/Dis key with a footswitch.

- Allow message-specific filtering.

- Have a single key for enabling all filters.

- Add a function to filter Sys Ex only.

Software Summary

States

Name	Objective
StFree	Filter in LED free run mode
StHold	Filter in LED hold mode

Actions

Name	Activity
IDLE	No action
FILINC	Increment message filter
FILDEC	Decrement message filter
FILTOG	Toggle filter status
RESET	Disable all filters
LHOLD	Clear LEDs and enter LED hold mode
LFREE	Clear LEDs and enter LED free run mode
SDISP	Update display for enabling filters
MDISP	Control LED message monitor

Events

Name	Cause
EvIdle	Idle
EvFree	LEDs FREE key
EvLeft	<— key
EvRight	—> key
EvHold	LEDs HOLD key
EvClear	STATUS CLEAR key
EvOnOff	STATUS OnOff key
EvMsg	MIDI Message

State Matrix

Event	State 0:StFree NextSt,Act	State 1:StHold NextSt,Act
EvIdle,	StFree,IDLE,	StHold,IDLE
EvLeft,	StFree,FILDEC,	StHold,FILDEC
EvRight,	StFree,FILINC,	StHold,FILINC
EvOnOff,	StFree,FILTOG,	StHold,FILTOG
EvClear,	StFree,RESET,	StHold,RESET
EvFree,	StFree,IDLE,	StFree,LFREE
EvHold,	StHold,LHOLD,	StHold,LHOLD
EvMsg,	StFree,MDISP,	StHold,MDISP

MIDI Implementation Chart

```
CHANNEL FILTER                                           Date: 9-30-93
MIDItool 10          MIDI Implementation Chart          Version: 1.0
```

Function		Transmitted	Recognized	Remarks
Basic	Default	***	1-16	note 1
Channel	Channel	***	1-16	note 2
	Default	***	Mode 1	
Mode	Messages	X	O	
	Altered	***	***	
Note		X	O	
Number	True Voice	***	***	
Velocity	Note ON	X	O	
	Note OFF	X	O	
Aftertouch	Key	X	O	
	Channel	X	O	
Pitch Bend		X	O	
Controllers		X	O	
Program		X	O	
Change	True #	***	***	
System Exclusive		X	X	
System	SPP	X	X	
Common	Song Select	X	X	
	Tune Request	X	X	
System	Clock	X	X	
Realtime	Commands	X	X	
Aux	Local ON/OFF	X	O	
	All Notes Off	X	O	
	Active Sensing	X	X	
	Reset	X	X	

```
Notes:
1: Device operates in OMNI mode
2: Filters for messages on any channel can be enabled or
   disabled by the user

Mode 1: Omni On, Poly      Mode 2: Omni On, Mono      O:Yes
Mode 3: Omni Off, Poly     Mode 4: Omni Off, Mono     X:No
```

Project 11: Data Filter

The MIDI data stream is like any other stream—you don't want to clog it up, or it won't flow as well. Some controllers generate data that is not needed by equipment in a MIDI system, but this data nonetheless becomes part of the MIDI stream along with data you do want.

The Data Filter analyzes incoming MIDI data and passes or rejects specific messages (note, program change, system exclusive, system common, system realtime, poly pressure, mono pressure, pitch bend, controllers) on all MIDI channels.

Typical applications include:

- Master Controller Filter. Suppose your keyboard generates aftertouch data. It produces this every time you press on the keys whether the data is used in the patch or not, which increases the MIDI stream's data density. If you record several parts in a sequencer, every part will record this aftertouch information. Although sequencers often let you filter out data while recording, the Data Filter does the same thing and is applicable to more than just sequencers.

- Drum Machine Helper. If you're using a drum machine as a drum module driven by a sequencer, you want to make sure the drum doesn't get triggered by the clock signals and start playing its own patterns. Hopefully the drum machine will let you disable MIDI sync, but if it doesn't (or if it defaults to external clock and you're tired of resetting it each time), the Data Filter can solve the problem once and for all by filtering out system real time messages.

- Slave Data Reducer. Use the Data Filter to process data on its way to the input of a slave device, and set the filter to remove any data types not implemented by the slave. This reduces the amount of data presented to the slave, and helps minimize situations where the slave's input overflows from excessive data.

- Data Monitor. The LEDs indicate the presence of various message types, regardless of the filter settings. This is useful for determining what type of MIDI signals a device transmits.

- MIDI Channel Doubler. Suppose you have only one MIDI channel left from your sequencer, but want to control both a drum sound module and change program settings on a MIDI-controlled signal processor. Use the Data Filter to either prevent notes from entering the signal processor, or program change messages from entering the drum module.

- Synchonizer Filter. Many of today's keyboards include a built-in sequencer. Synchronizing this to a computer-based sequencer expands the effective number of channels, but if the keyboard receives note messages as well as sync messages from the sequencer, it will attempt to play back the sequence from the computer as well as the one being generated internally. The Data Filter can filter everything out except sync messages between the computer and keyboard sequencer.

- Active Sensing Censor. Very old MIDI gear often generates Active Sensing messages. Few modern pieces of gear recognize this, and in fact, can even be confused by the presence of Active Sensing messages. Filtering out System Realtime messages, which include Active Sensing, takes care of that.

Data Filter Specs

Function: Filters various types of messages from the MIDI data stream.
Transmit/Receive/Both: Both
Inline Device: Yes
Internal Merging: No
PC Boards required: CPU, Hand H/I or Rack H/I
Inputs: MIDI In, Panel Keys (6), DC Power, On/Off Switch, LCD Contrast
Outputs: LCD, LEDs (9), MIDI Out, MIDI Thru
Enclosure: Hand Box or Rack Box
Complexity: Medium

Panel Layouts

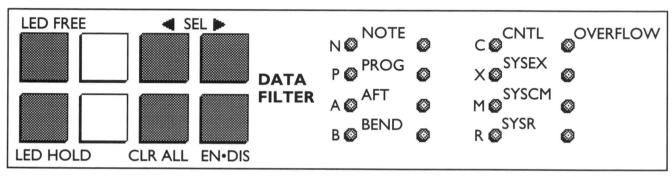

rack mount front panel

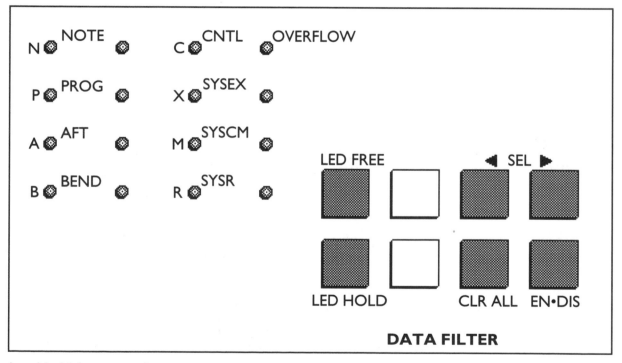

hand held front panel

Setup

1. Connect a suitable power supply (see Chapter 6) to the MIDItool power supply input.

2. Connect a MIDI cable from the master device's MIDI Out (this generates the data to be filtered) to the MIDItool's MIDI In.

3. Patch the Miditool's Midi Out to a slave device or Midi thru box Midi In.

4. Turn on the power switch.

5. Adjust LCD Contrast for the most readable display.

Data Filter Operations

Default Settings

On power-up, the display shows:

- All Filters—disabled

- LED Mode—free running (LEDs show data only as long as its present)

- Operational status—The first filter is available to be enabled, as shown by the arrow cursor pointing at it.

Select A Data Filter

Select a filter using the <– and –> Select keys; the LCD cursor arrow points to the selected filter. Eight independent data filters are available:

LCD Code	Message(s) Filtered	LED Code
N	Note on and note off	Note
P	Program Change	Prog
A	Channel and Key Aftertouch	Aft
B	Pitch Bend	Bend
C	Control Change (incl. Mode Messages)	Cntl
X	System EXclusive	Sysex
M	System CoMmon	Syscm
R	System Realtime	Sysr

Enable or Disable the Selected Filter

Press the Status En/Dis key to enable or disable the selected filter. When enabled, as indicated by an asterisk (*) under the associated LCD code letter for the filter, the filter rejects all messages of the corresponding type. These messages therefore do not appear at the Midi Out.

In the following example, Aftertouch, System Exclusive, and System Realtime messages are being filtered, and the System Common filter is ready for editing:

Disable All Filters

Press the Status Clear key to disable all filters. All asterisks will disappear.

Monitor the Received Data Stream

The LEDs monitor incoming data. If a message is received that matches the filter type, the appropriate LED lights regardless of the filter status.

Enable the Data Hold Display

Press the LEDs Hold key. The LEDs will light and stay lit when a matching message is received. Pressing the key again clears the LEDs without leaving this mode.

Enable the Free Running Display
Press the LEDs Free key; all LEDs will turn off, after which appropriate LEDs will blink when matching messages are received.

Data Buffer Overflow Indicator
The Overflow LED indicates when the MIDI receive buffer is full. Data errors may result from overflow. Then again, they may not (in any event, you've been warned!).

Advanced Applications
Here are some possible Data Filter modifications:

- Support a remote data monitor display with larger visual indicators.

- Interchange the LED/LCD displays (Data Monitor/Filter Status).

- Replace the Status En/Dis or Status Clear key with a footswitch.

- Allow channel-specific filtering.

- Let a single key enable all filters.

- Include a key for enabling all System Messages.

- Include a key for enabling a MIDI Clock filter.

Software Summary

States

Name	Objective
StFree	Filter in LED free run mode
StHold	Filter in LED hold mode

Actions

Name	Activity
IDLE	No action
FILINC	Increment message filter
FILDEC	Decrement message filter
FILTOG	Toggle filter status
RESET	Disable all filters
LHOLD	Clear LEDs and enter LED hold mode
LFREE	Clear LEDs and enter LED free run mode
SDISP	Update display for enabling filters
MDISP	Control LED message monitor

Events

Name	Interface
EvIdle	Idle
EvFree	LEDs FREE key
EvLeft	<— key
EvRight	—> key
EvHold	LEDs HOLD key
EvClear	STATUS CLEAR key
EvOnOff	STATUS OnOff key
EvMsg	MIDI message

State Matrix

```
                State 0:StFree      State 1:StHold
Event           NextSt,Act          NextSt,Act

EvIdle,         StFree,IDLE,        StHold,IDLE
EvLeft,         StFree,FILDEC,      StHold,FILDEC
EvRight,        StFree,FILINC,      StHold,FILINC
EvOnOff,        StFree,FILTOG,      StHold,FILTOG
EvClear,        StFree,RESET,       StHold,RESET
EvFree,         StFree,IDLE,        StFree,LFREE
EvHold,         StHold,LHOLD,       StHold,LHOLD
EvMsg,          StFree,MDISP,       StHold,MDISP
```

MIDI Implementation Chart

```
DATA FILTER                                    Date: 9-30-93
MIDItool 11         MIDI Implementation Chart  Version: 1.0
```

Function		Transmitted	Recognized	Remarks
Basic	Default	***	1-16	note 1
Channel	Channel	***	***	
	Default	***	Mode 1	note 2
Mode	Messages	X	O	
	Altered	***	***	
Note		X	O	note 2
Number	True Voice	***	***	
Velocity	Note ON	X	O	
	Note OFF	X	O	
Aftertouch	Key	X	O	note 2
	Channel	X	O	note 2
Pitch Bend		X	O	note 2
Controllers		X	O	note 2
Program		X	O	note 2
Change	True #	***	***	
System Exclusive		X	O	note 2
System	SPP	X	O	note 2
Common	Song Select	X	O	note 2
	Tune Request	X	O	note 2
System	Clock	X	O	note 2
Realtime	Commands	X	O	note 2
Aux	Local ON/OFF	X	O	note 2
	All Notes Off	X	O	note 2
	Active Sensing	X	O	note 2
	Reset	X	O	note 2

```
Notes:
1: Device operates in OMNI mode
2: Filters for messages of selected types can be enabled or
   disabled by the user

Mode 1: Omni On, Poly    Mode 2: Omni On, Mono     O:Yes
Mode 3: Omni Off, Poly   Mode 4: Omni Off, Mono    X:No
```

Project 12: Channel Mapper

This may not be the most glamorous project in the world, but in some situations it can be a real lifesaver. The Channel Mapper remaps incoming messages on one MIDI channel to a different MIDI channel, and sends the remapped data to the MIDI out. Operation is simple—just specify the channel number whose data you want to remap, then the channel number to which the data should be remapped. Typical uses include:

- Keyboard Enhancer. Some older keyboards, such as the Yamaha DX7, transmit on one channel only. The Channel Mapper lets it transmit on any channel.

- Sequencing Experimentation Tool. Set several sounds to different channels; remap a track to audition the different sounds.

- Track Router. Change the routing of a specific sequence track to various sounds in a multi-timbral module.

- Global Channel Selector. Route a track to the global channel of a multi-timbral sound module.

- Sequencer Enhancer. Simplify your life if your sequencer does not allow for easy channel modification.

- Drum Machine Enhancer. Some drum machines transmit on one channel only (usually channel 10), which can be limiting if you want to drive other drum sound modules or samplers with drum sounds. Use the Channel Mapper to remap data to any other channel.

- Diagnostic Tool. Loop a sequenced track, and map the data to each of the 16 channels to verify that all channels in your system are responding properly.

Channel Mapper Specs

Function: Modifies MIDI messages by changing the channel number.
Transmit/Receive/Both: Both
Inline Device: Yes
Internal Merging: No
PC Boards required: CPU, Hand H/I or Rack H/I
Inputs: MIDI In, Panel Keys (4), Fader, DC Power, On/Off Switch, LCD Contrast
Outputs: LCD, LED (1), MIDI Out, MIDI Thru
Enclosure: Hand Box or Rack Box
Complexity: Low

Panel Layouts

rack mount front panel

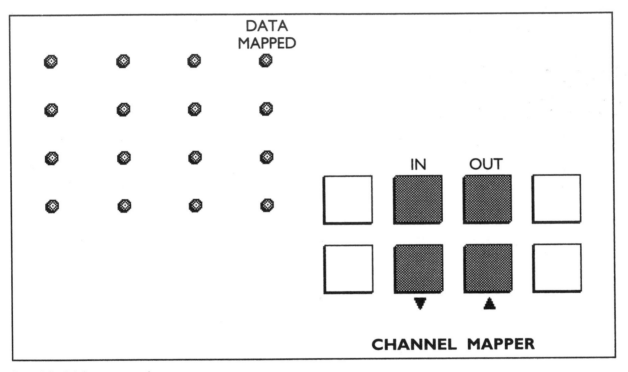

hand held front panel

Setup

1. Connect a suitable power supply (see Chapter 6) to the MIDItool power supply input.

2. Connect a MIDI cable from the master device's MIDI Out (this generates the data to be remapped) to the MIDItool's MIDI In.

3. Patch the MIDItool's MIDI Out to a slave device or MIDI thru box MIDI In.

4. Turn on the power switch.

5. Adjust LCD Contrast for the most readable display.

Channel Mapper Operation

Default Settings

When you first turn on power, the display shows:

The default settings are:

- In Channel—1

- Out Channel—1

- Operational status—The input channel is available for editing.

Remapping a Channel

The LCD's lower line shows both the input (original) and output (remapped) channels.

The variable, nn, represents the channel number and ranges from 1–16.

1. Press the Channel In key. The arrow points to the In parameter to indicate it's ready for editing.

2. Select the channel to be mapped using the +/– keys and/or Value fader.

3. Press the Channel Out key. The arrow points to the Out parameter to indicate it's ready for editing.

4. Select the new channel number with the +/– keys and/or Value fader.

All messages on the In channel are retransmitted on the new Out channel (data bytes are not modified). The Data Mapped LED lights when data is being mapped.

Advanced Applications

Here are some ideas on how to build a better mapper:

- Allow multiple mappings so that more than one MIDI channel can be remapped at a time.

- Be able to remap each channel to more than one channel.

- Remap any channel to all channels (a pseudo-omni mode).

- Allow for message-specific mapping and/or filtering (*e.g.*, remap only notes that meet particular criteria).

Software Summary

States

Name	Objective
StCIn	Select input channel
StCOut	Select output channel

Actions

Name	Activity
IDLE	No action (administer LED)
CIINC	Increment channel IN number
CIDEC	Decrement channel IN number
CIFDR	Set channel IN with fader
COINC	Increment channel OUT number
CODEC	Decrement channel OUT number
COFDR	Set channel OUT with fader
CIDISP	Update channel IN display
CODISP	Update channel OUT display

Events

Name	Interface
EvIdle	Idle
EvChanIn	CHANNEL IN key
EvChanOut	CHANNEL OUT key
EvMinus	- key
EvPlus	+ key
EvValue	VALUE fader

State Matrix

Event	State 0: StCin NextSt,Act	State 1: StCout NextSt,Act
EvIdle,	StCin,IDLE,	StCout,IDLE
EvPlus,	StCin,CIINC,	StCout,COINC
EvMinus,	StCin,CIDEC,	StCout,CODEC
EvValue,	StCin,CIFDR,	StCout,COFDR
EvChanIn,	StCin,IDLE,	StCin,CIDISP
EvChanOut,	StCout,CODISP,	StCout,IDLE

MIDI Implementation Chart

CHANNEL MAPPER   Date: 9-30-93
MIDItool 12   MIDI Implementation Chart   Version: 1.0

Function		Transmitted	Recognized	Remarks
Basic	Default	1	1	note 1
Channel	Channel	1-16	1-16	note 2
	Default	***	Mode 3	
Mode	Messages	X	O	
	Altered	***	***	
Note		X	O	
Number	True Voice	***	***	
Velocity	Note ON	X	O	
	Note OFF	X	O	
Aftertouch	Key	X	O	
	Channel	X	O	
Pitch Bend		X	O	
Controllers		X	O	
Program		X	O	
Change	True #	***	***	
System Exclusive		X	X	
System	SPP	X	X	
Common	Song Select	X	X	
	Tune Request	X	X	
System	Clock	X	X	
Realtime	Commands	X	X	
Aux	Local ON/OFF	X	O	
	All Notes Off	X	O	
	Active Sensing	X	X	
	Reset	X	X	

Notes:
1: The device maps channel 1 messages to channel 1
2: Receive channels and map channels are programmable

Mode 1: Omni On, Poly   Mode 2: Omni On, Mono   O:Yes
Mode 3: Omni Off, Poly   Mode 4: Omni Off, Mono   X:No

Project 13: Controller Mapper

Many synthesizers generate only a limited number of controllers, but this project can expand your options by transforming MIDI controller messages from one controller number to another. For example, if a slave module responds to controller 7 (master volume) and you want to control it from your master keyboard's mod wheel (controller 1) or footpedal (controller 4), simply remap either controller 1 or controller 4 to controller 7.

The Controller Mapper processes all channels passing through it, not just one channel.

Typical applications include:

- Sequencing Experimentation Tool. Try using volume or other messages to change modulation (or panning, or whatever), or to see if an instrument patch responds to specific controllers.

- Implementation Adjuster. Reroute controller information stored in a sequence as necessary when you change equipment (for example, patches on two different synths might assign filter cutoff to two different controller numbers).

- Sequencer Enhancer. Some sequencers, especially "scratchpad" sequencers built into keyboards, do not allow easy controller rerouting. You can even reroute signals within one keyboard by turning off local control, sending the keyboard MIDI Out to the MIDItool MIDI In, and the MIDItool MIDI Out to the keyboard MIDI In.

- Keyboard Enhancer. A keyboard controller with limited controller options can transmit any MIDI control change message. This can be particularly handy when controlling real time signal processor parameters from a keyboard.

- Diagnostic Tool. To identify which control change messages your equipment recognizes, loop a sequenced track while mapping a single controller (e.g., mod wheel) to various other control change numbers.

Controller Mapper Specs

Function: Modifies controller messages from one number to another on all MIDI channels
Transmit/Receive/Both: Both
Inline Device: Yes
Internal Merging: No
PC Boards required: CPU, Hand H/I or Rack H/I
Inputs: MIDI In, Panel Keys (4), Fader, DC Power, On/Off Switch, LCD Contrast
Outputs: LCD, LED (1), MIDI Out, MIDI Thru
Enclosure: Hand Box or Rack Box
Complexity: Low

Panel Layouts

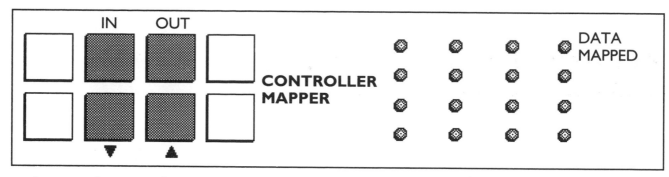

rack mount front panel

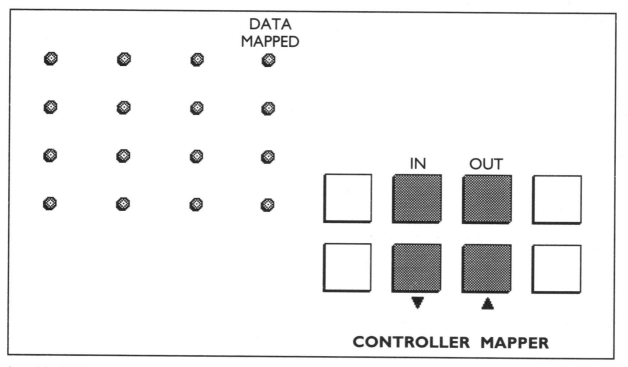

hand held front panel

Setup

1. Connect a suitable power supply (see Chapter 6) to the MIDItool power supply input.

2. Connect a MIDI cable from the master device's MIDI Out (this generates the data to be remapped) to the MIDItool's MIDI In.

3. Patch the MIDItool's MIDI Out to a slave device or MIDI thru box MIDI In.

4. Turn on the power switch.

5. Adjust LCD Contrast for the best display contrast.

Controller Mapper Operations

Default Settings
When you first turn on power, the LCD shows:

- Input Controller—0

- Output Controller—0

- Operational status—The input controller number is available for editing.

Remap A Controller
The LCD's lower line shows both the input (original) and output (remapped) controller numbers. The first two parameters monitor the data stream and show the most recently remapped controller message (channel and controller value).

The possible variable values are:

nn   = MIDI channel number (1 to 16)
bbb   = Controller number or value (0–127)

To remap a controller:

1. Press the Controller In key. The arrow points to the In parameter to indicate it's ready for editing.

2. Select the controller to be remapped using the +/– keys and/or Value fader.

3. Press the Controller Out key. The arrow points to the Out parameter to indicate it's ready for editing.

4. Select the new controller number using the +/– keys and/or Value fader.

All messages with the In controller number are retransmitted as the new Out controller (data bytes are not modified). In addition to the LCD's data monitor, the Data Mapped LED lights when data is being remapped.

Advanced Applications
Here are some suggested modifications for the Controller Mapper:

- Provide for multiple mappings (more than one controller).

- Allow a controller to be mapped to more than one controller simultaneously.

- Support channel-specific mapping.

- Include channel-specific and/or message-specific filtering.

Software Summary

States

Name	Objective
StCIn	Select input controller
StCOut	Select output controller

Actions

Name	Activity
IDLE	No action
CIINC	Increment controller IN number
CIDEC	Decrement controller IN number
CIFDR	Set controller IN with fader
COINC	Increment controller OUT number
CODEC	Decrement controller OUT number
COFDR	Set controller OUT with fader
CIDISP	Update display for controller IN
CODISP	Update display for controller OUT
MSGMAP	Update display with message info

Events

Name	Interface
EvIdle	Idle
EvCtlIn	CONTROLLER IN
EvCtlOut	CONTROLLER OUT
EvMinus	- key
EvPlus	+ key
EvValue	VALUE fader
EvMsgIn	MIDI message

State Matrix

Event	State 0: StCin NextSt,Act	State 1: StCout NextSt,Act
EvIdle,	StCin,IDLE,	StCout,IDLE
EvPlus,	StCin,CIINC,	StCout,COINC
EvMinus,	StCin,CIDEC,	StCout,CODEC
EvValue,	StCin,CIFDR,	StCout,COFDR
EvCtlIn,	StCin,IDLE,	StCin,CIDISP
EvCtlOut,	StCout,CODISP,	StCout,IDLE
EvMsgIn,	StCin,MSGMAP,	StCout,MSGMAP

MIDI Implementation Chart

CONTROL MAPPER   Date: 9-30-93
MIDItool 13   MIDI Implementation Chart   Version: 1.0

Function		Transmitted	Recognized	Remarks
Basic	Default	***	1-16	note 1
Channel	Channel	***	***	
	Default	***	***	note 2
Mode	Messages	X	***	
	Altered	***	***	
Note		X	***	
Number	True Voice	***	***	
Velocity	Note ON	X	X	
	Note OFF	X	X	
Aftertouch	Key	X	X	
	Channel	X	X	
Pitch Bend		X	X	
Controllers		X	O	note 3
Program		X	X	
Change	True #	***	***	
System Exclusive		X	X	
System	SPP	X	X	
Common	Song Select	X	X	
	Tune Request	X	X	
System	Clock	X	X	
Realtime	Commands	X	X	
Aux	Local ON/OFF	X	O	note 2
	All Notes Off	X	O	note 2
	Active Sensing	X	X	
	Reset	X	X	

Notes:
1: Device operates in OMNI mode
2: Channel Mode Messages can be mapped to any other
   controller number
3: Any controller message can be mapped to a different
   controller number

Mode 1: Omni On, Poly   Mode 2: Omni On, Mono   O:Yes
Mode 3: Omni Off, Poly   Mode 4: Omni Off, Mono   X:No

Project 14: Keyboard Mapper

This project processes the output from a MIDI keyboard or other controller by mapping note messages to one, two, or three channels, according to the note's velocity or number.

Splitting a keyboard according to note numbers lets you play up to three different sounds in different keyboard ranges (Zones) since each Zone sends out over a different MIDI channel. Example: With a five-octave keyboard, the lowest octave could play a bass sound assigned to channel 1, the middle three octaves a piano assigned to channel 2, and the top octave a string ensemble assigned to channel 3. Zones can overlap, allowing for layers along with splits.

Splitting according to velocity can give more dynamic sounds by triggering several different versions of the same sound. Example: Notes below a velocity value of 90 could trigger a softly hit drum, from 90–120 a drum hit somewhat harder, and from 120–127, the hardest-hit drum sample.

Velocity splits can also help give greater articulation to a part. Example: Low velocity notes could trigger a muted power guitar part, and high notes a power chord that "rings out."

Typical uses include:

- Keyboard Enhancer. This project can enhance inexpensive keyboards, which often lack sophisticated split capabilities.

- Voice Layering Tool. Triggering three MIDI channels from one note (*i.e.,* set all three channels to the same keyboard range) lets you layer instrument voices for thicker sounds.

- Sample Layering Tool. Use velocity switching to switch between three distinct samples of the same instrument to simulate different playing styles or dynamics.

- Effects Device Enhancer. To have a signal processor affect only certain note numbers or velocities, route their data to a sound module being processed by the effects device.

- Drum Machine Router. If your drum machine transmits all notes on one channel (*e.g.,* channel 10) and you want to layer it with other sounds, remap the note number of the drum to be layered to the destination drum sound's channel.

- Note Range Eliminator. Eliminate a particular range of notes by setting the zone boundaries accordingly. This is extremely useful if you're layering two keyboards but want some notes to remain unlayered.

Keyboard Mapper Specs

Function: Modifier that remaps note messages to a particular MIDI channel according to velocity or note number.
Transmit/Receive/Both: Both
Inline Device: Yes
Internal Merging: No
PC Boards required: CPU, Hand H/I or Rack H/I
Inputs: MIDI In, Panel Keys (8), Fader, DC Power, On/Off Switch, LCD Contrast
Outputs: LCD, LEDs (3), MIDI Out, MIDI Thru
Enclosure: Hand Box or Rack Box
Complexity: Medium

Panel Layouts

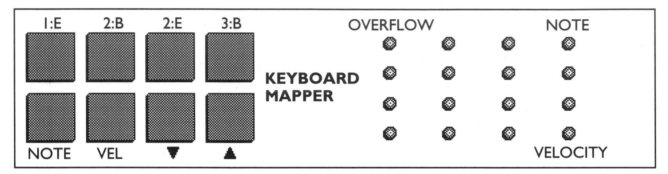

rack mount front panel

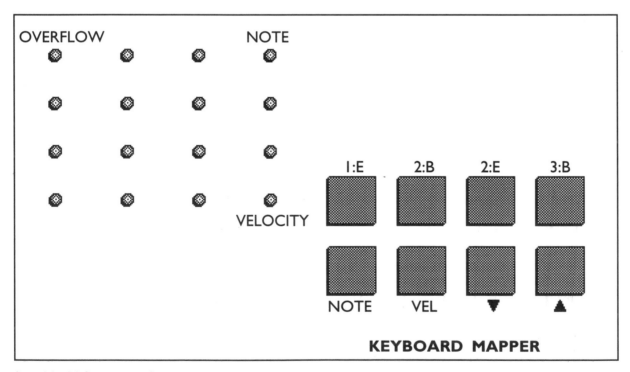

hand held front panel

Setup

1. Connect a suitable power supply (see Chapter 6) to the Miditool power supply input.

2. Patch the master controller's Midi Out to the Miditool Midi In.

3. Connect a midi cable from the Miditool Midi Out to the slave device's Midi In.

4. Turn on the power switch.

5. Adjust LCD Contrast for the most readable display.

Keyboard Mapper Operations

Default Settings

When you first apply power, the LCD shows:

The default settings are:

- Remapping is according to note number.

- The Zone 1 Endpoint (1:E)—127 (highest midi note number).

- The Zone 2 Beginning (2:B)—127.

- The Zone 2 Endpoint (2:E)—127.

- The Zone 3 Beginning (3:B)—127.

- Operational Status—the Zone 1 Endpoint is ready for editing, as indicated by the arrow pointing at the 1:E parameter.

Set Zone Boundaries

The LCD's upper line shows the labels for the Zone beginning and end points, and the lower line shows the value for these points.

The possible variable values are:

ccc   = midi note number or velocity value (0–127)

However, note that the Zone 2 end value must always be equal to or greater than the Zone 2 beginning value (naturally, the "higher" parameter can't be lower in value than the "lower" parameter).

Zone 1 extends from 0 (the lowest possible midi note or velocity value) to the note or velocity value specified under parameter 1:E.

Zone 2 extends from the low note or velocity value specified for 2:B to the high note or velocity value specified for 2:E.

Zone 3 extends from the low note or velocity value specified for 3:B to 127 (the highest possible midi note or velocity value).

To set Zone boundaries:

1. Select the Zone Boundary to be edited with one of the four Zone Boundary keys: 1:E, 2:B, 2:E, or 3:B. An arrow cursor will indicate the parameter to be edited.

2. Set the boundary value with the +/– keys and/or Value fader. Remember that 2:E cannot be lower than 2:B.

Set the Operating Mode

Zone values are assigned to one of two parameter groups: Note Numbers or Velocities. Select the mode using the Note and Vel keys. The appropriate Mode LED lights.

Examples: In Note mode, the following screen indicates that Zone 1 covers the entire keyboard, Zone 2 extends from middle C to two octaves above middle C, and Zone 3 ranges from two octaves above middle C to MIDI note number 127.

In velocity mode, this screen shows that Zone 1 consists of notes of any velocity, Zone 2 of notes with velocity values between 60 and 84, and Zone 3 of notes with velocity values between 84 and 127.

Mapper Channel Assignments

In either mode, notes received on channel N are retransmitted on channels assigned to each zone as follows:

Zone	Channel
1	N
2	N+1
3	N+2

Example: Suppose you're processing a keyboard that transmits on MIDI channel 7. Notes associated with Zone 1 will be retransmitted over MIDI channel 7, Zone 2 notes over MIDI channel 8, and Zone 3 notes over MIDI channel 9.

Data Buffer Overflow Indicator

If the receive data buffer becomes full, the Overflow LED will light. At this point you must reset the MIDItools computer by turning the power switch off, waiting a few seconds, and turning it on again. By the way—you have to play *a lot* of notes to create an overflow condition.

Advanced Applications

Here are some suggested mods for the Keyboard Mapper:

- Allow more zones.

- Map according to both note position and velocity simultaneously.

- Offset mapped notes or velocities.

- Support preset storage and retrieval of sets of Zone parameters.

- Provide for channel-specific mapping.

- Allow boundaries to be set with MIDI commands.

Software Summary

States

Name	Objective
StNote	Operate in Note Number Mode
StVel	Operate in Velocity Mode

Actions

Name	Activity
IDLE	No action
BRYINC	Increment Zone boundary
BRYDEC	Decrement Zone boundary
BRYFDR	Set Zone boundary with fader
NMODE	Select Note Number mode
VMODE	Select Velocity mode
Z1EDSP	Update display with Zone 1 endpoint
Z2BDSP	Update display with Zone 2 beginning
Z2EDSP	Update display with Zone 2 endpoint
Z3BDSP	Update display with Zone 3 beginning
ARWCLR	Clear LCD cursor arrow
KEYMAP	Map incoming messages

Events

Name	Interface
EvIdle	Idle
EvZ1E	ZONE BOUNDARIES Z1E key
EvZ2B	ZONE BOUNDARIES Z2B key
EvZ2E	ZONE BOUNDARIES Z2E key
EvZ3B	ZONE BOUNDARIES Z3B key
EvNote	MODE NOTE key
EvVel	MODE VEL key
EvMinus	VALUE - key
EvPlus	VALUE + key
EvValue	VALUE fader
EvMsgIn	MIDI message

State Matrix

Event	State 0:StNote NextSt,Act	State 1:StVel NextSt,Act
EvIdle,	StNote,IDLE,	StVel,IDLE
EvZ1E,	StNote,Z1EDSP,	StVel,Z1EDSP
EvZ2B,	StNote,Z2BDSP,	StVel,Z2BDSP
EvZ2E,	StNote,Z2EDSP,	StVel,Z2EDSP
EvZ3B,	StNote,Z3BDSP,	StVel,Z3BDSP
EvNote,	StNote,IDLE,	StNote,NMODE
EvVel,	StVel,VMODE,	StVel,IDLE
EvMinus,	StNote,BRYDEC,	StVel,BRYDEC
EvPlus,	StNote,BRYINC,	StVel,BRYINC
EvValue,	StNote,BRYFDR,	StVel,BRYFDR
EvMsgIn,	StNote,KEYMAP,	StVel,KEYMAP

Midi Implementation Chart

KEYBOARD MAPPER   Date: 9-30-93
Miditool 14   Midi Implementation Chart   Version: 1.0

Function		Transmitted	Recognized	Remarks
Basic	Default	***	1-16	note 1
Channel	Channel	**	***	
Mode	Default	**	Mode 3	
	Messages	X	X	
	Altered	***	***	
Note		X	O	note 2
Number	True Voice	***	***	
Velocity	Note ON	X	O	
	Note OFF	X	O	
Aftertouch	Key	X	X	
	Channel	X	X	
Pitch Bend		X	X	
Controllers		X	X	
Program		X	X	
Change	True #	***	***	
System Exclusive		X	X	
System	SPP	X	X	
Common	Song Select	X	X	
	Tune Request	X	X	
System	Clock	X	X	
Realtime	Commands	X	X	
Aux	Local ON/OFF	X	X	
	All Notes Off	X	X	
	Active Sensing	X	X	
	Reset	X	X	

Notes:
1: Device operates in OMNI mode
2: Midi note messages can be mapped to contiguous channels

Mode 1: Omni On, Poly   Mode 2: Omni On, Mono   O:Yes
Mode 3: Omni Off, Poly   Mode 4: Omni Off, Mono   X:No

Project 15: Translating Randomizer

When it's time to add a little variety to your MIDI life, this tool randomly alters MIDI note numbers, velocity, or program changes within a selectable range and in real time. It can also translate various MIDI channel messages from one type to another (*e.g.*, aftertouch to pitch bend). This can change music into interesting new permutations, some parts of which might even be pretty catchy.

There are 10 available modes (including off). Typical applications include:

- Composer's Assistant. Use randomizing modes 1 and 3 to experiment with random variations on what you play (or sequence).

- Drum Machine Chiller. Randomizing mode 2 shakes up the drum note velocities to relieve the boredom of mechanically correct drums.

- Keyboard Enhancer. Translation mode 9 generates channel aftertouch messages from a keyboard that has only a modulation wheel.

- Expressive Keyboard Expander. Translation modes 4, 5 and 6 convert channel aftertouch into pitch and volume changes.

- Realtime Panpot. Use the pitch bend wheel with translation mode 7 to pan a MIDI sound generator in real time (assuming, of course, that it implements MIDI-controlled panning).

- Realtime Balance Control. Use the pitch bend wheel with translation mode 8 to balance a track in real time.

- Performance Tool. Use randomizing modes 1 and 3 to create unique soundscapes during live performance.

- Practical joke. Randomizing the output of someone's keyboard is always good for a few laughs.

Translating Randomizer Specs

Function: Modifier that randomizes some types of MIDI data and also performs data translation.
Transmit/Receive/Both: Both
Inline Device: Yes
Internal Merging: No
PC Boards required: CPU, Hand H/I or Rack H/I
Inputs: MIDI In, Panel Keys (5), Fader, DC Power, On/Off Switch, LCD Contrast
Outputs: LCD, MIDI Out, MIDI Thru
Enclosure: Hand Box or Rack Box
Complexity: High

Panel Layouts

rack mount front panel

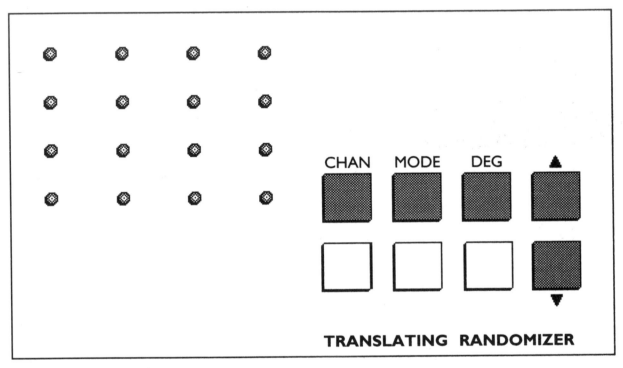

hand held front panel

Setup

1. Connect a suitable power supply (see Chapter 6) to the MIDItool power supply input.

2. Connect a MIDI cable from the master device's MIDI Out (this generates the data to be modified) to the MIDItool's MIDI In.

3. Patch the MIDItool's MIDI Out to a slave device or MIDI thru box MIDI In. To process a keyboard, patch back into the keyboard's MIDI In and turn the instrument's Local Control option to "off."

4. Turn on the power switch.

5. Adjust LCD Contrast for the most readable display.

Translating Randomizer Operations

Default Settings

On power-up, the display shows:

- Receive/Retransmit Channel—1

- Operating Mode—0 (off; effect is bypassed)

- Degree—0.

- Operational status—the Receive/Retransmit Channel is available for editing.

Set the Receive/Retransmit Channel

The screen's upper line shows the three available parameters, and the lower line, their values. The cursor arrow points to the parameter that will be modified by the +/– keys and Value fader.

The possible variable values are:

nnnn = MIDI channel (1 to 16, None, or All)
b   = Mode number (0 to 9)
ccc   = Degree of effect (0, 1, 3, 7, 15, 31, 63 or 127)

To set the channel:

1. Press the Setup Chan key. The arrow points to the Channel parameter to indicate it's ready for editing.

2. Set the MIDI channel on which messages will be received, as well as retransmitted by the Randomizer/Translator. The Value fader varies this from 1 to 16; the +/– keys cover this range as well as the All or None options. With All selected, messages received on *any* channel are re-transmitted on the same channel. With None selected, the MIDItools computer acts like a Thru box.

Choose the Mode of Operation

1. Press the Setup Mode key.

2. Select one of the following processor functions with the +/– keys:

Mode	Description
0	Translating randomizer Off
1	Randomize note numbers
2	Randomize velocity values
3	Randomize program change values
4	Translate channel pressure values to -bend messages
5	Translate channel pressure values to +bend messages
6	Translate channel pressure to volume
7	Translate pitch bend to pan
8	Translate pitch bend to balance
9	Translate mod wheel to channel pressure

Mode 1 randomizes Note On messages only. Since the processed output will probably be a different note, most retransmitted notes will not have a corresponding Note Off message. Therefore, any voices that play will sustain, so patches should be chosen with this in mind (e.g., use patches with natural decay).

Modes 4–6 and 9 respond only to channel aftertouch, not poly aftertouch.

Control the Degree of Each Effect

1. Press the Setup Deg key.

2. Set the degree of each effect with the +/– keys and/or the Value fader. The "degree" modifies messages according to the following rules:

Modes 1–3: Degree sets the "window" of possible values. The window is centered on the received value, and wraps around if the value goes below 0 or above 127.

Examples: (Mode 1) Processing note number 50 with Degree = 31 transmits a note with a random number between 35–66.

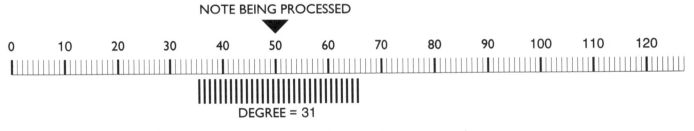

Processing note number = 110 with Degree = 63 transmits a note with a random number between 79–127, or 0–14 (due to wraparound).

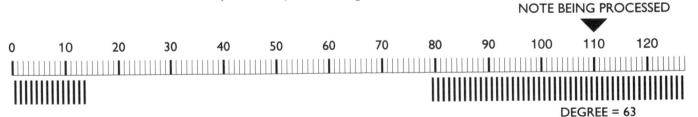

Modes 4–5: Degree sets the pitch bend's sensitivity to pressure messages. The lower the number, the greater the amount of pitch bend change in response to a given amount of channel pressure.

For math fans, here's the formula behind this. The starting pitch bend value is 64. Therefore, data is divided by the value of:

(Degree+1)/2, where Degree > 1

When Degree = 0 or 1, the data is divided by 2. After dividing, the data is subtracted (Mode 4) or added (Mode 5) to the starting pitch bend value of 64.

Mode 6: Degree sets the minimum transmitted volume value. Pressure messages increase volume level starting from this value.

Modes 7–8: Degree sets the pan and balance's sensitivity to pitch bend messages. The lower the number, the greater the amount of panning or balance change in response to a given amount of pitch bend.
The data is first divided by (Degree+1). The full range of new values is then centered around 64. The bend wheel center indent position corresponds to the center pan (Mode 7) or equal balance (Mode 8) position.

Mode 9: Scales the pressure messages according to the mod wheel. The lower the number, the greater the amount of pressure change in response to a given mod wheel position. The data is divided by (Degree+1) before being retransmitted.

Advanced Applications

Here are some ideas on Translating Randomizer modifications:

- Allow for time randomization ("dequantizing").

- Replace the fader with a foot pedal.

- Add more translation modes.

- Add more randomization modes.

- Support multiple modes simultaneously.

- Constrain retransmitted notes to harmonically related ones.

- Provide more control over the degree/damping factor.

Software Summary

States

Name	Objective
StCh	Set the receive/retransmit channel
StMode	Select the processing function
StDeg	Set the degree of processing

Actions

Name	Activity
IDLE	No action
CHINC	Increment channel
CHDEC	Decrement channel
CHFDR	Set channel with fader
MODINC	Increment mode number
MODDEC	Decrement mode number
DEGINC	Increment degree of processing
DEGDEC	Decrement degree of processing
DEGFDR	Set degree of processing with fader
CHDISP	Update display for changing channel
MODISP	Update display for changing mode number
DGDISP	Update display for changing degree
ARWCLR	Clear LCD cursor arrow

Events

Name	Interface
EvIdle	Idle
EvChan	SETUP CHAN key
EvMode	SETUP MODE key
EvDeg	SETUP DEG key
EvPlus	+ key
EvMinus	- key
EvValue	VALUE fader

State Matrix

Event	State 0:StCh NextSt,Act	State 1:StMode NextSt,Act	State 2:StDeg NextSt,Act
EvIdle,	StCh,IDLE,	StMode,IDLE,	StDeg,IDLE
EvPlus,	StCh,CHINC,	StMode,MODINC,	StDeg,DEGINC
EvMinus,	StCh,CHDEC,	StMode,MODDEC,	StDeg,DEGDEC
EvValue,	StCh,CHFDR,	StMode,IDLE,	StDeg,DEGFDR
EvChan,	StCh,IDLE,	StCh,CHDISP,	StCh,CHDISP
EvMode,	StMode,MODISP,	StMode,IDLE,	StMode,MODISP
EvDeg,	StDeg,DGDISP,	StDeg,DGDISP,	StDeg,IDLE

MIDI Implementation Chart

```
TRANSLATING  RANDOMIZER                              Date: 9-30-93
MIDItool 15           MIDI Implementation Chart      Version: 1.0
```

Function		Transmitted	Recognized	Remarks
Basic	Default	***	1-16	note 1
Channel	Channel	***	1-16	note 2
	Default	***	Mode 3	
Mode	Messages	X	X	
	Altered	***	***	
Note		X	O	note 3
Number	True Voice	***	***	
Velocity	Note ON	X	O	note 3
	Note OFF	X	O	
Aftertouch	Key	X	X	
	Channel	X	O	note 4
Pitch Bend		X	O	note 5
Controllers	1	X	O	note 6
Program		X	O	note 3
Change	True #	***	***	
System Exclusive		X	X	
System	SPP	X	X	
Common	Song Select	X	X	
	Tune Request	X	X	
System	Clock	X	X	
Realtime	Commands	X	X	
Aux	Local ON/OFF	X	X	
	All Notes Off	X	X	
	Active Sensing	X	X	
	Reset	X	X	

Notes:
1: The device receives on ALL channels at once
2: Receive channel is programmable (1-16, ALL, or NONE)
3: Device can be programmed to randomize data values (0-127)
4: Device can be programmed to translate channel aftertouch
   to negative bend, positive bend, or volume (controller 7)
5: Device can be programmed to translate pitch bend to pan
   (controller 10) or balance (controller 8)
6: Device can be programmed to translate modulation wheel
   (controller 1) to channel aftertouch

```
Mode 1: Omni On, Poly    Mode 2: Omni On, Mono     O:Yes
Mode 3: Omni Off, Poly   Mode 4: Omni Off, Mono    X:No
```

Project 16: Multi-Effector

This multi-effects unit for MIDI data offers real time data compression, limiting, noise gating, and delay. The effects are similar to those achieved by analog devices, but process MIDI data instead of audio data.

Typical uses include:

- Bad Note Eliminator. Brushing up against your controller's keys can produce spurious, low velocity notes (this is even more likely with MIDI guitar controllers, or drum pads that lack good isolation). Use the Gate to eliminate all notes with velocities below a certain level.

- Velocity Limiter. Use the Limit function to keep all note velocities below a maximum value, without affecting other notes. This is very handy with FM-based synthesizers (*e.g.*, Yamaha DX7) since they can be extremely sensitive to small differences in velocity values.

- Velocity Compressor. The Compressor restricts the data's dynamic range, which can often give a punchier sound and allow for raising a signal's average level. This effect is often used with bass to provide a more consistent "bottom."

- Velocity Expander. If the notes in a passage all play back at nearly the same level and this is undesirable because it sounds too mechanical, the Expander can increase the difference between the highest and lowest values.

- Delay Device. This works like a regular delay line by transmitting MIDI notes a programmable amount of time after they've been received, but adds the capability to have the echoes follow a programmable tempo.

Multi-Effector Specs

Function: Modifies and generates data
Transmit/Receive/Both: Both
Inline Device: Yes
Internal Merging: Yes
PC Boards required: CPU, Hand H/I or Rack H/I
Inputs: MIDI In, Panel Keys (8), Fader, DC Power, On/Off Switch, LCD Contrast
Outputs: LCD, LEDs (4), MIDI Out, MIDI Thru
Enclosure: Hand Box or Rack Box
Complexity: High

Panel Layouts

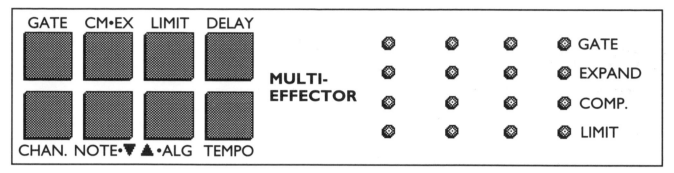

rack mount front panel

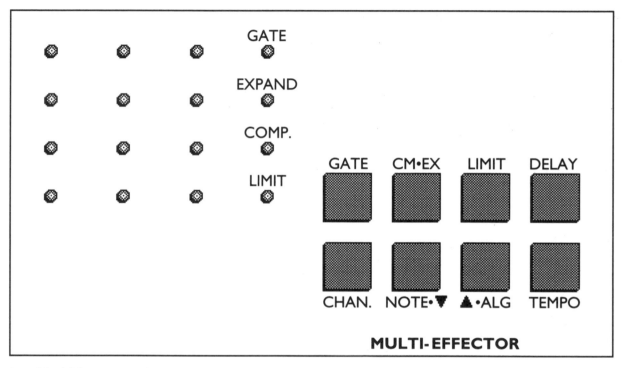

hand held front panel

Setup

1. Connect a suitable power supply (see Chapter 6) to the MIDItool power supply input.

2. Connect a MIDI cable from the master device's MIDI Out to the MIDItool's MIDI In.

3. Connect a MIDI cable from the MIDItool's MIDI Out to the receiver's MIDI in. This will often be a slave device or thru box, but can also be the MIDI In of the same keyboard you're playing if you want to process the keyboard data. In this case, the keyboard's "Local Control" parameter should be off.

4. Turn on the power switch.

5. Adjust LCD Contrast for the most readable display.

Multi-Effector Operations

Default Settings
When you first apply power, the display shows:

The default settings are:

- Gate Threshold—0

- Limit Threshold—127

- Compression—off

- Expansion—off

- Delayed Note Value—whole note

- Delay Generator—off

- Receive/Retransmit Channel—All!

- Delayed Note Tempo (Quarter Notes per Minute)—100

- Operational Status—the Receive/Retransmit channel is available for editing.

Set the Receive/Retransmit Channel
1. Press the Setup Chan key.

2. Set the Receive/Retransmit MIDI channel with the +/– keys and/or Value fader. The range of MIDI channels is 1–16, All, or None.

Set the Processor Parameters
1. The upper row of buttons select the four different effects. If the display currently shows the Channel or Tempo screens, pressing an Effect button will jump to the effects screen.

2. After pressing an Effect key, the display shows the following (CM, for compression, can also show EX for expansion):

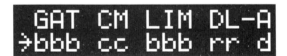

The possible variable values are:

bbb = Gate or limiter threshold (0 to 127)
cc = Compression/expansion ratio (63 to 0 and 0 to 63 respectively)
rr = Delayed note spacing (1, 2, 4, 8, 16 or 32)
d = Decay algorithm (options 0 thru 8)

The cursor arrow points to the parameter selected by the Effect key. This parameter can be edited by the +/– keys and Value fader.

3. Select the effect you want to edit with the appropriate Effect key, and adjust the parameter value with the +/– keys and/or Value fader.

Here are details on the various effects; each received note flows through the effects processors in the following order.

- **Gate**—All notes received with a velocity below the threshold will not be retransmitted. The Gate LED lights when a note is being gated.

- **Compressor/Expander**—Turning the Value fader completely counter-clockwise gives a compression ratio of 63. Turning the fader clockwise lowers this value until it reaches 0 at the fader midpoint. Continuing to turn the fader clockwise changes into expansion mode (as shown by the display label showing EX), and goes from value 1 (just right of fader midpoint) to 63 (fader full clockwise). The Compress LED lights when a note velocity is being compressed; the Expand LED does likewise for expansion.

- **Limiter**—All notes received with a velocity greater than this threshold will be retransmitted with the threshold velocity. The Limit LED lights when a note is being limited.

- **Delay**—Set the note delay spacing with the Note key. The range of values is 1, 2, 4, 8, 16, or 32 (respectively whole, half, quarter, eighth, sixteenth, and thirty-second notes). The delay generator affects the last note played only.

The Alg key chooses one of the following decay algorithms:

Alg	Description
0	Delay generator off
1	Repeat note at same velocity (endless)
2	Divide velocity by 2 until v = 0
3	Divide velocity by 4 until v = 0
4	Divide velocity by 8 until v = 0
5	Subtract 2 from velocity until v = 0
6	Subtract 4 from velocity until v = 0
7	Subtract 8 from velocity until v = 0
8	Subtract 16 from velocity until v = 0

Press the Setup Tempo key, then set the tempo at which the echoes occur with the +/− keys and/or the Value fader. The range extends from 20–255 quarter notes per minute.

When set to a tempo 100 QPM, the LCD shows:

```
MULTI-EFFECTOR
TEMPO          100
```

Troubleshooting

The various effects are subject to certain limitations of MɪDɪ gear. Each note that's delayed uses up a synthesizer voice, so if you play a complex part with lots of echo, you'll run out of voices and the echo effect will seem to diminish. Also, if a patch does not respond to velocity, then the delay will not seem to decay over time.

Advanced Applications

Here are some suggested Multi-Effector mods:

- Add more delay algorithms, such as reverse decay.

- Replace the delayed note value/tempo with absolute time.

- Add effects (harmonizing, polyrhythmic echoes, etc.).

- Replace the fader with a foot pedal.

- Add bypass switches to each effect.

- Separate the compression and expansion options.

Software Summary

States

Name	Objective
StSet	Set channel and tempo
StCmEx	Set compression/expansion parameters
StGtLm	Set gate/limit parameters
StDely	Set delay parameters

Actions

Name	Activity
IDLE	No action (administer delays & LEDs)
CTINC	Route setup increment action
CTDEC	Route setup decrement action
CTFDR	Route setup fader action
CHINC	Increment channel
CHDEC	Decrement channel
CHFDR	Set channel with fader
TEMINC	Increment delay tempo
TEMDEC	Decrement delay tempo
TEMFDR	Set delay tempo with fader
CEINC	Increment comp/exp value
CEDEC	Decrement comp/exp value
CEFDR	Set comp/exp value with fader
CECALC	Calculate comp/exp ratio
GLINC	Route gate/limit increment action
GLDEC	Route gate/limit decrement action
GLFDR	Route gate/limit fader action
GTINC	Increment gate threshold
GTDEC	Decrement gate threshold
GTFDR	Set gate threshold with fader
LMINC	Increment limit threshold
LMDEC	Decrement limit threshold
LMFDR	Set limit threshold with fader
DLINC	Increment value of delayed note
ALGINC	Increment decay algorithm
CHDISP	Update display for changing channel
TMDISP	Update display for changing tempo
LBDISP	Update display with comp/exp label
CXDISP	Update display with comp/exp ratio
GTDISP	Update display with gate threshold
LMDISP	Update display with limit threshold
DLDISP	Update display with delay note value
ALDISP	Update display with decay algorithm
ARWCLR	Clear LCD cursor arrow

Events

Name	Interface
EvIdle	Idle
EvGate	EFFECTS GATE key
EvCmEx	EFFECTS CM/EX key
EvLimit	EFFECTS LIMIT key
EvDelay	EFFECTS DELAY key
EvChan	SETUP CHAN key
EvMinus	SETUP NOTE- key
EvPlus	SETUP ALG+ key
EvTempo	SETUP TEMPO key
EvValue	VALUE fader

State Matrix

Event	State 0:StSet NextSt,Act	State 1:StCmEx NextSt,Act	State 2:StGtLm NextSt,Act	State 3:StDely NextSt,Act
EvIdle,	StSet,IDLE,	StCmEx,IDLE,	StGtLm,IDLE,	StDely,IDLE
EvPlus,	StSet,CTINC,	StCmEx,CEINC,	StGtLm,GLINC,	StDely,ALGINC
EvMinus,	StSet,CTDEC,	StCmEx,CEDEC,	StGtLm,GLDEC,	StDely,DLINC
EvValue,	StSet,CTFDR,	StCmEx,CEFDR,	StGtLm,GLFDR,	StDely,IDLE
EvChan,	StSet,CHDISP,	StSet,CHDISP,	StSet,CHDISP,	StSet,CHDISP
EvGate,	StGtLm,GTDISP,	StGtLm,GTDISP,	StGtLm,GTDISP,	StGtLm,GTDISP
EvLimit,	StGtLm,LMDISP,	StGtLm,LMDISP,	StGtLm,LMDISP,	StGtLm,LMDISP
EvTempo,	StSet,TMDISP,	StSet,TMDISP,	StSet,TMDISP,	StSet,TMDISP
EvDelay,	StDely,DLDISP,	StDely,DLDISP,	StDely,DLDISP,	StDely,DLDISP
EvCmEx,	StCmEx,CXDISP,	StCmEx,IDLE,	StCmEx,CXDISP,	StCmEx,CXDISP

MIDI Implementation Chart

```
MULTI-EFFECTOR                                    Date: 9-30-93
Miditool 16          MIDI Implementation Chart    Version: 1.0
```

Function		Transmitted	Recognized	Remarks
Basic	Default	***	1-16	note 1
Channel	Channel	***	1-16	note 2
Mode	Default	***	Mode 3	
	Messages	X	X	
	Altered	***	***	
Note		O	O	note 3
Number	True Voice	***	***	
Velocity	Note ON	O	O	note 4
	Note OFF	O	O	note 5
Aftertouch	Key	X	X	
	Channel	X	X	
Pitch Bend		X	X	
Controllers		X	X	
Program		X	X	
Change	True #	***	***	
System Exclusive		X	X	
System	SPP	X	X	
Common	Song Select	X	X	
	Tune Request	X	X	
System	Clock	X	X	
Realtime	Commands	X	X	
Aux	Local ON/OFF	X	X	
	All Notes Off	X	X	
	Active Sensing	X	X	
	Reset	X	X	

```
Notes:
1: The device receives on ALL channels at once
2: Receive channel is programmable (1-16, ALL, or NONE)
3: Device both receives and generates note numbers
4: Generated Note On velocities are between 1-127
5: Note On messages with velocity=0 are sent to turn
   generated notes off


Mode 1: Omni On, Poly     Mode 2: Omni On, Mono     O:Yes
Mode 3: Omni Off, Poly    Mode 4: Omni Off, Mono    X:No
```

Project 17: Sequencer Helper

This project takes your sequencer's output and provides a variety of useful, sequencer-oriented processing functions including selective transposition, controller reset, volume fades, etc. Typical uses include:

- Key Transposer. Transpose a sequence to match a vocalist's range without changing the sequence or transposing the drum tracks.

- Velocity Offsetter. Scale velocities upward to add a little bite and (usually) volume to your sequence.

- Master Mute Button. Mute the sequence without stopping it.

- Master Volume Control. During a mixdown situation that combines acoustic instruments recorded on tape with virtual MIDI tracks, you can match the overall level of the sequenced tracks volume to previously-recorded tracks. Or, add overall crescendos and accents.

- Master Fadeout/Fadein Control. Fade a song in or out smoothly.

- Controller Resetter. Starting and stopping a sequence during measures with controller data can result in "stuck" controller messages (volume stuck on full on or full off, pitch bend stuck in an out of tune setting, etc.). Use this function to reset the controllers to their nominal values.

- Panic Button. Use this to turn off any stuck notes, without having to stop and restart your sequence.

Sequencer Helper Specs

Function: Modifies sequencer data and generates commands
Transmit/Receive/Both: Both
Inline Device: Yes
Internal Merging: Yes
PC Boards required: CPU, Hand H/I or Rack H/I
Inputs: MIDI In, Panel Keys (8), Fader, DC Power, On/Off Switch, LCD Contrast
Outputs: LCD, LEDs (4), MIDI Out, MIDI Thru
Enclosure: Hand Box or Rack Box
Complexity: High

Panel Layouts

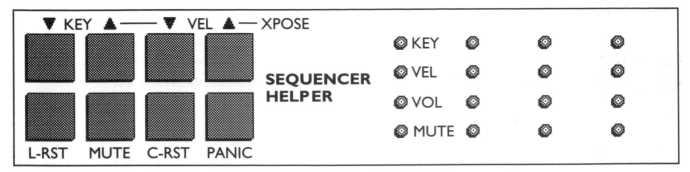

rack mount front panel

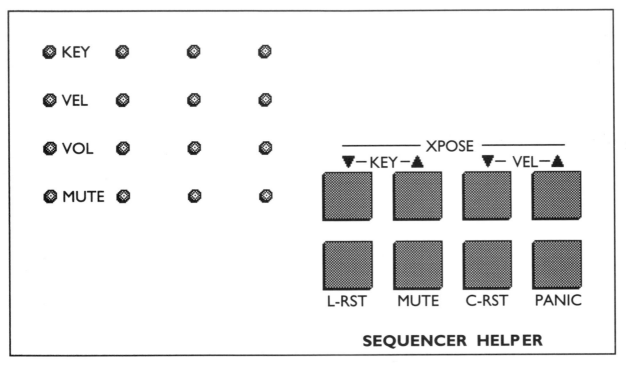

hand held front panel

Setup

1. Connect a suitable power supply (see Chapter 6) to the MIDItool power supply input.

2. Patch the sequencer's MIDI Out to the MIDItool MIDI In.

3. Connect a MIDI cable from the MIDItool MIDI Out to the target device's MIDI In (slave device, thru box, etc.).

4. Turn on the power switch.

5. Adjust LCD Contrast for the most readable display.

Sequencer Helper Operations

Default Settings

When you first apply power, the LCD shows:

The default settings are:

- Key Offset—0

- Velocity Offset—0

- Mute—off

- All channels—enabled for key transposition

- Operational status—The device is set for normal operation.

Set the Processor Parameters

The upper row of buttons provides Key Transposition and Velocity Offset. The lower row provides various individual functions. The possible variable values are:

```
Key:sddd  Vel:sddd
MMMMMMMMMMMMMMMM
```

s	= plus or minus symbol
ddd	= 0-127 (amount of Key Transposition or Velocity Offset)
mm	= one of five messages (Loc Reset - WAIT, Ctl Reset - WAIT, PANIC! - WAIT, MUTE ON, and blank)

Transpose the Key Signature

Each press of the Transpose Key + (the up arrow key) transposes the song 1/2 step higher, up to 127 semitones. Transposing above this "wraps around" to -127. Each press of the Transpose Key – (down arrow) transposes the song 1/2 step lower, down to -127. Transposing below this "wraps around" to +127. The Key Offset LED lights for nonzero offsets.

To disable key transposition for certain tracks (*e.g.*, drum parts), see Sequencer Setup for details on how to disable individual channels.

Offset All Sequence Velocity Values

Each press of the Transpose Vel + key adds 1 to all note velocities. Offsetting beyond 127 "wraps around" to -127. Each press of the Transpose Vel – key subtracts 1 from all note velocities. Offsetting below this "wraps around" to +127. The Vel Offset LED lights for nonzero offsets.

Mute Sequence Playback Without Stopping It

Press the Mute key to mute; press again to unmute. The Mute LED lights when notes are muted, and the LCD shows MUTE ON.

Control the Overall Volume

The Value fader acts as a Master Volume control that affects all MIDI instruments that respond to controller 7 (most do; some older ones don't). Rotating the fader fully counter-clockwise sets the minimum volume; rotating full clockwise sets the maximum volume. The Volume LED lights for all non-100% settings.

For proper operation of the master Volume fader, the sequencer should send the desired nominal volume settings (controller 7) on each MIDI channel used. Volume data is then scaled from this received volume data. For example, if a controller 7 message defines a certain unit's level as 80 and the MIDItools fader is set halfway, the unit's level will be 40. In the absence of any controller 7 data, the control defaults to a value of 127 (maximum volume).

You can also use this fader to create fade ins and outs.

Reset the MIDItool Parameters

Press the Local Reset (L-RST) key to return:

- Key Offset to 0

- Vel Offset to 0

- Mute to Off

- Volume to 100%

- All channels enabled for key transposition.

Reset All Controllers

Press the Ctl Reset (C-RST) key to reset controllers 0-95 on all channels to a value of zero, except for the following special cases:

- Volume (Ctl 7) is 127

- Pan (Ctl 10) is 64

- Balance (Ctl 8) is 64

This also transmits the "Reset All Controllers" Channel Mode Message (Controller 121) on each channel.

In addition to controller messages, pressing the Ctl Reset key returns (on all channels):

- Pitch Bend to MSB = 64 / LSB = 0 (No Bend)

- Channel Aftertouch to 0

- Key Aftertouch to 0 (all notes)

Turn Off All Notes

Pressing the Reset Panic key sends the following messages on all channels:

- All Notes Off (Controller 123, Channel Mode Message)

- Note Off (note numbers 0-127)

Enable/Disable Particular MIDI Channels

Generally, when transposing a sequence you don't want to transpose channels that contain drum parts, but only those that contain melodic parts. You can disable key transposition on any channel by using controller 16 messages. Receiving a controller 16 message with a value greater than 0 on a particular channel disables key transposition on that channel.

Example: Sending controller message $B3 10 7F to the Sequencer Helper disables key transposition on channel 4. Sending controller message $B3 10 00 later on in the sequence re-enables key transposition on channel 4.

Advanced Applications

Here are some ideas for Sequencer Helper modifications:

- Provide for "front panel" channel transposition disabling.

- Combine all reset functions into a master panic button.

- Parallel the panic key with a larger key or footswitch.

- Support muting of individual channels rather than just global muting.

- Allow message thinning.

- Allow message monitoring.

Software Summary
States

Name	Objective
StOp	Operate

Actions

Name	Activity
IDLE	No action
VOLSND	Send scaled volume messages
VELINC	Increment velocity offset
VELDEC	Decrement velocity offset
KEYINC	Increment key offset
KEYDEC	Decrement key offset
LOCALR	Reset local device parameters
CNTRLR	Reset all controllers
PANICR	Reset all instrument voices
MUTTOG	Toggle mute status
VDISP	Update display with velocity info
KDISP	Update display with key info
MDISP	Update display with mute info

Events

Name	Interface
EvIdle	Idle
EvKeyM	TRANSPOSE KEY- key
EvKeyP	TRANSPOSE KEY+ key
EvVelM	TRANSPOSE VEL- key
EvVelP	TRANSPOSE VEL+ key
EvReset	LOCAL RESET key
EvMute	MUTE key
EvRCtl	RESET R-CTL key
EvPanic	RESET PANIC key
EvVol	VOLUME fader

State Matrix

	State 0: StOp
Event	NextSt,Act
EvIdle,	StOp,IDLE
EvVelM,	StOp,VELDEC
EvVelP,	StOp,VELINC
EvKeyM,	StOp,KEYDEC
EvKeyP,	StOp,KEYINC
EvReset,	StOp,LOCALR
EvMute,	StOp,MUTTOG
EvRCtl,	StOp,CNTRLR
EvPanic,	StOp,PANICR
EvVol,	StOp,VOLSND

MIDI Implementation Chart

SEQUENCER HELPER   Date: 9-30-93
MIDItool 17   MIDI Implementation Chart   Version: 1.0

Function		Transmitted	Recognized	Remarks
Basic	Default	***	1-16	note 1
Channel	Channel	***	***	
	Default	***	Mode 1	
Mode	Messages	X	X	
	Altered	***	***	
Note		O	O	note 2
Number	True Voice	***	***	
Velocity	Note ON	X	O	note 3
	Note OFF	O	O	note 4
Aftertouch	Key	O	X	
	Channel	O	X	
Pitch Bend		O	X	
Controllers	7	O	O	note 5
	16	X	O	note 6
	121	O	X	reset conts
	0-95	O	X	note 7
Program		X	X	
Change	True #	***	***	
System Exclusive		X	X	
System	SPP	X	X	
Common	Song Select	X	X	
	Tune Request	X	X	
System	Clock	X	X	
Realtime	Commands	X	X	
Aux	Local ON/OFF	X	X	
	All Notes Off	O	X	
	Active Sensing	X	X	
	Reset	X	X	

Notes:
1: The device operates in OMNI mode
2: A programmable offset can be added to note numbers
3: A programmable offset can be added to Note On velocities
4: When muting, the device sets all velocities=0; when
   PANIC is pressed, device sends Note Off messages
5: Controller 7 is used to receive/set volume
6: Controller 16 disables key offset on individual channels
7: User can reset controllers 0-95 to their nominal values

Mode 1: Omni On, Poly   Mode 2: Omni On, Mono   O:Yes
Mode 3: Omni Off, Poly   Mode 4: Omni Off, Mono   X:No

Project 18: Chord Player

Play a single note line, and this box generates chordal accompaniment. What's more, these chords can be "strummed" to give guitar effects (with variable strumming speed) or arpeggiated.

Typical uses include:

- Sequenced guitar part enhancer. It's hard to sequence realistic-sounding guitar parts, but the Chord Player can help if you set the strum value to match a song's tempo.

- Enhanced "guitar player." A special range of strum values creates up and down strum effects. This also works well for arpeggios.

- One-fingered piano player. With minimum strum time, chord notes play simultaneously so you can play chord progressions with just one finger.

- Special Effects. Creating chords from a polyphonic keyboard controller creates some pretty weird effects since you can play many notes simultaneously.

- Fun brain vacation. Play with it, and you'll see what we mean.

Chord Player Specs

Function: Generates chords from individual MIDI notes.
Transmit/Receive/Both: Both
Inline Device: Yes
Internal Merging: Yes
PC Boards required: CPU, Hand H/I or Rack H/I
Inputs: MIDI In, Panel Keys (8), Fader, DC Power, On/Off Switch, LCD Contrast
Outputs: LCD, MIDI Out, MIDI Thru
Enclosure: Hand Box or Rack Box
Complexity: Medium

Panel Layouts

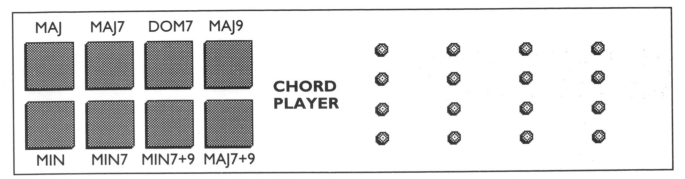

rack mount front panel

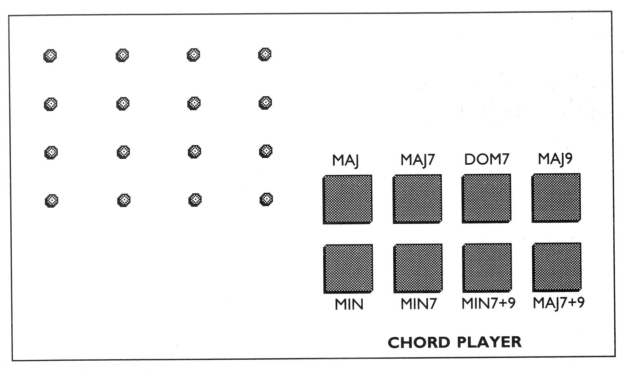

hand held front panel

Setup

1. Connect a suitable power supply (see Chapter 6) to the MIDItool power supply input.

2. Patch the MIDItool MIDI In to the master device's MIDI Out.

3. Patch the MIDItool MIDI Out to the target device MIDI In. This will often be a slave device or thru box, but can also be the MIDI In of the same keyboard you're playing if you want to process the keyboard data. In this case, the keyboard's "Local Control" parameter should be off.

4. Turn on the power switch.

5. Adjust LCD Contrast for the best contrast in the display.

Chord Player Operations

Default Settings
When you first apply power, the LCD shows:

The default settings are:

- Chord Type—major

- Strum Value—0

- Operational status—the device is set for normal operation.

Choosing the Chord Type and Strum Rate
The screen's upper line shows the parameter labels, and the lower line, their values.

The possible variable values are:

xxxxx   = chord type (major, minor, dominant 7, major 7, minor 7+9, minor 7, major 7+9, or major 9)

mmm   = strum setting (0 to 255)

To program the chord and strum:

1. Select the chord type with the appropriate key. Available chords types are: Major, Major 7, Dominant 7, Major 9, Minor, Minor 7, Minor 7+9, and Major 7+9.

2. Set the time between each note in the chord with the Value fader. A minimum setting simulates a piano chord (generated notes play simultaneously with no delay); a maximum setting simulates a slow guitar strum. Notes play from the lowest (root) note of the chord to the highest.

    Strum values between 16–31 are a special strum mode where a Note On triggers an upward strum, and the Note Off triggers a downward strum (at reduced velocity) that lasts half as long as the up strum. This is excellent for strummed guitar simulations.

3. Play a note and you should hear a chord. All non-note messages (*e.g.*, controllers, timing clock, etc.) are merged with any generated note messages. Single-note lines generally provide the best results; check your keyboard's manual to see if it has a monophonic mode (also called legato mode) that locks out the option to play chords.

Advanced Applications
Here are some ideas on how to modify the Chord Player:

- Add chord types.

- Parallel the keys with footswitches so you can change harmonies "on the fly."

- Add strum values.

- Add down strum capabilities for all strum values.

- Provide programmable upstrum velocities.

- Initiate chord changes by playing additional notes at the same time as the root.

- Add a low bass note to "root" the chord.

Software Summary

States

Name	Objective
StOp	Operate

Actions

Name	Activity
IDLE	No action (administer chords)
CMAJ	Set chord to major
CMAJ7	Set chord to major 7th
CDOM7	Set chord to dominant 7th
CMAJ9	Set chord to major 9th
CMIN	Set chord to minor
CMIN7	Set chord to minor 7th
CMIN79	Set chord to minor 7th+9th
CMAJ79	Set cord to major 7th+9th
STRSET	Set strum delay with fader
CDISP	Update display with chord type
SDISP	Update display with strum value

Events

Name	Interface
EvIdle	Idle
EvMajor	MAJOR key
EvMaj7	MAJ 7 key
EvDom7	DOM 7 key
EvMaj9	MAJ 9 key
EvMinor	MINOR key
EvMin7	MIN 7 key
EvMin79	MIN79 key
EvMaj79	MAJ79 key
EvStrum	STRUM fader

State Matrix

	State 0: StOp
Event	NextSt,Act
EvIdle,	StOp,IDLE
EvMajor,	StOp,CMAJ
EvMaj7,	StOp,CMAJ7
EvDom7,	StOp,CDOM7
EvMaj9,	StOp,CMAJ9
EvMinor,	StOp,CMIN
EvMin7,	StOp,CMIN7
EvMin79,	StOp,CMIN79
EvMaj79,	StOp,CMAJ79
EvStrum,	StOp,STRSET

MIDI Implementation Chart

CHORD PLAYER   Date: 9-30-93
MIDItool 18   MIDI Implementation Chart   Version: 1.0

Function		Transmitted	Recognized	Remarks
Basic	Default	***	1-16	note 1
Channel	Channel	***	***	
	Default	Mode 1	Mode 2	
Mode	Messages	X	X	
	Altered	***	***	
Note		O	O	note 2
Number	True Voice	***	***	
Velocity	Note ON	O	O	note 3
	Note OFF	O	O	note 4
Aftertouch	Key	X	X	
	Channel	X	X	
Pitch Bend		X	X	
Controllers	7	X	X	
	16,48	X	X	
	121	X	X	
	0-95	X	X	
Program		X	X	
Change	True #	***	***	
System Exclusive		X	X	
System	SPP	X	X	
Common	Song Select	X	X	
	Tune Request	X	X	
System	Clock	X	X	
Realtime	Commands	X	X	
Aux	Local ON/OFF	X	X	
	All Notes Off	X	X	
	Active Sensing	X	X	
	Reset	X	X	

Notes:
1: The device operates in OMNI mode
2: MIDI note messages are generated according to received
   root note messages
3: Generated notes have velocities that are equal to or
   slightly less than the received root note
4: Generated notes are turned off using Note On messages
   with velocity=0

Mode 1: Omni On, Poly   Mode 2: Omni On, Mono   O:Yes
Mode 3: Omni Off, Poly   Mode 4: Omni Off, Mono   X:No

Project 19: System Exclusive Folder

MIDI System Exclusive messages are used for many purposes; one common application is to express the parameter values in a device's memory in a form compatible with other MIDI data. As a result, data within a synthesizer, signal processor, or similar piece of programmable MIDI gear can be sent down the MIDI line to a System Exclusive storage device (such as a computer, or dedicated devices like the Alesis DataDisk or Peavey MIDI Streamer).

This project creates a non-volatile "folder" in the MIDItools Computer for storing up to 256 bytes of System Exclusive data. The data can be recalled later, and used to reload the memory of the gear from which it came. Typical uses include:

- Backup Device. Backup device presets in the System Exclusive folder.

- Interim Storage Device. While editing device preset parameters, use the Sys Ex folder to store a particular version until needed.

- Pseudo-Undo for synth programming. Before doing any major change to a patch, save it first to the Sys Ex folder. If you don't like the results of your edits, you can always revert to the most recently saved version.

System Exclusive Folder Specs

Function: Storage
Transmit/Receive/Both: Both
Inline Device: No
Internal Merging: No
PC Boards required: CPU, Hand H/I or Rack H/I
Inputs: MIDI In, Panel Keys (5), Fader, DC Power, On/Off Switch, LCD Contrast
Outputs: LCD, LEDs (2), MIDI Out, MIDI Thru
Enclosure: Hand Box or Rack Box
Complexity: High

Panel Layouts

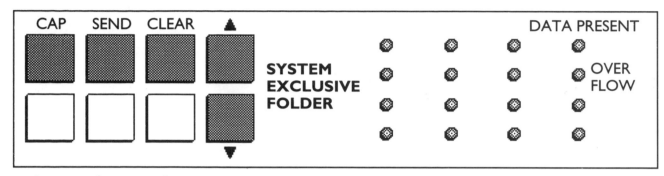

rack mount front panel

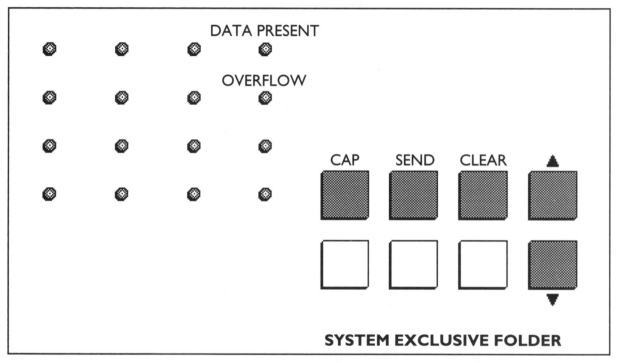

hand held front panel

Setup

1. Connect a suitable power supply (see Chapter 6) to the MIDItool power supply input.

2. Connect a MIDI cable from the transmitting device's MIDI Out to the MIDItool MIDI In.

3. Connect a MIDI cable from the MIDItool MIDI Out to the receiving device's MIDI In.

4. Turn on the power.

5. Adjust LCD Contrast for the most readable display.

System Exclusive Folder Operations

Default Settings
When power is first applied:

- The message stored at power-down is restored.

- Byte Displayed—1

- Operational status—the device is set for normal operation.

Capture System Exclusive Data
1. Press the Cap(ture) key to store the next System Exclusive message received at the Sys Ex Folder's MIDI input (data is saved automatically to non-volatile EEPROM). The LCD shows:

```
CAPTURING SYSEX
...waiting
```

2. Check the Data Present LED; it will light when data is present in the folder.

The Data Overflow LED lights if the folder overflows, meaning that the Sys Ex file is too large to be stored by the MIDItools computer.

Review the Folder Contents
Review the folder contents at any time by using the +/– keys and/or Value fader to select the desired byte. The LCD shows the data for the selected byte, as well as the total message length.

```
BYTE:bbb DATA:hh
MSG LENGTH: ccc
```

Possible variable values are:

bbb = 1–256 or "-"
hh = 00H–FFH or "-"
ccc = 0–255

Retransmit Stored Data
Press the Send key to transmit the folder contents. The LCD shows:

```
SENDING...
```

Clear the Folder
Press the Clear key to clear the folder contents and reset all parameters. The LCD shows:

```
CLEARING...
```

Advanced Applications

Here are some ideas for System Exclusive Folder modifications:

- Provide more internal memory to allow for storing longer messages.

- Allow multiple messages.

- Tag incoming messages with a number for selective recall.

- Support message data editing.

- List manufacturer by name (in other words, translate the Sys Ex ID header into a form that can be shown on the display).

- Allow manufacturer ID-specific storage.

- Further characterize Sys Ex extensions (*e.g.,* sample dump standards, MTC, etc.).

Software Summary

States

Name	Objective
StOp	Normal operation

Actions

Name	Activity
IDLE	No action
CAPINI	Initialize capture mode
MSGSTO	Store message
MSGSND	Send message
MSGCLR	Clear contents of folder
LENGET	Get length of folder message
REVINC	Increment message review pointer
REVDEC	Decrement review pointer
REVFDR	Set review pointer with fader
RDISP	Update display for review
DDISP	Update display with data
LDISP	Update display with message length
ADISP	Update display with everything

Events

Name	Interface
EvIdle	Idle
EvCap	CAP key
EvSend	SEND key
EvClear	CLEAR key
EvPlus	+ key
EvMinus	- key
EvValue	VALUE fader

State Matrix

	State 1: StOp
Event	NextSt,Act
EvIdle,	StOp,MSGSTO
EvCap,	StOp,CAPINI
EvSend,	StOp,MSGSND
EvClear,	StOp,MSGCLR
EvPlus,	StOp,REVINC
EvMinus,	StOp,REVDEC
EvValue,	StOp,REVFDR

MIDI Implementation Chart

SYSTEM EXCLUSIVE FOLDER   Date: 9-30-93
MIDItool 19   MIDI Implementation Chart   Version: 1.0

Function		Transmitted	Recognized	Remarks
Basic	Default	***	***	note 1
Channel	Channel	***	***	
	Default	***	***	
Mode	Messages	X	X	
	Altered	***	***	
Note		X	X	
Number	True Voice	***	***	
Velocity	Note ON	X	X	
	Note OFF	X	X	
Aftertouch	Key	X	X	
	Channel	X	X	
Pitch Bend		X	X	
Controllers	7	X	X	
	16,48	X	X	
	121	X	X	
	0-95	X	X	
Program		X	X	
Change	True #	***	***	
System Exclusive		O	O	note 1
System	SPP	X	X	
Common	Song Select	X	X	
	Tune Request	X	X	
System	Clock	X	X	
Realtime	Commands	X	X	
Aux	Local ON/OFF	X	X	
	All Notes Off	X	X	
	Active Sensing	X	X	
	Reset	X	X	

Notes:
1: The device transmits and recognizes only System Exclusive
   messages

Mode 1: Omni On, Poly   Mode 2: Omni On, Mono   O:Yes
Mode 3: Omni Off, Poly   Mode 4: Omni Off, Mono   X:No

Project 20: MIDI Patch Bay

If you're tired of patching and re-patching MIDI cables, this project's for you. Plug the MIDI In and Out connections from up to four pieces of MIDI gear into the Patch Bay, and program it to memorize 16 different routings. Typical applications include:

- When using several different keyboards with a sequencer, store different preset combinations of master and slave keyboards.

- Route various devices to a MIDI system exclusive storage "librarian," such as a suitably equipped keyboard, dedicated device, or Project 19 (Sys Ex folder).

- Set up assignments for different controllers (pedals, sliders, other MIDItools controller generators) to control signal processors, tone generators, etc.

- Switch between different master MIDI controllers (*e.g.,* MIDI guitar, MIDI drum pads, and MIDI keyboard).

This project requires the MIDI Patch Bay expansion PC board (see sidebar) to interface with the eight additional MIDI connectors. As a result, it cannot fit in the hand box and must be rack-mounted.

Please note that MIDI merging is not supported. Although a patch bay MIDI input can drive several patch bay MIDI outputs, a patch bay MIDI output cannot receive signals from more than one patch bay MIDI input.

MIDI Patch Bay Specs

Function: MIDI input/output router for up to four pieces of gear (translator)
Transmit/Receive/Both: Receive
Inline Device: No
Internal Merging: No
PC Boards required: CPU, Rack H/I, MIDI Patch Bay expansion board
Inputs: MIDI Ins (4), Panel Keys (8), Fader, DC Power, On/Off Switch, LCD Contrast
Outputs: LCD, LEDs (16), MIDI Outs (4)
Enclosure: Rack Box only
Complexity: High

Panel Layout

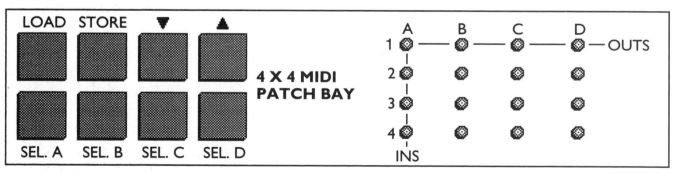

rack mount front panel

Setup

1. This tool uses the Patch Bay Expansion PC board (see sidebar) to provide an interface between the MIDItools computer and the four pieces of MIDI gear. Connect the Patch Bay board to the CPU board's expansion connector with a ribbon cable.

2. Connect a suitable power supply (see Chapter 6) to the MIDItool power supply input.

3. Connect MIDI cables from the MIDItool's four MIDI Ins to the MIDI Outs of four master devices.

4. Connect MIDI cables from the MIDItool's four MIDI Outs to the MIDI Ins of four slave devices.

5. Turn on the power switch.

6. Adjust LCD Contrast for the best display contrast.

MIDI Patch Bay Operations

Default Settings

Turn on power, and the screen initially shows something like:

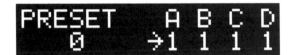

The default settings are:

- Preset—whichever was selected when power was last turned off (0 if no preset had been selected).

- Output A—selected for editing.

- Operational Status—The device is ready for normal operation.

Create a Patch to Route MIDI Connections

1. Press the desired Output key (A, B, C or D). Note: the outputs feed the MIDI Inputs of the devices connected to the patch bay.

2. Select the desired patch bay input (1–4) with the +/– keys and/or the Value fader. The arrow points to the parameter that will be modified by the +/– keys and Value fader. Inputs are fed by the MIDI Outs of devices connected to the patch bay.

The LCD's upper line shows the labels for the parameters on the bottom line.

The possible variable values are:

x   = MIDI patch bay input (1 to 4)
nn = Preset number (0–15)

An asterisk (*) next to the preset number indicates that the preset patch has been modified. Both the LCD and LED displays show the preset's patch routing.

Examples: The first diagram shows a MIDI system consisting of a keyboard synthesizer, drum machine, sequencer, and Sys Ex disk librarian. The following routing establishes these connections:

- The synth keyboard MIDI output feeds the sequencer's input to allow for recording parts into the sequencer.

- The sequencer MIDI Out drives the synthesizer MIDI In.

- The sequencer MIDI Out also drives the drumbox MIDI In. In this example, the drum box is being used as an expander module for its drum sounds.

For this routing, the LCD would show A= 3, C=1, and D=1. B could be set to 2 or 4.

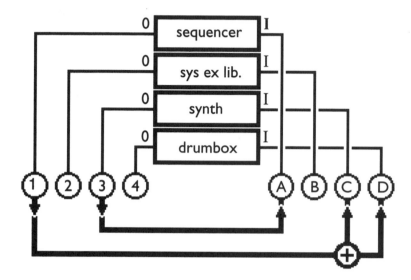

The next routing lets you save synthesizer patches as Sys Ex data into a Sys Ex librarian, then load the synthesizer with previously stored Sys Ex data.

The synth MIDI Out feeds the Sys Ex librarian MIDI In, so that the librarian can receive the synth data for storage. The librarian MIDI Out feeds the synth MIDI In so that the librarian can send patch data back into the synth.

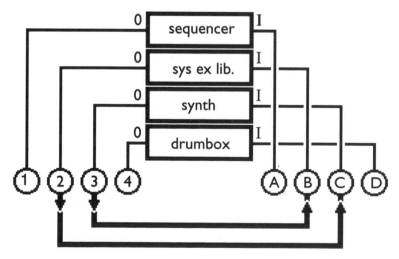

For this routing, the LCD would show B=3 and C=2. A and D could connect to 4.

In the final example, the drumbox serves as the master MIDI clock; it drives the sequencer and plays its own drum sounds. Meanwhile, the sequencer drives the synthesizer to play back sounds on the synth.

The drumbox MIDI Out drives the sequencer MIDI In, and the sequencer MIDI Out drives the synthesizer MIDI In. The LCD would show A=4 and C=1. B and D could connect to 2 so that they don't get in the way.

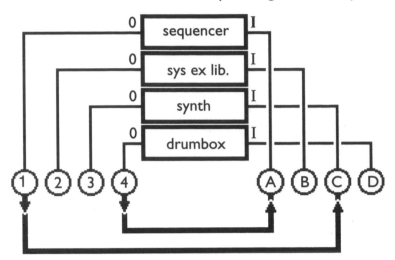

Store a Created Patch as a Preset

1. Press the Preset Store key. The LCD shows:

2. Use the +/– keys and/or the Value fader to select a preset number (nn, which ranges from 1–16). Routing data will be stored in this preset.

3. Press the Store key again to store the patch at the selected location. The LCD says "Storing!"

4. Press any Output key to resume patch editing.

Load a Preset Patch

1. Press the Preset Load key. The LCD shows:

2. Use the +/– keys and/or the Value fader to select the preset number (1–16) to be loaded.

3. Press the Load key again to load the preset. The LCD says "Loading!"

4. Press any Output key to resume patch editing.

Advanced Applications

Here are some ideas for possible MIDI Patch Bay modifications:

- Allow more user presets.

- Add an "off" option along with the four input selection options.

- Provide more inputs and/or outputs.

- Include MIDI merging of two or more inputs.

- Be able to name presets (e.g., "sequencing," "mixdown," etc.).

- Support a personal computer interface for patch storage and editing.

- Allow for programming the patch bay with Sys Ex messages.

- Accept real time patch changes via MIDI controller messages or a footswitch.

Software Summary

States

Name	Objective
StEdit	Edit patches
StLoad	Load patch from memory
StStore	Store patch to memory

Actions

Name	Activity
IDLE	No action
ASEL	Select Output A for patching
BSEL	Select Output B for patching
CSEL	Select Output C for patching
DSEL	Select Output D for patching
ININC	Increment selected input number
INDEC	Decrement selected input number
INFDR	Set selected input number with fader
PREINC	Increment selected preset number
PREDEC	Decrement selected preset number
PREFDR	Set selected preset number with fader
PTDISP	Update display for patch editing
STDISP	Update display for preset storing
LDDISP	Update display for preset loading
PRDISP	Update display with preset number
ADISP	Update Output A display
BDISP	Update Output B display
CDISP	Update Output C display
DDISP	Update Output D display
STORE	Store patch as preset
LOAD	Load preset patch and display values
HDUPD8	Configure hardware
LDUPD8	Update LED display
ARWDSP	Place LCD cursor arrow
ARWCLR	Clear LCD cursor arrow

Events

Name	Interface
EvIdle	Idle
EvLoad	PRESET LOAD key
EvStore	PRESET STORE key
EvMinus	PRESET - key
EvPlus	PRESET + key
EvA	OUTPUT A key
EvB	OUTPUT B key
EvC	OUTPUT C key
EvD	OUTPUT D key
EvValue	VALUE fader

State Matrix

Event	State 0: StEdit NextSt,Act	State 1: StLoad NextSt,Act	State 2: StStore NextSt,Act
EvIdle,	StEdit,IDLE,	StLoad,IDLE,	StStore,IDLE
EvA,	StEdit,ASEL,	StEdit,PTDISP,	StEdit,PTDISP
EvB,	StEdit,BSEL,	StEdit,PTDISP,	StEdit,PTDISP
EvC,	StEdit,CSEL,	StEdit,PTDISP,	StEdit,PTDISP
EvD,	StEdit,DSEL,	StEdit,PTDISP,	StEdit,PTDISP
EvPlus,	StEdit,ININC,	StLoad,PREINC,	StStore,PREINC
EvMinus,	StEdit,INDEC,	StLoad,PREDEC,	StStore,PREDEC
EvValue,	StEdit,INFDR,	StLoad,PREFDR,	StStore,PREFDR
EvLoad,	StLoad,LDDISP,	StEdit,LOAD,	StLoad,LDDISP
EvStore,	StStore,STDISP,	StStore,STDISP,	StEdit,STORE

MIDI Implementation Chart

MIDI PATCH BAY   Date: 9-30-93

MIDItool 20   MIDI Implementation Chart   Version: 1.0

Function		Transmitted	Recognized	Remarks
Basic	Default	***	***	note 1
Channel	Channel	***	***	
	Default	***	***	
Mode	Messages	X	X	
	Altered	***	***	
Note		X	X	
Number	True Voice	***	***	
Velocity	Note ON	X	X	
	Note OFF	X	X	
Aftertouch	Key	X	X	
	Channel	X	X	
Pitch Bend		X	X	
Controllers	7	X	X	
	16,48	X	X	
	121	X	X	
	0-95	X	X	
Program		X	X	
Change	True #	***	***	
System Exclusive		X	X	
System	SPP	X	X	
Common	Song Select	X	X	
	Tune Request	X	X	
System	Clock	X	X	
Realtime	Commands	X	X	
Aux	Local ON/OFF	X	X	
	All Notes Off	X	X	
	Active Sensing	X	X	
	Reset	X	X	

Notes:
1: The device has no available MIDI control

Mode 1: Omni On, Poly   Mode 2: Omni On, Mono   O:Yes
Mode 3: Omni Off, Poly   Mode 4: Omni Off, Mono   X:No

How the Expansion Board Works

The MIDI Patch Bay expansion PC board uses 74HC354 multiplexer chips to route MIDI data from each of the MIDI Inputs to the MIDI Outputs. The 74HC354 can actually route 8 channels, but a 4 x 4 router fits better in the available space.

Configuring each output channel involves feeding the 74CH354's two select lines (S0, S1) with a binary representation of the input to be connected. $00 selects Input 1, $01 selects Input 2, $02 selects Input 3, and $03 selects Input 4.

Example: Feeding $01 to an output assigns it to Input 2. Since there are four outputs, and each output requires two bits for the Input assignment, we need eight bits to configure all four outputs. The general purpose Parallel bus just happens to do this job perfectly. To write the configuration data into the 74HC354, feed the data to S0 and S1, then strobe the "Select Control" (SC) line to latch the data internally. SC connects to general purpose expansion port X0.

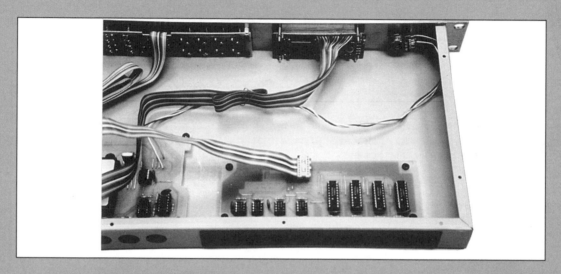

The patch bay expansion board mounts in the lower right corner; the connectors appear through the cutout in the rear panel.

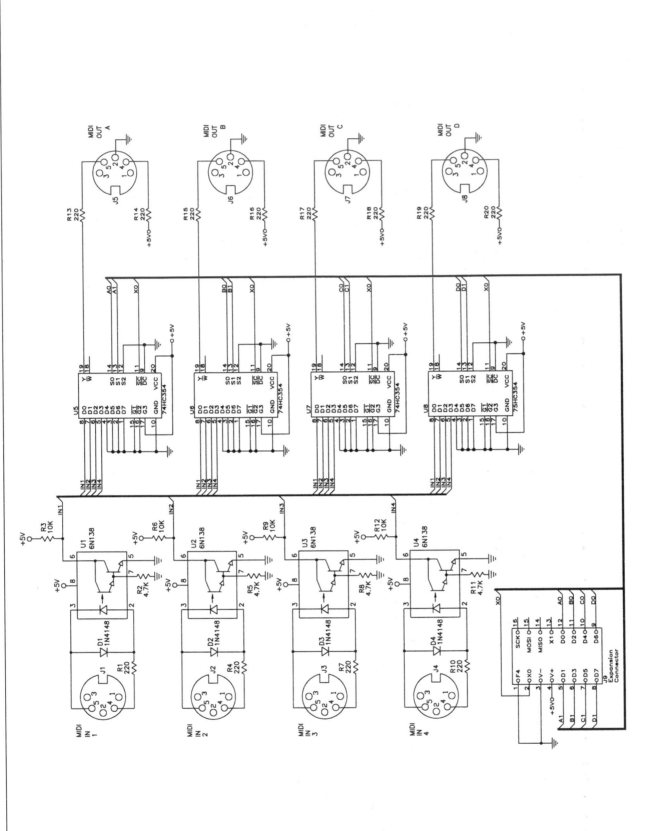

Notes:

(1) Expand power jumpers (J8 & J9 on CPU Board) must be in +5/GND position

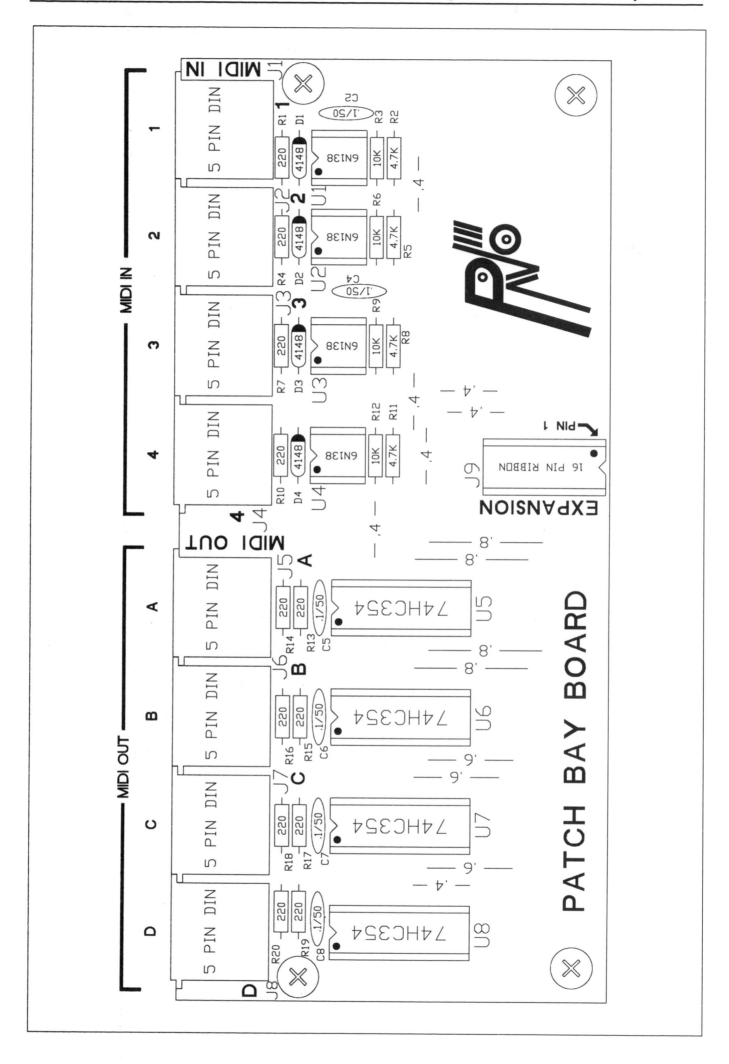

Chapter 8

Basic Digital Electronics Theory

MIDI is one application of *digital electronics*—the same technology that brought us computers, intelligent microwave ovens, remote controls, modern automobile ignition systems, and talking dolls that go to the bathroom.

Understanding digital electronics is the key to understanding MIDI devices on a nuts-and-bolts basis, but be warned that some of this involves math—yes, the subject that seemed like it was invented specifically to torment school-age kids. Fortunately, though, you don't need to be into math to get the MIDItools Computer up and running; this chapter is mostly for the benefit of those who want to get into MIDI programming eventually.

In the Beginning There Were Number Systems

A *number system* uses symbols to represent quantities, and is similar to a language. Like languages, there are many different number systems in use. Just as different languages provide different ways to express the same fundamental ideas, different number systems provide different ways to express the same quantities.

The most common number system is the *decimal* number system. It's based on tens because we have ten fingers, and it seems that's how people started counting. In the decimal number system any number can be made up from 10 different symbols, 0–9. For example, to express the number 107, we use the 1, 0, and 7 symbols, arranged in the proper order.

Different number systems express 107 differently. For example, the *binary* numbering system has only two symbols, 1 and 0. To express "107" in binary, we therefore end up with a string of 1s and 0s. (In case you wondered, the binary equivalent to 107 is 1101011. We'll find out why later.)

The *hexadecimal* system (*hex* for short) has 16 symbols, 0–9 and A–F. 107 in hexadecimal is 6B (trust us on this one, we'll explain it all later). The numbers "107," "1101011," and "6B" all describe exactly the same quantity—they just use different symbol systems to describe this quantity.

The difference between each of the above number systems is the number of symbols on which the system is *based*. Decimal is a *base 10* number system, which is to be expected since we have ten fingers and toes.

The binary system is a *base 2* number system because it's based on only two symbols. Binary is the number system of choice for digital systems because they only know "yes" and "no" (or "on" and "off"); they don't really grasp concepts such as "maybe." Just as decimal is well-suited for humans because of our ten fingers and toes, binary is ideal for machines that think in terms of only two possible options.

Hexadecimal is a *base 16* number system. Why bother with yet another system? The answer is convenience—more symbols allow expressing larger numbers with fewer characters. You saw how 107 in decimal became an unwieldy 1101011 in binary, and a sleek 6B in hex. With hex, we can write numbers up to 255 with only two digits, and numbers up to 65,536 with only four digits. Programmers are inherently lazy, so writing big numbers with fewer digits is a Big Deal.

Back to Binary

Since binary is the happening number system for digital electronics, we need to learn some of its high points. Not only is this essential knowledge if you want to program, but starting a discussion on binary theory is an excellent way to get rid of unwelcome house guests (unless they're programmers).

Bits

Bit is short for binary digit. Since binary is a base 2 number system, that digit can be only 0 or 1. These values represent any two states, such as "true" and "false," "high" and "low," "on" and "off," "5V" and "0V," "mark" and "space," "active" and "inactive," and so on.

Binary works well for digital electronics because you can represent the two states of a bit electrically by the presence or absence of a particular voltage (usually around 3 to 5 volts DC). We don't care what the exact voltage is, it just has to be there or not there. Since we don't care exactly how much voltage there is, digital systems can get pretty sloppy before they start to lose information. There can be hum or noise riding along with that voltage, but it doesn't matter—the system sees a voltage, and (in most cases) interprets it as "1." This eliminates almost any chance of misreading a bit, which is why you can make digital copies seemingly forever without losing data.

Anatomy of a Byte

Let's look at how to construct binary numbers, then how to add, subtract, multiply, and divide with them.

Grouping bits together lets you express more than 0 (no voltage) and 1 (voltage present and accounted for). For example, with two bits, there are four possible options:

Bit 1	Bit 2	Decimal equivalent
0	0	0
0	1	1
1	0	2
1	1	3

Adding another bit gives us eight options:

Bit 1	Bit 2	Bit 3	Decimal equivalent
0	0	0	0
0	0	1	1
0	1	0	2
0	1	1	3
1	0	0	4
1	0	1	5
1	1	0	6
1	1	1	7

A *byte* is a group of 8 bits. Each added bit doubles the number of options, so 4 bits gives 16 options, 5 bits 32 options, 6 bits 64 options, 7 bits 128 options, and 8 bits gives 256 options. Therefore, a byte can represent numbers that range from 1–256 (or 0–255).

An easy way to figure out the range of values available with a certain number of bits is to multiply 2 by itself for as many times as there are bits. For example, with 3 bits, you can have:

```
2 x 2 x 2 = 8
```

possible values (either 1–8 or 0–7).

With 5 bits:

```
2 x 2 x 2 x 2 x 2 = 32
```

possible values (1–32 or 0–31).

Since not only programmers but mathematicians are lazy, they get tired of writing out all those numbers. So, they use a kind of shorthand where the superscript shows the number of bits. Here's a different way to express the examples shown above:

$$2 \times 2 \times 2 = 2^3$$

$$2 \times 2 \times 2 \times 2 \times 2 \times 2 \times 2 \times 2 = 2^8$$

The way you'd say the first example is "2 to the 3rd power" and the second example, "2 to the 8th power." Just think, all this time you thought this kind of stuff was difficult! In reality, it's difficult only if you don't know what the shorthand symbols stand for.

Just to reinforce what we've learned so far, there are 8 bits in a byte. So how many possible values can a byte have?

$$2^8 = 2 \times 2 \times 2 \times 2 \times 2 \times 2 \times 2 \times 2 = 256$$

Columns and Values

With a decimal (base 10) number that has multiple digits, each digit has more "weight" as you move from the rightmost digit to the leftmost one: the rightmost digit is multiplied by 1, the next digit to the left is multiplied by 10, the next digit to the left is multiplied by 100, and so on. For example, the decimal number 357 is really shorthand for:

```
(3 x 100) + (5 x 10) + (7 x 1)
```

Another way to write this, using our newfound knowledge:

$$(3 \times 10^2) + (5 \times 10^1) + (7 \times 10^0)$$

(Incidentally, you might wonder about the "10 to the 0 power" part. Just remember that *any* number to the 0 power equals 1.)

As decimal numbers grow larger, we keep adding digits with higher powers of 10. For example, the digit to the left of hundreds stands for thousands, and so on.

Binary numbers work identically, except their digits come in powers of 2 instead of powers of 10. An 8-bit byte, therefore, has the following anatomy:

2^7	2^6	2^5	2^4	2^3	2^2	2^1	2^0	value of each bit
128	64	32	16	8	4	2	1	decimal value
b7	b6	b5	b4	b3	b2	b1	b0	bits

```
_____/
                    one byte
```

Each digit in a binary number has a weight of 2^n (where n is the position of the digit, starting from the right). For example, consider binary number 10101010:

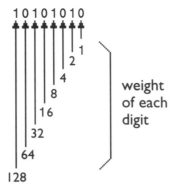

The above byte has a value of:

$(1 \times 128) + (0 \times 64) + (1 \times 32) + (0 \times 16) + (1 \times 8) + (0 \times 4) + (1 \times 2) + (0 \times 1) = 170$

If we were to count to ten in binary, the sequence would be:

```
00000000 (0)
00000001 (1)
00000010 (2)
00000011 (3)
00000100 (4)
00000101 (5)
00000110 (6)
00000111 (7)
00001000 (8)
00001001 (9)
00001010 (10)
```

Nibbles and Words

Two other binary terms are *nibble* and *word*. A nibble is half a byte (sounds reasonable, eh?), or four bits. A nibble has $2^4 = 16$ possible values.

In general, a word is the number of bits a particular computer uses internally for computation. This is often two bytes (16 bits total), with 2^{16} = 65,536 possibilities. For the purposes of this book, it is *always* 16 bits, even though sometimes people use the term "word" to describe other numbers of bits, such as 32 or 64. (Incidentally, some sampling keyboards that store digital audio samples 12 bits at a time consider 12 bits to be a word.)

Hexadecimal

Since hexadecimal is base 16, each digit in a hex number has a weight of 16^n (where n is the position of the digit, starting from the right). Since binary uses up 4 bits to represent what a single digit can express in hex, hex representation lets us write numbers with 25% as many digits as binary. For example, the number 250 needs 8 binary digits (11111010), but only two hex digits (FA). If you're anything like us, you'd rather write numbers like "FA" than "11111010" all day long.

Hex digits have sixteen possible values, so the normal numerals (0–9) don't cover the entire range. To fill in the gap, the letters A, B, C, D, E, and F represent the values 10–15. The first sixteen hex numbers are then:

0,1,2,3,4,5,6,7,8,9,A,B,C,D,E,F.

For example, sixteen in hex is "10." The "1" stands for 16^1, and the "0" stands for 16^0.

To differentiate a hex number like "14" from the decimal number that looks the same but represents a different value, precede the hex number with a $ or follow it with an H. For example, 20 in decimal becomes $14 or 14H in hex. If you see 14 by itself, assume it's decimal.

Binary Math

Now that you have an idea of what binary is, and what binary numbers look like, let's consider how to perform mathematical operations using the binary number system. Fortunately, the basic decimal arithmetic operations we do every day work very similarly in binary.

Binary Addition

Binary addition follows these simple rules:

0 + 0 = 0 (zero plus zero = zero)
0 + 1 = 1 (zero plus one = one)
1 + 0 = 1 (one plus zero = one)
1 + 1 = 10 (one plus one = two plus a carry)

The above rules can be represented by a *truth table* which shows inputs and outputs as a table. The truth table for binary addition is:

A +	B	Carry	Sum
0	0	0	0
0	1	0	1
1	0	0	1
1	1	1	0

Notice that 1 + 1 = 10. That's not a "ten," but a binary "two." Since two exceeds the range (0 to 1) of a binary digit, 1 + 1 requires a "carry" to the next digit. This is exactly what happens in decimal addition when the result of adding two digits exceeds 9.

Let's add two binary numbers.

```
      11 —carries
   0110001
  +1001011
   1111100
```

Addition begins with the rightmost bit (called "least-significant" or "lowest-order" because it has the least significant weight) and works to the left—just like adding decimal numbers. In the above example, the two least significant bits ("LSBs") add to 0, with a carry to the next significant digit. The bits in the second column (including the carry) add to 0 with a carry to the third column. The bits in the remaining columns add to ones.

Binary Subtraction

Here's the truth table for binary subtraction.

A -	B	Borrow	Diff
0	0	0	0
0	1	1	1
1	0	0	1
1	1	0	0

When subtracting a larger number from a smaller one, binary subtraction requires a "borrow," just like decimal subtraction. Borrowing works by looking to the left of the smaller number until we find a 1, changing it to 0, and changing all intervening 0s to 1s. Confused? Let's look at an example, 12 minus 1 (or 1100-0001 in binary):

```
 1100
-0001
```

The above subtraction begins with the LSB. According to the truth table, 0–1 = 1 and requires a borrow. Since the next significant digit is a 0, we must go on until we find a 1 to get our borrow. So, we borrow from the third digit by changing it from a 1 to a 0, and change the intervening (second) digit to a 1.

After the borrow, the problem looks like this:

```
  01
1̶1̶00
-0001
    1
```

Subtraction then proceeds according to the truth table, which gives us:

```
 1010
-0001
 1011
```

If we needed another borrow later on, we would perform that before proceeding.

Binary Multiplication

Here's the truth table for binary multiplication.

A ×	B	Product
0	0	0
0	1	0
1	0	0
1	1	1

As with decimal multiplication, the multiplicand (what's being multiplied) and multiplier (what's multiplying the multiplicand) are arranged like this:

```
 10110    multiplicand
×  101    multiplier
```

Now stay with us here—the following may sound complicated, but binary multiplication uses the same basic process as standard decimal multiplication. The main difference is that we don't analyze how we do decimal multiplication; it's something we've done all our lives. So with binary multiplication, we have to look at multiplication afresh. An example will tie it all together.

You do multiplication of any kind by computing partial products between each individual digit in the multiplier, and all the digits in the multiplicand. You then shift each partial product left one place with respect to the previous partial product. After computing all the partial products, you add them together to obtain the final result. Here's an example of decimal multiplication:

```
 346
× 24
```

We take the right-most individual digit in the multiplier, and multiply all the digits in the multiplicand, which gives us:

```
4 × 346 = 1384
```

We then put this under the multiplier, aligned with the right-most digit:

```
  346
× 24
1384
```

Now we take the next individual digit in the multiplier and multiply all the digits in the multiplicand. This gives us:

```
2 × 346 = 692
```

Remember, though, that it's necessary to shift each partial product left one place. So now we have:

```
  346
× 24
1384
692
```

Adding all the partial products together gives us:

```
   346
 × 24
 1384
+692
 8304
```

Now let's look at an example (10110 × 101) using binary numbers.

1. The multiplier's first digit (1) multiplies the multiplicand (10110) to provide the first partial product.

```
 10110
×   101
 10110
```

2. Multiplying the multiplier's second digit (0) by the multiplicand computes the next partial product, which is shifted left one position relative to the first partial product.

```
 10110
×   101
 10110
00000
```

3. Repeat this process once more to compute the third partial product.

```
  10110
 ×   101
  10110
  00000
+10110
```

4. Summing the three partial products provides the final answer:

```
  10110
 ×   101
  10110
  00000
+10110
 1101110
```

Binary Division

Binary division works similarly to decimal long division, and the dividend and divisor are arranged as in decimal division.

divisor ➔ 10)‾1‾1‾0‾1‾0‾ ← dividend

Like decimal division, binary division uses an *iterative* technique (meaning it goes through a process over and over again) to first determine how many times a divisor fits into a portion of the dividend, then uses multiplication to compute a partial quotient. You keep subtracting partial quotients until you run out of digits in the dividend.

To divide two binary numbers:

1. Compare the divisor to the dividend's highest order bits (use the same number of dividend bits as the number of bits in the divisor). In the example, the divisor is 10, and the same number of bits in the dividend is 11.

2. Check if the divisor "goes into" (is less than or equal to) the dividend bits. This determines the quotient's highest order bit, which becomes the first digit above the dividend. Here the divisor (10) goes into the first two bits of the dividend (11) once, so the quotient's most significant (leftmost) bit is 1.

$$
\begin{array}{r}
1 \\
10\overline{)11010}
\end{array}
$$

3. Multiply this bit by the divisor, then subtract the resulting partial product from the dividend's high order bits—just as in decimal long division.

$$
\begin{array}{r}
1 \\
10\overline{)11010} \\
-\underline{10} \\
1
\end{array}
$$

4. After the subtraction, "carry down" the dividend's next bit for the next iteration.

$$
\begin{array}{r}
1 \\
10\overline{)11010} \\
-\underline{10} \\
10
\end{array}
$$

5. Check if the divisor goes into this remainder to determine the quotient's next highest order bit. The divisor now goes into the result (10) once, so the next bit in the quotient is 1. Multiply this bit by the divisor, then subtract the resulting partial product from the previous result.

$$
\begin{array}{r}
11 \\
10\overline{)11010} \\
-\underline{10} \\
10 \\
-\underline{10} \\
0
\end{array}
$$

6. The next carry gives us a result of 01. Since the divisor (10) is not less than ("doesn't go into") the result, the next highest order bit in the quotient is 0. Multiplying this bit by the divisor, then subtracting the resulting partial product from the previous result, gives 1.

```
          110
    10 )11010
       -10
        10
       -10
        01
       -00
         1
```

7. Now we carry down the 0 and end up with a remainder of 10, so the divisor goes into this result once. Therefore the quotient's last bit is 1, and after multiplying this bit by the divisor, there's a remainder of zero and all the dividend bits have been used in the computation. So we're done! Here's the completed example:

```
         1101
    10 )11010
       -10
        10
       -10
        01
       -00
        10
       -10
         0
```

11010 divided by 10 equals 1101.

Decisions, Decisions: The World of Logic

It's not just enough for a computer to do arithmetic; it also has to make decisions based on the data. As in almost all other examples of decision-making, this requires logic (politics is one of the few examples where decisions can be made without the use of logic).

You use simple logical operations all the time to make decisions, but are often not aware of the thought processes behind it. For example, suppose you want to go out and hear some music. Your decision might go as follows:

IF my favorite band is playing tonight, AND I have enough money to buy a ticket OR can get on the comp list because I helped them troubleshoot the sound system last week, THEN I will go to the club.

A keyboard synthesizer might make a decision like:

IF middle C is down AND the amplitude envelope is on AND mute is NOT on, THEN send a middle C note to the audio output.

The simplest computer logic operations are AND, OR, and NOT. These are represented by standardized symbols, which we'll look at next.

Logical AND

The truth table (Fig. 8-1) specifies what output (Z) occurs with different input options (A and B). Since this is an AND operation, the output (Z) gives a 1 only if A is 1 AND B is 1.

You can also think of 1 as being "true" and 0 as being "false." Considered this way, the AND function reads "If A AND B are true, then Z is true."

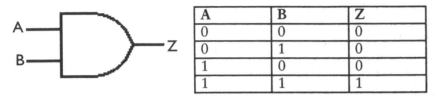

A	B	Z
0	0	0
0	1	0
1	0	0
1	1	1

Fig. 8-1: Symbol for the logical AND operation, and its accompanying truth table.

An AND operation can have any number of inputs, in which case all the inputs must be 1 to obtain a 1 at the output.

Logical OR

This table (Fig. 8-2) shows that the result of the OR operation is true if A OR B is true. Both A and B being true also gives a true result, since this satisfies the condition that at least one input is true. As with the logical AND, there can be any number of inputs.

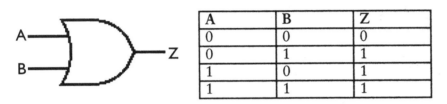

A	B	Z
0	0	0
0	1	1
1	0	1
1	1	1

Fig. 8-2: Symbol for the logical OR operation, and its accompanying truth table.

Logical NOT

The origin of saying a statement and then saying NOT to contradict it (such as "Madonna is the greatest operatic soprano who ever lived—NOT!") actually started with computers.

According to the table in Fig. 8-3, the result of a NOT operation is true (1) only if the input is false (0). Conversely, a true input gives a false output. In other words, the output is the opposite of (i.e., it's NOT) the input. Some people call this operation "complementing" or "inverting" a bit.

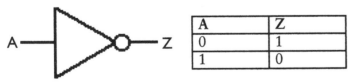

A	Z
0	1
1	0

Fig. 8-3: Symbol for the logical NOT operation, and its accompanying truth table.

Logical EXCLUSIVE OR

Although we don't mention this operation elsewhere in the book, for the sake of completeness let's look at the truth table for a two-input EXCLUSIVE OR operation (Fig. 8-4). This shows that the result is true whenever one OR another input is true, but not both inputs.

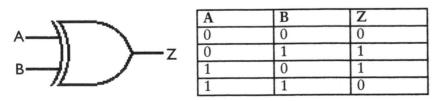

A	B	Z
0	0	0
0	1	1
1	0	1
1	1	0

Fig. 8-4: Symbol for the logical EXCLUSIVE OR (EX-OR for short) operation, and its accompanying truth table.

The EXCLUSIVE OR operation can have any number of inputs; for multiple input EXCLUSIVE OR functions, the output is true (1) if there is an odd number of 1s at the inputs, and false (0) if there is an even number of 1s.

Logical NAND

The NAND operation, a hybrid of the AND and NOT operations, follows an AND with a NOT (hence the name NOT AND, or NAND).

Its symbol (Fig. 8-5) is an AND with a dot at the output (the dot signifies the NOT operation). As expected, a NAND operation's result is the opposite of the AND operation since a NOT follows the AND. (Here's a piece of engineering trivia: all other logical operations—AND, OR, NOT, NOR, etc.—can be derived from connecting multiple NAND operations in various configurations.)

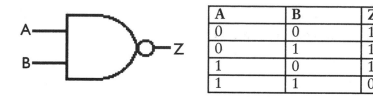

A	B	Z
0	0	1
0	1	1
1	0	1
1	1	0

Fig. 8-5: Symbol for the logical NAND operation, and its accompanying truth table.

Logical NOR

The NOR operation (Fig. 8-6), a hybrid of the OR and NOT functions, follows an OR with a NOT. As with NAND, the NOR symbol is an OR with the NOT dot at the output.

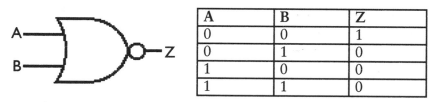

A	B	Z
0	0	1
0	1	0
1	0	0
1	1	0

Fig. 8-6: Symbol for the logical NOR operation, and its accompanying truth table.

Performing Binary Math with Logic Circuits

In case you're wondering about the connection between binary numbers, binary math, and logic, the basic idea is that you can use logic gates (ANDs, ORs, NOTs, and so on) to implement binary mathematical functions. Consider, for example, the truth table for binary addition:

A +	B	Sum	Carry
0	0	0	0
0	1	1	0
1	0	1	0
1	1	0	1

Let's see what logical functions we need to implement this table. The EX-OR function produces the binary sum:

A	B	EX-OR
0	0	0
0	1	1
1	0	1
1	1	0

The AND operation gives the carry in the binary carry:

A	B	Z
0	0	0
0	1	0
1	0	0
1	1	1

So, combining an EX-OR and AND function creates a binary adder (Fig. 8-7):

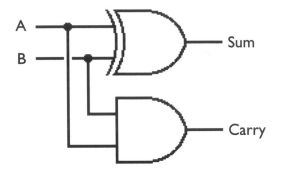

Fig. 8-7: *The EX-OR function provides the binary adder's sum, while the AND function gives the carry.*

This is only a 1-bit adder, so it's not very useful. In fact, the above circuit is normally called a "half adder," because it doesn't take into account the carry from the previous stage. A "full adder" does take the previous stage's carry into account, as shown in the following truth table:

A	B	C_{in}	Sum	C_{out}
0	0	0	0	0
1	0	0	1	0
0	1	0	1	0
1	1	0	0	1
0	0	1	1	0
1	0	1	0	1
0	1	1	0	1
1	1	1	1	1

Fig. 8-8 shows the logic circuitry needed to implement a full adder, which is simply two half adders and an extra OR gate.

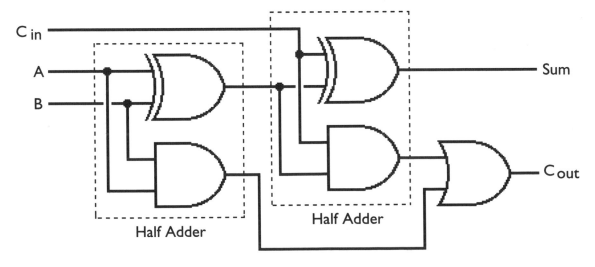

Fig. 8-8: *Creating a full adder from two half adders and an OR gate.*

Now, if you're the over-achieving type, you might be able to trace through the above logic circuit and verify that it operates according to the truth table. If not, don't worry. This "combination logic" stuff is beyond the scope of this book, since you don't need to understand it to build the projects or even program a microprocessor. What's important is the idea that logic functions can implement mathematical operations. Not just addition operations—*all* operations!

The full adder only adds two bits. Tying 8 full adders together (Fig. 8-9) creates an adder that can add two 8-bit numbers (bytes) and output a byte, which is much more useful.

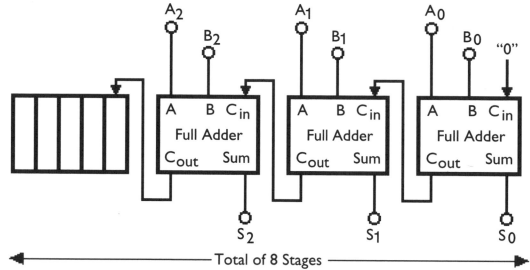

Fig. 8-9: *An adder that can add two 8-bit numbers.*

The point of all this is that you can carry out any mathematical operation with a suitable collection of logic gate circuitry. This is exactly what you find inside a microprocessor—lots of little logic circuits (see sidebar).

Two's Complement Representation

Our previous discussion of binary number representation considered only positive numbers (*i.e.*, from 0 to some big number). To be useful, binary must also represent negative quantities.

Putting a + or − sign in front of a decimal number represents positive or negative quantities. In binary there is no − symbol, only 1 and 0, so we have to somehow indicate negative numbers using 1 or 0.

Two's complement notation allows for this. With two's complement, all numbers with the MSB (most significant, or leftmost bit) equal to 0 are positive; if the MSB equals 1, the number is negative. In essence, the MSB is the + or − sign.

Two's complement numbers don't follow the normal pattern described earlier. The sequence from negative eight to positive seven is:

Decimal	Two's Complement
+7	0111
+6	0110
+5	0101
+4	0100
+3	0011
+2	0010
+1	0001
0	0000
−1	1111
−2	1110
−3	1101
−4	1100
−5	1011
−6	1010
−7	1001
−8	1000

Note that positive numbers count the same way as before (0001, 0010, 0011, etc.) but negative numbers are ordered differently. There is method behind this madness. Mathematically, a positive number plus a negative number (of the same magnitude) should equal zero. Notice what happens if we add +5 and −5 from the above table:

```
 111     carries
0101     (+5)
+1011    (−5)
10000
\_sum_/
```

If we limit the above sum to four bits (the same number of bits as the two numbers added), adding +5 and −5 gives 0. So, the +5 and −5 are indeed the same magnitude and opposite sign.

How do we derive that strange-looking two's complement sequence? Remember, positive numbers count as usual, with the MSB = 0. To derive the negative numbers, we negate the positive numbers with a simple procedure:

1. Complement the number (change all 0s to 1s and all 1s to 0s).

2. Add 1 to the result of step 1.

   Example: Negate +5 (0101) to −5

   Step 1: Complement +5

   ```
   complement of 0101 = 1010
   ```

   Step 2: add 1 to result of step 1

   ```
    1010
   +0001
    1011
   ```

   Result: 1011 equals −5

This process may seem a little odd, but the result is equivalent to multiplying by −1. Having a simple procedure to multiply by −1 makes two's complement very popular with computer people.

ASCII—The Computer's Alphabet

Although computers understand only numbers, they have to communicate with humans through written text on a display or printer. The computer therefore has to convert strings of numbers to written text (or vice-versa). For example, suppose we map numbers to text characters as shown below:

```
1 = "o"
2 = "c"
3 = "a"
4 = "y"
5 = "l"
6 = "w"
7 = "!"
8 = blank space
```

The computer can now compliment you by saying: "634821157." The display or printer translates the numbers to their associated characters so you can read them.

The American Standard Code for Information Interchange (ASCII) defines a standard mapping between numbers and characters so different computers, displays, etc. can share text. ASCII defines 128 unique letters, numbers, punctuation marks, and other characters as shown in Fig. 8-10.

Char	Hex	Char	Hex	Char	Hex	Char	Hex
nul	00	sp	20	@	40	`	60
soh	01	!	21	A	41	a	61
stx	02	"	22	B	42	b	62
etx	03	#	23	C	43	c	63
eot	04	$	24	D	44	d	64
enq	05	%	25	E	45	e	65
ack	06	&	26	F	46	f	66
bel	07	'	27	G	47	g	67
bs	08	(	28	H	48	h	68
ht	09	)	29	I	49	i	69
nl	0A	*	2A	J	4A	j	6A
vt	0B	+	2B	K	4B	k	6B
np	0C	,	2C	L	4C	l	6C
cr	0D	-	2D	M	4D	m	6D
so	0E	.	2E	N	4E	n	6E
si	0F	/	2F	O	4F	o	6F
dle	10	0	30	P	50	p	70
dc1	11	1	31	Q	51	q	71
dc2	12	2	32	R	52	r	72
dc3	13	3	33	S	53	s	73
dc4	14	4	34	T	54	t	74
nak	15	5	35	U	55	u	75
syn	16	6	36	V	56	v	76
etb	17	7	37	W	57	w	77
can	18	8	38	X	58	x	78
em	19	9	39	Y	59	y	79
sub	1A	:	3A	Z	5A	z	7A
esc	1B	;	3B	[	5B	{	7B
fs	1C	<	3C	\	5C	|	7C
gs	1D	=	3D	]	5D	}	7D
rs	1E	>	3E	^	5E	~	7E
us	1F	?	3F	_	5F	del	7F

Fig. 8-10: The ASCII character set

The first 32 codes ($00 – $1F) are "unprintable" characters. Data communications devices (such as computer keyboards and modems) use many of these unprintable characters to format and exchange strings of ASCII text. For example, *bel* makes your computer terminal beep, *esc* is the "escape" key on computer keyboards, *cr* corresponds to the "return" or "enter" key, and *sp* is space. Since ASCII is very old, many of the unprintable characters (e.g., *em* means "end of paper tape," which computers used before the advent of floppy disks!) are now obsolete and rarely used.

Most computers use a full byte (8 bits) to code text, which allows for 256 different characters. The first 128 are coded according to ASCII; the remainder provide foreign characters, mathematical symbols, graphics characters, and so on (this is where those evil little happy faces come from when your computer crashes). There is no standard for these extended characters.

The Parts Inside the Chips

Logic gates are simple circuits and require very few parts to build. This makes it easy to pack large numbers of gates on a chip.

Fig. 8-11 shows the circuits for AND and OR gates. Integrate a million or so of these little diode-resistor circuits in a chip, and you'd get a microprocessor.

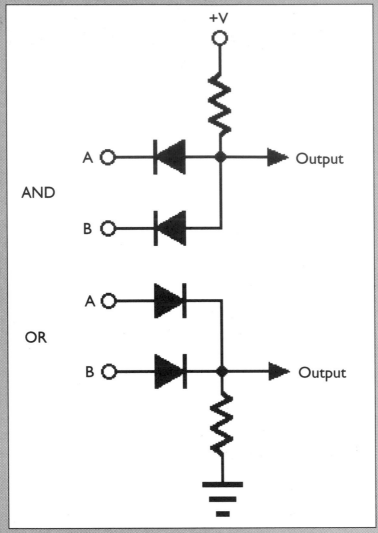

Fig. 8-11: Two diodes and a resistor are the only components needed to create an AND or OR gate.

In the real world, logic circuits rarely use diodes and resistors, but instead use transistors acting as diodes and resistors. If a chip is made of bipolar transistors, it's called a "Transistor Transistor Logic" (or "TTL") chip. Chips made of MOS transistors are called "CMOS" (the "C" stands for "complementary," which describes how the MOS transistors are hooked up inside).

Chapter 9
Computer Hardware Basics

Now you've been indoctrinated with enough digital electronics theory to look at how a computer works. Don't worry—it's really quite simple.

Actually, computers are very stupid. They can't learn anything we haven't taught them, don't know how to dance, and (as far as we know!) don't dream. What they *can* do is perform mathematical operations at blinding speed. As long as data can be expressed as numbers (and most data can) it can be analyzed, processed, and modified by the computer.

A computer generally has four components (Fig. 9-1):

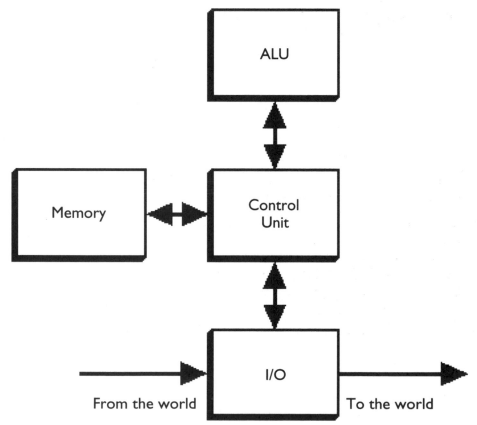

Fig. 9-1

- Memory. This is the computer's data repository. Data to be stored goes into memory, and data to be recalled comes from memory.

- Arithmetic Logic Unit (ALU). This is the computer's decision-maker, and does all the math and logic computations.

- Control Unit. This regulates the computer's operation by pulling instructions out of memory, in the right order, to accomplish specific tasks.

- Input/output (I/O). Just as we use paper, guitar, paint brush, or whatever as an output device for our brain, the computer uses *output* devices such as printers, synthesizers, tape recorders, and so on. *Input* is how the computer obtains data from the world—for example, playing a keyboard could provide note data that the computer then processes *(e.g.,* transposes it).

Incidentally, the term Central Processing Unit (CPU) refers to the combination of an ALU and Control Unit. Therefore, some people think of computers as having three elements: Memory, CPU, and I/O.

Memory

Since computers think of everything in terms of 1s and 0s, then each computer memory "cell" (bit) need only remember whether it's a 1 or a 0. The basic cell circuit is usually a *flip-flop,* which upon being triggered (set) generates a logic 1 and upon being cleared (reset) generates a logic 0. Even if the cell circuit is not a flip-flop, it will mimic the flip-flop's action—that is, remain in its existing state until told to change.

The flip-flop has "memory" because it remembers whether it is set or reset. This is one bit of memory. Computer memory chips, which consist of thousands or millions of tiny flip-flop circuits, store thousands or millions of bits.

To retrieve data from these millions of bits, the computer works like a post office. Just as every post office box has a unique number and set of contents, each byte (or word) of memory has a unique identification called an *address* and set of contents called *data.* In computer talk, the address specifies the memory location, and the data specifies what's stored at that location. Fig. 9-2 symbolically shows a typical chunk of memory; you can see that each address has a corresponding piece of data.

Computer memory comes in many flavors, but Random Access Memory (RAM) and Read Only Memory (ROM) are the most basic types.

RAM

The term "random access" is a bit misleading because RAM data is seldom accessed randomly (programmers usually know exactly where in memory their data lies). Perhaps a better term would be "read/writeable memory" because the computer can read its data or overwrite the data with new data.

There are several RAM technologies. *Dynamic RAM* (DRAM) is probably the most prevalent. Each cell consists of a *capacitor,* an electrical component that can hold a charge—sort of like a battery, except that it's easy to discharge rapidly. Each capacitor represents one bit of memory; a charged capacitor might indicate 1, and a discharged capacitor 0.

However, these capacitors are extremely "leaky," and as the charge leaks off, the memory contents are lost. So, special circuitry *refreshes* the charge if it exists—sort of as if you were trying to hold water in a leaky bucket, and more water gets thrown in to maintain the bucket's level. The refresh process happens hundreds or thousands of times a second.

Static RAM (SRAM) uses flip-flop circuits that don't require refreshing. However, since flip-flops are more complex than DRAM memory cells (the latter require only two transistors; flip-flops require many more), a given amount of memory requires more "real estate" with SRAM technology than DRAM technology. The tradeoff for DRAM's smaller size is less

Address	Data
15	$E4
14	$11
13	$B2
12	$ED
11	$6C
10	$00
09	$FF
08	$52
07	$A2
06	$DC
05	$74
04	$23
03	$B2
02	$84
01	$A3
00	$01

Fig. 9-2: Memory consists of addresses that specify particular locations in memory, and the data contained at each address.

convenience, since DRAM requires refreshing and SRAM does not. DRAM chips are also less expensive for a given amount of memory than SRAM. Many computers use both types of memory, although the MIDItools Computer uses only SRAM.

Most RAM requires power to retain its data—if the power goes away, so does the data. However, some SRAM can be backed up with battery power to protect data if the main power source fails.

ROM

Data is programmed into a ROM chip during the manufacturing process. From that point on, data can only be read from the ROM, and new data cannot be written to it.

A *Programmable ROM* (PROM) is a type of ROM that, using special programming devices, can be programmed after it leaves the factory. However, unlike RAM which can be rewritten with new data over and over (gazillions of times), once a PROM is written with data, it's permanent.

Erasable PROMs (EPROMs) have small, clear windows on top of the package. This isn't just so you can see how cool the inside of an IC looks, but for shining intense ultraviolet light on the chip itself to erase its memory. (In theory, sunlight could erase an EPROM over time, which is why EPROMs in commercial products usually have the window covered with a piece of opaque tape.) EPROMs can be programmed, erased, and reprogrammed thousands of times, making them convenient for prototyping new software. For production runs, once the software's been perfected it's customary to manufacture cheaper PROM or ROM versions.

Electrically erasable PROMs (EEPROMs) are erased not by ultraviolet light, but by applying a voltage (most new EEPROMs generate this voltage internally; older chips often had a special pin to which the voltage was applied). This allows a computer to erase parts of an EEPROM's memory and write to it as well as read from it. EEPROM is conceptually similar to RAM, but RAM loses its power when turned off, whereas EEPROMs are *non-volatile* and remember their data forever (or at least a hundred years or so).

Note that battery-backed SRAM (static RAM) is similar to the EEPROM since both types of memory can be read to or written from, and neither loses its data if the power supply is interrupted. The drawback of battery-backed SRAM is that once the battery dies, so does your data.

Arithmetic Logic Unit (ALU)

The ALU, which generally has two inputs and one output, performs all of the computer's arithmetic and logical functions. You can apply any of several operations to the inputs (addition, subtraction, logical AND, logical OR, logical NOT, etc.), and the result occurs at the output.

The Control Unit

The control unit regulates the computer's operation by fetching instructions stored in memory in the proper sequence, then decoding the instructions so they can be executed.

The most important part of the control unit is a collection of *registers*. These are special purpose memories, generally 8 or 16 bits wide. Two common registers are the *Program Counter* and the *Accumulator*.

The Program Counter (PC) keeps track of the address of the next instruction to be executed. After the computer fetches an instruction, the PC is updated to point to the next instruction. You can think of the PC as a compass that directs the computer through the program.

The Accumulator (ACCU) is a scratchpad memory for most ALU and memory operations. In particular, the ACCU holds the output of most ALU arithmetic and logic operations, and typically serves as one of the ALU's inputs. (The other ALU input can be an arbitrary memory address, another register, etc.) Most microprocessors contain at least one ACCU; many have more to allow for more powerful operations.

Getting on the Bus

A *bus* is a group of related connections that tie together the elements inside a circuit. For example, transferring a byte from one memory location to another occurs over a bus. A byte requires an 8-bit wide bus (since a byte is 8 bits), so a bus consists of eight separate wires (one for each bit).

Busses come in two flavors: *serial* and *parallel*. MIDI is an example of a serial bus, since it has only one cable connection between its two ends, and sends data one bit at a time, one right after the other.

Parallel buses provide more than one cable connection between the two ends in order to send several bits of data simultaneously. Parallel busses are faster than serial busses, because an 8 bit wide parallel bus can send an entire byte in the time it takes to send one bit over the serial bus. Another perspective is that it takes the serial bus eight times longer to send a byte than a parallel bus.

A good analogy is cars on two different types of roads. Suppose it takes a car 10 seconds to cover a particular piece of highway, and you want to move eight cars from one end of the highway to another. If it's an 8-lane highway, then all eight cars will reach the end of the road after 10 seconds. With a single-lane road, it would take 10 seconds for the first car to reach the end of the road, then another 10 seconds for the next car, another 10 seconds for the next car, and so on.

Although parallel busses are faster, having to use multiple conductors can make for unwieldy, fragile, and/or expensive cables.

Input/Output

I/O is the computer's connection to the outside world. Because there are a lot of things in the outside world that might interest a computer, there are many types of I/O.

An input or output connection is often called a *port*. The simplest I/O ports are general purpose input and output types. An *input port* typically connects to something outside the computer (like a keyboard switch, footpedal, etc.), and the computer program monitors data appearing at this port.

The *output port* sends data from the computer to an external device, which senses the data and acts on it. For example, the computer might send a piece of data that says "play middle C" to a MIDI-compatible output port; a MIDI synthesizer connected to the output would then sense the command and play middle C.

Interrupts

The computer reads from and writes to the I/O ports pretty much whenever it feels like it. In the real world, though, events often happen unpredictably that demand the computer's attention. These events must interrupt whatever the computer is doing and force it to service them. An example is receiving a MIDI message; the computer doesn't know when you're going to play a note on a keyboard, but when you do it must jump on the message immediately and deal with it.

Computers therefore support a special type of I/O called an *interrupt*. This temporarily suspends the program's normal execution. The computer then executes a special block of software (called an *Interrupt Service Routine* or ISR) written especially to handle the interrupt. In the example of MIDI reception, the ISR would probably store the message in memory somewhere for subsequent analysis.

Interrupts can be generated internally as well as from data at the I/O ports. For example, the computer's internal timer can generate a *timer interrupt*, an interrupt that occurs at specific intervals. The timer ISR could then execute a periodic software routine, such as blinking a light or sending a MIDI clock message.

Microprocessors and Peripherals

A microprocessor is a single chip that contains the computer's ALU and control unit portions (the CPU). Auxiliary ICs, called *peripheral ICs*, handle the memory and I/O functions.

A microprocessor is a very generic building block. Since microprocessors find their way into every conceivable application, no single part could ever have all the necessary I/O and memory needed for all applications. Consequently, most special I/O and memory functions are implemented in off-chip peripherals. Here's a brief description of some common peripherals (we'll go into more detail later):

- Analog to digital converters (ADCs). These measure analog signals from the real world (such as temperature, footpedal position, etc.) and translate the values into digital data the computer can understand. Example: The MIDItools Computer contains an ADC that converts the analog voltage from the data potentiometer to digital numbers that the computer can understand.

- Digital to analog converters (DACs). These convert a digital number, as created by the microprocessor, into an analog voltage. Example: A digital tone generator defines a waveform by a series of numbers; the DAC translates these into a varying voltage we can feed into an amplifier and hear as sound.

- UARTs. It's often necessary to send data to some other device over a communications link. A UART, which is used for MIDI communications, is considered an *asynchronous* communications link for reasons so boring that we'll save them for later.

There are as many different types of peripherals as there are microprocessor applications, so we'll discuss only the particular kinds of peripherals used in the MIDItools Computer hardware.

Latches

A *latch* is a bank of flip-flops. Most latches are 8 bits wide, and store one byte externally to the microprocessor. Once a byte is written into an external latch, the outside circuitry is free to do what it wants with the information. For example, each latch output might connect to an LED. To turn LEDs on and off, the microprocessor writes appropriate data to the latch.

Latches are either parallel or serial. A *parallel latch* loads eight bits simultaneously from a parallel bus. A *serial latch* (generally called a "shift register") transfers data over a serial bus.

A shift register works like people sitting in an empty row of chairs. Suppose the first person sits down in the first seat of the row. Then someone else wants to sit down, so the first person moves over one chair, and now the second person sits in the first chair. A third person comes, and the first and second people move down one chair to the second and third chairs respectively, while the third person sits down on the first chair. When eight seats are filled, you have a byte.

Most shift registers have either a serial input and parallel output, or a parallel input and serial output. These parts are called *Serial-To-Parallel* (S-P) or *Parallel-To-Serial* (P-S) registers respectively, since they convert one format to another.

These parts are useful in connecting a bus from one computer board to another. Rather than running eight separate connections to connect a byte-wide bus between each board, a parallel-to-serial shift register can convert the eight lines to a single serial line and send the serial data stream to the other board, where a serial-to-parallel shift register (S-P) converts the serial data back to parallel.

Analog to Digital Converters

Suppose you want to measure a battery's voltage with a computer. A battery doesn't put out digital data, so how is the computer going to know what the voltage is?

An *Analog to Digital Converter* (ADC) converts a voltage to a digital value that a microprocessor can read, forming a bridge between the analog-based "real world" and the digitally-based computer world. Not just batteries produce voltages; the waveforms of different instruments and sounds (even something as complicated as a symphony orchestra) can be converted by a microphone into a voltage that varies in a complex way over time. As a result, digital recording devices include ADCs to translate music into digital data a computer can store and process.

A typical ADC converts a voltage to a one-byte number, giving a resolution of 256 different values. Fig. 9-3 shows how an ADC digitizes a potentiometer's position; this is how a computer reads knob and pedal settings.

Digital to Analog Converters

Digital to analog converters (DACs) provide the complementary function to ADCs by converting a digital number into an analog voltage. A typical DAC converts a one-byte number to a voltage, providing a resolution of 256 different voltages. A typical DAC function is to convert the data in a keyboard sampler's "sound ROM" into a varying voltage that we can hear.

UART

A UART (Universal Asynchronous Receiver Transmitter) is basically an overachieving shift register.

Normal shift registers require synchronization. As one shift register shifts data to another, both the source and destination shift registers must know when the data is shifting (*i.e.*, when to look for each bit as it shifts).

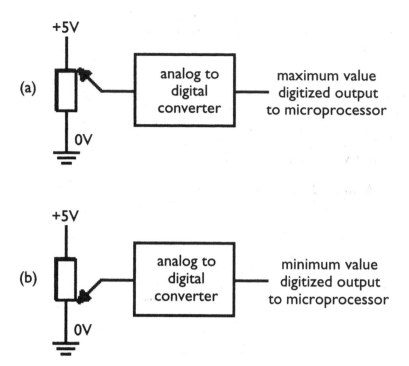

Fig. 9-3: With the control turned fully clockwise (a), the potentiometer "reads" the maximum voltage (5V). At the full counterclockwise position (b), the pot reads the minimum voltage (0V, or ground). In between these two extremes, the pot "picks off" different voltages. The ADC converts its input voltage into a binary number that goes to the microprocessor. Therefore, the microprocessor "knows" the pot's position by measuring the associated voltage.

A *clock* signal usually synchronizes the shift registers by telling the transmitting device when to send a bit and the receiving device when valid data is present on the data line, usually by toggling from one logic state to the other. Therefore, this type of serial interface requires two lines—one for the data, and one for the clock. In the "row of chairs" analogy, lack of a clock signal would cause some people to end up in other people's laps.

A UART does not need a clock synchronization line, which is why it's an *asynchronous* receiver-transmitter. To provide synchronization, the receiver and transmitter must agree ahead of time on the rate at which bits will be sent. To mark the beginning and ending of a block of bits *(e.g.,* a byte), the data transmitter generates special bits as part of the data stream. The receiver decodes these bits to determine when a block of bits starts and ends.

Most communications busses, such as MIDI and RS-232 (used with computers to tie into peripherals such as printers, modems, terminals, mice, etc.), use UARTs. Both ends of the interface know ahead of time how fast to transfer the bits, so once the receiver deciphers one valid block of bits from the encoded stream, it knows when to look for all future ones, thus providing synchronization.

What all this adds up to is that the UART can talk in either direction to another UART at a wide range of speeds and data formats, and without need for special synchronization—you can see why UARTs are very popular.

LCDs

LCDs (liquid crystal displays) provide our window on the microprocessor's world by carrying messages, displaying data, asking questions, and so on.

There are many different sizes and shapes of LCDs, as you have undoubtedly seen on digital watches, music equipment, and even computer monitors. The MIDItools Computer, like those devices, also uses an LCD.

Timers

A *timer* peripheral lets the microprocessor measure time. Timers are usually based on a free-running counter that counts at a given frequency. The microprocessor can read this counter whenever it wants to know what "time" it is (of course, this may not be hours, minutes, and seconds, but a much faster time standard—a second is eternity to a computer). Some timers provide sophisticated functions that allow the microprocessor to set up alarms, automatically set or reset I/O ports at pre-determined times, etc.

Timers can also interrupt the microprocessor so it can perform a function periodically (just like an alarm clock that interrupts our sleep periodically—each morning—to get us out of bed). The MIDItools Computer uses a timer to periodically remind the microprocessor to send MIDI clock messages.

Memory Peripherals

As mentioned, microprocessors are very generic parts. Perhaps the most variable aspect of all microprocessor applications is the amount and types of memory needed. Some applications need lots of RAM, others need lots of ROM. Some need lots of both, others need little of either.

For this reason, the microprocessor's internal memory is usually pretty minimal, with the appropriate levels of memory added as external peripherals. An example of a memory peripheral (and the kind we just happen to use in the MIDItools Computer) is a small EEPROM that holds 256 bytes of memory. The interface between this EEPROM and the microprocessor is a simple serial bus. The EEPROM shifts data to and from the microprocessor over the serial interface.

Microcontrollers

Despite the diverse applications for computer-based circuits, the hardware to implement many of them is generally very similar. For example, the microprocessor + UART + memory combination can be found in musical instruments as well as automobile dashboard readouts. Therefore, chip manufacturers offer *microcontrollers* that integrate a microprocessor and several of these generic peripherals. A microcontroller is a single-chip computer with the microprocessor (ALU and Control Unit), memory, I/O, and peripherals built into it.

Some people call the microcontroller a "microcomputer." Since the distinction is not very important for what we're doing, in this book we'll use the terms computer, microprocessor, processor, microcontroller, and microcomputer interchangeably.

The MIDItools hardware uses a very popular microcontroller called the 6805 (actually, its full name is MC68HC705C8). This microcontroller is very powerful as it has several built-in general purpose I/O ports (external latches), timer, UART, serial I/O port, lots of memory, and other useful built-in functions. We'll get more specific later, and even devote all of Chapter 13 to understanding this chip.

Chapter 10
Computer Software Basics

Up to now we've concentrated on computer hardware, but the computer's true power lies in its willingness to understand and perform a list of instructions designed to solve a problem. This list of instructions is called a *program* or *software*.

Your human computer executes programs all the time. For example, the "play the piano" program goes something like this:

(1) Sit down at the piano.

(2) Use your eye input devices to scan the page of sheet music.

(3) Put the first symbol in your brain's RAM.

(4) Compare that symbol to the symbols stored in your brain during music lessons (think of that as ROM).

(5) Send a signal to an output device (your finger) responsible for playing that note.

(6) Use another input device, your ear, to test whether the note was correct.

(7) If the note was correct, return to step 2 and play the next note. If not, you'll probably send a corrected output signal and try to play the note again.

A program's list of instructions includes the elementary binary functions we discussed earlier (addition, subtraction, AND, OR, etc.) and a number of other useful instructions. Different computers have different repertoires of instructions, with (naturally) some having a more powerful *instruction set* than others.

Machine Language

Since the computer understands nothing but binary numbers, computer languages are based on binary numbers. The computer's native language uses numbers and is called *machine language*. Many people are intimidated by machine language, but *any* language simply uses a particular set of symbols to represent something.

Expressing concepts in numbers isn't as weird as it sounds. For example, suppose we create our own language and represent the following English words with numbers:

do = 23   fine = 57   how = 16   just = 01   thank = 142   you = 09

Now, we can carry on a conversation with someone in our new language:

"16 23 09 23"
"01 57 142 09"

If you can decode the above exchange, then you can understand machine language.

Machine language simply assigns a unique number to each of the computer's instructions. For example, the 6805 assigns the following code numbers:

add = 171
subtract = 160
AND = 164
OR = 170

The above numbers are examples of machine language. A list of such numbers constitutes a program of instructions. Writing computer software is really that easy!

Of course, you also need the data that's going to be added, subtracted, multiplied, ANDed, or ORed. Therefore, a complete machine language instruction requires not just the operation codes shown above, but also the associated data. For example, a 6805 instruction to add 23 to a number is really:

171 23

Ultimately, every program is simply a sequence of instructions, expressed as numbers. The following typical sequence (shown in binary) is a 6805 program whose list of instructions adds 1 + 2 and stores the result in memory address $1000:

Address	Data
0	10100001
1	00000001
2	10101011
3	00000010
4	11000111
5	00010000
6	00000000

The program is 7 bytes long (addresses 0-6) and its instructions are organized in *contiguous* memory *(i.e.,* the address locations are consecutive). Each instruction in the above list consists of two parts: the operation code (or *op code*) and whatever data is necessary to complete the instruction (the *operand)*. We can rewrite the above program to show the op codes and operands:

Op code		Operand		Meaning
0)	10100001	1)	00000001	Instruction 1: fetch #1
2)	10101011	3)	00000010	Instruction 2: add above # to 2
4)	11000111	5)	00010000	Instruction 3: store result in address 0001000000000000 ($1000)
		6)	00000000	

Notice that the first two instructions in the above example (addresses 0 and 2) have one-byte operands and the third instruction (beginning at address 4) has a two-byte operand.

Now let's decipher the program. Data sheets and applications books for a particular microprocessor give a list of op codes and their meanings. In the example above, op code 10100001—the first instruction—means "fetch the number" given in the operand, which is binary 00000001 (or 1 in decimal).

The second instruction (op code 10101011) says "add the number fetched above to..." the operand, which is binary 00000010 (2 in decimal).

The final instruction, 11000111, says "store the result in the address" specified by the operand bytes, which is binary 00010000 00000000. In hex, this translates to sixteen-bit address $1000. Thus, this machine language block performs the operation 1+2 and stores the result in hex address $1000. That wasn't so bad, was it?

Addressing Modes

Operand data doesn't always automatically include the data for an instruction (as in the above example), but can sometimes point elsewhere to get the data. This leads us to different *addressing modes*, which determine where the op code finds its data. There are six main addressing modes implemented in most microcontrollers:

- **Inherent**—In *inherent* addressing mode, there is no operand byte—the instruction's op code contains all the information needed to perform an operation (the operand data is inherent to the instruction). Example: If the instruction says to "complement the accumulator register," no more data is needed; the computer simply inverts all the bits in the accumulator register.

- **Immediate**—In *immediate* addressing mode, the op code looks for its data in the memory location immediately following the op code byte. In the 1+2 example above, the first two instructions use immediate addressing mode.

- **Direct**—Instead of explicitly stating the data value to be used for the instruction (as in immediate addressing mode), *direct* addressing mode tells the computer to load the data from the address specified by the operand.

  Example: If the operand is $01, then the computer looks at address $01 and uses its contents as data for the instruction. Since the data at this address could be the result of another function or operation (for example, if I/O grabs a piece of data from the outside world and stuffs it at this address), direct addressing mode lets the computer use *variables (i.e.,* numbers that can change, depending on a variety of factors)—each variable is just an address of where to look for the data.

- **Extended**—*Extended* addressing mode is like direct addressing mode, except that the operand occupies the two bytes following the op code (instead of just one). This addressing mode was used in the third instruction in the 1+2 example above.

- **Indexed**—In *indexed* addressing mode, the operand provides an address which is added to the contents of an "index register," thereby deriving the address of the data used in the instruction.

  Example: If we have a table of data values, the operand tells the computer where the table starts (the address of the first value in the table) and the index register holds the index (position) into the table. By simply incrementing the number in the index register (an easy task), we can address our way through the table.

- **Relative**—*Relative* addressing mode allows for "branching" instructions, which tell the computer to start executing instructions somewhere else in memory. The "somewhere else" is specified by adding the operand to the address of the next op code. The operand is in two's complement format, so the computer can go forward or backward in memory (since the two's complement value can be positive or negative).

The op code always specifies the addressing mode, so the computer knows which addressing mode to use for a given instruction. Consider the ADD instruction; it has a different op code for each different addressing mode:

Instruction	Addressing Mode	Op code (shown in hex)
ADD	immediate	$AB
ADD	direct	$BB
ADD	extended	$CB
ADD	indexed	$EB

Because the computer knows what addressing mode is required from the op code, it therefore knows how many more data bytes are in the operand, and what to do with them to complete the instruction.

The Program Counter

Like a bus where the driver announces each "next stop," the Program Counter (PC) announces the address of the next op code to be fetched and executed. Technically speaking, the PC is a Control Unit register that always holds the memory address of the next op code.

About Instruction Cycles

The computer operates by repeating two basic steps:

(1) Fetch the next instruction from memory (the "fetch cycle").

(2) Perform the prescribed action defined by that instruction (the "execution cycle").

This sequence—fetch next instruction and then execute it, fetch next instruction and then execute it—goes on until the system shuts down.

Fetch Cycle

The fetch cycle always reads the first byte of the instruction (the op code) pointed to by the Program Counter. The Control Unit then looks at this new op code to find out what it's supposed to do. This leads us to the execution cycle.

Execution Cycle

During the execution cycle, the computer reads any additional operand bytes and performs the instruction. Recall that after the fetch cycle, the Program Counter points to the next byte after the op code. As we've seen, this next byte is the first byte of the operand. The op code inherently knows the operand's size, so the computer can reliably read the proper number of operand bytes for this instruction, advancing the Program Counter as it does so.

If the op code specifies *immediate* addressing mode, we have all the data needed to perform the instruction. With other addressing modes, the Control Unit must perform the additional steps of using the operand to go find the data somewhere else in memory. After locating and fetching this data, the instruction is finally performed.

After the execution cycle, the Program Counter now points one byte past the last byte of the operand, which is the first byte (op code) of the next instruction. The computer therefore loops back to perform the next fetch cycle, and the two-step process repeats indefinitely.

Computer Speed

The speed of performing the fetch and execution cycles determines the computer's overall speed—one of its most important parameters. Some high-speed computers have special mechanisms that fetch data in advance so it's ready as soon as it's needed, or perform the fetch and execution cycles simultaneously. (Most *Digital Signal Processor* chips—special types of microprocessors generally used for processing audio—use these tricks.

The topic of DSP is beyond the scope of this book, but we like using these parts, and never pass up an opportunity to mention them.)

Subroutines

Blocks of particular instructions often occur more than once in a program. Rather than rewrite this block several times (wasting time, memory, and making future maintenance of all the redundant versions a chore), we can create a *subroutine*. This is a block of instructions that can be "called" from any point in the program, then executed right after it's called. When the subroutine ends, the program resumes where it left off.

Example: The computer inside a keyboard synthesizer might have a subroutine that checks the keyboard at regular intervals to see if a new key has been pressed or released.

The process of executing a subroutine is called a *jump to subroutine*. Most microprocessors have an instruction to do this. When the computer jumps to a subroutine, it stores the Program Counter's contents so it knows where to return when the subroutine ends (called a *return from subroutine*).

Creating Software

To tell a computer what to do we simply give it a sequence of instructions encoded as numbers, according to the types of rules discussed above. It's an art form to create a sequence of instructions that can use a computer's resources efficiently and not have bugs. Beautifully crafted programs have many of the same elegant features of fine art: form, abstraction, clever wit, and even a dash of insanity. Let's look at how to create an actual program.

The 3-Step Program for Software Addicts

To create a computer program, the programmer must follow three steps:

(1) Define and understand the problem at hand and its solution.

(2) Design a step-by-step approach to solve it.

(3) Translate the solution into a sequence of numbers the computer can understand.

The 3-Step Program in Action:
A MIDI Sequencer Remote Control

Let's apply the 3 step program to designing a MIDI sequencer remote control.

Step 1: Understand the problem.

The sequencer remote control should operate like a VCR remote control. Press Play, and the sequencer starts to play; press Stop, and it stops. If you press Pause while the sequencer is playing, the sequencer pauses; if you press Play or Pause while the sequencer is paused, the sequencer will continue playing from the point where it was paused.

Step 2: Design a solution to the problem.

This step requires seeing a problem's solution as a sequence of many small steps. You have to specify these steps very carefully since the computer will take them literally; any ambiguities or discrepancies in the solution will mess with the computer's mind. Programmers use an assortment of tools, such as the *flow chart*, to break the solution of big problems into small steps.

Flow Charts

A flow chart represents the small steps necessary to solve a problem as a diagram, which consists of various symbols interconnected by arrows. Flow charts are very personal—no two programmers will draw the same diagram to solve the same problem. However, there is a common set of basic symbols.

Fig. 10-1: The termination box symbol for flow charts.

The oval symbol represents the beginning or end of a sequence of instructions (this may seem unnecessary, but you can't follow a flow chart if you don't know where it starts and stops). We'll call this symbol a *termination box*.

Fig. 10-2: The operation box symbol.

The rectangle symbol, an *operation box,* represents a processing or command operation. It contains a few words explaining what operation is performed.

Fig. 10-3: The decision box symbol.

The diamond symbol, a *decision box,* represents a decision point and asks a question. The answer to this question routes the program to one of two or more possible paths.

Fig. 10-4: The instruction flow symbol.

Arrows show the flow of instructions. All boxes in the flow chart have one arrow entering them and one (or more in the case of the decision box) exiting.

Fig. 10-5 shows a completed flow chart for the operation of a MIDI sequencer remote control.

Step 3: Translate the solution to a sequence of numbers understandable by the computer.

Translating the flow chart defined in step 2 into a list of instructions the computer can understand is often called *coding,* and represents the most varied element of programming. There are many different computer languages and tools to create code; the programmer's choice of a language is mainly up to personal preference and economics. Your options range from the computer's native *low level* machine language to many generic *high level* languages.

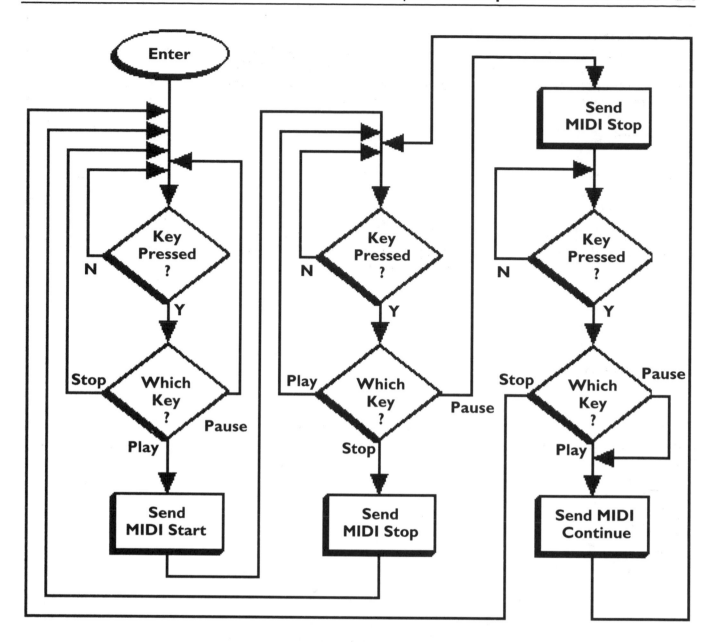

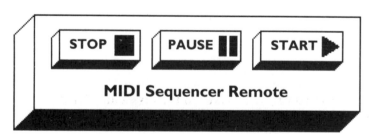

Fig. 10-5: MIDI sequencer remote flow chart. You can trace through all possible actions to test the program concept.

For very large programs, especially programs that are not critically dependent on speed or memory size, high level languages such as BASIC and C have advantages (such as being easier to program).

Assembly Language

For programs that work with tight timing or memory constraints, assembly language is often the best choice. While it's possible to write a program directly in a computer's raw machine language, in almost all cases programming in raw numbers is a horrible task fit for only the most fanatical nerds. Assembly language, which associates a little name (called a *mnemonic)* with each machine instruction, is a better choice. Instead of telling the computer to "$AB" ("add two numbers"), you can say "add" in assembly language. Unless you like to beat yourself up and have lots of time you need to kill, you will prefer the latter form of the instruction.

Assembly language not only represents the machine code instructions with names, it also lets you represent variables (a variable is simply an address where a piece of data is stored), as well as constant values, with meaningful names. For example, when doing an addition we can use the assembly language instruction "STA RESULT" to tell the computer to store the contents of the accumulator register ("STA" instruction) in address "$1000," providing that RESULT was defined as address $1000 earlier in the program. The variable names are meaningful to the human programmer; the corresponding numbers are meaningful to the computer.

High Level Languages

People normally think in different terms from a computer. Since the computer's instruction set (and therefore assembly language) is oriented around twiddling bits of data in memory, solving real world problems in assembly language can be awkward—we normally don't consider problems from the perspective of binary data manipulation. Moreover, since different computers generally speak different sets of machine instructions, a program written in assembly language for one computer will rarely execute on a different computer.

High level languages such as C and *BASIC* (an acronym for Beginner's All-purpose Symbolic Instruction Code) provide the programmer a set of instructions that more closely resemble a human language. For example, some typical instructions in BASIC include "print," "C = A + B," and "IF this is true THEN do that."

Eventually, though, high level instructions need to be translated to the low level numbers the computer wants to see. Special computer programs called *compilers* translate (compile) the high level instructions into the low level (machine code) instructions understood by the computer. As a result, a high level language will work in any computer that has a compiler (translator) available for that language. Programs written in high level languages are therefore more readily understood by programmers, and more portable to other computers.

Back to Step 3

Let's return to the task of translating the flow chart to computer code. First we'll write the MIDI sequencer remote control program in BASIC, and then in 6805 assembly language. *Don't worry if these programs don't make complete sense to you,* they are provided to give you an example of what a program looks like. However, you might find that some of it actually does make sense! We'll investigate 6805 assembly language in Chapter 13. For now, see if you can follow each program's flow of instructions against the flow chart.

The BASIC Program

BASIC is aptly named. It is a very simple high level language that is easy to understand, and is the first language learned by most people. BASIC is popular in schools, but rarely used by professional programmers (programs written in BASIC are generally very slow).

Only four different high level BASIC instructions can code the entire sequencer remote control example:

REM—Text following this instruction is a remark intended for humans (programmers) who are looking over the code and want to understand what's going on. The computer ignores REM instructions, so they have no effect on the computer's processing.

CALL—This calls a *subroutine,* another block of instructions somewhere else in the computer's memory. In this example, the READ_KEYS subroutine is a pre-existing block of instructions that takes care of reading the computer's keypad. (Remember, a subroutine can be called as many times as desired from other parts of the program to eliminate duplicate code.)

IF...THEN...—IF the condition after the *if* part of the instruction is true, THEN do the action declared after the *then* part of the instruction. For example, "IF NEWKEY = 0 THEN GOTO 220" means "if the variable NEWKEY has value 0 in it, then go execute instructions starting at line number 220."

GOTO—This forces the program to start executing instructions beginning at the specified line number.

You'll notice that each line in the BASIC program starts with a *line number*. These define the order in which instructions are executed, from the lowest number to the highest. GOTO instructions also specify line numbers so the program knows where to GO TO. Line numbers are often not consecutive to allow for inserting additional lines later on if needed without changing the existing order.

Following each block of lines is an explanation of what the lines mean.

```
10   REM MIDI SEQUENCER REMOTE CONTROL
20   REM 8JUN93 B.MOSES
30   REM
40   REM     SUBROUTINES CALLED ARE:
50   REM
60   REM     READ_KEYS—reads keys and loads the "NEWKEY"
70   REM     variable with a code corresponding to the
80   REM     key status.
90   REM
100  REM     "NEWKEY" codes:
110  REM          0  No key is pressed
120  REM          1  Play key is pressed
130  REM          2  Pause key is pressed
140  REM          3  Stop key is pressed
150  REM
160  REM     MIDI_START—sends a MIDI START command
170  REM
180  REM     MIDI_STOP—sends a MIDI STOP command
190  REM
200  REM     MIDI_CONT—sends a MIDI CONTINUE command
210  REM
```

Lines 10-210 are simply remarks. When someone prints out the *program listing* of instructions to see what makes the program, these remarks indicate the name of the program, the author, and some notes on labels used in the program. Some lines are left blank to format the text in an easier-to-read way.

```
220 REM — key pressed?
230 CALL READ_KEYS
240 IF NEWKEY = 0 THEN GOTO 220
```

This block calls the READ_KEYS subroutine to check if a key is pressed. If the result of reading the keys is 0, no key is pressed (as noted in REMark line 110) so the program goes back to line 220.

```
250 REM — which key?
260 IF NEWKEY = 2 THEN GOTO 220
270 IF NEWKEY = 3 THEN GOTO 220
280 REM — send MIDI Start
290 CALL MIDI_START
```

If the result of READ_KEYs was not 0, then the program doesn't loop back to line 220 and instead keeps moving through the program. If READ_KEYS returns 2 or 3, the program goes back to line 220. However, if READ_KEYS returns 1 *(i.e., the Play key is pressed)*, then the program goes to line 290, and sends a MIDI start command.

```
300 REM — key pressed?
310 CALL READ_KEYS
320 IF NEWKEY = 0 THEN GOTO 300
```

We've sent the MIDI start command, so the sequence is going. Now it's time to check whether another button is pressed. If READ_KEYS returns 0, meaning no key is pressed, then the program loops back to line 300 until READ_KEYS returns something other than 0.

```
330 REM — which key?
340 IF NEWKEY = 1 THEN GOTO 300
350 IF NEWKEY = 2 THEN GOTO 390
```

If the NEWKEY variable is 1, then the play key is pressed. Since to get this far into the program it would have been necessary to already have the sequencer in Play mode, the program loops back to line 300 to read the keys and see if a value other than 0 or 1 shows up. If the NEWKEY variable read by READ_KEYS is 2, meaning that Pause has been pressed, then the program jumps to line 390. If the variable is 3, then the stop key has been pressed, and the program moves on to the next block of code.

```
360 REM — send MIDI Stop
370 CALL MIDI_STOP
380 GOTO 220
```

If the variable was 3, then the program knows to send a MIDI Stop command. After doing that, the program jumps back to line 220 and gets ready for the next button press.

```
390 REM — send MIDI Stop
400 CALL MIDI_STOP
```

If the variable was 2, then line 350 instructed the program to jump to line 390. The program sends a Stop command to pause the sequencer.

```
410 REM — key pressed?
420 CALL READ_KEYS
430 IF NEWKEY = 0 THEN GOTO 410
```

This block of code is very similar to lines 300-320. If no key is pressed (NEWKEY = 0), then the program keeps looping back to line 410 until a key is pressed.

```
440 REM — which key?
450 IF NEWKEY = 3 THEN GOTO 220
```

Since the program already sent a STOP command in line 400, the program goes back to line 220 and gets ready for the next button press.

```
460 REM — send MIDI Continue
470 CALL MIDI_CONT
480 GOTO 300
```

But what happens if READ_KEYS returned a 1 or 2 back in line 420? The program goes past lines 420-460, and then line 470 sends a MIDI Continue command.

If you trace through the various options of having different keys pressed at different times, you'll see that the program always knows what to do with this data. Try comparing this program to the flow chart (Fig. 10-5).

6805 Assembly Language Program

Now that we've spoiled you with the simplicity of BASIC, we will torment you by coding the sequencer remote control in 6805 assembly language. This example is meant to give you an idea of what an assembly language program looks like, so some of the instructions will probably look like Swahili. Consider this an introduction only; we'll get to the specific details of the 6805 assembly language in Chapter 13.

Since assembly language is a lower level language than BASIC, we'll need to use more types of instructions, and they will have less intuitive meanings compared to BASIC. However, there are some similarities between the two languages. Both languages (indeed, all languages) support comments for human eyes only (assembly language comments are typically prefaced with a semicolon rather than BASIC's "REM"), both use subroutines to do the generic stuff, and both follow the same flow chart.

Assembly language does not use line numbers. Instructions are executed in the order they appear—in essence, the address of each instruction in memory is its line number. *Labels* refer to specific instructions when the program must jump to somewhere else in the program. Programmers usually prefer to keep labels short (to keep the code readable), so labels often resemble words on personalized license plates.

```
; Sequencer Remote Control example in 6805 assembly language
; 8JUN93 B.Moses
;
; Subroutines called by this program:
;
;       READ_KEYS—reads keys and loads the "NEWKEY"
;                  variable (declared somewhere else) with
;                  a code corresponding to the key status.
;
;                  "NEWKEY" codes:
;                    0  No key is pressed
;                    1  Play key is pressed
;                    2  Pause key is pressed
;                    3  Stop key is pressed
;
;       MIDI_START—sends a MIDI START command
;       MIDI_STOP—sends a MIDI STOP command
;       MIDI_CONT—sends a MIDI CONTINUE command


;— Program Entry

BEGIN:

;— key pressed?

RDKY1:  jsr    READ_KEYS      ;read the latest key status
        lda    NEWKEY         ;
        cmp    #0             ;NEWKEY = "No key pressed"?
        beq    RDKY1          ;yup

;— which key?

        cmp    #2             ;pause?
        beq    RDKY1          ;yup
        cmp    #3             ;stop?
```

```
        beq     RDKY1           ;yup

        ;if we get here it must be play

;— send MIDI Start

        jsr     MIDI_START      ;subroutine sends MIDI Start

;— key pressed?

RDKY2:  jsr     READ_KEYS        ;read the latest key status
        lda     NEWKEY          ;
        cmp     #0              ;NEWKEY = "No key pressed"?
        beq     RDKY2           ;yup

;— which key?

        cmp     #1              ;play?
        beq     RDKY2           ;yup
        cmp     #2              ;pause?
        beq     RDKY2A          ;yup

        ;if we get here it must be stop

;— send MIDI Stop

        jsr     MIDI_STOP       ;subroutine sends MIDI Stop
        jmp     RDKY1           ;go wait for Play

RDKY2A:

;— send MIDI Stop

        jsr     MIDI_STOP       ;subroutine sends MIDI Stop

;— key pressed?

RDKY3:  jsr     READ_KEYS        ;read the latest key status
        lda     NEWKEY          ;
        cmp     #0              ;NEWKEY = "No key pressed"?
        beq     RDKY3           ;yup

:— which key?

        cmp     #1              ;stop?
        beq     RDKY1           ;yup

        ;if we get here it must pause or play

;— send MIDI Continue

        jsr     MIDI_CONT       ;subroutine sends MIDI Continue
        jmp     RDKY2           ;go wait for stop or pause

;— program exit

        ;actually, this program never ends—but call this the
        ;end anyway...
```

```
       rts                          ;traditionally, this program
                                    ;would have been called as a
                                    ;subroutine so execute a "return
                                    ;from subroutine" when it ends
```

Okay, so maybe it's not the most readable prose you've ever seen. But you may be able to see that some of this is starting to make sense. The important point is that we've defined our problem, come up with a solution, and coded that solution in a form the computer can understand. The further you advance in this book, the more you'll understand.

State Machines

The flow chart is just one way to document a solution to a particular problem. It works well for problems of simple or intermediate complexity. However, with more sophisticated problems, the flow chart can grow unwieldy and sprout hundreds of boxes and arrows. In particular, flow charts aren't very useful for *event-driven* control applications where you have many inputs (*e.g.*, pushbuttons) and functions. For these problems, the State Machine provides an alternative model.

Whereas the flow chart gives the designer complete freedom to create any possible web of instructions, the State Machine prescribes one rigid generic model which can implement a huge number of different systems. In other words, the state machine is a pre-determined program structure which adapts to the application. Let's investigate what this means.

The Mechanics of the State Machine

The fundamental tenet of the State Machine is that its *output* is always a function of its current *state* and its *inputs*.

State—The state machine is always sitting in a known *state*. A state is a condition. The sequencer remote control has three states: stopped, playing, and paused. Each state defines what is happening *right now*.

Input Events—The state machine is responsive to a known set of *input events*. For example, the sequencer remote control recognizes three input events:

- Play button pushed

- Stop button pushed

- Pause button pushed

These are the only things you can do to the remote. When any of these input events occur, the remote control changes state (if necessary, it can "change" to the same state if it wants). Example: When the sequencer is playing and you press stop, the remote enters the *stopped* state. When you press play, it enters the *playing* state, and so on.

Output Actions—The final ingredient of the state machine is *output actions*, the tasks performed by the device. The sequencer remote control's actions are send MIDI Start message, send MIDI Stop message, and send MIDI Continue message.

The state machine, like any intelligent living organism, is always doing something. So, we also need to include the equivalent of twiddling our thumbs while waiting for something to do. We call this the *idle* action.

Output actions occur only whenever an input event occurs (for the record, this type of state machine is called a "Mealy Machine"). Therefore, an input event causes two things to happen:

(1) The state machine changes state.

(2) It performs an output action.

State Machine Implementation of the Sequencer Remote Control

The best way to understand a state machine is to actually build one. So, let's build the sequencer remote control based on a state machine.

The remote control has three states:

State 1: Stopped
State 2: Playing
State 3: Paused

Three input events:

Event 1: Play key pressed
Event 2: Pause key pressed
Event 3: Stop key pressed

And four output actions:

Action 1: Send MIDI Start message
Action 2: Send MIDI Stop message
Action 3: Send MIDI Continue message
Action 4: Idle (sit around and twiddle thumbs)

After defining these states, events, and actions, we can draw a *state transition* (also called *bubble)* diagram of the state machine. The bubble diagram consists of two symbols:

- A bubble represents a state

- An arrow represents a response to an input event

Written adjacent to each arrow is the input event corresponding to this arrow, and (separated by a / symbol) the output action executed as the state machine transitions to the next state pointed to by the arrow. Let's draw the bubble diagram for the sequencer remote control (Fig. 10-6):

The bubble diagram fully describes the operation of the state machine. If we know the current state (that is, what we're doing), and detect an input event, the bubble diagram tells us what to do (the output action) and what state to transition to (what to wait for next). See if you can read the operation of the sequencer remote control directly from the bubble diagram. We'll get you started: "When the sequencer is stopped (state), and you hit the play key (event), you send a MIDI Start (output action) and start playing (next state)...."

State Transition Matrix

Bubble diagrams are fun to draw, and when you show them to your friends they'll think you're cool. But, computers aren't exactly designed to read them, so your beautiful bubble diagram must be translated to the computer's machine code (numbers).

One way is to translate the operation of the state machine to a table of numbers called a *State Matrix.* Input events are arranged in the rows of the state matrix, and the states are represented by columns. Each column-row intersection in the state matrix defines the next state and output action performed when that event occurs during that state. Let's write the state matrix for the sequencer remote control.

Events	States		
	Stopped	*Playing*	*Paused*
Play key pressed:	Playing/send Start message	Playing/Idle	Playing/send Contin. message
Pause key pressed:	Stopped/Idle	Paused/send Stop message	Playing/send Contin. message
Stop key pressed:	Stopped/Idle	Stopped/send Stop message	Stopped/Idle

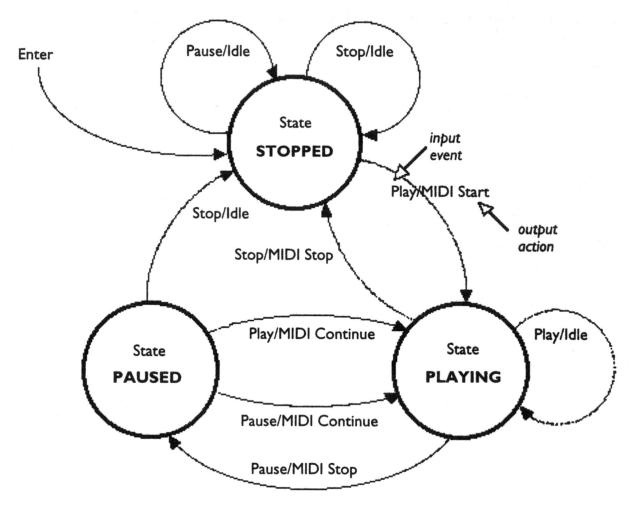

Fig. 10-6: Typical state transition diagram.

Each row/column intersection shows the resulting "next state"/"output action" when the row's input event occurs during the column's state.

The above state matrix describes the operation of the sequencer remote control, just as the bubble diagram did. You should be able to read the entire operation of the system directly from it. Go back and reread the description of the system as told by the bubble diagram and you will see it describes the operation defined by this state matrix.

Notice that the matrix is defined with labels corresponding to each event, state, and action. These labels can be assigned unique numbers that get programmed into the computer. If we use the numbers we originally assigned to the states, events, and actions of the sequencer remote (just before Fig. 10-6), we get the following matrix:

```
2,1    2,4    2,3
1,4    3,2    2,3
1,4    1,2    1,4
```

This matrix can be written directly into the computer's memory as 2,1,2,4,2,3,1,4,3,2,2,3,1,4,1,2,1,4. Only 18 numbers describe the sequencer remote control's operation! Therein lies the beauty of the state machine.

State Machines Are Our Friends

Poorly written programs often malfunction because the programmer overlooked a peculiar input event at an unanticipated time. One of the charms of the state machine is it defines a reaction for every possible input event during every possible state, as you can see in the previous bubble diagram and state matrix. The state machine forces the programmer to take complete responsibility for all possible circumstances. There is no ambiguity and no holes in the design of the system. State machines are very robust—it's hard to crash them. State machines are our friends.

Coding a State Machine

Refer back to the 3 Step Program for software creation and notice that the bubble diagram and state matrix help you perform step 2. Now we are ready for step 3: translate the solution into code the computer can understand.

The actual code for a state machine simply tells the computer how to use the data in the state matrix. A state machine operates in a simple loop, forever:

(1) Did we get an input event? No: goto 1. Yes: goto 2

(2) Look up output action from state matrix

(3) Perform output action

(4) Look up next state from state matrix

(5) Transition to new state

(6) Go back to number 1.

This small *generic* (works no matter which state you are in) block of instructions waits for an input event and then executes the output action specified by the state matrix. The state changes, then the process repeats again and again and again and again.

The entire program only requires these 6 lines of code, the state matrix, and the simple output actions. The state machine is a very efficient model for event-driven programs.

The MIDItools software is based on a state machine. Typical input events are push button presses, data fader moves, and MIDI data reception. Typical states are "Select MIDI channel," "Select this," and "Select That." Typical output actions are "send a MIDI message," "write something into the LCD display," "set the MIDI Channel to the value specified by the data fader," and so on. When we discuss the software for each MIDI tool, you'll see that each application consists of a simple State Matrix and a few simple output action subroutines.

Software Development

Producing a tangible program you can hold in your bare hands involves several steps. The program must be written, converted to a list of machine instructions the computer can understand, and debugged. These steps are almost always performed on a computer, often the same computer for which the software is being written. This requires an assortment of software development tools—programs that help you write, convert, and debug software.

Source Code

Regardless of the language used to write a program, it is initially written on a computer with a word processing program. The resulting file is called the *source code* file. This is the program's master record; future modifications are generated by modifying the source code.

Assembler

Source files written in assembly language require an *assembler* program to translate the source file (which is, of course, a list of assembly instructions) into machine language instructions (which is the only thing the computer can understand). The result is called *object code* and is stored in an *object file*.

Compiler

As mentioned previously, *compiling* a source file written in a high level language generates the final machine language version. Depending on the high level language, compilation can involve a number of steps. Often, the high level language is first translated to assembly language, and then an assembler translates this to machine language.

Linker

An individual source file frequently does not present a complete program, but only a portion. Programs are typically split into several source files to isolate certain parts of the program, which we've done with the MIDItools software. Each file covers only one particular resource in the computer. For example, one source file contains all LCD code, another all the MIDI code. By partitioning a large program like this, several programmers can work on one project, and you can modify certain pieces without disturbing the rest of the program. If we want to change the program to support a different LCD, we simply replace the LCD file and leave the rest of the program files alone.

Since a program can consist of many source files, something needs to tie them all together before they can feed the computer. This is the *linker*'s job. Linkers link object code, so each source file must first be individually assembled (assuming they are assembly language source files), and the resulting object files are linked into one big object file. High level language compilers generally take care of linking for you.

Debugging

A bug is a piece of a program that doesn't work. The name arose from an early computer glitch which literally was the result of a bug crawling inside the computer. Debugging is the act of removing bugs from the program. Programmers like to say they are debugging, rather than admit they are fixing their mistakes.

There are a variety of debugging tools available. We won't mention any here, because there are too many and this would lead us astray from our focus. Debugging tools generally aid the programmer in finding flaws in the object code, which must then be traced to the source code and fixed.

Loading and Running a Program

So, you've gone through all the above steps and have an object file ready to load into a computer and execute. How do you get it in there?

The answer to the above question varies from computer to computer. If the computer has an *operating system,* you tell the operating system to go find this object file and load the program counter (PC) with the address of the first instruction (well, that's the basic idea anyway). If the program is destined for a small microprocessor, things may be different.

Loading and running a program in the MIDItools Computer is similar to the process used in most microprocessor-based systems, so let's take a look at how it works.

A program for the MIDItools Computer is written, assembled, and linked on a personal computer as explained above. You then transfer the resulting object code to a device called an *EPROM programmer,* which writes the object code into an EPROM. The EPROM is then plugged into the computer.

Resetting the microprocessor, by connecting the "reset" pin on the chip to logic 0, sets its PC at the first op code in the program (which is at a well-defined address) and starts cranking out the fetch/execute cycles. It's that simple!

The MIDItools EPROM can be erased by exposing the chip to intense ultraviolet light. So, if your program doesn't work, just erase the EPROM, change the program's source code, assemble, link, and reprogram the EPROM. Life is so simple.

Chapter 11

MIDI—The Bits and Bytes

We've already looked at MIDI from a musical perspective in Chapter 3; now it's time to look at MIDI from a programmer's standpoint. We'll begin with the interface hardware.

MIDI Interface Hardware

Fig. 11-1 (next page) shows the circuitry for MIDI In, Out, and Thru stages. These are the "classic" circuits from the original MIDI spec; the MIDItools Computer adds some variations, mostly by using a 6N138 optoisolator, which is somewhat faster and has a different pinout from the PC900. Since the MIDI Thru circuitry is optional, it's shown surrounded by a dashed line.

The triangles represent inverters, which can be implemented using IC or transistor circuitry.

These stages are linked by three-conductor cables that use twisted-pair wire surrounded by a shield.

The twisted pair wires connect to pins 4 and 5 of a 5-pin DIN plug, and the shield connects to pin 2 at both ends of the cable. (Pins 1 and 3 are currently not used; for more information on building MIDI cables, see *MIDI Projects for Musicians*.) To prevent ground loops from forming with MIDI cables, the MIDI Out and Thru jacks have pin 2 connected to ground, but the MIDI In jack leaves pin 2 disconnected.

Longer cables increase the amount of signal distortion. For standard cables, lengths longer than 50 feet (15 meters) are not recommended. However, with technological improvements such as radio and infrared transceivers, wireless LANs, etc., it is likely that MIDI cables (and their inherent limitations) will disappear from MIDI systems of the future.

The MIDI Protocol

MIDI operates within the following definitions and constraints.

Serial Communication

Transmitting data one bit at a time (serially) is slower than transmitting multiple bits simultaneously (parallel). However, parallel systems are much more complex and expensive. Besides, MIDI's speed is not the limiting factor in current systems, but rather the speed of the device reacting to the MIDI messages.

Byte Length

MIDI's serial nature requires differentiating the beginning and end of a particular string of data. Therefore, a complete MIDI byte consists of:

- One Start Bit (logic 0). The start bit indicates that a message is about to begin by transitioning from logic 1 to logic 0.

- Eight message-specific bits (D0–D7), starting with the LSB (Least Significant Bit, or D0).

- One Stop Bit (logic 1). The stop bit indicates that a particular message is complete by transitioning from logic 0 to logic 1.

Transmission Speed

MIDI data is transmitted at 31,250 bits per second. Therefore, transmitting a single bit takes 1/31,250 or 0.000032 seconds (32 microseconds). Transmitting a complete byte (10 bits) requires 320 microseconds.

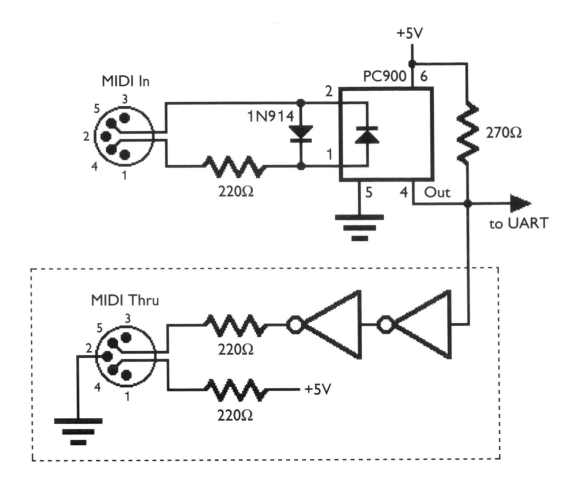

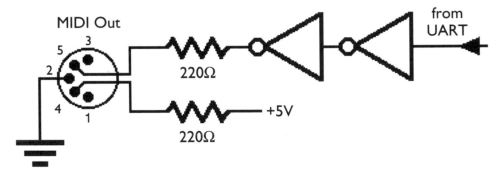

Fig. 11-1: MIDI interface electronic circuitry.

The Dreaded MIDI Delay

Although MIDI's transmission speed is adequate for most applications, not being able to send pieces of data simultaneously can lead to timing delays, since bytes must "wait in line" until it is their turn to be transmitted.

To illustrate this, assume you want to play 100 notes (played by various multi-timbral instruments) at the same time. Each transmitted MIDI note message consists of three serial bytes, and each byte requires 320 microseconds to transmit. So, the first note's 3-byte package will be sent immediately, the second 3-byte package 960 microseconds after the first one, the third 3-byte package 1,920 microseconds after the first one, and so on. The last note will play about 1/10th of a second after the first note, since:

100 notes = 300 bytes
300 bytes × 0.000320 seconds per byte = 0.096 seconds

Granted that playing 100 notes at the same time is not something you do every day, but there's more to MIDI than notes. Any 3-byte message—pitch bend, note on or off, controllers, etc.—requires the same 960 microseconds of transmission time. If you rotate a pitch bend wheel, it will spew out lots of messages. If you rotate a pitch bend wheel, move a footpedal, *and* use a keyboard with pressure response, the amount of data can hog the MIDI transmission medium and end up delaying important data like note messages.

Interestingly, the MIDI specification recognizes this limitation when it comes to timing messages. As a result, MIDI clock messages are given top priority and can be transmitted at any time, even in the middle of another message.

Getting Around MIDI Channel Constraints

16 channels seemed like all the channels you'd ever need back in the days when synthesizers cost $5,000 and could respond to only one channel at a time. However, with modern multi-timbral sound modules capable of responding to as many as 16 independent channels all by themselves, 16 channels is often insufficient.

Fortunately, many sequencers can drive multiple MIDI Out ports, each carrying 16 channels. For example, Macintosh sequencers can usually send data for 16 MIDI channels out the modem port and 16 more channels out the printer port. The receivers don't care where they get their messages from; if a synth is set to receive on channel 1 and you hook it up to the modem MIDI port, it will receive the channel 1 data assigned to that port. Hook that same synth up to the printer MIDI port, and it will receive the channel 1 data assigned to *that* port.

However, the sequencer does need to know where to send the data. It usually does this by letting you assign data not only to 1 of 16 channels, but one of several *cables*. For example, the modem port might be A and the printer port B; assigning an instrument to B16 would therefore send the data on channel 16, over the printer port.

There are now interfaces that provide literally hundreds of MIDI channels, thus circumventing the 16 channel limit once and for all. Unfortunately, these can be somewhat costly (as predicted by Murphy's Law of Digital Devices: Problems can generally be solved by throwing money at them).

The MIDI Language

MIDI communication succeeds only when valid messages (those in the MIDI vocabulary) are sent according to the proper "rules of grammar."

Grammar

MIDI messages are groupings of one or more bytes. Bytes can be either *Status bytes* (which indicate the type of message) or *Data bytes* (which indicate specific values). Status bytes can be transmitted once per message, or they may be transmitted according to the rules of Running Status (described later).

Byte Format

Both Status bytes and Data bytes must follow a particular format.

- Status bytes have eight bits, with the MSB set high (logic 1). Status bytes indicate the type of message, which defines the quantity and nature of the Data bytes that follow.

  Valid Status byte values range from $80–$FF. Certain byte values within this range are undefined, or invalid, and should never be transmitted. If received, they should be ignored.

- Data bytes have eight bits, with the MSB set low (logic 0). The number of Data bytes following a Status byte depends on the message type. MIDI receivers wait until all Data bytes in a message have been received before processing the message.

  Valid Data byte values range from $00–$7F. All byte values within this range may be valid, depending on the message type. Data bytes not preceded by the appropriate Status byte are considered invalid, and should be ignored by the receiver.

Message Format

The structure of a MIDI message depends on whether it is a Channel message or System message. Channel Messages are encoded with a MIDI channel number. As explained in Chapter 3, there are two types of Channel Messages:

- Channel *Voice* Messages control an instrument's sound generators (voices).

- Channel *Mode* Messages control an instrument's mode of operation.

System Messages are not encoded with a MIDI channel number, so are available to all receivers in a MIDI system. There are three types of System Messages:

- System Common Messages are intended for all receivers in a system.

- System Realtime Messages are intended for all receivers controlled by a MIDI timing clock

- System Exclusive Messages are intended only for equipment made by a particular manufacturer.

Message Structure

MIDI messages (except System Exclusive) consist of a Status byte followed by up to two Data bytes. The following chart shows the number of Data bytes transmitted for each valid Status byte's name and value.

In the Status Byte Value column, n stands for the channel number nibble and can range from $0 to $F, corresponding to channels 1 ($0) through 16 ($F).

Message Family	Message Type	Message Name	Status Byte Value	# of Data Bytes
Channel	Voice	Note Off	$8n	2
		Note On	$9n	2
		Key Pressure	$An	2
		Control Change	$Bn	2
		Program Change	$Cn	1
		Channel Pressure	$Dn	1
		Pitch Bend	$En	2
Channel	Mode	(note 1)	$Bn	2
System	Common	MTC 1/4 Frame	$F1	1
		Song Pointer	$F2	2
		Song Select	$F3	1
		Tune Request	$F6	0
		EOX	$F7	0
System	Realtime	Timing Clock	$F8	0
		Start	$FA	0
		Continue	$FB	0
		Stop	$FC	0
		Active Sensing	$FE	0
		System Reset	$FF	0
System	Exclusive		$F0	(note 2)

Note 1: Channel Mode messages are sent under the same status byte as Control Change messages

Note 2: System exclusive messages include bytes to indicate Status, Identification, Data, and EOX ("End Of system eXclusive").

Running Status

A device that provides for running status retains the status specified by a Channel Message Status byte until it receives a different valid Status byte (System Realtime messages will not terminate Running Status). This allows transmitters to send message strings of the same type with Data bytes only.

Running Status greatly improves MIDI Channel Message throughput. For example, suppose a MIDI transmitter sends four consecutive channel aftertouch messages without running status. The message would have four status byte/data byte pairs and require 8 bytes:

Status Byte 1	Data Byte 1	Status Byte 2	Data Byte 2	Status Byte 3	Data Byte 3	Status Byte 4	Data Byte 4

With running status, status bytes 2, 3, and 4 are not necessary since they are the same as status byte 1. This message requires only 5 bytes:

Status Byte 1	Data Byte 1	Data Byte 2	Data Byte 3	Data Byte 4

Running status is also one of the primary reasons that MIDI merge boxes are so much more expensive than MIDI thru boxes—merging requires a microprocessor to sort out and synchronize two independent streams of running status data.

The MIDI Vocabulary

Let's look at each of the individual messages that make up these five main message types (Channel Voice, Channel Mode, System Common, System Realtime, and System Exclusive).

Channel Voice Messages

Channel Voice messages are the most prevalent in MIDI communications. The following chart summarizes the data structure for particular messages; the range of valid Data byte values is in decimal. After the chart, we'll look at each message in detail.

Message Name	Status Byte	Data Byte 1	Data Byte 2
Note Off	$8n	0–127	0–127
Note On	$9n	0–127	0–127
Key Pressure	$An	0–127	0–127
Control Change	$Bn	0–120	0–127
Program Change	$Cn	0–127	
Channel Pressure	$Dn	0–127	
Pitch Bend	$En	0–127	0–127

In the Status Byte column, *n* stands for the channel number nibble and can range from $0 to $F, corresponding to channels 1 ($0) through 16 ($F).

Note On

A Note On message contains three bytes:

Status Byte	Data Byte 1	Data Byte 2
$9n (n=channel)	Note Number (0–127)	Velocity (0–127)

Example: The Hex equivalent of "Start note 49 on channel 11 with an attack velocity of 35" is $9A $31 $23.

Note that a Note On message with velocity = 0 is equivalent to sending a Note Off message. This allows a system to take full advantage of running status, since it is not necessary to change the Note On status to Note Off to turn off a note. Because running status is a common and useful part of MIDI, most MIDI transmitters do not transmit Note Off messages.

Note Off
A Note Off message contains three bytes:

Status Byte	Data Byte 1	Data Byte 2
$8n (n=channel)	Note Number (0–127)	Rel. Velocity (0–127)

Example: The Hex equivalent of "Stop note 49 on channel 11 with a release velocity of 35" is $8A $31 $23.

Key Pressure
A Key Pressure (also called Polyphonic Pressure) message contains three bytes:

Status Byte	Data Byte 1	Data Byte 2
$An (n=channel)	Note Number (0–127)	Press. Value (0–127)

Example: The Hex equivalent of "Add aftertouch to note 49 on channel 11 with a value of 35" is $AA $31 $23.

Control Change
A Control Change message contains three bytes:

Status Byte	Data Byte 1	Data Byte 2
$Bn (n=channel)	Controller # (0–120)	Cont. Value (0–127)

Example: The Hex equivalent of "Add controller 1 (modulation wheel) to all notes on channel 11 with a value of 35" is $BA $01 $23.

Controller numbers are not constrained to specific functions, but some have become more or less standardized, while others remain unassigned. Following is the current list of assigned controllers; numbers in parenthesis indicate the controller's range of possible values.

1	Modulation Wheel (0–127)
2	Breath Controller (0–127)
3	Early DX7 Aftertouch (0–127)
4	Foot Controller (0–127)
5	Portamento Time (0–127)
6	Data Slider (0–127)
7	Main Volume (0–127)
8	Balance (0–127)
10	Pan (0–127)
11	Expression (0–127)
16	General Purpose #1 (0–127)
17	General Purpose #2 (0–127)
18	General Purpose #3 (0–127)
19	General Purpose #4 (0–127)
32–63	Least Significant Bits, Controllers 0–31 (0–127)
64	Sustain Pedal (0 or 127)
65	Portamento On/Off (0 or 127)
66	Sustenuto Pedal (0 or 127)
67	Soft Pedal (0 or 127)
69	Hold 2 (0 or 127)
80	General Purpose #5 (0 or 127)
81	General Purpose #6 (0 or 127)
82	General Purpose #7 (0 or 127)
83	General Purpose #8 (0 or 127)
92	Tremolo Depth (0–127)
93	Chorus Depth (0–127)
94	Celeste Depth (0–127)
95	Phase Depth (0–127)
96	Data Increment (0 or 127)

97   Data Decrement (0 or 127)
98   Non-Registered Parameter MSB (0–127)
99   Non-Registered Parameter LSB (0–127)
100   Registered Parameter MSB (0–127)
101   Registered Parameter LSB (0–127)

Note that controller numbers 121–127 are reserved for Channel Mode messages (described later).

Program Change

A Program Change message contains two bytes:

Status Byte	Data Byte
$Cn (n=channel)	Program # (0–127)

Example: The Hex equivalent of "On channel 11, change the instrument's preset patch number to 35" is $CA $23.

Channel Pressure

A Channel Pressure message contains two bytes:

Status Byte	Data Byte
$Dn (n=channel)	Pressure Value (0–127)

Example: The Hex equivalent of "Add an aftertouch value of 35 to all notes on channel 11" is $DA $23.

Pitch Bend

A Pitch Bend message contains three bytes:

Status Byte	Data Byte 1	Data Byte 2
$En (n=channel)	LSB Value (0–127)	MSB Value (0–127)

The two Data bytes encode a 14-bit value, allowing for a maximum decimal value of 16,383. To obtain the 14-bit value, combine the last seven bits of data byte 1—the least significant byte—with the last seven bits of data byte 2, the most significant byte. (The reason why we use only the last seven bits is because, as you may recall, the first bit of a data byte is always 0.)

Let's show how to figure out the decimal equivalent of a Pitch Bend message.

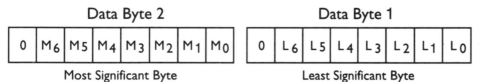

Combining these gives a 14-bit number:

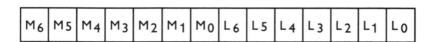

The formula for calculating the decimal value is:

LSB + (MSB × 128)

Examples: The Hex equivalent of "Transmit a pitch bend value of 11,427 on Channel 11" is $EA $23 $59. Here's how to derive the decimal value:

Data Byte 1 (the Least Significant Byte) is $23 (00100011 in binary or 35 in decimal). Data Byte 2 (the Most Significant Byte) is $59 (01011001 in binary or 89 in decimal). According to the formula given above, this works out to:

$$35 + (89 \times 128) = 11,427$$

Note that the minimum pitch bend value in decimal is 0 and the maximum is 16383; therefore, the no pitch bend value (i.e., pitch bend wheel at center position) is halfway between these two extremes, or 8192.

Examples: The Hex equivalent of "Maximize pitch bend (decimal value 16383) on channel 11" is $EA $7F $7F. "Return pitch bend to its no-effect position (decimal value 8192) on channel 11" would be $EA $00 $40, and the message "Minimize pitch bend (decimal value 0) on channel 11" would be $EA $00 $00.

Channel Mode Messages

The following chart summarizes the data structure for the various mode messages. The range of valid Data byte values is in decimal. After the chart, we'll look at each message in detail.

Message Name	Status Byte	Data Byte 1	Data Byte 2
Reset All Controllers	$Bn	121	0
Local Control	$Bn	122	0, 127
All Notes Off	$Bn	123	0
Omni Mode Off	$Bn	124	0
Omni Mode On	$Bn	125	0
Mono Mode On	$Bn	126	0–16
Poly Mode On	$Bn	127	0

In the Status Byte Value column, n stands for the channel number nibble and can range from $0 to $F, corresponding to channels 1 ($0) through 16 ($F). Channel Mode messages are recognized only when transmitted on the receiver's Basic channel.

The four mode messages (Omni Mode On/Off, Mono/Poly Mode On) set the receiver mode, and can also turn off all notes on the associated channel.

Reset All Controllers

The Reset All Controllers message resets the receiver's pitch bend, controllers, and aftertouch to their initial settings (e.g., pitch bend set to the midpoint, and controllers and aftertouch set to 0). This message contains three bytes:

Status Byte	Data Byte 1	Data Byte 2
$Bn (n=channel)	121	0

Example: The Hex equivalent of "Reset all controllers on channel 11 to their initial settings" is $BA $79 $00.

Local Control

The Local Control message determines whether a keyboard's internal sound generators are triggered by the keyboard and incoming MIDI messages (Local Control On), or incoming MIDI messages only (Local Control Off). In either case, the keyboard still transmits to the MIDI Out. This message contains three bytes:

Status Byte	Data Byte 1	Data Byte 2
$Bn (n=channel)	122	0=LC Off 127=LC On

Examples: The Hex equivalent of "Enable local control on the device connected to channel 11" is $BA $7A $7F. "Disable local control on the device connected to channel 11" is $BA $7A $00.

All Notes Off

The All Notes Off message turns off all notes playing on the receiver's Basic channel and contains three bytes:

Status Byte	Data Byte 1	Data Byte 2
$Bn (n=channel)	123	0

Example: The Hex equivalent of "Stop all notes playing on channel 11" is $BA $7B $00.

Omni Mode Off

The Omni Mode Off message contains three bytes:

Status Byte	Data Byte 1	Data Byte 2
$Bn (n=channel)	124	0

Example: The Hex equivalent of "Turn off omni mode in the receiver connected to channel 11" is $BA $7C $00.

Omni Mode On

The Omni Mode On message contains three bytes:

Status Byte	Data Byte 1	Data Byte 2
$Bn (n=channel)	125	0

Example: The Hex equivalent of "Turn on omni mode in the receiver connected to channel 11" is $BA $7D $00.

Mono Mode On (Poly Mode Off)

The Mono Mode On message contains three bytes:

Status Byte	Data Byte 1	Data Byte 2
$Bn (n=channel)	126	# of channels, 0–16

We'll call the number of channels M and the receiver's basic channel N. If the receiver is set to Omni Off, all Channel Voice messages received on channels N through N+M−1 will monophonically control internal voices 1 through M, respectively. Example: If N is Basic Channel 9 and M specifies 4 channels, then messages received on channels 9 through 9+4−1 (*i.e.*, 12) will trigger the first four synth voices (1–4).

When M=0, the receiver assigns internal voices starting with N and ending with 16 (or until all the receiver's available voices have been used up).

If the receiver is set to Omni On, it will ignore any values of M that are greater than 1.

Example: The Hex equivalent of "Turn on monophonic mode in the receiver connected to channel 11 with 4 voice channels activated" is $BA $7E $04.

Poly Mode On (Mono Mode Off)

The Poly Mode On message contains three bytes:

Status Byte	Data Byte 1	Data Byte 2
$Bn (n=channel)	127	0

Example: The Hex equivalent of "Turn on polyphonic mode in the receiver connected to channel 11" is $BA $7F $00.

System Common Messages

The following chart summarizes the data structure for the various system common messages. The range of valid Data byte values is in decimal. Following the chart, we'll look at each message in detail.

Message Name	Status Byte	Data Byte 1	Data Byte 2
MTC Quarter Frame	$F1	0–127	
Song Position Pointer	$F2	0–127	0–127
Song Select	$F3	0–127	
Tune Request	$F6		
EOX	$F7		

MIDI Time Code Quarter Frame

MTC Quarter Frame messages contain two bytes. The Data byte for a single MTC message does not contain all the information needed to specify a particular SMPTE time; eight consecutive messages must be received to completely decode a SMPTE time code number. (Actually, these should be considered as four pairs of messages, since you need two MTC messages to describe each of the four SMPTE time fields—hours, minutes, seconds, frames.) Messages 0 and 1 give the frame count, 2 and 3 the seconds count, 4 and 5 the minutes count, and 6 and 7 the hours count.

As a result, let's look at a pair of MTC messages instead of just a single message. The structure for expressing the hour, minute, second, or frame count is:

Status Byte	Data Byte
$F1	$nd
Status Byte	Data Byte
$F1	$nd

The first nibble (n) specifies the message number (0–7, since there are eight messages needed to specify a SMPTE time). Taking the second nibbles of the pair of messages and combining them gives the time. The first nibble is the Least Significant nibble, the second the Most Significant nibble.

Example: Suppose a pair of MTC messages is $F1 $0D and $F1 $11. The first nibble of the first data byte tells us this is message 0; the first nibble of the second data byte specifies that this is message 1. Therefore, this message pair expresses the frame count.

Combining the pair of second nibbles gives $1D. If we write this out as a byte in binary (remember that D is the Least Significant nibble), we get 0001 (1) and 1101 (D), or 00011101. Translating this from binary gives us 29. Therefore, $F1 $0D and $F1 $11 expresses a frame count of 29.

All MTC message pairs are treated similarly. However, there are slight variations between how to interpret the byte formed by combining the pair of second nibbles.

- With frames, the first three bits of the byte are unused and not defined. The remaining five bits express the frame count. Valid values are 0–29.

- With seconds, the first two bits of the byte are unused and not defined. The remaining six bits express the seconds count. Valid values are 0–59.

- With minutes, the first two bits of the byte are unused and not defined. The remaining six bits express the minutes count. Valid values are 0–59.

- With hours, the first bit of the byte is unused and not defined. The next two bits determine the time code type. SMPTE allows for different frame rates to accommodate several different technologies (film, video, American TV, European TV, etc.):

```
0 (00 in binary) = 24 frames/second
1 (01 in binary) = 25 frames/second
2 (10 in binary) = 30 frames/second (drop frame)
3 (11 in binary) = 30 frames/second (non-drop frame)
```

The remaining five bits express the hours count. Valid values are 0–23.

Let's tie all this together with an example. The hex equivalent of "Synchronize to SMPTE timecode 23:59:59:29" is:

```
$F1 $0D    D=Frame Least Significant (LS) nibble
$F1 $11    1=Frame Most Significant (MS) nibble
$F1 $2B    B=Seconds LS nibble
$F1 $33    3=Seconds MS nibble
$F1 $4B    B=Minutes LS nibble
$F1 $53    3=Minutes MS nibble
$F1 $67    7=Hours LS nibble
$F1 $75    5=Time Code Type and Hours MS nibble
```

Regarding the last two messages, combining the pair of second nibbles gives 01010111. This breaks down to 0 10 10111, where the first bit is ignored, the next two specify the Time Code type (30 frames/second, drop frame), and the final five bits indicate that the number of hours is 23.

Song Position Pointer

A Song Position Pointer (SPP) message, which represents the value of the number of sixteenth notes (1 sixteenth note = 6 MIDI timing clocks) since the start of a song, contains three bytes:

Status Byte	Data Byte 1	Data Byte 2
$F2	0–127 (LSB)	0–127 (MSB)

The two Data bytes encode a 14-bit value in a manner similar to the way pitch bend messages encode a 14-bit value, thus allowing for a maximum decimal value of 16,383. As with pitch bend messages, combining the last seven bits of data byte 1 (the least significant byte) with the last seven bits of data byte 2 (the most significant byte) gives the Song Position Pointer value. For an explanation of how this is done, refer back to the section on pitch bend messages.

Example: The Hex equivalent of "Locate measure 100 of the current 4/4 time signature sequence" is $F2 $40 $0C. (The decimal SPP value is 100 measures × 16 sixteenth notes per measure, or 1,600.)

Song Select

A Song Select message selects which song or sequence will play when a MIDI Start message is transmitted, and contains two bytes:

Status Byte	Data Byte
$F3	Song # (0–127)

Example: The Hex equivalent of "Select song 5" is $F3 $05.

Tune Request

A Tune Request message requests that an analog synthesizer tune its internal oscillators and contains one byte:

Status Byte
$F6

Example: The Hex equivalent of "Tune thyself, dinosaur synthesizer!" is $F6.

End of System Exclusive Flag

An End of System Exclusive (EOX) message indicates the end of a System Exclusive message and contains one byte:

Status Byte
$F7

Example: The Hex equivalent of "Terminate this System Exclusive transmission" is $F7.

System Realtime Messages

All System Realtime messages contain one byte, and can be transmitted in the middle of other messages (even in the middle of System Exclusive). Giving priority to timing messages assures proper synchronization. Setting a MIDI receiver to "MIDI Sync" lets it respond to System Realtime messages.

The following chart summarizes the data structure for system realtime messages. Following the chart, we'll look at each message in detail.

Message Name	Status Byte
Timing Clock	$F8
Start	$FA
Continue	$FB
Stop	$FC
Active Sensing	$FE
System Reset	$FF

Timing Clock

The Timing Clock message is transmitted at a periodic rate of 24 times per quarter note and contains one byte:

Status Byte
$F8

Example: The Hex equivalent of "Here comes a timing clock pulse, dude" is $F8.

Start

The Start message initiates a sequence/song playback and contains one byte:

Status Byte
$FA

Example: The Hex equivalent of "Start sequencer playback from the beginning (SPP=0)" is $FA.

Continue

The Continue message resumes playback of a sequence/song from its current location and contains one byte:

Status Byte
$FB

Example: The Hex equivalent of "Start sequencer playback from the current position" is $FB.

Stop

The Stop message terminates sequence/song playback and contains one byte:

Status Byte
$FC

Example: The Hex equivalent of "Stop sequencer playback" is $FC.

Active Sensing

Active Sensing messages are sent every 299 milliseconds or less when no other MIDI data is being transmitted. The message contains one byte:

Status Byte
$FE

Example: The Hex equivalent of "Hello synthesizer, the MIDI line is still here" is $FE.

System Reset

A System Reset message returns all MIDI devices to their default (power-up) configurations and contains one byte:

Status Byte
$FF

Example: The Hex equivalent of "Take cover! I'm resetting the entire system!" is $FF.

System Exclusive Messages

System Exclusive messages encode internal device parameter data (synth patches, rhythm machine patterns, etc.) as data that can be sent and received via MIDI.

The following chart summarizes the data structure for System Exclusive messages, which can be any length. Following the chart, we'll look at each message in detail.

Message Component	Number of Bytes
Status	1 ($F0)
ID	1 ($01–$7C), or 3 if first byte = $00 (remaining 2 bytes are $00–$7F)
Data	Any number; values are $00–$7F
EOX	1 ($F7)

Manufacturer ID Numbers

Manufacturer ID Codes consist of either one or three bytes. If the first byte value is between $01 and $7C, that value is the Manufacturer ID Number. If the first byte value is $00, the following two bytes give the Manufacturer ID Number.

For non-commercial use, the System Exclusive ID Number $7D is reserved for any product not offered for sale to the public.

If the first byte value is $7E or 7F, there are special applications which we'll cover later under Non-Realtime Extensions and Realtime Extensions.

Data Bytes

System Exclusive Data bytes can be any value between 0–127. (However, for realtime and non-realtime extension messages, some Data byte values are constrained; this is fairly esoteric stuff, so see the MIDI Specification for further details.)

Message Termination

There are two ways to terminate a System Exclusive message:

- EOX Message: The System Common message EOX ($F7) is the proper way to terminate a System Exclusive message. This should be the last byte transmitted in a string of System Exclusive bytes.

- Non-Realtime Status Byte: A System Exclusive message will automatically terminate upon receipt of a Channel Message, a System Common Message, or another System Exclusive Message. System Realtime messages will *not* terminate a System Exclusive message.

Non-Realtime Extensions

System Exclusive ID Number $7E is reserved for extending the MIDI Specification's non-realtime applications. A complete message consists of:

- 1 System Exclusive Status byte ($F0)

- 1 Special ID Code byte ($7E)

- 1 Channel number byte

- 1 or 2 Sub-ID Code bytes

- 1 or more Data bytes

- 1 EOX byte ($F7).

Following are some non-realtime extensions.

Sample Dump Standard

The Sample Dump Standard allows digital audio to be sent and received via midi. The following Sub-ID Codes are used for sampler data dumps:

Byte Value	Function
$01	Dump Header
$02	Data Packet
$03	Dump Request
$7C	Wait
$7D	Cancel
$7E	NAK (no acknowledge)
$7F	ACK (acknowledge)

Loop Point Messages

The following Sub-ID Codes can specify up to 16,383 pairs of loop points per sample:

Byte Values	Function
$05 $01	Loop Points Transmission
$05 $02	Loop Points Request

Inquiry Message

The following Sub-ID Codes request the identity of any receiving device:

Byte Values	Function
$06 $01	Send General Inquiry
$06 $02	Send Response to Gen. Inquiry

Midi Cueing

The following Sub-ID Codes address individual devices in a synchronized midi system:

Byte Values	Function
$04 $00	Special
$04 $01	Punch In Point
$04 $02	Punch Out Point
$04 $03	Delete Punch In Point
$04 $04	Delete Punch Out Point
$04 $05	Event Start Point
$04 $06	Event Stop Point
$04 $07	Event Start Point with Info
$04 $08	Event Stop Point with Info
$04 $09	Delete Event Start Point
$04 $0A	Delete Event Stop Point
$04 $0B	Cue Point
$04 $0C	Cue Point with Info
$04 $0D	Delete Cue Point
$04 $0E	Event Name in Additional Info

Realtime Extensions

System Exclusive ID Number $7F is reserved for extending the MIDI specification's realtime applications. A complete message consists of:

- 1 System Exclusive Status byte ($F0)

- 1 ID Code byte ($7F)

- 1 channel number byte

- 2 Sub-ID Code bytes

- 1 or more Data bytes

- 1 EOX byte ($F7)

Full MTC Message

The following Sub-ID Code transmits a complete SMPTE timecode value to tape-transport equipment that is not running:

Byte Values	Function
$01 $01	Send Complete Time Code Message

SMPTE User Bits

The following Sub-ID Code transmits "User Bits" that can be programmed by dedicated equipment for special functions (sure, that's a vague definition, but this is *not* the kind of thing you run into every day):

Byte Values	Function
$01 $02	User-Defined

So much for the bits and bytes of MIDI; now let's delve a little deeper into the MIDItools software itself.

Chapter 12

MIDItools Software

Software is a craft. Programmers are artists. There is no right or wrong way to write software, just elegant or inept ways. Writing software always involves judgment calls, just as a painter judges how to mix paint and brush it onto a canvas. What we're about to cover is not necessarily the "right" way to write software; it's just "a" way.

The MIDItools software follows three ground rules:

- Simplicity, so people at all levels of computer literacy have a chance of understanding it.

- Flexibility, so it can be adapted to many different applications.

- Efficiency and reliability, so a program doesn't crash on you in the middle of a crucial gig or recording session.

Be forewarned: this chapter and the following one may be somewhat daunting to novices. (If it isn't daunting, you're a natural-born computer hacker and probably have a high-paying job just waiting for you in the software industry.) The subject of software is sort of like a big jigsaw puzzle, where each piece may not make sense by itself—but put them all together, and the picture becomes clear.

Those familiar with the 6805 processor should find this chapter relatively easy reading; those who lack experience with this chip can still derive useful background information. However, for a better understanding of the MIDItools software, you might want to skim Chapter 13 to familiarize yourself with the 6805's operation. You may have to go back and forth between this chapter and Chapter 13 a few times for the pieces to fall into place and make sense.

The Big Overview

As mentioned in the beginning, this book is written primarily for those who want to build and use the MIDItools Computer. However, we also hope to inspire quite a few of you to become interested enough in software to write some MIDItools programs of your own, and maybe even share them with other musicians.

One of the stumbling blocks to writing a program is the sheer complexity of all the little details. However, the MIDItools Computer contains a collection of basic input/output service routines (the BIOS) that contain all the code needed to handle various low-level actions—check switch presses, put characters on the LCD, and so on.

Since you're relieved of dealing with all those messy parts, you're free to concentrate on writing the application itself. To do that, you need two pieces of knowledge in addition to what we've covered to far:

- How the 6805 processor works, and its repertoire of available instructions (see Chapter 13).

- The BIOS routines available in the MIDItools Computer software.

We've already covered the concept of a State Matrix in Chapter 10. The State Matrix is crucial to writing MIDItools applications, as it represents a very simple and rapid way to define and solve a problem. You'll recall that the basic principle is that you set up a matrix of inputs (button presses, MIDI data received at the MIDI input, and analog to digital converter readings), states (what the device is doing *now)*, and outputs (characters to write on the LCD, MIDI data sent to the MIDI out port, LEDs to light, etc.). At the intersection of each input and state, you tell the computer what to do in response to a given input to create the desired output.

Once you've figured out the state matrix, you're well on your way. All that remains is to put it into the correct format to burn into the MIDItools EPROM, and you're ready to go. Of course, this is not exactly a trivial undertaking, but it's not too difficult either (if we can do it, so can you). For more information, see Chapter 14 and the Appendix.

Coding Conventions

One secret to writing good software is adhering to a consistent set of conventions. Conventions provide code which is more readable, maintainable, and generally less bug-prone. Following are some of the MIDItools Computer's software conventions.

Labels

All MIDItools software labels are written with capital letters so that they stick out from the instructions, which are written in lower case. Macros (labels assigned to blocks of code) are also written in all capital letters, as are variables and constants.

Comments

Virtually every line of code in the MIDItools software carries a corresponding programmer's comment. Commenting is extremely important as it reveals the programmer's intent for each instruction. If a program is not working properly, you should be able to compare each instruction with its comment to verify that the instruction correlates with the programmer's intentions.

Comments should not merely state the *behavior* of each instruction, but document the *purpose* behind the instruction *(e.g.,* a comment for an add instruction should not state "add two numbers" but something more meaningful, such as "compute total number of CDs sold"). You should be able to follow what's happening in a program just by reading the comments.

Delineating between major and minor sections of code helps break a program into logical pieces and make it more readable. In the MIDItools software, major comments mark major sections of code, and minor comments mark subsections. Consider the following block of code, taken from a MIDItools BIOS subroutine:

```
;- see if switch status has changed

SGE1:
    jsr   SW_READ            ;read switches
    cmp   PREVSW             ;has switch status changed?
    FAR_BEQ    CIFF          ;nope, go check faders
    tax                      ;buffer new status in index reg
    eor   PREVSW             ;bit set for each changed switch

    ;release all switches in PREVSW that just got released

    txa                      ;A = new switch status
    eor   PREVSW             ;A = what changed
    and   PREVSW             ;A = what released
    eor   PREVSW             ;A = old switch status-releases
    sta   PREVSW             ;update switch history
```

```
;process one newly pushed switch

comx                                    ;X still = new switch status
txa                                     ;A = complemented switch status
ora     PREVSW                          ;A = switches that didn't change
coma                                    ;A = switches that did change
```

The major section of code is identified by the three leading dashes (";—
see if_"). Minor sections are identified by indented comments (";release all
switches_" and ";process one newly pushed switch"). Also note that each
instruction is followed by a comment that reveals its purpose.

The final type of comment is a *subroutine header*. Subroutines are blocks
of code which are called from other parts of the program to perform a
general service. When a subroutine finishes, it returns to where it was called
from. Since subroutines generally accept and return variables, use other
resources in the computer and make other assumptions, it is good practice
to document all these underlying details in a header.

The header format used by MIDItools subroutines follows this convention:

Subroutine name
Brief description of routine
Arguments: Returns: Registers: Variables: Calls: Macros:

The above header provides the name of the subroutine, a brief explanation of the what the routine does, and a list of parameters:

- Arguments accepted

- Returned values

- CPU registers used

- Variables used

- Other subroutines called by this one

- Macros used

This header helps future programmers (you!) maintain the routine.

Naming

Names assigned to subroutines follow an "object_procedure" convention. The beginning of a subroutine's name is the name of the *object* the
routine relates to—like the noun in a sentence. An underscore separates the
object name from the *procedure* name, which describes what the subroutine
does to the object (like the verb in a sentence).

Example: A MIDItools subroutine that puts a character in the LCD
display is called "LCD_PUT_C." "LCD" designates the LCD object.
"PUT" implies something is put into the display. The "C" stands for
character. This naming convention is consistent, so you should always be
able to tell what a routine does just by decoding its name.

Software Structure

All MIDItools software is partitioned into two general modules:

- Basic Input Output Services (BIOS). The BIOS contains basic routines that control the computer's hardware and provides a foundation on which applications are built. It contains all the generic stuff that is used repeatedly in different applications.

- Application. The Application contains the routines unique to a particular application. Since the BIOS is generic, to create a new tool you simply create an "Application file" that contains the application's unique code.

The State Machine

All MIDItools are based on a state machine. As discussed in Chapter 10, a state machine is a standard program structure that translates input events to output actions. The MIDItools state machine recognizes three types of input events from its peripherals: button pushes, ADC (analog to digital converter) changes, and MIDI reception.

Since the state machine is common to all applications, most of its software is located in the BIOS. Output actions are defined in Application files since they define unique reactions to input events.

BIOS Basics

The BIOS consists of 11 BIOS source code files. Ten of the files govern individual resources in the computer. The eleventh, MAIN.ASM, is the mother of all source code files and specifies which BIOS and Application files to include for a particular tool.

The BIOS files are:

MAIN.ASM	The main source code file
SYS05C8.ASM	MC68HC705C8 system routines
SPI.ASM	SPI routines
TIMER.ASM	Timer routines
MIDI.ASM	SCI and MIDI routines
LCD.ASM	LCD routines
LED.ASM	LED routines
SW.ASM	Switch routines
ADC.ASM	ADC routines
EEPROM.ASM	EEPROM routines
STMACH.ASM	State machine routines

Each BIOS file contains two types of routines: *private* routines and *public* routines.

To understand the difference, consider your telephone dial. It provides a simple interface to the telephone company's complex labyrinth of cables, switches, and routing technology. The dial is your simple, *public* interface to the underlying telephone network. You don't care about what fills telephone company buildings; all that complicated stuff is *private*.

Private Routines

Private routines hide the BIOS's most intimate operations. They generally transfer raw data between the 6805 and peripherals, hiding the application from the complexity of the interfaces. Application files are discouraged from accessing these routines since it's seldom necessary.

Public Routines

Public routines provide the public interface to the computer's resources. These routines simplify the interface between an application and the resources by shielding the application from all the gory details (which are handled by the private routines). Example: Public LCD routines write information into the LCD by passing simple commands to the BIOS. The private routines handle all the messy details of what data to send to what chips over what ports.

Interrupt Service Routines

Some MIDItools Computer peripherals initiate interrupts. BIOS files that support such peripherals contain an additional type of routine, the *Interrupt Service Routine* (ISR). An ISR is executed whenever its associated interrupt occurs. For example, the Serial Communications Interface (SCI) can issue an interrupt (if it's enabled) whenever the MIDI In port receives a byte. When this interrupt occurs, the program turns control over to the SCI ISR, located in the MIDI.ASM BIOS file.

ISR Call Backs

You can ignore all interrupts and ISRs if you don't want to deal with them, or go crazy and take full control of the interrupts.

You can override each BIOS ISR by using an *ISR call back*, which calls a custom routine at a known location in the Application file. The first thing a BIOS ISR does is jump to this address. When the Application file receives control, it has the option of immediately returning back to the BIOS ISR, or executing its own. So, if you don't want to service a particular interrupt in the Application file you simply jump back to the BIOS.

That's about it for BIOS basics. Now, let's look at each routine inside the BIOS. To understand more of the background behind terms like Serial Peripheral Interface, Master Output/Slave Input, etc., please refer to Chapter 13.

SPI Routines (file: SPI.ASM)

The SPI routines provide basic access to the Serial Peripheral Interface Bus. These routines initialize the SPI, check to see if it's ready for a data transfer, then perform the bi-directional data transfer.

Private Routines

SPI_RDY—Waits for SPIF flag to set. This routine is called before accessing the SPI bus to ensure that the bus is ready for new data.

SPI_INIT—Initializes SPI. A reset causes the BIOS to call this routine automatically.

Public Routines

SPI_IO—Outputs a byte to MOSI (Master Output/Slave Input) and inputs a byte from MISO (Master Input/Slave Output). This routine is your main access to reading and writing data from and to the SPI bus.

Timer Routines (file: TIMER.ASM)

The timer is dedicated exclusively to generating precision MIDI clocks. Many applications need timing services other than MIDI clocks, mainly delays. We implement these delay routines without using the timer by constructing blocks of instructions with known execution times. These routines really don't do anything, they just take a known amount of time to do nothing. So, the delay routines in the TIMER.ASM file don't actually use the timer (but don't tell anyone).

Private Routines

TIMER_ISR—Timer Interrupt Service routine. Whenever its associated interrupt occurs, the program turns control over to this routine.

TIMER_INIT—Initializes timer. A reset causes the BIOS to call this routine automatically.

Public Routines

DELAY_1MS—Waits 1 ms.

DELAY_10MS—Waits 10 ms.

DELAY_100MS—Waits 100 ms.

DELAY_1SEC—Waits 1 second.

Midi Routines (file: MIDI.ASM)

The MIDI routines perform MIDI input and output processing. The private routines transfer raw data between the MC68HC705C8's Serial Communications Interface (SCI) and the MIDI interface hardware. The public routines speak the MIDI protocol.

Queues

All MIDI data, transmitted or received, is buffered in a "queue." A queue is a line, like what you stand in when you go to see a popular movie. This queue forms because incoming people arrive faster than the cashier can service them (without a queue, you'd need a superhuman cashier—preferably one with a couple dozen arms—so that each person could be serviced the instant they appear).

Similarly, without a queue for MIDI data every received MIDI byte would have to be serviced before the next one came along, which allows only about 320 μs (microseconds) to do all that work! The MIDI queue collects data to ease timing requirements, since the queue gives the microprocessor more latitude in deciding when it's going to process the collected pieces of data.

Midi Reception

Properly receiving and processing MIDI data is not a trivial task. Data pours into the computer asynchronously —you don't know when to expect it. When it appears, you have to figure out what it means and process it (this is called *parsing)*.

To simplify our job in writing an application, the BIOS takes care of all the details of parsing received MIDI data. Once the BIOS receives and translates a complete MIDI message, it issues a MIDI Reception event to the state machine and records the Status and Data byte(s) in special variables. So, when creating an application, you just define an output action for the state machine to call in response to MIDI data reception. Upon calling this output action, the BIOS hands you the parsed message via simple variables. This greatly simplifies the process of creating MIDItools applications.

Midi Message Classes

Since we're processing a data stream, in the interest of efficiency the processor should deal only with messages that are of interest to a particular application and ignore the rest. All MIDI messages are partitioned into eight different classes:

- System Real Time

- System Common

- System Exclusive

- Control Change

- Pitch Bend

- Aftertouch

- Program Change

- Note On/Off

The MIDI receive queue receives MIDI messages corresponding to each class only if the M_RX_Q_XPT ("Midi Receive Queue Accept") variable is suitably configured. M_RX_Q_XPT is bit-mapped with each bit corresponding to a particular class:

bit	7	6	5	4	3	2	1	0
	SysReal	SysCom	SysEx	Ctlr	PchBnd	AftTch	PrgChg	NoteOn/Off

If an application is interested in accepting messages in a particular MIDI class, it must set the corresponding bit in M_RX_Q_XPT to a logical 1. Likewise, if an application is uninterested in messages in a particular class it can ignore them (not enqueue them) by resetting the corresponding bit in M_RX_Q_XPT to a logical 0.

MIDI Transmission

MIDI transmission is much simpler. To transmit a MIDI message an application writes the Status and Data bytes to the transmit queue with the public routine MIDI_PUT. Timing is not a concern to the application, thanks to the transmit queue; the BIOS invisibly handles all details of transmitting this data out the MIDI interface, including the correct format and timing.

Interrupt Service Routine Call Backs

The BIOS SCI Interrupt Service Routine (ISR) provides several call backs.

SCI_RX_CB and SCI_TX_CB are called when the SCI (Serial Communications Interface) recognizes SCI receive and transmit interrupts, respectively. The BIOS SCI Receive ISR parses incoming MIDI bytes on the fly, so the application can process Status and Data bytes as they are detected.

SCI_RX_CB_S is called when a Status byte is received. SCI_RX_CB_D1 and SCI_RX_CB_D2 are called when the first and second MIDI Data bytes are received. These call back routines are called regardless of the MIDI receive queue class enables (M_RX_Q_XPT).

When the SCI_RX_CB_S, SCI_RX_CB_D1, and SCI_RX_CB_D2 routines are called, the accumulator holds the class (see codes for M_RX_Q_XPT) of the current message, and the index register holds the byte. You can process the incoming MIDI in the call back routines, or return control to the BIOS and allow it to buffer the messages in the MIDI receive queue. As messages are buffered in this queue, the state machine parses them and issues MIDI In events.

Therefore, there are two options for receiving MIDI, each with different tradeoffs:

- Process incoming MIDI in the MIDI receive call back routines. This requires strict control over timing—since you are processing data within the SCI ISR, you have a maximum of about 250µs (320µs minus the overhead of getting in and out of the BIOS ISR) for all processing.

- Allow the BIOS to buffer the incoming MIDI, and process messages as the state machine issues MIDI In events. This allows plenty of time to process the incoming MIDI bytes, but there is a considerable time delay between when the message comes in and when the state machine dispatches events to you.

The bottom line on the two options: use the call back routines for short, critical processing functions. Use the state machine if timing is not a concern.

MIDI Sequencer Routines

The MIDItools Computer cannot implement a sequencer application because it does not contain enough RAM to hold a sequence of any reasonable length. It does, however, provide public routines to generate accurate MIDI clocks, and Start, Stop, Continue, and Song Position Pointer messages.

Private Routines

UART_RX_INT_EN	Enables receiver interrupts.
UART_RX_INT_DIS	Disables receiver interrupts.
UART_TX_INT_EN	Enables transmitter interrupts.
UART_TX_INT_DIS	Disables transmitter interrupts.
UART_TX_MT_W8	Waits for empty UART tx (transmit) register.
MIDI_CLASS	Returns class mask for a MIDI message.
MIDI_ISR	SCI (MIDI) Interrupt Service Routine.
MIDI_INIT	Initializes MIDI primitives (*i.e.,* basic MIDI routines). A reset causes the BIOS to call this routine automatically.

Public Routines

MIDI_PUT	Writes the byte in the accumulator to the MIDI transmit queue.
MIDI_GET	Reads a byte from the MIDI receive queue and writes it to the accumulator.
MIDI_PARSE	Parses data in the MIDI receive queue. The MP_FLAGS variable is updated, and the Status and Data byte(s) are written to MP_RSTAT, MP_DATA1, and MP_DATA2 respectively. Note: Since the state machine uses this routine to detect MIDI In events, to prevent conflicts don't call this routine if you are using the state machine.
MIDI_TEMPO	Sets tempo of outgoing MIDI Clock messages according to the tempo (20-255) in the accumulator.
MIDI_METER	Computes numerator and denominator of meter. The numerator (1-16) is passed along from the accumulator, and the denominator (1,2,4,8,16) from the index register.
MIDI_COMPUTE_SPP	Computes Song Position Pointer, determined by the current MEASURE and BEAT.
MIDI_POSN	Sets MEASURE and BEAT; the measure is passed along from the accumulator, and the beat from the index register.

MIDI_PLAY   Play a remote sequencer. The starting measure is passed along from the accumulator and the beat from the index register. This subroutine is used to implement both the MIDI Play and MIDI Continue functions.

MIDI_STOP   Stops a remote sequencer.

MIDI_SPP   Sends MIDI Song Position Pointer message.

LCD Routines (file: LCD.ASM)

The LCD routines control the LCD. Private routines exchange raw data between the 6805 and the LCD driver chip. Public routines place words and numbers in the display, and control the cursor.

The HD44780 LCD Driver Chip

Almost all character-based LCD modules are controlled by a driver chip called the HD44780, which accepts data from the microprocessor and places it in the display. Thanks to this standard interface chip it is easy to write software that supports LCD modules from virtually any manufacturer.

You control the chip by writing specially coded data bytes to two internal registers:

- The *Instruction Register* (IR) accepts coded instructions, such as "move the cursor," "place a character in the display," "blink the display," etc.

- The *Data Register* (DR) accepts data for the various Instruction Register commands. Example: To execute the command that places a character in the LCD, you write a special code to the IR that says "place the following character in the display," followed by writing the character to the DR. This is very similar to MIDI's Status/Data byte combination.

Operating the LCD

There are two basic public LCD routines:

- Routines that control the cursor

- Routines that place characters in the display.

Controlling the Cursor

The LCD cursor tracks the position where the next character will be written. You can program this cursor to be visible or invisible, and position it to any location (even outside the display's visible area if you're not careful). Two routines control the cursor:

LCD_CURSOR   allows you to make it visible or invisible

LCD_GOTOXY   allows you to position it at any X,Y position in the display.

Writing Characters to the LCD

You can write numbers, characters, and sentences to the LCD by calling the various "LCD_PUT__" routines. When you call each routine you give it the information to be written to the display; the details of formatting and placing the information are all handled invisibly. You may also clear the entire display by calling LCD_CLEAR.

Private Routines

LCD_IR_RD	Reads from LCD Instruction Register (IR).
LCD_IR_WR	Writes to LCD IR.
LCD_DR_RD	Reads from LCD Data Register (DR).
LCD_DR_WR	Writes to LCD DR.
LCD_W8_BSY	Waits for LCD busy flag to clear. This routine is called before accessing the LCD to ensure that it's ready to receive.
LCD_INIT	Initializes LCD. A reset causes the BIOS to call this routine automatically.

Public Routines

LCD_CLEAR	Clears LCD. The cursor is sent to "home" (X,Y position 0,0—the upper left corner).
LCD_CURSOR	Turns cursor on or off, as defined by the data in the accumulator (0 for off, 1 for on).
LCD_GOTOXY	Positions cursor at X,Y as defined by the coordinates in the accumulator and index register respectively. Valid X,Y ranges are 0-15 and 0-1 respectively. 0,0 is the upper left corner.
LCD_PUT_C	Writes a character to the LCD as defined by the character in the accumulator. The character is coded according to the ASCII convention.
LCD_PUT_S	Writes a string to the LCD. This is a macro, which writes the entire string (enclosed in quotes) to the display. Example: "LCD_PUT_S "Hello, world"" writes "Hello, world" in the display. In this example, the character "H" appears at the current cursor position.
LCD_PUT_I	Writes an integer (0-255) to the LCD as defined by the data in the accumulator.
LCD_PUT_H	Writes a hex value ($00 - $FF) to the LCD as defined by the number in the accumulator.
LCD_PUT_RJ2_I	Writes a 2-digit right justified integer (0-99) to the LCD as defined by the data in the accumulator.

LCD_PUT_RJ3_SI	Writes a 3-digit right justified signed integer (-127 to +128) to the LCD as defined by the data in the accumulator.
LCD_PUT_RJ3_I	Writes a 3-digit right justified integer (0-255) to the LCD as defined by the data in the accumulator.
LCD_PUT_ARROW	Writes an arrow at position X,Y, as defined by the coordinates in the accumulator and index register respectively. Valid X,Y ranges are 0-15 and 0-1 respectively.

LED Routines (file: LED.ASM)

The LED routines control the LEDs. Private routines transfer raw data to the LED driver chips in the Human Interface board, while public routines turn individual LEDs on or off.

LED Driver Chips

The Human Interface Board LEDs are driven by two 74HC595 chips. These chips accept a serial input, and output the received data in parallel form. LEDs connect to each parallel output, and therefore turn off and on as the input data bits are logical 0 and 1, respectively.

LED RAM Image

Two bytes of RAM are allocated in the BIOS to maintain an "image" (status) of the lit and unlit LEDs. Each bit in the two-byte image corresponds to a particular LED. The private "LED_REFRESH" routine sends this 16-bit image to the 74HC595 chips, thus setting the state of each LED to the state of its respective bit in the RAM image. Public Routines turn these image bits on and off, and call LED_REFRESH to transfer the image to the driver chips.

Operating the LEDs

The following routines handle the LED image, as well as turn LEDs on and off.

Private Routines

LED_REFRESH	Writes current LED image to driver chips.
LED_INIT	Initializes LED display. A reset causes the BIOS to call this routine automatically.

Public Routines

LED_CLEAR	Clears all LEDs.
LED_ON	Turns on the specified LED as defined by the corresponding code number in the accumulator.
LED_OFF	Turns off the specified LED as defined by the corresponding code number in the accumulator.

Switch Routines (file: SW.ASM)

The switch routines provide basic access to the switches (not too surprising, eh?).

Operating the Switches

The BIOS automatically takes care of reading and processing the switches; the state machine continuously monitors all switches, and issues events when they are pushed and released. All an application needs to do is specify which switch events correspond to which output actions, according to the State Matrix. If the state machine is unused, or you want to read switches independently of the state machine, calling the public SW_READ routine retrieves the latest status of each switch.

Private Routines

SW_INIT   Initializes switches. A reset causes the BIOS to call this routine automatically.

Public Routines

SW_READ   Reads switches and returns current status via the accumulator. Each bit in the accumulator corresponds to each switch; logical 0 indicates the switch is "off" and logical 1 indicates it's "on."

ADC Routines (file: ADC.ASM)

The ADC routines control the analog to digital converter.

Operating the ADC

The ADC is very simple to operate. Call the public ADC_READ routine, and the BIOS hands you measurements of the ADC's four analog inputs via four variables: ADC0, ADC1, ADC2, and ADC3. Each variable corresponds to one ADC channel.

The Human Interface Fader

The Human Interface fader connects to ADC channel 0. As you move the fader, the state machine recognizes changes to ADC0 and issues "Fader Move" events. This all happens automatically in the BIOS; you don't need to read the ADC directly.

Private Routines

ADC_INIT   Initializes ADC. A reset causes the BIOS to call this routine automatically.

Public Routines

ADC_READ   Reads all four channels of the ADC. BIOS variables ADC0, ADC1, ADC2, ADC3 are refreshed with the latest status of each ADC channel.

EEPROM Routines (file: EEPROM.ASM)

The EEPROM routines provide basic access to the EEPROM. Private routines transfer raw data between the EEPROM and the 6805. Public routines provide high level read and write operations.

Operating the EEPROM

To read or write data to the EEPROM, call public routines EE_READ or EE_WRITE respectively. EE_READ requires one argument—the address you want to read. EE_WRITE requires two arguments: the address you want to write to, and the data you want to put there.

Private Routines

EE_WREN	Set Write Enable latch.
EE_WRDI	Reset Write Enable latch.
EE_INIT	Initializes EEPROM. A reset causes the BIOS to call this routine automatically.

Public Routines

EE_READ	Read byte from EEPROM. The address you want to read is defined in the accumulator. The data read from this address returns to you via the accumulator.
EE_WRITE	Write byte to EEPROM. The address you want to write to is passed along from the accumulator, and the data to write is passed along from the index register.

State Machine Routines (file: STMACH.ASM)

The BIOS provides the basic routines necessary to implement a state machine with up to four states. The private routines maintain the State Matrix and take care of recognizing input events and executing output actions (which you specify in the Application file). One public routine, STM_RUN, puts the state machine into perpetual motion—it runs forever in an infinite loop.

When writing an application, you simply define the State Matrix and provide the output actions. The BIOS does everything else for you.

The State Matrix

The State Matrix defines the state machine's behavior. State Matrix columns correspond to each state, and rows correspond to each input event. The intersection of each column/row specifies the next state and which output action to execute when that row's input event occurs during that column's state.

Defining the State Matrix at the Application level is straightforward. A simple public macro, "STM_ROW," lets you specify each row in the matrix by transferring the corresponding event for this row, and the next-state/output-action pairs for each column.

Input Events

Input events come from three sources: switch presses/releases, ADC changes (*e.g.,* fader moves), and MIDI input. The STM_GET_EVENT routine detects these events and registers them via the "EVENT" variable. This routine is called in the BIOS' main state machine loop. You need not call it at the application level.

Output Actions

Output actions are defined in the Application file, and define the unique behavior of each MIDI tool. Whenever an input event occurs in the State Matrix, the state machine calls a corresponding output action automatically. All output actions must end with a "return from subroutine" ("rts") instruction to return control to the BIOS.

Defining the State Matrix

Putting all the pieces together, here's a typical State Matrix:

```
;- Build State Matrix

     STM_BEGIN

;                       State 0:StB1    State 1:StB2    State 2:StB3        Not
;               Event   NextSt,Act      NextSt,Act      NextSt,Act          Used
;                       ─────────────────────────────────────────────────────────
 STM_ROW    EvIdle,     StB1,IDLE,      StB2,IDLE,      StB3,IDLE,      StB1,IDLE
 STM_ROW    EvPlus,     StB1,B1INC,     StB2,B2INC,     StB3,B3INC,     StB1,IDLE
 STM_ROW    EvMinus,    StB1,B1DEC,     StB2,B2DEC,     StB3,B3DEC,     StB1,IDLE
 STM_ROW    EvValue,    StB1,B1FDR,     StB2,B2FDR,     StB3,B3FDR,     StB1,IDLE
 STM_ROW    EvNull,     StB1,B1OFF,     StB2,B2OFF,     StB3,B3OFF,     StB1,IDLE
 STM_ROW    EvClear,    StB1,MSGCLR,    StB1,MSGCLR,    StB1,MSGCLR,    StB1,IDLE
 STM_ROW    EvSend,     StB1,MSGSND,    StB2,MSGSND,    StB3,MSGSND,    StB1,IDLE
 STM_ROW    EvByte1,    StB1,IDLE,      StB1,B1DISP,    StB1,B1DISP,    StB1,IDLE
 STM_ROW    EvByte2,    StB2,B2DISP,    StB2,IDLE,      StB2,B2DISP,    StB1,IDLE
 STM_ROW    EvByte3,    StB3,B3DISP,    StB3,B3DISP,    StB3,IDLE,      StB1,IDLE

     STM_END
```

The above State Matrix came right out of the TOOL01.ASM file, the application file for the first MIDI tool. You'll notice three major components of the State Matrix definition:

- The public STM_BEGIN macro initiates definition of the matrix.

- STM_ROW defines each row of the State Matrix.

- STM_END terminates definition of the State Matrix.

Notice how using labels makes the State Matrix easier to read.

State Machine Main Loop

Calling the public STM_RUN routine executes the main state machine loop. This loop cycles the following sequence: Get event, look up output action in the State Matrix and execute, transition to the next state, go back and get next event, and repeat.

Private Routines

STM_GO_NEXT   Transitions to the next state in State Matrix.

STM_DO_ACTION   Calls action in State Matrix.

STM_GET_EVENT   Gets latest event.

STM_INIT   Initializes the state machine. A reset causes the BIOS to call this routine automatically.

Public Routines

STM_BEGIN   This macro initiates State Matrix definition. It must be called prior to State Matrix definition to prevent assembler errors.

STM_END   This macro terminates State Matrix definition. It must be called following State Matrix definition to prevent assembler errors.

STM_ROW   This macro writes rows into the State Matrix. You provide it with the event corresponding to this row, and four next state/output action pairs.

STM_RUN   Main state machine loop.

BIOS Summary

Even though the MIDItools Computer handles a lot of resources of varying complexity, accessing and operating these resources is fairly straightforward. Remember, you really don't want to mess with the private routines. Use the public routines. They give you full access to each resource, with minimal headache. Go ahead and play with the private routines if you want, but be careful.

As you work with the MIDItools library, you will undoubtedly come up with new routines. Feel free to add them to the library. Nothing in there is sacred—dive in and have fun.

If you add new peripherals to the MIDItools Computer, we suggest you define a new BIOS file with private and public routines consistent with the rest of the resources. This keeps your code clean, consistent, and maintainable. Don't forget to include your new file(s) in MAIN.ASM.

The Application Files

Software for each MIDItool consists of the BIOS and one Application file. As mentioned previously, the BIOS contains routines common to all applications. Application files contain routines that are unique for each application.

Although each Application file is unique, they all follow the same general format. Each Application file contains six primary ingredients:

(1) A comment header at the top of the file that describes everything you need to know about the application.

(2) Declaration of constants and variables.

(3) Specification of the State Matrix.

(4) Initialization code. This resets all variables to default values, and writes defaults to the LED and LCD displays.

(5) Output action subroutines. These routines perform the unique functions of the application. They are referenced in the state machine and called automatically whenever their corresponding input events occur.

(6) Interrupt Service Routine (ISR) call back routines. Some peripherals in the MIDItools Computer execute interrupts that are serviced either at the BIOS level or the application level. The BIOS receives an interrupt first, but immediately transfers control to the application in case the application wants to service the interrupt. This passing of the interrupt baton is referred to as a "call back."

Each of the above six items is unique for each application. To design a new MIDI tool, you just fill in the six sections. In most cases, it takes only a couple of hours to implement a new tool! The following example Application file, "Adjust a number and display it in the LCD," outlines this process. See the end of the listing for an explanation of the various sections.

```
1 ;===============================================================;
1 ;                                                               ;
1 ;      EXAMPLE.ASM    Rev 1.0                                    ;
1 ;      Adjust a number                                          ;
1 ;                                                               ;
1 ;      The user can set the value of a number.                  ;
1 ;                                                               ;
1 ;===============================================================;
1 ;                                                               ;
1 ;      Operation:                                               ;
1 ;                                                               ;
1 ;      HOW DO I...                                              ;
1 ;                                                               ;
1 ;      ...INCREMENT THE NUMBER?                                 ;
1 ;      The number is incremented by pressing the + key.         ;
1 ;      The LCD shows the current number.                        ;
1 ;                                                               ;
1 ;                                                               ;
1 ;      ...DECREMENT THE NUMBER?                                 ;
1 ;      The number is decremented by pressing the - key.         ;
1 ;      The LCD shows the current number.                        ;
1 ;                                                               ;
1 ;                                                               ;
1 ;      ...ADJUST THE NUMBER WITH THE FADER?                     ;
1 ;      The number is adjusted with the fader.                   ;
1 ;      The LCD shows the current number.                        ;
1 ;                                                               ;
1 ;-------------------------------                                ;
1 ;                                                               ;
1 ;      LCD Screens:                                             ;
1 ;;
1 ;      |Number: XXX  |    where XXX= 0-255                      ;
1 ;      |             |                                          ;
1 ;                                                               ;
1 ;-------------------------------                                ;
1 ;                                                               ;
1 ;      Hardware:                                                ;
1 ;                                                               ;
1 ;      This MIDItool uses the CPU board and one HUMAN           ;
1 ;      INTERFACE board.                                         ;
1 ;                                                               ;
1 ;-------------------------------                                ;
1 ;                                                               ;
1 ;      States:                                                  ;
1 ;                                                               ;
1 ;      StNum       Set the number                               ;
1 ;                                                               ;
1 ;      Actions:                                                 ;
1 ;                                                               ;
1 ;      IDLE     No Action                                       ;
1 ;      NUMINC   Increment the number                            ;
1 ;      NUMDEC   Decrement the number                            ;
1 ;      NUMFDR   Set number value with fader                     ;
1 ;                                                               ;
1 ;===============================================================;
```

```
2 ;————————————————————————————
2 ; Variables
2 ;————————————————————————————
2
2    .PAGE0
2    .ABSOLUTE
2
2 NUMBER          .DS   1              ;value of the number


3 ;————————————————————————————
3 ;          State Matrix
3 ;————————————————————————————
3
3 ;— Enumerate states
3
3 StNum           EQU   0
3
3 ;— Map application events to BIOS events
3
3 EvIdle          EQU   EV_IDLE
3 EvInc           EQU   EV_SW4_ON
3 EvDec           EQU   EV_SW8_ON
3 EvFdr           EQU   EV_FDR_MOVE
3
3 ;— Build State Matrix
3
3  STM_BEGIN
3
3 ;                    State 0:StNum                          Not
3 ;         Event      NextSt,Act                             Used
3 ;————————————————————————————
3  STM_ROW  EvIdle,    StNum,IDLE,      StNum,IDLE,StNum,IDLE,StNum,IDLE
3  STM_ROW  EvInc,     StNum,NUMINC,    StNum,IDLE,StNum,IDLE,StNum,IDLE
3  STM_ROW  EvDec,     StNum,NUMDEC,    StNum,IDLE,StNum,IDLE,StNum,IDLE
3  STM_ROW  EvFdr,     StNum,NUMFDR,    StNum,IDLE,StNum,IDLE,StNum,IDLE
3
3  STM_END


4 ;————————————————————————————
4 ;     Application
4 ;————————————————————————————
4
4    .CODE
4    .RELATIVE
4
4 APPLICATION:
4
4 ;— Initialize variables
4
4        lda      #0             ;default values
4        sta      NUMBER         ;
4
4 ;— Initialize display
4
4     ;greet the human
4
4          jsr    LCD_CLEAR
```

```
4
4          LCD_PUT_S "Example. . .    "
4
4          lda    #0
4          ldx    #1
4          jsr    LCD_GOTOXY
4
4          LCD_PUT_S "Adjust a Number!"
4          jsr    DELAY_1SEC
4
4          ;set up static labels
4
4          jsr    LCD_CLEAR
4
4          LCD_PUT_S "Number:      "
4
4          jsr    NUMDISP        ;update display
4
4 ;- Execute state machine
4
4          jmp    STM_RUN


5 ;--------------------------------------
5 ;          Actions
5 ;--------------------------------------
5
5 ;- No action
5
5 IDLE:    rts
5
5 ;- Increment Number
5
5 NUMINC:  lda    NUMBER         ;fetch number
5          inca                  ;increment value
5          sta    NUMBER         ;save new value
5          jsr    NUMDISP        ;update display
5          rts
5
5 ;- Decrement Number
5
5 NUMDEC:  lda    NUMBER         ;fetch number
5          deca                  ;decrement value
5          sta    NUMBER         ;save new value
5          jsr    NUMDISP        ;update display
5          rts
5
5 ;- Set number value with fader
5
5 NUMFDR:  lda    FDR            ;fetch fader value
5          sta    NUMBER         ;save new number value
5          jsr    NUMDISP        ;update display
5          rts
5
5 ;- Update display
5
5 NUMDISP:
5          lda    #15            ;position cursor
```

```
5              ldx     #0                ;
5              jsr     LCD_GOTOXY        ;
5
5              lda     NUMBER            ;fetch number
5              jsr     LCD_PUT_RJ3_I     ;display it
5              rts

6  ;————————————————————————————
6  ;         Interrupt Call Backs
6  ;————————————————————————————
6
6              IGNORE_IRQ_SWI_SPI
6
6  TIMER_CB:
6              jmp     TIMER_HOOK_RET
6
6  SCI_TX_CB:
6              jmp     SCI_TX_HOOK_RET
6
6  SCI_RX_CB:
6              jmp     SCI_RX_HOOK_RET
6
6  SCI_RX_CB_S:
6              jmp     SCI_RX_HOOK_S_RET
6
6  SCI_RX_CB_D1:
6              jmp     SCI_RX_HOOK_D1_RET
6
6  SCI_RX_CB_D2:
6              jmp     SCI_RX_HOOK_D2_RET
6
6
```

In the above example, the numbers at the left of each line indicate the six application file "ingredients." They wouldn't appear in a real program.

(1) Comment Header. The comment header provides all the useful information about the application—the hardware configuration, operating the application, displaying info in the LCD, and the input events and output actions implemented by the state machine.

(2) Constants and Variables. This application defines one variable, NUMBER. No constants are defined.

(3) State Matrix. State Matrix definition begins by defining a constant for this application's one state: StNum. This constant makes the State Matrix easier to read. Constants are also defined for each input event. The BIOS input events have generic names (EV_SW4_ON, EV_SW8_ON, and EV_FDR_MOVE). By renaming these with application-specific names, the State Matrix is easier to read. Finally, the State Matrix rows are defined with the STM_ROW macro. This macro receives the input event corresponding to each row, followed by the next state/output action pairs.

Since this application only defines one state, only the first column (State 0, referred to as "StNum") has meaningful entries. The three unused states are defaulted to transition to StNum with the IDLE output action. Even though these states really don't exist, they must be included in the State Matrix definition to plug in the empty holes. You should be able to read the State Matrix and understand the entire operation of the application from it.

(4) Initialization. Executable code starts with the initialization section (starting with the line labeled "APPLICATION") which sets all variables (in this case, just NUMBER) to default values, and initializes the display. Display initialization begins with a greeting message, and finishes by writing the static text (in this case, the "Number:" label) in the LCD. Calling the BIOS STM_RUN routine executes the state machine.

(5) Output Actions. The output actions are next. The first action, IDLE, doesn't do anything; it's called whenever the input event is idle (*e.g.,* no switches were pressed, and the fader hasn't moved). The other three actions, NUMINC, NUMDEC, and NUMFDR, adjust the value of NUMBER. Notice that each action calls the NUMDISP routine, which writes the latest value of NUMBER into the LCD.

(6) Interrupt Call Backs. All interrupt call backs are serviced at the end of the file. They all simply return control back to the BIOS ISR. If we want to override a BIOS ISR, we could insert our own routine.

That's it! See how simple it is to define an application? Of course, this application is not very exciting, but you will find that most MIDItools applications are not significantly more complicated.

Chapter 13

Getting to Know the MC68HC705C8

To enter the world of MIDItools programming, we need to look into the MC68HC705C8 microcontroller. By understanding its *instruction set*—the repertoire of ways to manipulate data—we can understand the most basic level of computer programming.

Be forewarned that this kind of stuff can sprain your brain at first. There are many interlocking aspects of using microprocessors—*e.g.,* if A happens and B happens while C is showing some particular status, *then* D happens. It's easy enough to learn what A *is* but what it *does* depends on what's happening with B, C, and D.

Probably the best strategy for neophytes is to read this chapter once in its entirety. Don't become discouraged if only 5 to 10% of it "sticks." Get away from the book for a little bit, then read the chapter again; more of it will make sense. Eventually, as you put theory into practice and become more familiar with the instructions and how they affect a program's performance, the remaining pieces will fall into place.

Just because this is a chapter with finite length doesn't mean that one read-through will do the job, any more than reading a book about music theory will make you a musician. That's both the charm and the problem with microprocessors: they're pretty open-ended. It's like learning any software—you can grasp the big concepts pretty quickly, but the details take a while to figure out.

The MC68HC705C8 Microcontroller

The MC68HC705C8 microcontroller, part of the 68HC05 family of microprocessors, is the heart of the MIDItools Computer. Motorola publishes an excellent book on the 68HC05 family, *68HC05 Applications Guide,* that covers everything in much greater detail than we can here. If you really want to dig into this part, contact Motorola (see Chapter 14) about their book.

Up until now we've called the MC68HC705C8 the "6805" for short. However, since not all of the information in this chapter relates to other members of the 6805 family, we'll be more specific and use the name "6805C8."

6805C8 Features

This chip comes with some really great features, including:

- High speed operation (good for musicians) and low power consumption (good for the environment, among other things).

- 24 bidirectional input/output ports. This is how you get information in and out of the chip.

- 7 input-only ports. These let the chip receive data, and also double as ports for the on-board special peripherals.

- 2 timer I/O ports. These can automatically time an input signal or generate an output signal.

- Lots of memory (for a chip). There's 7,584 bytes of ROM and 304 bytes of RAM. The ROM is actually EPROM, so you can load a program into it, erase the program, load another one, erase that one, and so on. The part includes a built-in "bootstrap" program that handles the details of loading in other programs.

- A friendly, straightforward instruction set. The instruction set is the "repertoire" of tasks the microprocessor can perform. Some microprocessors are fun and easy to work with, and others are painfully complicated; overall, the 6805C8 is one of the most friendly microprocessors to work (and especially to learn) with.

- A built-in timer. This peripheral has a number of powerful functions, which we'll cover later.

- A built-in UART. Motorola calls it the "Serial Communications Interface" (SCI), which is a fine name because that's what it is. However, we'll call it a UART more often than SCI because UART is a more common term.

- A built-in Serial Peripheral Interface (SPI). This serial port allows the 6805C8 to communicate with external peripherals on a serial bus. The SPI can input and output data on the serial interface at various speeds, data formats, and using different software options.

- Interrupts. Getting interrupted can be one of life's more annoying experiences, but for the microprocessor it is essential so that it can give priority to urgent tasks. The 6805C8 allows five different ways to interrupt it: from the timer, SCI, SPI, a special software interrupt instruction, or the external interrupt pin.

- Easy to use, 40-pin DIP package. You need no special tools or machinery to work with this chip.

See Fig. 13-1 for the 6805C8's basic anatomy. The CPU consists of a control unit, arithmetic logic unit, and various registers. There are several blocks of RAM and ROM memory, the SCI, SPI, and timer peripherals, input/output ports, and auxiliary modules (power supply, COP watchdog, oscillator, and programming control). These terms should all make sense by the end of this chapter.

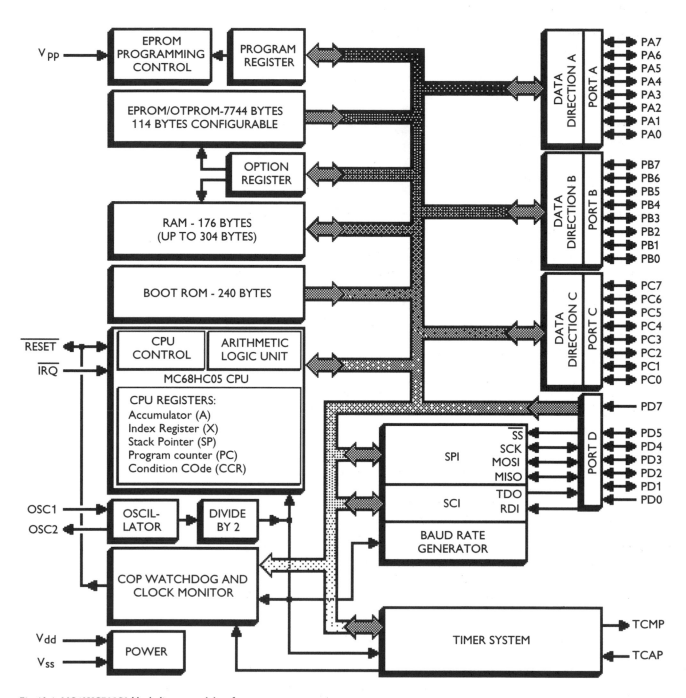

Fig. 13-1: MC68HC705C8 block diagram and data flow.

Pin Assignments

Fig. 13-2 shows the names and numbers of the 6805C8's pins.

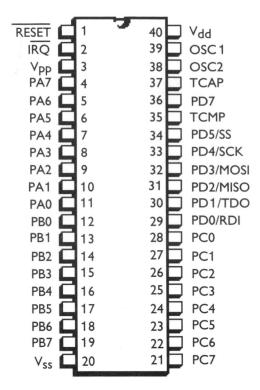

Fig. 13-2: MC68HC705 pinout.

Here's what the various pin names mean (pin numbers are in parenthesis).

V_{dd} (40) and V_{ss} (20)—These hook up to the power supply—V_{dd} to +5 VDC, and V_{ss} to ground (0 VDC).

V_{pp} (3)—When programming the EPROM, applying +15.0 VDC to this pin forces the 6805C8 into "receive a program from the outside world" mode. In normal operation, this pin isn't used.

OSC1 (39) and OSC2 (38)—These two pins connect a quartz crystal or ceramic oscillator to the 6805C8, thus completing the on-chip clock oscillator circuit (these parts are too big to integrate into the chip). The clock is the processor's "heartbeat"—each *machine cycle,* the frequency at which the chip performs the basic fetch and execute cycles, is half the frequency of this oscillator.

Input Capture (TCAP, pin 37)—Controls the programmable timer's input capture feature. We'll discuss this pin in the Timer section.

Output Compare (TCMP, 35)—Provides the output for the timer's output compare feature, as covered in the Timer section.

Reset (1)—Resets the processor when it receives a logical 0. Once reset, the 6805C8 loads the program counter (PC) register with the *reset vector* (think of it as a placemarker) at address $1FFE in memory. The program starts executing from there.

IRQ (2)—Feed this pin a logical zero to trigger an external interrupt.

Ports (4–19, 21–34, 36)—PA0–PA7, PB0–PB7, PC0–PC7, and PD0–PD5, PD7 are all input/output ports, whose functions we'll discuss soon.

MC68HC705C8 Memory

The 6805C8's memory is divided into several ranges of RAM and ROM (Fig. 13-3).

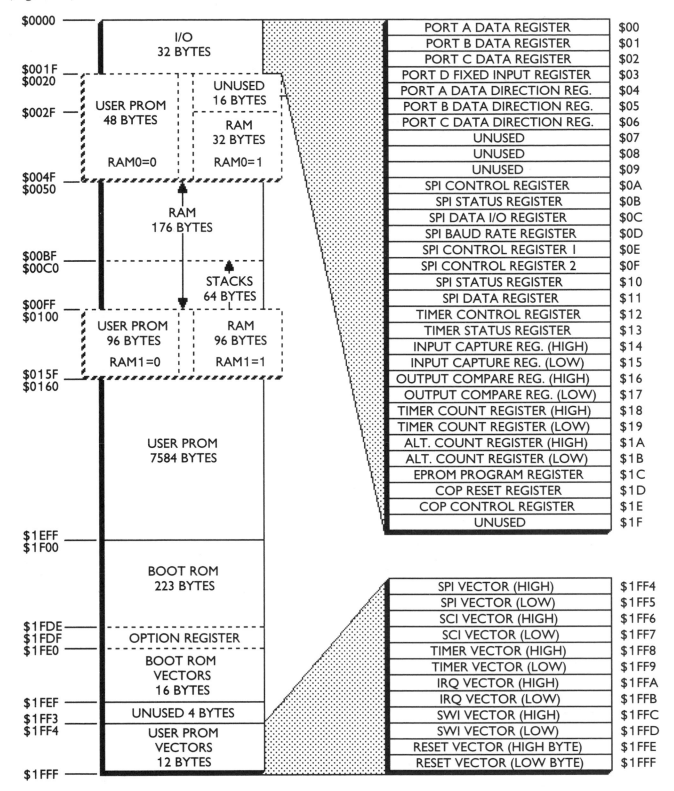

Fig. 13-3: The 6805C8's memory map.

RAM

The 6805C8 has three major blocks of RAM. The first 32 bytes (addresses $0000–$001F) are the various I/O peripheral registers, which provide access to the 6805C8's I/O ports and peripherals.

Addresses $0050 through $00BF provide 112 bytes of general purpose RAM we can use any way we want. The MIDItools Computer uses it for variables.

Addresses $00C0–$00FF are the *stack,* a special range of RAM that stores data temporarily. The 6805C8 uses the stack for two applications:

- Store the state of the CPU registers (A, X, CC, and PC) when the CPU is interrupted.

- Store the program counter (PC) when the program jumps or branches to a subroutine.

Registers are "pushed" onto the stack in last in, first out (LIFO) order.

Address ranges $0020–$004F and $0100–$015F are selectable as either RAM or ROM. The MIDItools Computer configures both ranges as RAM since RAM is in much shorter supply than ROM in this particular processor.

ROM

The 6805C8 has three types of ROM:

- General purpose ROM, which lives in address range $0160–$1EFF and is where the program resides. This ROM is EPROM, so you can program and erase it many times.

- ROM that holds six special 16-bit *vectors* at addresses $1FF4–$1FFF. A vector is the address of the first instruction of a certain block of instructions in the program. The blocks corresponding to the 6805C8's six vectors contain the code that's executed upon receiving an interrupt from one of the six interrupt sources (SPI, SCI, timer, reset pin, external interrupt pin, or software interrupt instruction).

- What we'll call "programming ROM," which can program and select certain chip options. This has two parts, the *Boot ROM* and the *Option Register.*

The Boot ROM block resides in addresses $1F00–$1FDE. This small block holds a special utility program that runs automatically when the Vpp pin gets hit with the +15.0 VDC programming voltage. This utility talks to an external device that transfers your program, byte by byte, to the 6805C8 via this block of code. The 6805C8, in turn, writes the data into EPROM.

The Option Register (OR), located at address $1FDF, maps each option to a bit:

bit	7	6	5	4	3	2	1	0
	RAM0	RAM1			SEC		IRQ	

Here's what each option means.

Input Request Sensitivity (IRQ)

Setting this bit to logical 0 causes the 6805C8 to initiate an interrupt whenever the IRQ pin changes from logic 1 to logic 0, and continues to register additional interrupts as long as the pin remains at logic 0. Setting the bit to logical 1 initiates interrupts only on the negative transition (IRQ pin goes from logic 1 to logic 0).

Security (SEC)

Programming the part sets this bit, which disables the Boot ROM until the part is erased.

RAM1

Specifies whether the RAM1 range (addresses $0100–$015F) is RAM (RAM1 = 1) or ROM (RAM1 = 0).

RAM0

Specifies whether the RAM0 range (addresses $0020–$004F) is RAM (RAM0 = 1) or ROM (RAM0 = 0).

The MC68HC705C8 CPU

The 6805C8 ALU and Control Unit have five registers.

Accumulator (A)

The accumulator is a general-purpose 8-bit register that holds operands and results of arithmetic, logic, and data manipulations. It can also be a "scratch pad" register that holds the intermediate values of most processor operations.

Index Register (X)

Indexed addressing mode instructions use the 8-bit index register. Adding its 8-bit value to another value creates the operand address for an indexed addressing mode instruction (we'll jump into more detail on this later). The index register, like the accumulator, can also be a general purpose scratch pad register.

Program Counter (PC)

The program counter register holds the address of the next instruction to be fetched and executed. The PC allows the processor to keep track of where it is in the program. The PC's 13-bit length allows it to address 2^{13} (8,192) bytes of memory.

Condition Code Register (CCR)

The CCR is a 5-bit register. The H, N, Z, and C bits indicate certain conditions resulting from the previous instruction. The I bit enables interrupts. A program can test each of these bits individually, and take specific actions as a result of their state. (Note: Even though the CCR has only 5 bits, it is considered an 8-bit register with three upper bits that are always logical 1s.)

Here's the CCR bit map:

bit	7	6	5	4	3	2	1	0
	1	1	1	H	I	N	Z	C

Carry/Borrow (C)

This bit is set if a carry or borrow occurred during the previous arithmetic operation. (It's also affected during bit test and branch instructions, and during shifts and rotates—something that's not of vital importance right now, but mentioned for the sake of completeness.)

Zero (Z)

The Z bit is set whenever the result of an arithmetic, logical, or data manipulation instruction is 0.

Negative (N)

The N bit is set whenever the result of an arithmetic, logical, or data manipulation instruction is negative *(i.e.,* the two's complement MSB = 1).

Interrupt Mask Bit (I)

When an interrupt occurs, the program can set the I bit to disable any interrupts from the timer, SCI, SPI, and external interrupt pin until the original interrupt is serviced. Once that's done, the program always executes a "Return From Interrupt" (RTI) instruction to return the CPU to the state it was in prior to the interrupt (more on this shortly).

Half-Carry Bit (H)

This bit is set during addition instructions to indicate that a carry occurred between bits 3 and 4. Operations on binary coded decimal (BCD) values require this status indicator.

Stack Pointer (SP)

The stack pointer is a 13-bit register that contains the address of the next free location on the stack; it resets to location $00FF during an MCU reset or after executing the "Reset Stack Pointer" (RSP) instruction. Pushing data onto the stack decrements the SP, and pulling data from the stack increments it. We have hardly any control over this register, so it's mentioned only for completeness and since you are no doubt a naturally curious type.

MC68HC705C8 Interrupts

The 6805C8 has six interrupt sources. There are several ways to generate an interrupt from an external source (setting the CCR's I bit disables all these interrupts):

- Apply a logical 0 signal (0 VDC) to the IRQ or Reset pin

- Execute a "Software Interrupt" instruction (SWI) in your program

- Generate special events with the SPI, SCI, and timer peripherals.

If we interrupt the processor and perform some other task, the interrupting task will alter various registers. When the interruption ends and the processor resumes where it left off, these altered registers could disrupt the original task. To solve this problem, the processor saves the state of all the registers in the stack. The "Return From Interrupt" (RTI) instruction ends each interrupt service routine, recovers the stack register data, and allows normal processing to resume.

External Interrupt

The 6805 continuously watches the state of the external interrupt pin; when it changes, the 6805 initiates an interrupt.

Software Interrupt

The SWI instruction generates a "software" interrupt. Software interrupts are recognized regardless of the state of the CCR's I bit.

Timer Interrupt

There are three different timer interrupt flags that cause a timer interrupt whenever they are set and enabled. The interrupt flags are in the timer status register (TSR), and the enable bits are in the timer control register (TCR). We'll discuss these further in the Timer section.

SCI Interrupts

An interrupt in the SCI (serial communications interface) occurs after this interface receives or transmits a byte. To enable an SCI interrupt:

- The I bit in the CCR must be clear

- The enable bit in the "Serial Communications Control Register" (SCCR) must be set.

SPI Interrupts

An interrupt in the SPI occurs after this interface receives or transmits a byte. To enable an SPI interrupt:

- The I bit in the CCR must be clear

- The enable bit in the "Serial Peripheral Control Register" (SPCR) must be set.

MC68HC705C8 I/O Ports

Input/Output Ports (PA0–PA7, PB0–PB7, PC0–PC7)

These 24 lines are organized as three 8-bit general purpose ports: Ports A, B, and C. Each one can be either an input or output.

Fixed Input Port (Port D)

Port D has seven lines: PD0–PD5, and PD7 (there is no PD6). All can serve as general purpose inputs, or as pins for the 6805C8's peripheral functions. These pins do double duty so that if you don't need one or more of the peripheral functions, it's still available as a general purpose input.

PD0 and PD1 provide pins for the Serial Communications Interface (SCI). PD2–PD5 provide pins for the Serial Peripheral Interface (SPI). PD7 is just an input; it has no alternate function.

I/O Port Operation

All pins in Ports A–C are programmable as either inputs or outputs via special memory locations called "Data Direction Registers" (DDRs). Each port pin corresponds to a bit in the DDR; writing a logic 1 to a particular bit programs its associated port as an output, and writing a logic 0 programs an input. A reset initializes all DDRs to logic zero (input ports).

Writing data to a port requires writing to another special purpose memory location for the port—its *Data Register* (DR). Port A–C Data Registers are located at addresses $0000–$0002. When a port serves as an output, the output pin reflects the corresponding bit in the DR. When a port is an input, this location in memory takes its data from the voltages applied to the pin(s) on the chip.

Since the Data Register is memory mapped, the program considers the DR (and therefore the port itself) the same as any other memory location. Reading and writing values to the ports is no different from accessing normal memory locations.

Fixed Input Port Programming

Port D is the oddball of the crowd. It provides seven input-only lines (PD7, PD5–PD0) which double as the pins for the SPI and SCI interfaces. The SCI requires two pins (PD1–PD0) for its *Transmit Data Output* (TDO) and *Receive Data Input* (RDI). The SPI function requires four of the pins (PD5–PD2) for its *Slave Select* (SS), *Serial Clock* (SCK), *Master Output/Slave Input* (MOSI), and *Master Input/Slave Output* (MISO) ports. A pin can be a general purpose input or a peripheral pin, but not both.

The pins are programmed for input or peripheral mode via special registers which we'll cover shortly.

MC68HC705 Peripherals

The Timer

The 6805C8's timer consists of a 16-bit counter. This timer can do many things, such as measure waveform inputs or generate waveform outputs. Timed pulse widths can vary from several microseconds to many seconds.

Because the timer has a 16-bit architecture, each function is represented by two *concatenated* (linked) registers. These registers contain a "low" byte (bits 0–7) and a "high" byte (bits 8–15).

The Counter

The key element in the programmable timer is a 16-bit free-running counter register, preceded by a prescaler. This divides the internal processor clock by four to give the timer a resolution of 2.0 microseconds if the internal bus clock is 2.0 MHz (which is the case if the external oscillator is 4.0 MHz). Software can read the counter at any time without affecting its value.

The double-byte, free-running counter can be read from either of two locations, $0018–$0019 (Counter Register) or $001A–$001B (Counter Alternate Register). Reading from only the least significant byte (LSB) of the free-running counter ($0019–$001B) receives the count value at the time of the read. If reading the free-running counter or Counter Alternate Register addresses the most significant byte (MSB) first, the LSB is transferred to a buffer.

The value in this buffer remains fixed after reading the first MSB (even if you read the Counter Alternate Register LSB), which allows a sequential reading of the total counter value. When reading either the free-running counter or Counter Alternate Register, if the MSB is read, the LSB must also be read to complete the sequence.

The Counter Alternate Register differs from the Counter Register in one respect: reading the Counter Register LSB can clear the "Timer Overflow Flag" (TOF). Therefore, you can read the Counter Alternate Register at any time without missing timer overflow interrupts due to unintentional clearing of the TOF.

The value in the free-running counter repeats every 262,144 internal bus clock cycles. When the counter rolls over from $FFFF to $0000, it sets the TOF. It's also possible to enable a timer interrupt when counter rollover occurs by setting its interrupt enable bit (TOIE).

Timer Registers

Output Compare Register (OCR—addresses $0016–$0017)

The 16-bit *Output Compare Register* (OCR) comprises two 8-bit registers at locations $0016 (MSB) and $0017 (LSB). The OCR contents are always being compared with the contents of the free-running counter. If they match, that sets the corresponding *Output Compare Flag* (OCF) bit, and clocks the corresponding *Output Level* (OLVL) bit to an output level register. The Output Compare Register values and the output level bit can be changed after each successful comparison to establish a new timeout threshold. An interrupt can also accompany a successful output compare, provided the corresponding interrupt enable bit (OCIE) is set.

A processor write cycle to the Output Compare Register MSB ($0016) inhibits the output compare function until the LSB ($0017) is also written. The programmer must write both bytes if the MSB is written first; a write made only to the LSB ($0017) will not inhibit the compare function.

The free-running counter is updated every four internal bus clock cycles. The minimum time required to update the Output Compare Register is a function of the program rather than the internal hardware.

Input Capture Register (ICR—addresses $0014–$0015)

Two 8-bit, read-only registers make up the 16-bit "Input Capture Register" (ICR), which latches the value of the free-running counter after the corresponding input capture edge detector senses a transition defined by the corresponding "Input Edge Bit" (IEDG). Reset does not affect the Input Capture Register contents.

Each proper signal transition transfers the free-running counter contents to the Input Capture Register, regardless of whether the input capture flag (ICF) is set or clear. The Input Capture Register always contains the free-running counter value that corresponds to the most recent input capture.

Reading the Input Capture Register MSB ($0014) inhibits the counter transfer until the LSB ($0015) is also read.

Timer Control Register (TCR—address $0012)

This read/write register contains five control bits. Three bits control interrupts associated with Timer Status Register flags ICF, OCF, and TOF:

bit	7	6	5	4	3	2	1	0
	ICIE	OCIE	TOIE				IEDG	OLVL

Output Level (OLVL)

When the output compare register shows a match, the processor clocks the Output Level value into the output level register. This value appears on the TCMP pin.

  0 = Low output
  1 = High output

Input Edge (IEDG)

The value of Input Edge determines which level transition on the TCAP pin will transfer the free-running counter to the Input Capture Register.

  0 = Negative edge (reset does not affect the IEDG bit)
  1 = Positive edge

Timer Overflow Interrupt Enable (TOIE)

The next three interrupt enables have already been described; the associated value determines whether the interrupt is enabled or disabled.

  0 = Interrupt disabled
  1 = Interrupt enabled

Output Compare Interrupt Enable (OCIE)

  0 = Interrupt disabled
  1 = Interrupt enabled

Input Capture Interrupt Enable (ICIE)

  0 = Interrupt disabled
  1 = Interrupt enabled

Bits 2–4 are unused and always read zero.

Timer Status Register (TSR—address $0013)

This read-only register contains three status flag bits:

bit	7	6	5	4	3	2	1	0
	ICF	OCF	TOF					

Timer Overflow Flag (TOF)

  0 = To clear the flag, read the free-running counter low register ($0019) after reading TSR while TOF was set.
  1 = A free-running counter transition from $FFFF to $0000 sets the flag.

Output Compare Flag (OCF)

  0 = To clear the flag, write to the Output Compare low Register ($0017) after reading TSR while OCF was set.
  1 = The flag is set when the output compare register contents match the free-running counter contents.

Input Capture Flag (ICF)

  0 = To clear the flag, read the Input Capture low Register ($0015) after reading TSR while ICF was set.
  1 = Flag is set when the input capture edge detector senses the selected polarity edge.

Bits 0–4 are unused and always read zero.

The first step in clearing status bits is to access the Timer Status Register. The second step is to access the register corresponding to the status bit.

Serial Communications Interface (SCI)

The Serial Communications Interface communicates with other devices through a UART. It is very flexible and features:

- Full-duplex operation (simultaneous transmit and receive).

- Software programmable for one of 32 different baud rates.

- Several software-selectable data formats.

- Advanced error detection.

- SCI can trigger interrupts from four different conditions.

Data Format

The SCI system communicates via the *Receive Data Input* (RDI) and *Transmit Data Out* (TDO) pins. The following diagram shows the data format, as programmed for MIDI communication:

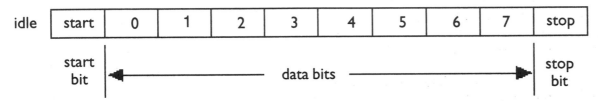

The state of the SCI link is normally logical 1 during idle conditions. The *start bit*, a logical 0, marks the start of a transmitted byte. The byte's 8 data bits are then transmitted serially, followed by a logical 1 *stop bit*. This will remain in the logical 1 (idle) state until the next byte occurs, as signaled by a logical 0 start bit.

Receive Data Input (RDI)

This pin takes data from the outside world and feeds it to the *Receive Data Register* (RDR).

Transmit Data Output (TDO)

This pin delivers serial data, formatted as shown above, from the *Transmit Data Register* (TDR).

How It Works

The Serial Communications Control Register 1 (SCCR1) control bits specify the SCI wake-up method and data word length. The Serial Communications Control Register 2 (SCCR2) control bits individually enable or disable the transmitter or receiver, enable system interrupts, provide wake-up enable, and send break code bits (a break is a long string of zeroes).

The Baud Rate Register bits select different baud rates for the transmitter and receiver, as explained later on.

Sending a Byte out the SCI

To send a byte out the SCI:

(1) Enable the transmitter.

(2) Write data to the Serial Communications Data Register (SCDAT).

(3) This transfers data to the transmit data shift register, with the LSB sent first. The receiver bit rate clock synchronizes the transfer.

This transfer does the following:

- Sets the SCI Status Register (SCSR) Transmit Data Register Empty (TDRE) bit.

- Generates an interrupt if Transmit Interrupt is enabled.

Completing the transmission does the following:

- Sets the Transmission Complete (TC) bit.

- Generates an interrupt if the Transmit Complete interrupt is enabled.

Receiving a Byte from the SCI

When the SCDAT is read, it contains the last data byte received (assuming that the receiver is enabled). Setting the SCSR Receive Data Register Full (RDRF) bit indicates a data byte transfer from the input serial shift register to the SCDAT, which can cause an interrupt if the receiver interrupt is enabled. The receiver bit rate clock synchronizes data from the input serial shift register to the SCDAT. Data reception errors set the SCSR overrun (OR), noise flag (NF), or FE bits.

The Five SCI Registers

Serial Communications Data Register (SCDAT—address $0011)

The SCDAT is a read/write register that receives and transmits SCI data. SCDAT functions as two separate registers:

- The *Transmit Data Register* (TDR) provides the parallel interface from the internal data bus to the transmit shift register.

- The *Receive Data Register* (RDR) interfaces the receive shift register to the internal data bus.

Serial Communications Control Register 1 (SCCR1—address $000E)

The SCCR1 provides control bits that determine word length and select the wake-up method.

bit	7	6	5	4	3	2	1	0
	R8	T8		M	WAKE			

Wake-Up Select (WAKE)

This bit selects the receiver wake-up method.

0 = Wakes up if there's an idle line condition.
1 = Wakes up if the received character's most significant bit (the eighth or ninth bit, depending on the M bit) is 1.

SCI Character Word Length (M)

This determines whether the word length is 8 or 9 bits long.

0 = One start bit, eight data bits, one stop bit
1 = One start bit, nine data bits, one stop bit

Transmit Data Bit 8 (T8)

If M=1, then we need a ninth bit for transmitted data. The T8 bit provides a storage location for this ninth bit.

Receive Data Bit 8 (R8)

If M=1, then we also need a ninth bit for received data. The R8 bit provides a storage location for this ninth bit.

Serial Communications Control Register 2 (SCCR2—address $000F)

The SCCR2 controls individual SCI functions such as interrupts, transmit/receive enabling, receiver wake-up, and send break code.

bit	7	6	5	4	3	2	1	0
	TIE	TCIE	RIE	ILIE	TE	RE	RWU	SBK

Send Break (SBK)

0 = Transmitter sends a set of 10 (M=0) or 11 (M=1) logical zeroes, then reverts to an idle state or continues sending data. (If the transmitter is empty and idle, setting and clearing the SBK bit may send out two break characters because the first break transfers almost immediately to the shift register, but the second is queued into the parallel transmit buffer. A break is a long string of zeros.)

1 = Transmitter continually sends blocks of logical zeroes (sets of 10 or 11) until cleared. After sending the break code, the transmitter sends a single logical 1 bit, which the rest of the system recognizes as a valid start bit.

Receiver Wake-Up (RWU)

0 = If the WAKE bit = 1, receiving a data word with the MSB set clears the RWU bit. If WAKE=0, receiving 10 (M=0) or 11 (M=1) consecutive logical 1s clears the RWU bit.

1 = Places receiver in sleep mode and enables the wake-up function.

Receive Enable (RE)

0 = Disables the receiver and inhibits the RDRF, IDLE, OR, NF, and FE status bits.

1 = Applies the RDI line to the receiver shift register input.

Transmit Enable (TE)

0 = TE going to zero disables the transmitter after the transmit shifter completes any serial transfer that was in progress when TE went to zero. After transmitting the last byte, the TD0 line becomes a high-impedance line.

1 = Applies the transmit shift register output to the TD0 line and, depending on the SCCR1 M bit, transmits a preamble of 10 (M=0) or 11 (M=1) consecutive ones.

Idle Line Interrupt Enable (ILIE)

0 = IDLE interrupt disabled
1 = SCI interrupt enabled

Receive Interrupt Enable (RIE)

0 = RDRF and OR interrupts disabled
1 = SCI interrupt enabled

Transmit Complete Interrupt Enable (TCIE)

0 = TC interrupt musabled
1 = SCI interrupt enabled

Transmit Interrupt Enable (TIE)

0 = TDRE interrupt disabled
1 = SCI interrupt enabled

Serial Communications Status Register (SCSR—address $0010)

The SCSR provides inputs to the SCI interrupt logic circuits, and also includes noise flag and framing error bits.

bit	7	6	5	4	3	2	1	0
	TDRE	TC	RDRF	IDLE	OR	NF	FE	

Framing Error (FE)

When set to 1, the receiver detected a framing error.

Noise Flag (NF)

When set to 1, noisy data was detected.

Overrun (OR)

When set to 1, there was a data overrun in the receiver.

Idle Line Detect (IDLE)

0 =   To clear the IDLE, read the SCSR then read the RDR. Once IDLE is cleared, IDLE cannot become set until the RDI line becomes active and idle again.

1 =   Indicates receiver has detected an idle line.

Receive Data Register Full (RDRF)

0 =   No significant data is in the RDR. To clear the RDRF, read the SCSR then read the RDR.

1 =   Transferring the receive data shift register contents to the RDR sets this bit.

Transmit Complete (TC)

0 =   Transmitter is currently active. To clear the RC bit, read the SCSR then write to the TDR.

1 =   Indicates that the end of the data frame, preamble, or break condition has occurred (transmitter is empty, including shifter).

Transmit Data Register Empty (TDRE)

0 =   TDR still contains data. To clear the TDRE, read the SCSR then write to the TDR.

1 =   TDR is empty and can accept new data for transmission.

Baud Rate Register

The Baud Rate register selects the SCI transmitter and receiver baud rate. The SCP0 and SCP1 bits provide prescaling; using them with the SCR0 through SCR2 baud rate bits provides multiple baud rate combinations for a given crystal frequency. Bits 3, 6, and 7 always read zero.

bit	7	6	5	4	3	2	1	0
			SCP1	SCP0		SCR2	SCR1	SCR0

SCI Baud Rate Bit 0 (SCR0), SCI Baud Rate Bit 1 (SCR1), SCI Baud Rate Bit 2 (SCR2)

Figs. 13-4 and 13-5 tabulate the divider chain used to obtain a particular baud rate clock (transmit clock), according to the setting of the SCP0–SCP1 and SCR0–SCR2 bits in the baud rate register.

The three SCR0–SCR2 bits select the SCI transmitter and receiver baud rate (Fig. 13-4).

SCR bits			div. by	Representative Highest Prescaler Baud Rate Output				
2	1	0		131.072 kHz	32.768 kHz	761.80 kHz	19.20 kHz	9600 Hz
0	0	0	1	131.072 kHz	32.768 kHz	76.80 kHz	19.20 kHz	9600 Hz
0	0	1	2	65.536 kHz	16.384 kHz	38.40 kHz	9600 Hz	4800 Hz
0	1	0	4	32.768 kHz	8.192 kHz	19.20 kHz	4800 Hz	2400 Hz
0	1	1	8	16.384 kHz	4.096 kHz	9600 Hz	2400 Hz	1200 Hz
1	0	0	16	8.192 kHz	2.048 kHz	4800 Hz	1200 Hz	600 Hz
1	0	1	32	4.096 kHz	1.024 kHz	2400 Hz	600 Hz	300 Hz
1	1	0	64	2.048 kHz	512 Hz	1200 Hz	300 Hz	150 Hz
1	1	1	128	1.024 kHz	256 Hz	600 Hz	150 Hz	75 Hz

Fig. 13-4: Transmit baud rate output for a given prescaler input. This illustrates how the SCI select bits can provide lower transmitter baud rates by further dividing the prescaler output frequency. These five example frequencies are only representative samples; in all cases, the baud rates shown are transmit baud rates (transmit clock), and the receive clock is 16 times higher in frequency than the actual baud rate.

SCI Prescaler Bit 0 (SCP0), SCI Prescaler Bit 1 (SCP1)

Two prescaler bits allow dividing the internal processor clock to alter the baud rates controlled by the SCR0–SCR2 bits (Fig. 13-4). All divided frequencies shown in Fig. 13-5 represent the final baud rate resulting from the internal processor clock division shown in the divided-by column.

SCP bit		Clock *	Crystal Frequency (f_{osc}) MHz				
1	0	(f_{op}) ÷ by	4.194304	4.0	2.4576	2.0	1.8432
0	0	1	131.072 kHz	125.000 kHz	76.80 kHz	62.50 kHz	57.60 kHz
0	1	3	43.691 kHz	41.666 kHz	25.60 kHz	20.833 kHz	19.20 kHz
1	0	4	32.768 kHz	31.250 kHz	19.20 kHz	15.625 kHz	14.40 kHz
1	1	13	10.082 kHz	9600 Hz	5.907 kHz	4800 Hz	4430 Hz

* refers to the internal processor clock

Fig. 13-5: Prescaler highest baud rate frequency output. The divided frequencies shown in this table represent baud rates that are the highest transmit baud rate (Tx) obtainable by a specific crystal frequency and only using the prescaler division. To obtain lower baud rates, divide further using the SCI rate select bits. See Fig. 13-4 for some representative prescaler outputs.

Serial Peripheral Interface

The serial peripheral interface (SPI) provides a serial link between the 6805C8 and external peripherals with serial interfaces. The SPI transfers data between a master device and slave device in either direction. The master is in charge of the transfer and supplies the synchronizing "clock" signal.

The 6805C8 can act as either the master or the slave. The MIDItools Computer assigns the 6805C8 as the master.

SPI Block Diagram

Fig. 13-6 shows the block diagram of an SPI link. The master (6805C8) device sends two signals, *Master Out Slave In* (MOSI) and *Serial Clock* (SCK) to the slave peripheral device. Data is read back from the slave via the *Master In Slave Out* (MISO) pin.

SPI Signals

The SPI interface consists of four basic signals (MOSI, MISO, SCK, and SS). We will consider each pin's master mode function, since that is the MIDItools Computer's SPI operating mode.

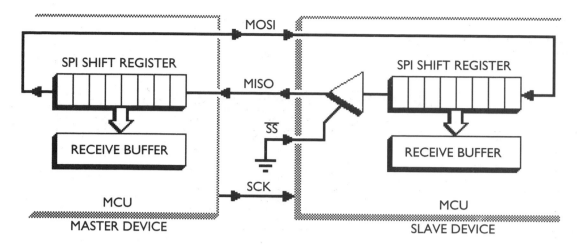

Fig. 13-6: SPI Master-Slave interconnections for the MOSI, MISO, and SCK lines.

Master Out/Slave In (MOSI)—This line is the output for a master device and the input for a slave device. Since the 6805C8 is the master, the MOSI line transfers serial data from the 6805C8 to the peripheral device. Serial bus data transfers send the most significant bit (MSB) first.

Master In/Slave Out (MISO)—This line is the input in a master device and the output in a slave device, so in our application the MISO line transfers serial data from the peripheral device to the 6805C8. Serial bus data transfers send the most significant bit (MSB) first.

Serial Clock (SCK)—This line synchronizes the data on the MOSI and MISO lines. The master and slave devices exchange a byte of information during a sequence of eight SCK cycles. Since SCK is generated by the master device, this line is an input on the slave device.

Figure 13-7 shows the timing relationship between the data signals (MOSI and MISO) and SCK. Actually, the SPI interface allows us to choose from four possibilities. We have chosen the format which is compatible with the peripheral devices implemented in the MIDItools Computer. The other formats could be chosen by using control bits CPOL and CPHA in the *Serial Peripheral Control Register* (SPCR). Two bits (SPR0 and SPR1) in the SPCR select the clock rate.

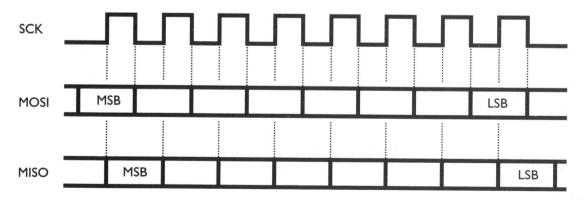

Fig. 13-7: SCK, MOSI, MISO timing diagram.

Slave Select (SS)—This input line selects whether the 6805C8 is the master device (line connects to +5 VDC) or slave device (line connects to 0 VDC) in the SPI link.

SPI Registers

Three SPI registers provide control, status, and data storage functions.

Serial Peripheral Control Register (SPCR—address $000A)

The SPCR controls individual SPI functions such as interrupt and system enabling/disabling, master/slave mode select, and clock polarity/phase/bit rate select. Bit 5 is not used and can read either one or zero.

bit	7	6	5	4	3	2	1	0
	SPIE	SPE		MSTR	CPOL	CPHA	SPR1	SPR0

SPI Clock Rate Bits (SPR0, SPR1)

These two bits select one of four clock rates for SCK when the 6805C8 is in the master mode. In slave mode, these bits have no effect since SCK is supplied from outside. The following table shows the clock rate selection.

SPR1	SPR0	Internal processor clock* divided by:
0	0	2
0	1	4
1	0	16
1	1	32

*Internal processor clock equals the oscillator frequency divided by two.

Clock Phase (CPHA)

This bit along with CPOL (see next) controls the clock-data relationship between the master and slave devices. CPHA selects one of two fundamentally different clocking protocols.

0 = Shift clock is the OR of SCK with SS (Slave Select). When SS is low, the first edge of SCK (whether this is the rising or falling edge depends on the configuration of CPOL) invokes the first data sample.

1 = SS is an output enable control.

Clock Polarity (CPOL)

This bit, in conjunction with the clock phase (CPHA) bit, controls the clock value.

0 = SCK line idles in low state.

1 = SCK line idles high.

Master Mode Select (MSTR)

0 = Slave mode

1 = Master mode

Serial Peripheral System Enable (SPE)

0 = SPI system off

1 = SPI system on

Serial Peripheral Interrupt Enable (SPIE)

0 = SPI interrupt disabled

1 = SPI interrupt enabled

Serial Peripheral Status Register (SPSR—address $000B)

The SPSR has three status bits. Bits 0–3 and 5 are unused and can read either zero or one.

bit	7	6	5	4	3	2	1	0
	SPIF	SCOL		MODF				

Mode Fault Flag (MODF)

0 = To clear, read SPSR (with MODF = 1) then write to the SPCR.
1 = Indicates multi-master system control conflict.

Write Collision (WCOL)

0 = To clear, read SPSR (with WCOL = 1) then access the SPDR.
1 = Indicates an attempt was made to write to SPDR while the data transfer was in process.

Serial Peripheral Data Transfer Flag (SPIF)

0 = To clear, read SPSR (with SPIF = 1) then access the SPDR.
1 = Indicates data transfer completed between processor and external device. (SPIF = 1 and SPIE = 1 enables SPI interrupt.)

Serial Peripheral Data I/0 Register (SPDR—address $000C)

The SPDR is a read/write register that receives and transmits SPI data.

bit	7	6	5	4	3	2	1	0
	SPD7	SPD6	SPD5	SPD4	SPD3	SPD2	SPD1	SPD0

A write to the SPDR places data directly into the SPI shift register and initiates the transmission/reception of a byte. Completing the byte transmission sets the SPIF status bit.

The SPDR can also be read. The SPIF status bit must be cleared by the time a new data transfer finishes and data is transferred from the shift register to the read buffer, or an overrun will occur. In overrun cases, the new byte is written into the read buffer, whether the previous data was read or not.

The MC68HC705C8 Instruction Set

The 6805C8 has five types of instructions:

- Register/memory

- Read-modify-write

- Branch

- Bit manipulation

- Control

This section gives a brief glimpse of each instruction. The Motorola manual referenced at the beginning of this chapter gives a more thorough discussion.

Register/Memory Instructions

These instructions perform an operation on a register (accumulator, A or index register, X) and the operand. The operand is obtained from memory according to the specified addressing mode. The jump unconditional (JMP) and jump to subroutine (JSR) instructions don't use a register.

The following shows each Assembly Language mnemonic, followed by its function.

lda	Load the accumulator from source specified by the operand.
ldx	Load the index register from source specified by the operand.
sta	Store the accumulator into destination specified by the operand.
stx	Store the index register into destination specified by the operand.
add	Add the operand to the contents of the accumulator, ignore the carry bit, and place result in A.
adc	Add the operand to the contents of the accumulator, take into account the carry bit, and place the result in A.
sub	Subtract the operand from the contents of the accumulator, ignore the borrow bit, and place the result in A.
sbc	Subtract the operand from the contents of the accumulator, take into account the borrow (carry) bit, and place the result in A.
and	Perform logical AND between the operand and the accumulator contents, and place the result in A.
ora	Perform logical OR between the operand and the contents of the accumulator, and place the result in A.
eor	Perform logical Exclusive OR between the operand and the accumulator contents, and place the result in A.
cmp	Perform an arithmetic compare between the accumulator contents and the operand, then update the condition codes accordingly.
cpx	Perform an arithmetic compare between the index register contents and the operand, and update the condition codes accordingly.
bit	Perform a logical compare between the accumulator contents and the operand, and update the condition codes accordingly.
jmp	Jump unconditionally to address specified by the operand.
jsr	Jump unconditionally to the subroutine specified by the operand and save current program counter (PC) on the stack.

Read-Modify-Write Instructions

These instructions read a memory location or a register, modify or test its contents, then write the modified value back to memory or the register. The *Test for Negative or Zero* (TST) instruction is an exception to the read-modify-write sequence since it does not modify the value.

inc	Increment the operand.
dec	Decrement the operand.
clr	Clear the operand.
com	Complement (invert) the operand.
neg	Negate (twos complement) the operand.
rol	Rotate the operand left, shift old carry bit into LSB, and shift old MSB into the carry bit.
ror	Rotate the operand right, shift old carry bit into MSB, and shift old LSB into the carry bit.
lsl	Logical-shift the operand left, shift a logical 0 into LSB, and shift old MSB into the carry bit.
lsr	Logical-shift the operand right, shift a logical 0 into MSB, and shift old LSB into the carry bit.
asl	Arithmetic-shift the operand left, shift a logical 0 into LSB, and shift old MSB into the carry bit.
asr	Arithmetic-shift the operand right, shift old LSB into the carry bit, and hold the MSB constant.
tst	Test for negative or zero. Tests the operand and updates the condition codes accordingly.
mul	Multiply the contents of the accumulator and the contents of the index register, place the low byte of the result in A and the high byte of the result in X.

If the accumulator or index register provides the operand for a read-modify-write instruction (not including MUL), the register name can be appended to the mnemonic:

inca	Increment A
incx	Increment X
deca	Decrement A
decx	Decrement X
clra	Clear A
clrx	Clear X
coma	Complement A
comx	Complement X
nega	Negate (twos complement) A
negx	Negate (twos complement) X
rola	Rotate left A
rolx	Rotate left X
rora	Rotate right A
rorx	Rotate right X
lsla	Logical shift left A
lslx	Logical shift left X
lsra	Logical shift right A
lsrx	Logical shift right X
asla	Arithmetic shift left A
aslx	Arithmetic shift left X
asra	Arithmetic shift right A
asrx	Arithmetic shift right X
tsta	Test A
tstx	Test X

Branch Instructions

This class of instructions causes a branch if a particular condition is met. Otherwise, no operation occurs. Branch instructions all have a one-byte operand that specifies how many bytes away (in two's-complement format) to branch. Branch instructions look at the state of particular conditional codes in the condition code register (CCR) to determine if they should branch.

bra	Branch always (unconditionally).
brn	Branch never.
bhi	Branch if higher. Branches if condition codes C and Z are logical 0.
bls	Branch if lower or same. Branches if condition codes C or Z are logical 1.
bcc	Branch if carry clear. Branches if condition code C is logical 0.
bhs	Branch if higher or same. Branches if condition code C is logical 0.
bcs	Branch if carry set. Branches if condition code C is logical 1.
blo	Branch if lower. Branches if condition code C is logical 1.
bne	Branch if not equal. Branches if condition code Z is logical 0.
beq	Branch if equal. Branches if condition code Z is logical 1.
bhcc	Branch if half carry clear. Branches if condition code H is logical 0.
bhcs	Branch if half carry set. Branches if condition code H is logical 1.
bpl	Branch if plus. Branches if condition code N is logical 0.
bmi	Branch if minus. Branches if condition code N is logical 1.
bmc	Branch if interrupt mask clear. Branches if condition code I is logical 0.
bms	Branch if interrupt mask set. Branches if condition code I is logical 1.
bil	Branch if interrupt low. Branches if external interrupt pin is logical 0.
bih	Branch if interrupt high. Branches if external interrupt pin is logical 1.
bsr	Branch to subroutine. Branches unconditionally to subroutine, saves current program counter (PC) on the stack.

Bit Manipulation Instructions

These instructions allow the processor to set or clear any writable bit that resides in the first 256 bytes of memory (addresses $0000–$00FF). This memory space is where all port registers, port DDRs, timer, timer control, and on-chip RAM reside.

An additional feature allows the software to test and branch on the state of any bit within these 256 locations. The value of the tested bit is also placed in the condition code register C bit.

brset n (n = 0_7)	Branch if bit n of the operand is set (logical 1).
brclr n (n = 0_7)	Branch if bit n of the operand is clear (logical 0).
bset n (n = 0_7)	Set (logical 1) bit n of the operand.
bclr n (n = 0 _7)	Clear (logical 0) bit n of the operand.

Control Instructions

These instructions manipulate the A, X, and CCR register directly, and control processor operation during program execution.

tax	Transfer contents of accumulator to index register.
txa	Transfer contents of index register to accumulator.
sec	Set condition code C to logical 1.
clc	Clear condition code C to logical 0.
sei	Set condition code I to logical 1.
cli	Clear condition code I to logical 0.
swi	Software Interrupt. Saves current registers A, X, CCR, and PC on the stack and loads the program counter (PC) with the contents of the software interrupt vector. Program execution then proceeds from this new PC location.
rts	Return from subroutine. Retrieves program counter (PC) from the stack.
rti	Return from interrupt. Retrieves registers A, X, CCR, and PC from the stack.
rsp	Reset stack pointer to top of the stack.
nop	No operation. Does nothing, just takes space and stalls for one fetch/execute cycle.
stop	Stop. Stops everything in the processor, except external interrupt, to save power.
wait	Wait. Stops everything in the processor, except timer and external interrupt, to save power.

Addressing Modes

Immediate

The one-byte operand contains the argument. Use immediate addressing mode to access constants that do not change during program execution.

Assembly instructions specify the immediate addressing mode by preceding the operand with a # symbol. Examples: *lda #40* loads A with immediate value 40. *ldx #WORM* loads X with immediate value WORM. (The label WORM is assigned a value less than $0100 elsewhere in the program.)

Direct

The one-byte operand contains the argument address. Direct addressing allows the program to address directly the lowest 256 bytes in memory.

Assembly instructions specify this addressing mode by including the explicit address (or label assigned to the address). Examples: *ldx 40* loads X with the contents of address 40. *lda GUIT* loads A with the contents of address GUIT. The label GUIT is assigned to an address less than $0100 elsewhere in the program.

Extended

The two-byte operand contains the argument address. Instructions using extended addressing mode can reference arguments anywhere in memory.

Assembly instructions specify extended addressing mode by using the explicit address (or label assigned to an address). Examples: *lda 440* loads A with the contents of address 440. *cpx FISH* compares X to the contents of address FISH. The label FISH is assigned to an address greater than $0100 elsewhere in the program.

Relative

This mode is used for branch instructions. In relative addressing, adding the contents of the one-byte two's complement signed operand to the program counter (PC) derives the branch's destination address.

Branching occurs only if the branch conditions of the instruction are true. Otherwise, control proceeds to the next instruction. The range of relative addressing is from −127 to +128 bytes away from the current PC location.

Assembly language instructions never specify the actual offset, but rather, the destination for the branch instruction. The assembler takes care of calculating the offset between the current PC address and the specified branch destination. Examples: *beq $1000* causes a branch to address hex $1000 if the previous compare instruction was true. *bhs DOG* causes a branch to address DOG if the previous compare instruction was true. The label DOG is assigned to an address within +128/−127 bytes from this instruction.

Indexed, No Offset

Indexed addressing modes make it possible to define tables of data in memory. In the indexed, no offset addressing mode, the index register contains the argument address. Since the index register is 8 bits wide, this addressing mode can access the first 256 memory locations. This addressing mode can move a pointer through a table located in the lowest 256 addresses, or hold the address of a frequently referenced RAM or I/O location. Examples: *lda ,X* loads the accumulator with the address specified by the contents of X. *inc ,X* increments the contents of address specified by the contents of X.

Indexed, 8-Bit Offset

The address is the sum of the contents of the unsigned index register and the unsigned one-byte operand. This addressing mode is useful for selecting the "Kth" element in an "n" element table. With this instruction K would typically be in X, with the address of the beginning of the table in the operand. As such, tables may begin anywhere within the first 256 addressable locations and extend as far as location 510 (address $01FE). Examples: *lda 7,X* loads the accumulator with the address specified by adding the contents of X to 7. *inc TREE,X* increments the contents of the address specified by adding the contents of X to TREE. The label TREE is assigned a value less than $0100 elsewhere in the program.

Indexed, 16-Bit Offset

The address is the sum of the contents of the unsigned index register and the two-byte operand. This is similar to indexed, 8-bit offset mode except that the two-byte operand allows tables to be located anywhere in memory. Examples: *lda $567,X* loads the accumulator with the address specified by adding the contents of X to $567. *inc OINK,X* increments the contents of address specified by adding the contents of X to OINK. The label OINK is assigned a value greater than $0100 elsewhere in the program.

Bit Set/Clear

The bit to be set or cleared is part of the opcode, and the one-byte operand specifies the direct address of the byte containing the bit to be set or cleared. This addressing mode can selectively set or clear any read/writeable bit in the first 256 locations of memory, including I/O. Examples:

bset 5,NOSE sets bit 5 of contents of address NOSE. The label NOSE is assigned a value less than $0100 elsewhere in the program. *bclr 2,$36* clears bit 2 of the contents at address $36.

Bit Test and Branch

This is a combination of direct addressing and relative addressing. The opcode includes the bit to be tested, and its condition (set or clear). The address of the byte to be tested is in the first operand byte. Setting or clearing the specified bit in the specified memory location adds the signed relative offset in the operand to the program counter (PC).

This instruction allows the program to branch based on the condition of any readable bit in the first 256 locations of memory. The span of branching is from −125 to +130 from the opcode address. The state of the tested bit is also transferred to the carry bit of the condition code register. Example: *brset 5,BLACK,WHITE* tests bit 5 of contents of address BLACK and causes a branch to address WHITE if the bit is set. Labels BLACK and WHITE follow the rules for Direct and Relative addressing modes, respectively.

Inherent

The opcode contains all the information necessary to execute the instruction; no operand is necessary. Control instructions with no arguments, and operations on the accumulator or index register, use this mode. Examples: *inca* increments A. *rorx* rotates X right.

Chapter 14

Where to Learn More

Learning about musical electronics is not necessarily simple because it is not a large industry, and both the technology and æsthetic considerations change as often as spring fashions. Fortunately, there is much material available on general electronics; it's a small step from learning about electronics to figuring out how to apply circuits to musical ends. And since computers are very general-purpose devices, you don't need to learn different instruction sets for different applications—the raw materials are the same, so all that matters is how you apply those materials.

It's important to recognize that much of the responsibility for your education rests on your shoulders. There are few books and fewer authorities, and in any event we still know very little about the nature of sound and how it affects the human body and psyche. If you really want to learn, you need motivation, tenacity, interest, curiosity, and patience; there are no magic short cuts or formulas. Learning is a lifelong process anyway, because nothing remains static.

There are seven major sources for educating yourself about musical electronics:

- People

- Educational institutions

- Magazines

- Libraries

- "Hands-on" learning

- Books

- Semiconductor manufacturers

Let's look at the various options.

People

Nothing increases knowledge as fast, or inspires as thoroughly, as mutual brain picking with similarly inclined enthusiasts. The problem is finding these people. One option: take out a classified ad in the local newspaper or "musician's paper" (such as BAM in California) asking if any like-minded musical electronics enthusiasts in your area want to form a user's group. Another good bet is schools and colleges with experimental music departments; put your name up on a bulletin board and hang around the music classrooms. Another advantage of music schools is that their libraries often contain books and magazines about electronic music and synthesizers.

Another way to meet people is at conventions and trade shows. If you live near a large city, there are often mini-conventions (generally sponsored by local music stores or colleges) that cover audio and related fields like electronic music. One of the best-known national conventions open to the public is the Audio Engineering Society (AES) convention, which alternates yearly shows between the east and west coast (typically New York and either Los Angeles or San Francisco). There you can see the latest in studio equipment, sound synthesis technology, and the like. There's often an admission charge for this kind of affair, but it's well worth it.

There is one warning about learning from other people: sometimes, you'll find that a little knowledge is a dangerous thing, and someone who really doesn't know that much about musical electronics will feel qualified to expound on it by virtue of managing to fix a toaster once. Although advice can be helpful, we have seen some projects that had nothing wrong with them except for a bad solder joint until an "expert" tried to trouble-shoot it and made matters far worse. But if you know someone who can be a partner in learning, then you've got it made. Anyone who is successful in this industry owes a lot to the people who are kind enough to share what they know.

Educational Institutions

Don't expect to learn about musical electronics in traditional college engineering courses, since engineering and art courses (such as music) are often segregated. To obtain a specific degree, you generally undertake a fixed and formulated set of courses that lead towards that degree. As an electrical engineering student you may become proficient in designing hydroelectric dams, instrumentation amps, power supplies, and other circuits, but little (if any) of your experience will involve hands-on knowledge concerning musical electronics.

This is not meant to sound like a general indictment against colleges; it's just that many of the skills involved in creating electronic music devices are not the skills traditionally associated with engineering. For example, when trying to decide what type of tone control *sounds* best, having a good ear will help you more than knowing calculus.

In many cases, a musician with a minimal amount of electronic knowledge can often create more useful (and musically valid) devices than someone with a Ph.D. in physics, just as untrained musicians can sometimes play more emotionally arresting music than a conservatory-trained musician. However, as with music theory the more background you have, the further you can take your natural talents.

Fortunately, several more specialized schools now recognize that musical engineering is an important part of the total engineering picture. Some concentrate more on hardware, while others emphasize musical skills such as production and mixing. For information on these schools, check the ads in recording-related magazines; representatives of schools often attend local music-oriented events and conventions as well. (Remember, they want to find you as much as you want to find them.)

Regarding correspondence courses, they seldom emphasize musical electronics. These are generally job- and career-oriented and deal with subjects like getting an FCC license, computer repair, etc. Although some correspondence courses can be helpful for getting a general background in the field, you're usually better off learning from more specialized sources.

Magazines

Virtually all industrial countries have magazines devoted to electronics hobbyists, such as *Elektor* for the United Kingdom, *Electronics Now* and *Popular Electronics* in the USA, etc. Many of these publications recognize that a portion of their audience is interested in music and publish musical or music-related stories and projects; you can get quite an education in electronics just by subscribing to a few of the various available periodicals. If you can't afford subscriptions, many libraries take a number of publications devoted to electronics, and some subscribe to fairly esoteric journals.

Magazines also keep you posted on hot news. For example, if some company comes up with a faster way to make printed circuit boards in the home, chances are you'll see it first in a magazine ad. By reading the ads, you can find what's available, from whom, and for how much.

The best place to find suitable magazines is music stores and large book stores, such as Waldenbooks or B. Dalton's. Although they don't carry some of the smaller-circulation periodicals, you can find out about these by talking to educators or recording studio personnel, or from ads in larger magazines.

The following technically oriented music magazines sometimes include do-it-yourself projects. Write them for information on obtaining a sample issue, or check them out on the newsstand. Remember that magazines come, go, and merge, so this list is not meant to be comprehensive.

Audio Amateur, P.O. Box 576, Peterborough, NH 03458. Mostly intended for more of an audiophile audience, but deals with everything from how to get the most out of tubes to esoteric digital audio issues.

Electronic Musician, 6400 Hollis St. #12, Emeryville, CA 94608. General-interest magazine for computerphiles who are into music, and musicians who use computers. Occasional do-it-yourself projects.

EQ, 939 Port Washington Ave, Port Washington, NY 11050. Special-interest magazine devoted to project studio users; covers recording techniques, MIDI, computers, and digital audio. Regularly runs do-it-yourself projects.

Guitar Player and *Keyboard*, 411 Borel Ave., Suite 100, San Mateo, CA 94402. These instrument-specific magazines are well respected, established publications that also cover recording and MIDI issues as they relate to the instruments they cover. *Keyboard* is the more high-tech of the two. Occasional do-it-yourself projects.

Home and Studio Recording, 7318 Topanga Canyon Blvd., Suite 200, Canoga Park, CA 91303. Special-interest magazine for home and studio recording enthusiasts. Runs construction projects fairly regularly.

Sound on Sound, PO Box 30, St. Ives, Cambs PE17 4XQ, England. *SOS* is England's premier high-tech music publication, and covers occasional do-it-yourself projects for music and studio applications.

A final note about publications: If you want to see more articles on musical electronics, write them and make your wishes known. Editors do read letters and act on them—just a few letters of approval actually stand for thousands of happy readers.

Libraries

It's baffling why so many people overlook libraries as a source of knowledge; but now that you've been warned, you won't have to make that mistake. You can even spend hours in engineering libraries without ever attending the schools, but that's another story (try not to act conspicuous).

Anyway, libraries not only have books, but also magazines, and a listing of periodicals so that you can find out what's going on in the great, wide world out there. One suggestion: Suppose you and a couple of friends want to subscribe to a magazine, but don't have the bucks. Well, if each of you contributes one-third of the subscription price and then donate that subscription to the library, not only will it arrive every month for you and your friends to read, but it will also be there for the use of others in your community, and you'll be doing a good deed at the same time.

"Hands-on" Ways to Learn Electronics

Book learning isn't all there is to knowledge; there's also the need for practical experience to which you can relate this theory. Towards this end, check out the "100-in-1" lab kits. Electronic stores such as Radio Shack often carry miniature electronic "labs" that allow you to perform a variety of electronic experiments— you know, little amplifiers, wireless microphones, that sort of thing. These are aimed at high school science fair types, but are eminently suitable for anyone wanting to learn basic electronics. They don't cost too much, and sometimes you can learn more from one of these in four weeks than you can from a year in college.

Another option is the "solderless breadboard," made by a number of manufacturers, and available both from stores and via mail order. By getting one of these and a bunch of parts, you can build up circuits without soldering—thus, you can use the same parts over and over again.

Solderless breadboards (also called prototype boards) have a grid of holes that connect together electrically; plugging a lead from a capacitor and a lead from a resistor into adjacently connected holes hooks them together electrically to make a completed circuit. In many ways, this is the grown-up extension of the 100-in-1 type kit mentioned above. Get yourself a fistful of parts, and you're ready to go.

Prototype boards aren't real cheap but they're worth every penny, both in terms of knowledge gained and in parts that aren't destroyed. If you want to expand the basic breadboard, bolt it onto a metal chassis that includes extras like a couple of power supplies, some pots and switches, signal generator, etc.

If you would like a relatively painless introduction to electronics, you might want to check out some of the offerings of various kit manufacturers. Aside from the PAVO products that support this book (see Appendix), request a catalog from Paia Electronics, 3200 Teakwood Lane, Edmond, OK 73013. Many of the Paia kits are music-related, including rack mount studio gear (several designed by Craig Anderton), MIDI-to-CV converters, etc.

Books

MIDI Books and Information

The International MIDI Association provides documentation on all parts of the MIDI spec. For example, they offer the complete MIDI 1.0 Detailed Specification, as well as specs for Standard MIDI Files, MIDI Machine Control, and General MIDI. IMA, 526 W. 57th St., Los Angeles, CA 90056.

There are also many books that relate to MIDI. Other books published by Amsco Publications, a division of Music Sales Corporation are:

MIDI For Musicians (Craig Anderton, 1986). This was written specifically for those with no background in MIDI. It is the best-selling book on the topic, and has been used as a textbook in many schools and music programs.

MIDI For The Professional (Tim Tully and Paul D. Lehrman, 1993). Provides in-depth, hands-on data for those who work with MIDI in film, video, multimedia, and other pro applications.

The Electronic Musician's Dictionary (Craig Anderton, 1988). This book defines approximately 1,000 music, electronic, and computer terms relating to musical electronics; it serves as a useful glossary complement to *Digital Projects for Musicians*.

MIDI Projects for Musicians (Alan Gary Campbell and Craig Anderton, scheduled 2nd quarter 1994). This presents plans for simple MIDI do-it-yourself projects such as switchers, mergers, patchers, MIDI cables, etc.

The above books are available from Mix Bookshelf, 6400 Hollis St. #12, Emeryville, CA 94608, and can be ordered through book and music stores.

Books About Digital Electronics, Microprocessors, and Computer Programming

If you peruse the shelves of your local book store you'll find lots and lots of books about digital electronics and computer programming. Many are written for engineering students, others are written for people. We recommend you scan them to see which ones meet your needs. We have, and a few of our personal favorites are:

The Art of Programming Embedded Systems (Jack G. Ganssle, Academic Press, Inc., 1992). This describes the general ideas behind programming microprocessor systems. Topics include choosing the right microprocessor and peripherals for your application, debugging techniques, interrupt management, writing mathematical routines, and how to write a real time operating system. This is an excellent book for people who want to graduate from "amateur hacker" status to "seasoned pro" status. Highly recommended.

Musical Applications of Microprocessors (Hal Chamberlin, Hayden Books, 1985). The title says all you need to know about this nearly 800 page book that covers just about every imaginable detail concerning the history, theory, and implementation of analog, digital, and microprocessor synthesis (including extensive coverage of the inner working of many vintage synths). It also explains digital signal processing and how digital filters work. It's a little light on MIDI (it was written right after MIDI came out), but that's okay because *Digital Projects for Musicians* fills in the gap. (In fact, these two books taken together pretty much cover the spectrum of combining music, microprocessors, and MIDI.) *Byte* magazine declared "this book is a milestone in microcomputer history," and we wholeheartedly agree. Buy it!

Intuitive Digital Computer Basics: An Introduction to the Digital World (Thomas M. Frederiksen, McGraw Hill, Inc., 1988). This book provides a basic look at digital electronics. You'll learn what electrons do, how the various electronic components (resistors, capacitors, diodes, transistors, etc.) do their thing, basic digital circuitry, and how software is constructed. It's written for normal people, and is a good place to learn the basics.

CMOS Cookbook (Don Lancaster, Howard W. Sams & Company, 1977). This is one of those classic books that every digital hardware designer hides in their bottom desk drawer but never admits to using ("cookbooks" are considered cheating by snobby design engineers). The book covers the "4000" family of CMOS logic chips, and describes lots of interesting and useful applications as well as how to design digital logic circuits, oscillators and frequency synthesizers, digital displays, an ASCII keyboard, and even a "76 note polytonic music system." The book is fairly old, and most of the chips it covers are basically obsolete today—but the design techniques remain invaluable.

Don Lancaster is somewhat of a guru to electronics hackers, and has collected a lot of his writings into books that cover topics ranging from Postscript printing to where to find bargain electronic components. It's worth writing to his company, Synergetics (3860 West 1st. St., Box 809-DP, Thatcher, AZ 85552) for a listing of what's currently available—you'll find information in Lancaster's publications you won't find anywhere else (including some of the straightest talk you'll ever hear about the patent system).

Data Books About Parts Designed into the MIDItools Computer

IC manufacturers publish lots of information about their parts since it's in their best interest to make it as easy as possible for you to use them. Data books list the characteristics of different parts—how much voltage you can give them before they blow up, some representative circuits using the device, software instruction set, test rigs for determining optimum performance, and other data of use to engineers. These are often available from both mail-order suppliers and stores.

You'll want to get your hands on Motorola's data books about the 6805 (listed below) and an HCMOS logic data book (available from Motorola, National Semiconductor, Texas Instruments, Signetics, and other digital logic IC manufacturers). You'll find these data books at most electronics retailers, and even some large general book stores. If you're brave, you can call an IC manufacturer directly and ask them to send you a free copy (they will if you can convince them you're a valuable customer).

M68HC05 Applications Guide (Motorola, Motorola Part #M68HC05AG/AD, 1989). This book is indispensable. Even though the 6805 family consists of literally hundreds of different variations, this generic 6805 book focuses on our friend the MC680HC705C8. It explains every nuance of the part, and provides an excellent reference to the 6805's assembly programming language.

MC68HC705C8 Technical Data (Motorola, Motorola Part #M68HC705C8/D, 1990). This is the reference book on the MC68HC705C8 microcontroller. You won't find any basic theory or applications hints, but you will find every detail about every feature of the part—including how to build a MC68HC705C8 PROM programmer so you can burn your own programs into the chip.

You can reach the Motorola Literature Distribution Center at Box 20912, Phoenix, AZ 85036, or in Europe at 88 Tanners Drive, Blakelands Milton Keynes, MK 145BP, England.

Magazines About Digital Electronics, Microprocessors, and Computer Programming

There are a few magazines covering digital electronics, and many magazines targeted at the world of software programming. Some are very technical and seem to be of interest mostly to people who accessorize their basic wardrobe with a pocket protector. Others provide down-to-earth information for the rest of us. A few of our favorites are listed below.

Circuit Cellar INK—The Computer Applications Journal, Circuit Cellar, Inc., Subscriptions, Box 3050-C, Southeastern, PA 19398. This is one of the very best magazines in print—no question. Every issue is packed with excellent information about digital electronics and microprocessors, written especially for people who want a no-nonsense, hands-on approach. Past articles have explained how to build a MC68HC705C8 programmer, create a home automation system, how to use the latest, hippest, new microprocessor peripheral chips, and so on. You'll also find ads for lots of parts and kits. Be sure to check out their kit for an "EEG Biofeedback Brainwave Analyzer"! We shake with excitement every time a new issue comes in the mail.

Embedded Systems Programming, Miller Freeman, Inc., Box 41094, Nashville, TN 37204. This excellent magazine covers—you guessed it— topics related to embedded programming. An excellent reference for anyone serious about this stuff, the magazine is written by professional programmers, and covers issues such as how to write really efficient interrupt service routines, little operating systems for microprocessors, routines that crunch numbers, and so on. Highly recommended if you really want to know what you're doing.

Dr. Dobb's Journal, Miller Freeman, Inc., Box 56188, Boulder, CO 80322-6188. Dr. Dobb's is a very popular magazine for programmers. It focuses mainly on writing software for personal computers, but you'll often find an article that concerns embedded programming. It's an ideal publication for people who want to keep up to date on the latest programming trends.

Computer Language, Miller Freeman, Inc., Box 53525, Boulder, CO 80322-3525. This magazine doesn't offer a lot of specific information for embedded programmers (it covers issues of general interest to all breeds of programmers) but is another useful reference if you want to keep up to date on modern programming issues.

Semiconductor Manufacturers

In addition to publishing data books, manufacturers print data sheets and application notes for newer parts, as well as supplemental applications material for older parts as new applications develop. Better yet, some companies put on seminars at low or nominal cost in major metropolitan areas. If you purchase data books directly from the company, you will probably get on a mailing list that advises you of these opportunities.

Corresponding with the Authors

One of the best parts of writing a book is getting feedback from readers. Not only does this provide valuable insights on what to add or delete in future printings, we get to meet some pretty nice people that way (even if it is only through the mail). Readers also come up with nifty mods and applications that we would never think of ourselves.

We answer as many letters as possible, within present limitations of the time-space continuum. However, there are some things you can do that increase the odds of getting a fast and detailed answer to any questions you might have.

- Avoid asking questions that are already answered elsewhere in the book. This is unproductive for all concerned because you just end up getting referred back to the book anyway.

- Include a self-addressed, stamped envelope. People in countries outside the USA who don't have access to USA stamps can purchase an International Reply Coupon at their local post office, provided that their country is a member of the Universal Postal Union (just about every country is).

- Keep your questions short, to the point, and *legible*. Feel free to make comments, ramble on about yourself, present your views of the world, computers, or music—just don't let the questions pile up too high, or we won't be able to answer any of them.

- Do not ask for custom designs or schematics. It is simply not possible to spend the time needed to do a particular mod unless there is a great deal of interest.

- The main rule when writing any author is that letters that are easy to answer will get dealt with the fastest.

We're hoping that sales of this book justify a newsletter about new programs and circuit updates. We are indebted to you for your interest in this book, and hope to continue the dialog in the future—after all, this is software, and subject to change without notice.

Appendix

Venturing Out on Your Own

You are now approaching expert status, and should be ready to tackle the exciting world of programming microprocessors and building custom MIDI equipment. This section points you in the direction you need to go to venture out on your own and create your own MIDItools projects.

Development Tools You Need

You need the following tools to develop your own software:

- A text editor for writing source code. You can use almost any word processor that can save and load ASCII files. Be sure you don't operate your text editor in "document mode," which imbeds alien characters in your file that will drive the 6805 assembler crazy (and possibly you, if you're not aware of the problem).

- A 6805 assembler/linker. We use a package from the 2500AD company, but many others are available. Make sure that whatever package you get is compatible with the MC68HC705C8. Be aware that some of the "assembler-specific" assembler directives in the MIDItools source code may not be compatible with assemblers other than the one from 2500AD.

- An MC68HC705C8-compatible EPROM programmer. Motorola provides a schematic diagram in the *MC68HC705C8 Technical Data Guide*. Several others are available commercially. Most standard EPROM programmers are not compatible with the MC68HC705C8; make sure yours is before using it.

- An optional MC68HC705C8 Evaluation Module (EVM) from Motorola lets you test your code before you program it into an actual microprocessor. The EVM provides full debugging support, allowing you to load a program, step through each instruction, watch all the registers, fiddle with any part of memory, and so on. It is an indispensable tool for debugging. It also contains an on-board programmer so you can zap a chip when you get your program working.

- A personal computer for running all the above software, EPROM programmer, and EVM.

What You Do

We outlined the general process of creating a program and pumping it into a microprocessor back in Chapter 10. The actual process depends on the specific software and hardware tools you have. Follow the instructions which came with your development tools. In general, the process will resemble:

(1) Write the source code. For standard MIDI tools, you create an Application file with the six ingredients outlined in Chapter 10. Make sure you specify your new Application file in the file MAIN.ASM. Save your new Application file as a standard ASCII file (not a proprietary word processing document file; this is usually done with the "export" or "text only" option when saving).

(2) Assemble the MIDItools source code file, MAIN.ASM. MAIN.ASM includes all the BIOS files and your new Application file (assuming you told it to). The output of the assembler is a MAIN.OBJ object file.

(3) Link the MAIN.OBJ file. This links all the various components of the program together and gives all the instructions in the program addresses. The output of the linker is a "load module." Load modules contain machine code with some additional formatting so the computer can pass them to an EPROM programmer. The EPROM programmer will strip out this extra formatting, yielding the raw machine code of your program. Two standard load module types are .HEX and .S19 files.

(4) Load the .HEX (or .S19, or whatever load module you have) into the EPROM programmer or EVM. You are now free to program a C8 or debug your program if you have an EVM. Go back to step 1 and edit your source code if you need to make changes to the program.

That's it! You are now in full control of your MIDI system. If you need a special tool, build it yourself. Happy programming, and good luck!